The Art of Travel

HENRY JAMES

1905

The Art of Travel

Scenes and Journeys in America, England, France and Italy from the Travel Writings of

Henry James

Edited and with an Introduction by

Morton Dauwen Zabel

Essay Index Reprint Series

BOOKS FOR LIBRARIES PRESS
FREEPORT, NEW YORK

Reprinted 1970 by arrangement with
Doubleday & Company, Inc.

STANDARD BOOK NUMBER:
8369-1663-8

LIBRARY OF CONGRESS CATALOG CARD NUMBER:
76-111839

PRINTED IN THE UNITED STATES OF AMERICA

Contents

IV: The Lover of Italy

Travels in Italy 1873–1900

V: The Return of the Native

The American Scene 1904–1905

The Art of Travel

Introduction

Caelum non animum mutant
qui trans mare currunt

I

It appears to be the chosen destiny of a writer like Henry James to mean many things to many readers. This was true enough during his lifetime; it has become increasingly so in the forty years since his death. Like the work of all writers of large dimensions and searching vision—like that of Baudelaire, Rimbaud, Melville, and Dostoevski among his contemporaries—his art, restless in craft and insight, indefatigable to the end in curiosity, subtlety, and symbolic impulse, has arrived at a result he must certainly have foreseen and, with the claims he made for "mystification," doubtless intended. "The work of the valid artist," he once said, "must, if it counts for anything, constitute an experience for us." The one thing James's readers are bound to have in common, whatever they bring to his work or take away from it, and whether they resist it critically or embrace it with enthusiasm, is that his books count as an experience in their lives—bring them to share an activity of thought and imagination that in one degree or another becomes an active part of their own intelligence. The "wondrous adventure" James called his career when he looked back on it in old age can become an adventure equally challenging and unpredictable to those who trace it through the fifty years of its development—a drama of craft, discovery, and critical inquisition that soon carries them beyond the external charms of the teller of tales into the explorations of a mind inexhaustibly curious, a sensibility endlessly avid and undiscouraged, until it brings them into regions of daring speculation, heights of rarefied vision and difficult breathing, that touch the farthest boundaries to which the craft of fiction has yet been carried.

> Experience is never limited, and it is never complete; it is an immense sensibility, a kind of huge spider-web of the finest silken threads suspended in the chamber of consciousness, and catching every air-borne particle in its tissue. It is the very atmosphere of the mind; and when the mind is imaginative—much more when it happens to be that of a man of genius—it takes to itself the faintest hints of life, it converts the very pulses of the air into revelations.

When James said this in his essay on "The Art of Fiction" he might have been defining the kind of participation he expected his own work to demand of its readers. "A great suspended swinging crystal—huge lucid lustrous, a block of light—flashing back every impression of life and every possibility of thought": his figure for Saltram in "The Coxon Fund" can be applied to himself. And such an experience is bound to include another result he set up as an aim of whatever confidence the artist seeks in the minds of those who share his work. It will impart that "intimacy with a man's specific behaviour, with his given case," which is "desperately certain to make us see it as a whole" and to enforce the discovery that "what a man thinks and what he feels are the history and the character of what he does."

James's given case has accordingly been examined under any number of tests and tenets. He has been studied as an American, as a European, and as a man who could never successfully be either; as an aesthete, a social historian, a psychologist, and a religious allegorist; as the realist he claimed to be and as the idealist or abstract thinker he repudiated being; as a systematic moral critic and as a poet of metaphysical vision. If it is only the most dedicated who will follow him into the remote and perilous "country of the blue" of his ultimate values, there are less strenuous ways of gaining access to his work and discovering in it the clues to the history and character of the man who created it.

II

There has always been one clue particularly, one means of intimacy with James's mind and character, that few of his readers have ever missed or failed to respond to. It shows itself so pervasively in his pages, becomes so much the radical imagery and music of his fiction, that it has probably given most of his readers their clearest impression of what he represents in the art of the novel. A novelist as much as a poet is likely to be distinguished by a characteristic vein of imagery. If he is the conscious artist James was, his imagery will run deep in his work—will persist, ramify, and enrich itself from book to book, and so become a key to his mind and to the revelation it seeks to impart. Only quotation can suggest it adequately, and since to quote is to be tempted to anthologize,[1] quotation here must be brief.

The early Roman spring had filled the air with bloom

[1] As was done twice with James's encouragement—by Evelyn Garnaut Smalley in *The Henry James Year Book* (1911), and by Ruth Head in *Pictures and Other Passages from Henry James* (1916).

> and perfume, and the rugged surface of the Palatine was muffled with tender verdure. . . . It seemed to him he had never known Rome so lovely as just then. He looked off at the enchanting harmony of line and colour that remotely encircles the city—he inhaled the softly humid odours and felt the freshness of the year and the antiquity of the place reaffirm themselves in deep interfusion. . . .

Thus an early visitor in Rome. Here is a later one:

> I may not attempt to report in its fulness our young woman's response to the deep appeal of Rome, to analyse her feelings as she trod the pavement of the Forum or to number her pulsations as she crossed the threshold of Saint Peter's. It is enough to say that her impression was such as might have been expected of a person of her freshness and her eagerness. She had always been fond of history, and here was history in the stones of the street and the atoms of the sunshine. She had an imagination that kindled at the mention of great deeds, and wherever she turned some great deed had been acted. . . . The sense of the terrible human past was heavy to her, but that of something altogether contemporary would suddenly give it wings that it could wave in the blue. . . . The herd of re-echoing tourists had departed and most of the solemn places had relapsed into solemnity. The sky was a blaze of blue, and the plash of the fountains in their mossy niches had lost its chill and doubled its music. . . .

Here is another city:

> We swept in the course of five minutes into the Grand Canal; whereupon she uttered a murmur of ecstasy as fresh as if she had been a tourist just arrived. She had forgotten the splendour of the great water-way on a clear

> summer evening, and how the sense of floating between marble palaces and reflected lights disposed the mind to freedom and ease. We floated long and far, and though my friend gave no high-pitched voice to her glee I was sure of her full surrender. . . . The gondola moved with slow strokes, to give her time to enjoy it, and she listened to the plash of the oars, which grew louder and more musically liquid as we passed into narrow canals, as if it were a revelation of Venice. . . .

But there are scenes of a different kind and of another country:

> . . . the influences of the hour were such as to make the excursion very agreeable to our young man, who liked the streets at all times, but especially at nightfall in the autumn, of a Saturday, when in the vulgar districts the smaller shops and open-air industries were doubly active, and big clumsy torches flared and smoked over hand-carts and costermongers' barrows drawn up in the gutters. . . . He liked the reflexion of the lamps on the wet pavements, the feeling and smell of the carboniferous London damp; the way the winter fog blurred and suffused the whole place, made it seem bigger and more crowded, produced halos and dim radiations, trickles and evaporations on the plates of glass. He moved in the midst of these impressions this evening, but he enjoyed them in silence. . . .

Thus the "great grey Babylon" of London, with "the assault directly made by the great city upon an imagination quick to react." Here is another Babylon, the "vast bright Babylon" across the Channel:

> The Boulevard was all alive, brilliant with illuminations, with the variety and gaiety of the crowd, the dazzle of shops and cafés seen through uncovered fronts or

> immense lucid plates, the flamboyant porches of theatres and the flashing lamps of carriages, the far-spreading murmur of talkers and strollers, the uproar of pleasure and prosperity, the general magnificence of Paris on a perfect evening in June. . . . "Splendid Paris, charming Paris"—that refrain, the fragment of an invocation, a beginning without an end, hummed itself perpetually in [his] ears; the only articulate words that got themselves uttered in the hymn of praise his imagination had been addressing to the French capital from the first hour of his stay . . . and his comprehension gave him wings—appeared to transport him to still wider fields of knowledge, still higher sensations.

So a young man walks the city, but it casts its spell on an older one too:

> . . . he came down the Rue de la Paix in the sun and, passing across the Tuileries and the river, indulged more than once—as if on finding himself determined—in a sudden pause before the book-stalls of the opposite quay. In the garden of the Tuileries he had lingered, on two or three spots, to look; it was as if the wonderful Paris spring had stayed him as he roamed. The prompt Paris morning struck its cheerful notes—in a soft breeze and a sprinkled smell, in the light flit, over the garden-floor, of bareheaded girls with the buckled strap of oblong boxes, in the type of ancient thrifty persons basking betimes where terrace-walls were warm, in the blue-frocked brass-labelled officialism of humble rakers and scrapers, in the deep references of a straight-pacing priest or the sharp ones of a white-gaitered red-legged soldier. He watched little brisk figures, figures whose movement was as the tick of the great Paris clock. . . .

"Was it at all possible for instance to like Paris enough without liking it too much?" this stroller presently asks himself. The question hovers over scores of such scenes in James, of which any few examples must serve as scant suggestive tokens. There are scenes that reach back to his earliest tales and his earliest memories—the old New York of his boyhood in *Washington Square* which later becomes the new New York of a more modern day in "Crapy Cornelia," "A Round of Visits," and "The Jolly Corner"; the early Newport of "An International Episode" and the later Newport of *The Ivory Tower;* the New England of "Four Meetings," "A New England Winter," *The Europeans,* and *The Bostonians,* and the old England, dense in its saturation of history and ancient tone of time, in "The Passionate Pilgrim," "The Author of Beltraffio," *The Portrait of a Lady, The Spoils of Poynton, The Golden Bowl, The Sense of the Past,* and with its country houses and broad estates whose names chime their charm, amenity, and age-seasoned beatitude—Medley, Fawns, Beccles, Gardencourt, Lockleigh, Flickerbridge, Summersoft. Then the France and Paris of *The American, The Princess Casamassima,* and *The Ambassadors;* scenes farther afield—high-fashioned Homburg in "Louisa Pallant," sparkling Vevey in *Daisy Miller,* the Switzerland of Alpine passes and bristling glaciers in "At Isella," "The Private Life," or Milly Theale's vision of the kingdoms of the world; and so southward to the great stage of Italy—Venice, Florence, Rome as they lend their resonance of splendor and history to *Roderick Hudson, The Portrait of a Lady, The Aspern Papers, The Wings of the Dove.*

But this is to suggest only a few of the pictures that pass in the great panorama of James's drama. No reader can ever have missed their spell in his pages, forgotten their evocative magic, or, once having experienced them, failed to remember them when he himself comes to explore the cities and countries they describe. They carry unmistakably the signature of his particular mind and emotion, and reveal him as one of the great artists of scene and atmosphere in modern literature. They reveal, of course, something more. They constitute the appropriate imagery of his subject matter, are part and substance of the theme he made basic to his lifework, and so become the matrix of the moral and historical drama his fiction unfolds. Where some novelists find their material and imagery in a given locality or fixed orbit of experience, others are impelled abroad to find the theater their imagination requires. James is classic in their company. Whatever else his work shows him to be—and it shows much—he is an artist and poet of travel. He became so by the requirements of his imagination, but he also became so by the special conditions and circumstances of his life—his origins, his nationality, his sense of history, and the moment of modern history he was given to record.

III

Travel was not the first condition of James's existence but it has a clear claim to having been the second. The popular legend of his career has for eighty years set him down as the classic example of the exile, expatriate, and voluntary fugitive of American literature; and of course his remains a pre-eminent case of the writer who finds his destiny and fulfills himself as an artist in foreign parts. But it is still necessary to take first things first in James's life, for without the fact of his origins and point of departure neither his travels, his expatriation, nor the art he made of them can be seen in their actual perspective and significance. The first condition of his career was his birth, as the second son of Henry James, Senior, and his wife, Mary Robertson Walsh, on Washington Place in New York City on April 15, 1843, and his thereby becoming enlisted at a stroke in a dual nationality—a citizen of the American republic and as what his brother William was to call his real nationality, "a native of the James family." That birth, with its double allegiance and division of loyalty, can be taken as basic to everything James was by origin, became by heredity and temperament, and remained by instinctive commitment to the end of his life. But the second portent of his history was soon to declare itself, and like the first it befell him, as he liked to say, "antecedent to choice." Six months had hardly elapsed before he was transported by his parents, an infant in arms, from the United States to Europe on the first of the journeys that were to become the habit and recurring feature of almost seventy years. He was initiated into travel before he was a year old.

The modern taste for finding symbolism at work in the lives of artists as much as in the products of their imagination need feel no scruple in reading into these two primary facts of James's career the clues to his destiny and vocation. It can be taken as no chance accident but as an ordained event that the elder Jameses delayed their voyage to France and England long enough for him to be born in America. It can be taken as an equal signal of his fate that he first crossed the Atlantic while he was still unconscious of the momentous displacement that interrupted the normal course of his American babyhood. Not wholly unconscious, however. It was to be James's boast seventy years later, when he came to write the account of his childhood in *A Small Boy and Others,* that the earliest "vibration of [his] very most infantine sensibility" which he could recall from his faraway infancy was the memory of having seen in Paris "as a baby in long clothes"—"while I waggled my small feet, as I definitely remember doing, under my flowing robe"—the "view, framed by the clear window of the vehicle as we passed, of a great stately square surrounded with high-roofed houses and having in its center a tall and glorious column," and thus of having "taken in, for all my time, the admirable aspect of the Place and the Colonne

Vendôme." This precocious feat of observation, a "marvel" in after-years to his family and to himself a matter of boyish pride, was never forgotten as the first hint he caught of his destiny—a "mystic gage" of what the future held in store for him.

The signal was soon to be repeated. After returning with his family to America at the age of three, he was taken back to Europe at twelve, in 1855, for three years of schooling in Switzerland, England, and France with his brothers and sister, and for his first avid explorations of the foreign world that now opened itself to his curiosity in Geneva, London, Paris, and Boulogne-sur-Mer. He returned to New York and Newport in 1858, but another fifteen months found him back in Europe for a third time. His third homecoming fell in 1860; and for nine years New York, Newport, Cambridge, a short term at the Harvard Law School, and the deeply stirring experience of the Civil War stamped his American birthright on his mind and impelled him, by successive stages, into the career in letters he chose for himself. By the time he was ready to make his first adult journey to Europe in 1869, James approached her shores as a practiced traveler, already a seasoned cosmopolite of two continents.

The design of his future life had by that time assumed another dimension. The first story he succeeded in getting published, "A Tragedy of Error," in 1864, was a tale with a European setting, as his second, "The Story of a Year" in 1865, was, in appropriate antithesis, a tale of America and its Civil War. Other tales soon followed, with American themes alternating with dramas of Europe or European travel, some of them so elaborately equipped with scenic or touristic description—"Traveling Companions," "At Isella," "The Madonna of the Future"—as to give an impression of being travelogues with a story attached. When James was ready to publish his first book of fiction in 1875 its title announced one of the key phrases of his lifework, *A Passionate Pilgrim.* So did his second, *Transatlantic Sketches,* in the same year, with its account of his own pilgrimages, undisguisedly passionate in their emotion of homage and discovery in spite of the fact that they constituted not his first advent in Europe but his fourth and fifth, among the scenes and shrines of England, Switzerland, Holland, Belgium, Germany, and Italy.

When James's first long novel appeared in 1876 it was *Roderick Hudson,* the story of another passionate pilgrimage to Europe. Still another appeared in his next one, *The American,* in 1877. And both of them, like a dozen of the early tales, offered heroes who combined in their characters and fortunes two of the classic American types of the age, his own passionate pilgrim and the "innocent abroad" which another American of the time immortalized. When James was ready to publish his first book of essays in 1878 it was *French Poets and Novelists,* an account of what he had learned in the literary and aesthetic schools of Paris. His shorter tales up to this time had been roughly divided between American and European themes, but the two that won him his first popular success, *Daisy Miller* and *An International Episode* in 1878–9, were again tales of Americans—innocents or pilgrims—in Europe, and both their titles gave catchwords to the language of their day. *Confidence* in 1880 once more pictured the American abroad. So did *The Portrait of a Lady* in 1881, the theme now deepening into moral conflict and tragedy. *The Europeans* in 1878 had reversed the subject: it brought Europeans to America. It was not until *Washington Square* in 1880 that James applied his full strength (leaving aside the slighter effort of *Watch and Ward* ten years earlier) to the American scene and drama that were to engage him as a counter-subject intermittently in the future. The central theme of his lifework, the "international subject," had defined itself as the special demesne and incentive of his imagination. He had established the basis and design of the huge creation that lay ahead. And that work was to include six further volumes and a continuous flow of essays on his travels.

IV

James's account with travel was never to be closed. It appears, still a question for moral debate and inquisition, in the two novels he left unfinished at his death in 1916. He is notable among novelists in a number of the salient traits of his genius—in, among others, his union of the imaginative and the critical faculties in everything he wrote. But he is particularly marked among modern writers by the use to which he put the call and experience of travel. Marked, yet far from unique. Travel, displacement, quest, and exploration have become so pervasive in the literature of the modern age of restlessness and mobility, have so widely reasserted themselves in their ancient function as incentives to the personal and moral imagination, as to have become radical impulses in a host of writers. The novel of displacement has become a major genre in a century of unrest and dislocation. The opposite tradition will presumably always exist—the regionalists, local-colorists, and historians of a concentrated microcosm of human life, with Jane Austen, Balzac, Dickens, Manzoni, and Hardy among their masters. But those who have ranged abroad for their drama have come almost to outnumber them—Stendhal, Goethe, and Turgenev leading a procession that includes most of the nineteenth century Americans, from Irving, Cooper, and Melville to Howells, Fuller, Stephen Crane, and Edith Wharton; twentieth century writers of every rank and nationality—Gide, Malraux, Saint-Exupéry, and Camus; Mann and Kafka; Conrad, Lawrence, Forster, Greene, and Waugh; and again a troop of Americans: Fitzgerald, Lewis,

Wolfe, Miller, Porter, Hemingway. But if James is far from alone or singular in his practice of the genre, he probably did more than anyone else to define and establish it, to make its claim and status recognized.

The point to be emphasized is that it was not from his personal experience alone that he took his incentive. It was from the age, moment, and situation in which he was born and lived, the pulse of one of whose radical necessities he felt with the accuracy of a diagnostician. Travel is not in his work a marginal matter of romantic atmosphere, arbitrary impulse, or escapist appeal. It is a cognate of the moral and historical drama to which he addressed himself; of the conflict of culture he saw as basic to his century; of the "complex fate" which he discovered "being an American," but being no less a man of full modern sensibility and responsible intelligence, imposed on him.

Travel, of course, is far from being the privilege or prerogative of modern times. It is one of the earliest and oldest of man's activities, its history coextensive with that of the race itself, a primary impulse of the human species and a major determinant of history. Whether as migration or exploration, science or pleasure, enforced displacement or irrational wanderlust, it has figured as a condition of every race and age, era or culture. So far it is a recognized fact of human record and experience. But two other facts soon appear: that there are as many kinds of travel as there are men and occasions, and that throughout its long history travel has had not only a mixed reputation but what may be called a mixed press. In some periods its repute is high, in others surprisingly low. In some times or societies it becomes a criterion of the cultivated life, a standard of civilized action and purpose. In others—of which obvious contemporary instances suggest themselves—it falls under the reproof of patriots, nationalists, and xenophobes as a demoralizer of states or a threat to the integrity of races.

If it has been praised for its civilizing value, it has also given large scope to moral self-righteousness and warning, and it has required of its chroniclers a great deal of apology and justification. Some have made a science of it, others a means of survival or rehabilitation, still others a function of politics and propaganda. The one ambition that appears always to have animated the civilized traveler has been to make an art of it; and to many people even today it is one of the few means of art or creative action they find open to them.

But if the one definable feature of travel is that it has been a constant in human history, an irresistible lure to ambition or imagination, it has never achieved a reliable standing in literature. There has, in fact, always attached to it a hint of the deceptive or the deluding. "There is nothing worse for mortals than a wandering life": the warning is as old as Homer, if its opposite—"Many shall run to and fro, and knowledge shall be increased"—is also as old as the Old Testament. Seneca's "Every change of scene is a delight," Hesiod's "New air gives new life," are reproved by Talmudic censure: "Three things are weakening: fear, sin, and travel." If one man, Sterne, says that "Nothing is so perfectly amusement as a total change of ideas," another, Chesterfield, holds that "Those who travel heedlessly from place to place . . . set out fools, and will certainly return so." If Johnson advises that "the use of traveling is to regulate imagination by reality, and, instead of thinking how things may be, to see them as they are," Shakespeare says, "When I was at home, I was in a better place." Hazlitt's enthusiasm—"The soul of a journey is liberty, perfect liberty, to think, feel, do just as one pleases"—is corrected by French realism: *Voyager, c'est travailler.* And men seem never to have rid themselves of one of the stubbornest irritants of the footloose conscience—that escape and change are equally impossible and that a man carries himself and his soul with him wherever he goes. *Caelum non animum mutant qui trans mare currunt.*

Possibly no nation has been as uneasy in its view of travel as America. The one Western country that has always held expatriation to be something of a misdemeanor, if not an actual offense to patriotism or a form of social betrayal, it has never freed itself of the sense of guilt apparently rooted in a society which originated in deracination and grew into its modern dimensions through incessant migration and restlessness. The American celebrants of wanderlust have been as eloquent as any—Melville with his "I love to sail forbidden seas and land on barbarous coasts"; Whitman with his hymn of the footloose:

> Afoot and lighthearted I take to the open road,
> Healthy, free, the world before me,
> The long brown path before me leading wherever I
> choose . . .

But reproof or skepticism has always been ready to correct these enthusiasms. Franklin's came as early as 1767—"Traveling is one way of lengthening life, at least in appearance"; Jefferson's in 1787:

> Traveling makes men wiser, but less happy. When men of sober age travel, they gather knowledge which they may apply usefully for their country; but they are subject ever after to recollections mixed with regret; their affections are weakened by being extended over more objects; and they learn new habits which cannot be gratified when they return home.

Emerson's rasps insistently in his essays of forty years: in 1841:

> It is for want of self-culture that the superstition of

> traveling, whose idols are Italy, England, Egypt, retains its fascination for all educated Americans;

and in 1860:

> Men run away to other countries because they are not good in their own, and run back to their own because they pass for nothing in the new places. For the most part, only the light characters travel.

Hawthorne's, whatever the charms he found in the "old home" of England or on his hilltop at Bellosguardo, sounds throughout his letters and journals with the incurable ache of the homesick and the unreconciled:

> I remember to this day the dreary feeling with which I sat by our first English fireside and watched the chill and rainy twilight of an autumn day darkening down upon the garden, while the preceding occupant of the house (evidently a most unamiable personage in his lifetime), scowled inhospitably from above the mantelpiece, as if indignant that an American should try to make himself at home there. Possibly it may appease his sulky shade to know that I quitted his abode as much a stranger as I entered it . . .

or again:

> I consider it a great piece of good fortune that I have had experience of the discomforts and miseries of Italy, and did not go directly home from England. Anything will seem like a Paradise after a Roman winter.

Men like Henry Adams, Charles Eliot Norton, Santayana, and the later expatriates of the 1920's have had a different counsel to offer, though even their consciences were often far from clear on the matter. But the debate between the romantic and the realistic attitudes among American travelers that was set in motion by Irving and Cooper in the earlier nineteenth century has never been conclusively resolved. It is a debate that has been applied more severely to Henry James by his American critics and apologists than to any other American writer.

The debate exists within his own work. He made it basic to his moral drama and international theme. It was he, more than any other man of his time, who brought it into focus and gave it its classic expression in American literature. But it was not as a didactic philosopher or moralist that he achieved his expression of it, any more than he did so as a nationalist, politician, or sociologist. The morality of the problem, personal as well as nationalistic, was sufficiently evident to him, yet it was not on ethical or moralistic grounds that he chose to argue it. He chose the grounds and terms of his art, and of the critical vision, moral justice, and "quality of mind" he held his art to embody. It was his business to make an art of his travel writings and fictions, but this required that he first make an art of travel itself.

V

He was, as we now look back on it across a century, enviably privileged in his opportunity. All the conditions of his liberal parentage, family circumstances, native temperament, as well as his age and nationality, joined to make him so. He was possessed as much as his father was by the "subjective passion" that endowed every action he took part in, every sight he beheld, with an incentive "largely educative," an emotion "supremely determinant." Even as a boy he saw his parents "homesick" for "the ancient order, and distressed and inconvenienced by many of the more immediate features of the modern, as the modern pressed about us, and since," as he said, "their theory of our better living was from an early time that we should renew the question of the ancient on the very first possibility I simply grew greater in the faith that somehow to manage that would constitute success in life." The "nostalgic cup," he recognized, had "been applied to my lips before I was conscious of it"; and though he was later to call its potion a "poison" that "had entered my veins," he drank from it without fear or foreboding. "The sense of change" had from the beginning rested "with a most warm and comfortable weight on my soul." He knew from his earliest years that he had "taken over, under suggestion and with singular infant promptitude, a particular throbbing consciousness" of what travel and the past were to mean to him, and of "the source at which it could best be refreshed"—a consciousness of "certain impressions, certain *sources* of impression again, proceeding from over the sea and situated beyond it." The "mild forces" that had shaped his youth and temperament had done one thing for which he never ceased to be grateful. They had succeeded in "pushing the door to Europe definitely open," and even as a youth he hoped it would never be closed to his access and exploration. It never was.

Moreover, the time and place of his birth were as propitious for his opportunity as the family into which he was born. James was an American in an age when it was one of the recognized duties of every cultivated American to recover and examine, weigh and estimate, his legacy of breed, culture, and tradition in the Old World. The impulse that had impelled Englishmen or Europeans of James's century—Goethe, Byron, Stendhal, Heine, Gautier—toward the classic lands of southern Europe in their search for a spiritual ancestry or inheritance became, among Americans of the nineteenth century, an even more urgent and comprehensive ambition. The past meant not only Italy and Greece. It meant England, France, Germany, Italy, Spain

—every country that had fathered, sponsored, or initiated, in the discovery and settlement of America, the greatest human venture of modern times. The problem of defining the point at which America had arrived in her venture of nationhood—of determining her debt, responsibility, and relationship to the parent and rival civilizations of Europe—was one to which every serious American writer felt in one degree or another obligated to address himself. When James later said of himself that this problem "was implied in every question I asked, every answer I got, and every plan I formed," he was speaking for almost every inquisitive member of his generation and for most of the major American writers of his time.

If it was not yet the moment for searching out a "usable past" in America itself, it was decidedly the moment for seeking such a past in the older world. Virtually every serious American writer of the age—Thoreau, Whitman, and Emily Dickinson are the obvious exceptions—was to make his journey overseas. The program of inquiry and assessment that had been initiated by Franklin, Adams, and Jefferson was continued under a variety of tenets—romantic, critical, skeptical, moralistic, inquisitive—by Irving, Cooper, and Poe, by Emerson, Hawthorne, Melville, Lowell, Mark Twain, Howells, and Henry Adams, and so by their followers in a new century: Henry B. Fuller, Stephen Crane, Edith Wharton, Willa Cather, Eliot, Pound, Lewis, Dos Passos, Fitzgerald—the list is a long one. But it was the nineteenth century traveler who had the advantage of a stronger compulsion, a more intimate personal need, and of a time when travel was still as much an opportunity for romantic education as for moral self-determination.

"The romance of travel": James was to call it such when he retold this part of his life many years later in his memoirs. And as we now see it across the distance of a hundred years of reckless change and dislocation, it is the romance as much as the high-minded scruples of American travel in that age that gives cause for envy. Romantic travel was in its last great age. The tradition of the Grand Tour, though waning, was not yet spent. The cities and monuments of Europe still stood in their appointed places. Space had not yet been annihilated by engines, wires, wireless, and air flight. The sanctity of time and tradition still blessed the holy places of historical and aesthetic pilgrimage. Nations still lived in comparative friendship and mutual respect. Physically as much as spiritually, there still prevailed a sense of historical proportion in the conditions of the world, and in the relation of the New World to the Old. The traveler traced his steps slowly, methodically, and with a necessary deliberation of movement and intention. He was not yet hurtled across the ocean in a day or from one hemisphere to another in a night. His emotions and reflexes were not wrenched out of their normal habits and logic by scientific speed. History, except in minds like Rimbaud's, had not yet become "foreshortened by violence." Whatever distortion of tradition or culture was in the making through machinery, industry, and commerce, the nations, cities, and shrines of the earth still respected the roles that had been assigned to them by long centuries of historic process and order. The conformities of standardization, the leveling destructiveness of scientific progress and warfare, were still biding their hour. It was, as James later called it, "a moment of a golden age"—perhaps the last golden age the traveler will ever know.

When James wrote his biography of William Wetmore Story in 1903 he felt that that moment had already passed its zenith in his youth and slipped irrecoverably into the lost past. He opened the memoir by paying his tribute to the men of the earlier time who had prepared the way for his own generation—"the light skirmishers, the *éclaireurs,* who have gone before." He did so not only with a sense of his personal debt to them but with a sense of how much they did to preserve for their followers a feeling for the traditional continuities of European civilization which had already, when he himself began to travel, begun to disintegrate. "Europe, for Americans, has, in a word, been *made* easy," he admitted. The "old relation, social, personal, aesthetic, of the American world to the European" had largely disappeared. The "American initiation" to the delights and lessons of travel had become darkened by "a comparative historic twilight." "The pure and precious time —the time of the early flowering—was the matter of a moment and lasted but while it could."

It was the "good faith" of the old pilgrims that had "supported them through the tribulations from which we are exempt, and their good faith thus becomes for us the constant key to their pleasure, or at least to their endurance." And while he argued that "the dawn of the American consciousness of the complicated world it was so persistently to annex is the more touching the more primitive we make that consciousness," he was willing to admit that "we must recognise that the latter can scarcely be interesting to us in proportion as we make it purely primitive." But he also felt that he had enjoyed an advantage soon to be lost to his successors when he touched the last moments of the romantic age of travel:

> I think of the American who started on his *Wanderjahre* after the Civil War quite as one of the moderns divided by a chasm from his progenitors and elder brothers, carried on the wave as they were not, and all supplied with introductions, photographs, travelers' tales, and other aids to knowingness. He has been, this child of enlightenment, very well in his way; but his way has not, on many sides, been equally well, save as we think of it all as the way of railroads and hotels.

And, he concluded, "'a vanished society' is a label before which, wherever it be applied, the man of imagination must inevitably pause and muse":

> Do we know why it is we all ruefully, but quite instinctively, think of the persons grouped in such an air as having had, though they were not to know it, a better "time" than we? For we are surely conscious of that conviction, the source of which we perceive to be excess of our modern bliss. We have more things than they, but we have less and less room for them, either in our lives or in our minds; so that even if our taste is superior we have less the use of it, and thereby, to our loss, less enjoyment of our relations. The quality of these suffers more and more from the quantity, and it is in the quantity alone that we today make anything of a show. The theory would perfectly be workable that we have not time for friendships—any more, doubtless, than for enmities; luxuries, both, as to which time is essential. Friendships live on the possibility of contact, that contact which requires in some degree margin and space. We are planted at present so close that selection is smothered; contact we have indeed, but only in the general form which is cruel to the particular. That is logically the ground of our envy of other generations.

It is certainly the ground of our own envy of the nineteenth century traveler—of James himself, whose sense of shrunken zest and opportunity in his travels becomes almost incredible when we consider it in the light of the almost total disappearance of his kind of pleasure—the pleasure of "margin and space"—which has taken place during the forty years of progress, violence, and calamity since his death. What he defined when he wrote the above paragraph was an age he still had, whatever his regrets, the good fortune to share. The conditions for making travel a mode of civilized education were still available to him; he was still able to apply to his journeys the resources of his artist's intelligence.

Yet however much his age gave him that opportunity, his role as an American obliged him to be something more than a connoisseur of travel. The obligation of comparison, assessment, and judgment was as urgent in him as the prospect of delight. Europe might be a "threshold of expectation," a "scene for the reverential spirit," a world "immemorial, complex, accumulated." He could still approach it as a passionate pilgrim, an "heir of all the ages," a participator in "history as a still-felt past and a complacently personal future," in "society, manners, types, characters, possibilities and prodigies and mysteries of fifty sorts." He was free to discover that Europe meant "ever so many things at once, not only beauty and art and supreme design, but history and fame and power, the world in fine raised to the richest and noblest expression." But with whatever innocence or enthusiasm he approached the shrine, there worked in him another faculty, his "incurable critical impulse," which forced him both to identify himself with what he saw and to hold it under critical and moral scrutiny. To "criticise" meant by definition "to appreciate, to appropriate, to take intellectual possession, to establish in fine a relation with the criticised thing and make it one's own." That was what art of any kind meant to him. Which in turn leads us to ask what kind of artist of travel James was, what he made of his excursions at home or abroad, and what these count for in the sum of his achievement.

VI

A distinction is needed at the outset, and one comes conveniently to hand. There is "the traveler who writes" and there is "the professional writer, the novelist, the critic, the poet, who travels." There are travelers "who will themselves into movement with a strategic purpose, which is partly professional, partly temperamental," and there are "the travelers impelled from within."[2] Both classes have been large, at times they overlap, and each has included famous chroniclers. The first begins with the ancient geographers and explorers, the scribes of conquistadors, discoverers, and empire builders; includes masters of adventure like Marco Polo, Hakluyt, Bernál Diáz, Fernão Mendes Pinto, and the historians of the *grandes peregrinaciones;* and continues down to Mungo Park, Livingstone, Darwin, Doughty, the men driven by later dreams of discovery, fervors of missionary zeal, schemes of conquest or scientific mastery, into the dark or waste lands of the earth, and whose successors are the specialists–biologists, anthropologists, and ethnologists–of the past hundred years. The second category shows an even longer descent and it has shaped a major department of modern literature–the legionary seekers and searchers of our own day.

Further distinctions follow. The traveler who writes either belongs to a primitive age or prefers an objective that is still primitive. The unknown exists for him either as *terra incognita* or as civilized ignorance. He is an explorer less in his own interests than in the interests of humanity at large. The unknown promises an extension of knowledge, new opportunities for conquest, trade, power, or moral influence, for the civilization of which he is the agent. The strange, the inaccessible, and the savage are his chosen territory: Asia, Africa, or America in their unconquered darkness, or regions of a later age still shrouded in primitive violence or unpenetrated mystery–Arabia, Amazonas, Antipodes, South Seas, the East, the Poles–the *Lawless*

[2] V. S. Pritchett, "The Writer as a Traveler," *The New Statesman and Nation* (London), Vol. LI, pp. 693–94 (June 16, 1956).

Roads, the *Enchafèd Flood, Journey without Maps, Journey to a War, Le Mystère bestial, L'Espace du Dedans.* "The modern educational journey is not the Grand Tour but the territories of the *Grand Débâcle.*" Poets and novelists sometimes venture on it, but they take explorers and scientists for their guides.

The writer who travels is less likely to choose virgin territory (though he may, like Melville, Conrad, Saint-Exupéry, or Michaux, make forays into it). He is not so much a discoverer as a rediscoverer. His values are as much those he brings with him as those he finds waiting for him. The professional or scientific traveler works under a great initial advantage. He profits by the unprejudiced truth of his material, the objective reality of the life he encounters. If he happens to have an artist's skill in reporting it, as Park, Doughty, and Parkman had, his expressive powers will be strengthened by the objective truth he deals with. Imaginative writers sometimes draw on that kind of strength also.[3] But it is not his first business to create or impose. It is to observe and impart.

The writer who travels may enjoy greater advantages of access, transport, preparation, and comfort, but his task, whether as poet, novelist, or chronicler, is a much more complex one. He comes as a predisposed, purposive, and highly subjective sensibility, a prepared and sensitized in-

[3] Cf. T. S. Eliot: "There are, perhaps, only two ways in which a writer can acquire the understanding of environment which he can later turn to account: by having spent his childhood in that environment—that is, living in it at a period of life in which one experiences much more than one is aware of; and by having had to struggle for a livelihood in that environment—a livelihood bearing no direct relation to any intention of writing about it, of *using* it as literary material. Most of Joseph Conrad's understanding came to him in the latter way. Mark Twain knew the Mississippi in both ways: he had spent his childhood on its banks, and he had earned his living matching his wits against its currents." Introduction to *The Adventures of Huckleberry Finn* (1950).

strument. He brings with him a complicated conditioning and a prepared insight, to which he must remain faithful. But he encounters phenomena of place and time, history and society, culture and achievement, and the values they embody, and he has to be faithful to these likewise. He travels under a double responsibility. He must bring into single focus two aspects of reality—his own truth and the truth of what he sees. He owes a duty to his phenomena but he also owes a duty to himself. It is not every writer, however gifted, who is capable of sustaining the dual honesty of the reporter and of the man of creative insight and imagination. His predicament has been defined by a modern poet who has subjected himself to the test of travel:

> Of all possible subjects, travel is the most difficult for an artist, as it is the easiest for a journalist. For the latter, the interesting event is the new, the extraordinary, the comic, the shocking, and all that the peripatetic journalist requires is a flair for being on the spot where and when such events happen—the rest is merely passive typewriter thumping: meaning, relation, importance, are not his quarry. The artist, on the other hand, is deprived of his most treasured liberty, the freedom to invent; successfully to extract importance from historical personal events without ever departing from them, free only to select and never to modify or to add, calls for imagination of a very high order.[4]

VII

When Henry James wrote his earlier travel essays he put himself in the middle ground where the journalist and the artist are expected to collaborate. Though already fully

[4] W. H. Auden, Introduction to James's *The American Scene* (1946).

aware of which of these two roles he had dedicated himself to, he took on the office of the traveler who writes, and as such he sent his reports to *The Nation*, the *New York Tribune*, and *The Atlantic Monthly*. (It is significant that almost none of his travel writings were done for English periodicals. Though some enjoyed circulation among continental tourists in the Tauchnitz editions, until 1900 only one of his travel books, *Portraits of Places*, was published in England. He wrote about his travels expressly for Americans and only incidentally or until his last years for the English.) He made himself as efficient a journalist as it lay in his capacity to do. But he was never wholly comfortable in this role, least of all when journalism put pressure on his prose and required it to be simple or newsworthy. When he engaged to write Paris letters for the *New York Tribune* in the 1870's, he made his one effort to become a systematic reporter of public events and history, and to do his duty by French politics, social news, and theatrical events; it was not to be until many years later, when he made his first return journey in twenty-one years to the United States in 1904–5 and produced *The American Scene*, that he applied himself to anything resembling systematic critical or social observation. But when Whitelaw Reid, the editor of the *Tribune*, complained that his reports were not the lively topical article his readers wanted, James was quite willing to throw up the game.[5]

[5] James to Whitelaw Reid from France, August 30, 1876: "I have just received your letter of August 10th. I quite appreciate what you say about the character of my letters, and about their not being the right sort of thing for a newspaper. I have been half expecting to hear from you to that effect. . . . I can easily imagine that the general reader should feel indisposed to give them the time requisite for reading them. They would, as you say, be more in place in a magazine. But I am afraid I can't assent to your proposal that I should try and write otherwise. I know the sort of letter you mean—it is doubtless the proper sort of thing for the *Tribune* to have. But I can't

James, in fact, was not prepared to treat history in motion, or, outside his fiction, life in action. How far he was from being an active sociologist or systematic reporter can be seen if one compares all but his last travel writings with some of the classics of systematic observation in the nineteenth century—Tocqueville's *La Démocratie en Amérique,* Taine's *Notes sur l'Angleterre,* or Livingstone's *Journals,* just as his distance from the efficient topical journalism of his time can be seen by any comparison of his essays with the flood of contemporary reporting and history that poured from the presses of his day, to a large share of which he at one time gave his attention as a reviewer.[6]

---

produce it—I don't know how and I couldn't learn how. It would cost me really more trouble than to write as I have been doing (which comes tolerably easy to me) and it would be poor economy for me to try and become 'newsy' and gossipy. I am too finical a writer and I should be constantly becoming more 'literary' than is desirable. To resist this tendency would be rowing upstream and would take much time and pains. If my letters have been 'too good' I am honestly afraid that they are the poorest I can do, especially for the money! I had better, therefore, suspend them, altogether. I have enjoyed writing them, however, and if the *Tribune* has not been the better for them I hope it has not been too much the worse. I shall doubtless have sooner or later a discreet successor." (*The Selected Letters of Henry James,* edited by Leon Edel, 1955, pp. 67–68.) James's *Parisian Sketches* from the *New York Tribune* have now been assembled by Leon Edel and Ilse Dusoir Lind (New York, 1957). His reports on the American, French, and British drama and theater, written intermittently over the years 1872–1901, are likewise unsystematic, and were never written for any one specific editor or journal; they form, however, one of James's most valuable series of criticisms, and can now be read in Allan Wade's edition of *The Scenic Art: Notes on Acting and the Drama* by Henry James (1948).

[6] James reviewed Taine's *Notes sur l'Angleterre* for the New York *Nation* of January 25, 1872, as well as Taine's *Italy: Rome and Naples* (May 7, 1868) and *Notes on Paris* (May 6, 1875). He reviewed Livingstone's *Last Journals* in *The Nation* of March 11, 1875. He seems never to have written on Tocqueville. Between 1868 and 1877 he covered a large number of works of travel, exploration, contemporary history, and journalistic re-

James preferred his history and subject matter fixed for scrutiny, composed for observation, arrested so far as possible in their moment of time for his study or diversion. In one or two of his English essays—"An English Easter," "London at Midsummer," both of 1877, and in a few paragraphs of his long London study of 1888—he touches briefly on the social undercurrent, the life of the working class and the poor, but any attempt at a serious portrayal of that life such as he undertook in writing *The Princess Casamassima* is soon skirted. When he found himself surrounded by the Roman carnival in 1873 ("A Roman Holiday"), he found it to be a distraction from his Roman preferences. ("I turned my back accordingly on the Corso and wandered away to the grass-grown quarters. . . . I have been keeping Carnival by strolling perversely along the silent circumference of Rome. . . . The place has passed so completely for the winter months into the hands of the barbarians that that estimable character the passionate pilgrim finds it constantly harder to keep his passion clear.") Arriving on another journey in Genoa ("Italy Revisited"), he saw the spectacle of toil and poverty in the palatial streets as a rough intrusion on his pleasure:

---

search, all of which gave him opportunity to discuss the literary principles of these species. Most of these reviews appeared in *The Nation*. The books included travel writings by Gautier, Augustus Hare, Howells, Sir Samuel Baker, and many minor writers, and the subjects included Russia, Constantinople, Italy, England, Portugal, the United States and Canada, France, Africa, Australia, Ismailia, Spain, China, Indo-China, *Lost Empires, Communistic Societies,* Parkman's *Jesuits in North America* and *The Old Régime in Canada,* etc. These articles remain uncollected but they compose into a valuable account of James's dealings with the literature of travel and history; several quotations in this introduction are drawn from them. His important study of the art critic as traveler is his review of Fromentin's *Les Maîtres d'Autrefois, The Nation,* July 13, 1876 (now included in *The Painter's Eye* by Henry James, edited by J. L. Sweeney, 1956).

> A traveler is very often disposed to ask himself whether it has been worth while to leave his home—whatever his home may have been—only to see new forms of human suffering, only to be reminded that toil and privation, hunger and sorrow and sordid effort, are the portion of the great majority of his fellow-men. To travel is, as it were, to go to the play, to attend a spectacle; and there is something heartless in stepping forth into the streets of a foreign town to feast upon novelty when the novelty consists simply of the slightly different costume in which hunger and labour present themselves.

France gave him a stronger challenge and a richer opportunity for social analysis: he made a fairly serious effort to provide it in his *Tribune* dispatches; but it was at a place like the Théâtre Français that he found French civilization best displayed: "a copious source of instruction as to French ideas, manners, and philosophy." Even when, thirty years later, he returned to the United States to observe the new energy at work in his native land, whatever the zest, astonishment, or fascination he applied to studying the teeming forces of the New World—the business, commerce, immigrant life, and headlong progress of New York and other cities—they were exercised under a kind of protest. "The huge American rattle of gold," the " 'business' field," the "movement of a breathless civilization," the "whole play of wealth and energy and untutored liberty"—these, he confessed, offered "a line of research closed to me, alas, by my fatally uninitiated state." The push and thrust of the "ubiquitous American force," the stir of aggressive life, the turbulence of sheer animal energy, stimulated him to the most acute social observation he ever arrived at, and they helped to make *The American Scene* a masterpiece of its kind; but they were not the stimulus his own kind of vision most required or best could use. On certain occasions they served him importantly in his fictions; in his travels they confused his purpose and distracted his contemplation. The kind of book Taine and Engels wrote about England, or Tocqueville, Dickens, and the Trollopes about America, was beyond his capacity and outside his purpose. "Such failures of opportunity and of penetration, however, are but the daily bread of the visionary tourist," he admitted. He looked in another direction for his success.

VIII

A "visionary tourist"—it was by some such term that he habitually called himself: sometimes a "sentimental tourist," frequently a "seeker of aesthetic pleasure" or a "lover of the picturesque," often a "cosmopolite," most characteristically a "passionate pilgrim." He belongs in fact to a distinctly nineteenth century race of travelers. The race has largely disappeared today. If they survive they seek their subjects in places as remote from the harassed West as possible—Claudel in China, Freya Stark in Asia Minor, Isak Dinesen in Africa. Their high moment fell between the strain and danger of early exploration and the scientific inquiry or political engagement of our own age. Their century was the century of the *genius loci,* and their bibles were Murray, Baedeker, and the *Guide Joanne.* Goethe, Byron, Chateaubriand, Stendhal, and Browning were the heroes in whose wake a large class of lesser wanderers and seekers of the place spirit trailed—Clough with the *Amours de Voyage;* Gissing with a masterpiece, *By the Ionian Sea;* Symonds, Hearn, Howells, Loti, Vernon Lee; with Norman Douglas as one of the last of the line. They might have taken their motto from a modern poet:

> We were the last romantics—chose for theme
> Traditional sanctity and loveliness.

When James presented himself as a devotee of "constituted beauty"; when he made it his business to discover "the classic quality of the French nature"; when he said that among England's abbeys and castles "you feast upon the pictorial, you inhale the historic"; when he asked with some uneasiness "How far should a lover of old cathedrals let his hands be tied by the sanctity of their traditions?"; when he felt in American resorts of pleasure "the absence of serious associations"; when he asserted that "the flower of art blooms only where the soil is deep" and that "it takes a great deal of beauty to produce a little literature"; when he began his elaborate evocation of the history and splendors of Venice by saying, "I write these lines with the full consciousness of having no information whatever to offer," and added that "I hold any writer sufficiently justified who is himself in love with his topic," he set himself down as a member of that company.

To steep himself in "the tone of time," to cultivate and nourish his "sense of the past," was his constant and ruling passion; and the one discomfort he seems to have felt in indulging it came from the fact that, as a tourist at least partially disabled by the romantic fallacy inseparable from the role of the spectator, he could not more completely identify himself with what he saw. "Our observation in any foreign land is extremely superficial," he more than once confessed; and the hero of one of his early stories, "Travelling Companions," beholding the "palpable, material sanctity" of a great Italian church, exclaims to his companion: "What a real pity that we are not Catholics; that that dazzling monument is not something more to us than a mere splendid show! What a different thing this visiting of churches would be for us, if we occasionally felt the prompting to fall on our knees. I begin to grow ashamed of this perpetual attitude of bald curiosity."

Curiosity, bald or furtive, successfully concealed or not,

was nevertheless the first incentive of James's explorations, and he never discarded his native American passion or innocence sufficiently to disguise it. But the mind that directed it could never let it remain curiosity and nothing more. Conscious as he admitted himself to be of "missed occasions and delays overdone," much as he could "regret that [he] might not, first or last, have gone farther, penetrated deeper, spoken oftener—closed, in short, more intimately with the great general subject," he was fully aware that "from the moment the principle of selection and expression, with a tourist, is not the delight of the eyes and the play of fancy, it should be an energy in every way much larger," and that "there is no happy mean . . . between the sense and the quest of the picture, and the surrender to it, and the sense and the quest of the constitution, the inner springs of the subject—springs and connections social, economic, historic."

> There are relations that soon get beyond all merely showy appearances of value for us. Their value becomes thus private and practical, and is represented by the process—the quieter, mostly, the better—of absorption and assimilation of what the relation has done for us.

Such value was bound to be a critical value for him: it was what his role as a traveling American and native of the James family required him to seek. It was as a traveling critic and observer preparing himself for a professional career in writing that he always felt himself obliged to justify his foreign sojourns and indulgences, both to his uneasy family back home and to his editors and readers in America.[7] But rigorous critical application was never the whole

[7] Leon Edel, discussing James's first adult trip to Europe in 1869–70 and the means he took to allay the financial and other doubts that came to him from his family in the States, says: "He defined his situation as a need to lay the foundations for an education in the great works of painting and sculpture 'which

duty of travel to him. Criticism might mean something better than systematic analysis and dissection. "To appreciate, to appropriate, to take intellectual possession," and to make the criticized thing "one's own," as well as "the quest of the constitution, the inner springs of the subject," were important. Without them he would have considered himself a spendthrift of time and opportunity and a failure in his task. But James emphasizes equally the necessity of "surrendering" to the picture before him, of making it his own in more than an energetic or possessive sense. He may have traveled as a critic but he also traveled as a seeking spirit and an artist in sensations, an explorer of "a world of reflection and emotion." When he undertook to write his sketches he might try his best to sit down to journalism; he invariably rose from authorship.

And it was more than sketches he made of his travels. He made tales and novels of them as well. Delightful, charming, amusing, and instructive as his essays are—for pure pleasure and grace of writing they have few equals in English—the greater value and profit of his explorings shows itself in his fiction. There his images of travel take on their deepest insight and resonance; there his experience in the landscape, cities, monuments, and history of Europe and America joins most profoundly with his sense of human fate and character, with the comedy and tragedy of life, and

---

may be of future use to me.' He also had to make the most of the opportunity to visit the great cities and historic places on the Continent. . . . 'I shall hang on to a place till it has yielded me its drop of life-blood,' he said, explaining his method of intensive study of each town he visited. 'I promise you there shall be a method in my madness. In this way I hope to get a good deal for my money and to make it last a long time. How long I know not. When it is gone I shall come home,' and he added, 'a new man.'" *Henry James: The Untried Years 1843–1870* (1953), pp. 298–99. This major biography details James's travels up to 1870 in full; and its sequels, *The Middle Years* and *The Master,* will presumably complete the chronicle.

with the dramas of conflict, evil, or spiritual triumph he created from the age he witnessed and the wide international stage he took for his province.

IX

His critical consciousness was most active the closer he found himself involved, personally, professionally, or socially, in the scene around him. It is possible to define the degrees of this activity in James according to the relations he established with the countries he frequented. The early American essays of 1870–71 quickly establish their tone as one of urbanity and amused sophistication. Saratoga is "the least complete of all the cities of pleasure"; he finds he has made "a cruelly small allowance for the stern vulgarities of life"; and though he admits that "one's visions, on the whole, gain more than they lose by being transmuted into fact," that "there is an essential indignity in indefiniteness," and that facts "give more to the imagination than they receive from it," it is "the eloquent silence of undedicated nature" in the rude surrounding country that makes "you wonder what it is you so deeply and calmly enjoy." At Newport, with which he had from boyhood such intimate family associations, he held himself

> very far from professing a cynical contempt for the gaieties and vanities of Newport life: they are, as a spectacle, extremely amusing; . . . they are worth observing, if only to conclude against them; they possess at least the dignity of all extreme and emphatic expressions of a social tendency; but they are not so untouched with Philistinism that I do not seem to overhear at times the still, small voice of this tender sense of the sweet, superior beauty of the natural things that surround them, pleading gently in their favour to the fastidious critic.

But he soon admits "that to speak of a place with abundance you must know it, but not too well," and "I suffer from knowing the natural elements of Newport too well to describe them." Quebec, being Canadian, French, and foreign, gives him as a first impression the notion "that not America, but Europe, should have the credit" of its existence. It reminds him of Balzac. There "the historic sense, conscious of a general solidarity in the picturesque, ekes out the romance and deepens the colouring"; and the patriotic American's reflection on "the ultimate possibility of their becoming absorbed into his own huge state" produces in "this sentimental tourist of ours" "little but regret." America is decidedly held at the full length of the critical arm. It is only when the tourist confronts Niagara in the grandeur and desolation of its untamed magnificence that he abandons all caution and launches into one of the great bravura descriptive feats of his early prose.

France offered a challenge even more rigorous than America did in James's earlier years, and its complexity taxed him throughout his life, from *The American* to *The Ambassadors*. Of all European countries it offered an example of the highest civilization, the purest historic idea, the most impressive order in culture, art, manners, and society. As a writer he put himself to school among the *cénacles* and arts of Paris, but the apprenticeship was never wholly congenial or comfortable and it ended in withdrawal. No country so attracted and charmed him, and yet none so definitely marked him as a foreigner, moralist, puritan, and outsider. "Surrender" was never possible there though other reactions were—an overwhelming boyhood revelation in the Galerie d'Apollon of the Louvre, where the "sense of glory" and the triumph of style were first impressed on him; a lifelong passion for Balzac; a lifetime's respect and admiration; and the sense of being "deeply devoted always to the revelations" and "indebted to the genius of France." Strether's capitulation represents one side of James's relations with French life and culture; Christopher Newman's betrayal represents another, and it was never wholly effaced.

It is significant that when James wrote his first essay on Paris in 1877 he set himself down as a "cosmopolite" and found the role uncomfortable. The "baleful spirit of the cosmopolite" came as an "uncomfortable consequence of seeing many lands and feeling at home in none":

> To be a cosmopolite is not, I think, an ideal; the ideal should be to be a concentrated patriot. Being a cosmopolite is an accident, but one must make the best of it. If you have lived about, as the phrase is, you have lost that sense of the absoluteness and the sanctity of the habits of your fellow-patriots which once made you so happy in the midst of them. You have seen that there are a great many *patriae* in the world, and that each of these is filled with excellent people for whom the local idiosyncrasies are the only thing that is not rather barbarous. There comes a time when one set of customs, wherever it may be found, grows to seem to you about as provincial as another; and then I suppose it may be said of you that you have become a cosmopolite.

The "best of it" is "the habit of comparing, of looking for points of difference and resemblance," of coming "to think well of mankind," and there is "something to be said for it." But France kept him too busy comparing, contrasting, balancing, and subtracting, ever to give a sense of ease and free assimilation. It remained from first to last a test of his critical acumen: invaluable, indispensable, intellectually rewarding, imaginatively bracing, but never a home for himself or his art.

England may have offered an equal challenge to James, but here a deeper and more viable sympathy operated, and it ended in his making England his home. There he could feel, in his early days, as homesick and estranged as he ever felt anywhere. It was the country and London the city of Dickens and a hundred early enthusiasms. But, he wrote his sister, "I have been crushed under a sense of the mere magnitude of London—its inconceivable immensity—in such a way as to paralyse my mind for any appreciation of details." It induces "an extraordinary intellectual depression . . . an indefinable flatness of mind. The place sits on you, broods on you, stamps on you with the feet of its myriad bipeds and quadrupeds." It is "dreadful," it is "delightful." Its "low black houses [are] like so many rows of coal scuttles and as inanimate"; and "What terrible places are these English hotels!"

> I have [he wrote eight years later] every disposition to think better of the English race than of any other except my own. There are things which make it natural I should; there are inducements, provocations, temptations, almost bribes. There have been moments when I have almost burned my ships behind me . . . I am convinced that if I had taken this reckless engagement, I should greatly have regretted it. . . . If one were to give up the privilege of comparing the English with other people, one would very soon, in a moment of reaction, make once for all (and most unjustly) such a comparison as would leave the English nowhere.

It was the era of the "certain condescension" Lowell defined as constitutionally and unconsciously endemic to the island race, and the ranklement of it could stir James to the sharpest satire and sarcasm he ever applied to a people—as witness *An International Episode,* "Lady Barbarina," "A London Life," "The Point of View," or the Cassandra-like prophecy of the Princess Casamassima: "the old régime again, bristling with every iniquity and every abuse, over which the French Revolution passed like a whirlwind; or perhaps even more a reproduction of Roman society in its decadence, gouty, apoplectic, depraved, gorged and clogged with wealth and spoils, selfishness and scepticism, and waiting for the onset of the barbarians."

Yet England was also the country of James's "banquet of initiation." She gave him her stories of memory, tradition, amenity, recognition; gave him friendship, hospitality, and fame; and by 1881 he could write in his journal:

> *J'y suis absolument comme chez moi.* Such an experience is an education—it fortifies the character and embellishes the mind. It is difficult to speak adequately or justly of London. It is not a pleasant place; it is not agreeable, or cheerful, or easy, or exempt from reproach. It is only magnificent. You can draw up a tremendous list of reasons why it should be insupportable. The fogs, the smoke, the dirt, the darkness, the wet, the distances, the ugliness, the brutal size of the place, the horrible numerosity of society, the manner in which this senseless bigness is fatal to amenity, to convenience, to conversation, to good manners—all this and much more you may expatiate upon. You may call it dreary, heavy, stupid, dull, inhuman, vulgar at heart and tiresome in form. I have felt all these things at times so strongly that I have said—"Ah London, you too then are impossible?" But these are occasional moods; and for one who takes it as I take it, London is on the whole the most possible form of life. I take it as an artist and as a bachelor; as one who has the passion for observation and whose business is the study of human life. It is the biggest aggregation of human life—the most complete compendium of the world. The human race is better represented there than anywhere else, and if you learn to know your London you learn a great many things.

By 1913 he could tell his English friends that "I was drawn to London long years ago as by the sense, felt from still earlier, of all the interest and association I should find here, and I now see how my faith was to sink deeper foundations than I could presume ever to measure." And in 1915, breaking the news of his British naturalization to his nephew, he laid down his final commitment: "I have spent here all the best years of my life—they practically have *been* my life. . . . My practical relation has been to this [country] for so long, and now my 'spiritual' or 'sentimental' quite ideally matches it."

Here James felt the most complete test of identification of his lifetime—except for one other; and he experienced the test in all it meant to him of grateful sympathy and stubborn self-assertion, submissive affection and recalcitrant pride, sense of kinship and sense of difference, the right to love but the right also to criticize. He wrote these contrary emotions and mutually necessary judgments into everything he wrote about England. They provide the dialectic substance of his English fictions as well as his English essays, making these a central bulwark of his lifework.

But the same debate of attitudes, in an even subtler form and with a more profound sense of personal participation, comes in his treatment of America and Americans. The debate began with his birth and childhood; it continued as the vital thread or lifeline of his tales and novels from first to last. It extends from *Roderick Hudson* and *The American* to *The Sense of the Past* and *The Ivory Tower*. It is enacted by his salient characters, from Hudson, Clement Searle, Christopher Newman, and Isabel Archer, to Strether, Milly Theale, Adam and Maggie Verver, Ralph Pendrel, Graham Fielder. It is James's own, original, persistent, incontestible, first and final subject; and *The American Scene* of 1907 is the book that gives it its fullest objective critical statement.

Until now he had been, whatever his European commitment, an American abroad or an American at home. In *The American Scene* all the complex elements of his history and character combined—the American and the European, the native and the expatriate, exile and homecomer, critic and patriot. The book has the curious effect of thrusting on James the protean role of summarizing in himself all his American predecessors who had attempted to locate themselves in time and place at home or abroad: of being a conscious synthesis or end product of *Home as Found, Our Old Home, The American Scholar* and *English Traits, Mardi* and *Moby Dick, Innocents Abroad* and *The Gilded Age, Song of Myself* and *Democratic Vistas*. And it forecasts the day of *An American Tragedy, U.S.A., Eimi, The People, Yes,* and *The Bridge.*

There is now no possibility of presenting himself as a sentimental tourist, passionate pilgrim, cosmopolite, devotee of aesthetic pleasure or the picturesque, or visionary traveler. He becomes the "restless analyst." America, as he had long ago recognized, had long ceased to be a country where "the elements of high civilisation, as it exists in other countries . . . are absent." The deficiencies he had ascribed to Hawthorne's time in his book of 1879—"No State, in the European sense of the word," "barely a specific national name," "no sovereign, no court, no personal loyalty, no aristocracy, no church, no clergy, no army, no diplomatic service, no country gentlemen, no palaces, no castles, nor manors, nor old country-houses, nor parsonages, nor thatched cottages, nor ivied ruins; no cathedrals, nor abbeys, nor little Norman churches; no great Universities nor public schools—no Oxford, nor Eton, nor Harrow; no literature, no novels, no museums, no pictures, no political society, no sporting class—no Epsom nor Ascot!"—these had been repaired and compensated for by a "staggering superabundance of everything." The void had been filled and more than filled. He faced the task of matching himself against "the great adventure of a society reaching out into the apparent void for the amenities, the consummations, after having earnestly gathered in so many of the preparations and necessities." The Civil War, as he had perceived a quarter-century earlier, had marked "an era in the history of the American mind": it had "introduced into the national consciousness a certain sense of proportion and relation, of the world being a more complicated place than it had hitherto seemed, the future more treacherous, success more difficult." "The good American" had all too truly "eaten of the tree of knowledge." James, coming home with all Europe had given him of complexity, success in life, and a sense of proportion, relation, and treachery, "'fresh' as an enquiring stranger" but also "acute as an initiated native," found himself standing up to a challenge more forcible than even Europe or England had given him.

The result, while unquestionably a work of art, is also a critical and documentary landmark that marks a stage in America's coming-of-age. Its author is no longer simply a traveler. His internationalism is now not a matter of transatlantic contrasts and comparisons. It is a question of discovering that good and evil, tradition and discontinuity, progress and privation, even America and Europe, can exist simultaneously in a nation that is more physically and materially an "heir of all the ages" than he himself had been. James now knew himself as never before to be an initiated native of everything he saw—a Jamesian native, moreover, on whom nothing he discovered in America could be lost, and for whom retreat into the past or into the glory of order and tradition was no longer—even at the age of sixty-four—possible. The American journey of 1904–5 gave him more than *The American Scene*. It gave him the task of reassessing his entire life and lifework for the New York Edition of his novels and tales. It gave him "Crapy Cornelia," "A Round of Visits," and "The Jolly Corner." It led him toward his three books of autobiography, and it spurred him to take up the two novels, both of them revivals of the international subject, which occupied him as a recapitulation of the great theme of his career in his final years—*The Sense of the Past* and *The Ivory Tower.*

Thus James's dealings with the three countries in whose life and culture he was most deeply involved—France, England, America—imposed on him tests of moral judgment, self-assessment, and personal choice which never permitted them to remain passive or purely spectacular in his writings. They were at all times active agents in his destiny, and he knew himself to be an active participant in their destinies as well. He wrote about all three of them as more than a traveler: they obliged him to be critic, analyst, and moralist. There remained one country, however (his dealings with Germany, Switzerland, Holland, and Belgium are slight and transitory), in which his personal fate was never involved or challenged; in which he could escape from the intellectual or moral strain of criticism and judgment; and in which he perhaps found the deepest spiritual and aesthetic affinity of his life.

"And which country do you prefer?" asks the New England heroine in "Four Meetings" of the gentleman who tells her story.

"'There's one I love beyond any. I think you'd do the same.'

"Her gaze rested as on a dim revelation and then she breathed, 'Italy?'

"'Italy,' I answered softly too; and for a moment we communed over it." And Isabel Archer, in *The Portrait of a Lady,* pausing at San Remo, found that "the charm of the Mediterranean coast only deepened . . . on acquaintance, for it was the threshold of Italy, the gate of admirations"; and Italy "stretched before her as a land of promise, a land in which a love of the beautiful might be comforted by endless knowledge."

In no other country did James find his spirit so freed of confinement, of fixed and conscious identity; so liberated from practical personal decision and responsibility, and so inspired to his profoundest sense of beauty, his most passionate instinct for the meaning of art and history. There, far more than in Paris or England, art and faith were "blind, generous instincts"; there the "solemnity of time" and the "sublimity of eternity" best measured the brevity and vanity of life and set the seal of wisdom, pity, tragedy, and spiritual triumph on mortal things. The surging excitement that had possessed him when he first descended from the North in 1869, down through Lombardy, Venezia, and Tuscany to make his first entry into Rome ("At last—for the first time—I live!") never released him from the enchantment of "the Spirit of the South." The "beautiful dishevelled nymph" became the muse of a lifetime. Venice, Florence, and Rome remained "shrines for the reverential spirit" to the last.

They and what they gave him—the art of Titian, Tintoretto, Michelangelo; the Campagna, the Campidoglio, Bellosguardo, St. Mark's; the "aesthetic presence of the past," the "felicity of picturesqueness," the "supreme perception of luxury," and a hundred other testimonies of "mind, spirit, harmony, creation"—inspired James to his richest expression as an artist of travel. It was Italy that gave his fiction its moments of deepest resonance, his drama and tragedy their most memorable images of knowledge, recognition, and justice. It is she who witnesses, with her ancient wisdom and time-tested sense of destiny, the fates of Roderick Hudson, of Daisy Miller, of Isabel Archer as her doom closes down on her—

> she wished to be far away, under the sky, where she could descend from her carriage and tread upon the dai-

> sies. She had long before this taken old Rome into her confidence, for in a world of ruins the ruin of her happiness seemed a less unnatural catastrophe. She rested her weariness upon things that had crumbled for centuries and yet still were upright; she dropped her secret sadness into the silence of lonely places. . . . She had become deeply, tenderly acquainted with Rome; it interfused and moderated her passion. But she had grown to think of it chiefly as the place where people had suffered—

of Milly Theale as betrayal overtakes her and of her betrayer in his hour of recognition:

> It was a Venice all of evil that had broken out for them alike, so that they were together in their anxiety, if they really could have met on it; a Venice of cold lashing rain from a low black sky, of wicked wind raging through narrow passes, of general arrest and interruption, with the people engaged in all the water-life huddled, stranded and wageless, bored and cynical, under archways and bridges. . . . Here, in the high arcade, half Venice was crowded close, while, on the Molo, at the limit of the expanse, the old columns of the Saint Theodore and of the Lion were the frame of a door wide open to the storm . . . and the whole place, in its huge elegance, the grace of its conception and the beauty of its detail, was more than ever like a great drawing-room, the drawing-room of Europe, profaned and bewildered by some reverse of fortune.

In America, England, and France, James could exercise himself in all the parts his active and engaged intelligence imposed on him—as sentimentalist, pilgrim, critic, analyst, or cosmopolite. When he crossed the Alps he became something else. He was possessed by a "passion," and hardly a page he wrote on the South fails to present him as "a lover." It is as "a lover of Italy" that his love becomes a full surrender and expresses itself in a poetry of history, harmony, and art that issued from the deepest springs of his nature.

X

How essential to his experience James's travels were; how much they gave his genius its appropriate voice and opportunity; how necessary a part he made them of his achievement and of the moment of history that made the achievement possible—all this becomes apparent as soon as his character as an artist is realized and his work is experienced in its full meaning. All achievement in art, once its authority and truth are clear, takes on a retrospective logic. It is one of the functions of art to do so. We profit in our own lives by seeing the use to which a talent puts the opportunity that is given it, and every feature of that opportunity—good fortune or bad, privilege or privation, success or failure—counts in the sum.

James's opportunity was a rich one and he met it fully prepared. He came to it as an American, as a man of the nineteenth century, as a member of the James family; as a product of the "sensuous education" his father provided him and as a nature schooled from childhood in enthusiasm, curiosity, and a sense of the past. It was this equipment that he brought with him into his excursions at home and abroad; and, as we see what he made of it, it is impossible to think of his life or his work apart from the great scene in which they were tested and fulfilled. Dubious as he might sometimes feel about yielding to "the baleful spirit of the cosmopolite" or of "seeing many lands and feeling at home in none"; much as he might warn one friend of the "drawback" of "not having the homeliness and the inevitability and the happy limitation and the affluent poverty of a Country of your Own," or confess to another that "the mixture of Europe and America which you see in me has proved disastrous," there could have been for him, as there can be for his readers today, no question of the fitness to his character and purpose which he made of these conditions of his life. He was given a subject to record, a moment of history to dramatize, and a penetrating sense of past and present to express. For their faithful expression no other stage was possible than the international scene he chose as the theater of his imagination.

Nor was it possible for him, however widely he ranged through the scenes and nations that gave him the settings and characters of his drama, to disown the endowment of spirit and curiosity his origins had given him. This remained his point of vantage and departure in everything he wrote. It came of being born in 1843 in New York City, the son of his particular parents, a child of his century, and the heir not merely "of all the ages" but of what must always count as a greater advantage for a writer who puts his talent to the service of realism and justice—a specific, concrete, and imperative moment in time. There could be little risk of such a character losing itself abroad. There was only the severe task for that character of proving itself worthy of its opportunity as the chosen instrument of the moment, subject, and experience that were given it to record.

James was right in thinking of his as a "given" case. So is everyone's case, and failure or success are measured by the degree to which a man is able to prove the justice of it. Few men have exposed themselves more fully than James did to the tests of such an assignment, and few have confessed their exposure by a more complete exercise of consciousness and perception. He changed his skies. He did not and could not change the character or spirit he took with him. These remained the animus of his explorings of the world of his time, and the art by which he fulfilled them testifies as much to the truth of insight and imagination he carried into that world as to the truth of the revelation with which the world repaid him. His travel writings, with their acuteness of observation, integrity of interest, and brilliance of detail and expression, share with his writings on literature and art the resources of intelligence, sympathy, and imagination that produced the greater art of his fiction. They are part and substance of that art, and they are an indispensable share of James's gift to his inheritors.

Morton Dauwen Zabel

Part I

The Sentimental Tourist

Early American Travels

1870—1871

Editor's Note

*James had been contributing stories and book reviews to American magazines—*The Continental Monthly, The North American Review, The Atlantic Monthly, The Nation, The Galaxy*—for six years before he began to write his first travel sketches in 1870; and though they followed not only his youthful sojourns abroad but his first adult journey to Europe in 1869–70, they were not on European subjects but on American. They antedate even the European essays assembled in his first book of travel,* Transatlantic Sketches, *in 1875, and were first printed in* The Nation *in 1870–71. When James included them in* Portraits of Places *in 1883 he described them as "the earliest published" of those travel writings and added that they could "now have (in some slight degree) only the value of history." Besides the four on Saratoga, Newport, Quebec, and Niagara included here from* Portraits of Places, *he wrote on "Lake George" (in* The Nation, *August 25, 1870) and on "From Lake George to Burlington" (September 1, 1870). He was to use American scenes and backgrounds in many of his tales and novels in these and future years, but he was not again to treat of American scenic and social subjects in his essays until he returned to America many years later, in 1904–5, to gather* *material for* The American Scene (1907). *Thus James's earliest experiments in the art of travel were devoted to his own country, and they serve as an appropriate prelude to his excursions in foreign parts.*

The dates printed at the head of essays throughout this book are wherever possible those affixed to them by James himself. Where he did not supply them, the dates given here are, so far as they can be determined, those of the journeys on which the essays were based or, failing that, of first magazine publication (as indicated in the Bibliography at the end of this volume). When collecting his travel writings in book form James was usually apologetic about the passage of time. "It is obvious that the impressions and observations they for the most part embody [have] sprung from an early stage of acquaintance with their general subject-matter," he more than once remarked. Since the essays include a good deal of local, topical, or passing historical allusion, it has been considered advisable here to date them as close to the time of the journeys they record as possible. "They represent a good many wonderments and judgments and emotions, whether felicities or mistakes, the fine freshness of which the author has—to his misfortune, no doubt—sufficiently outlived," James said in the preface to English Hours *in 1905; "But they may perhaps on that very account present something of a curious interest." It is this interest they hold for James's readers now, and the dates of their writing are pertinent not only to the times they reflect but to the stages of his own progress as a traveler, a maturing intelligence, and an artist in language.*

Saratoga

1870

The sentimental tourist makes images in advance; they grow up in his mind by a logic of their own. He finds himself thinking of an unknown, unseen place, as having such and such a shape and figure rather than such another. It assumes in his mind a certain complexion, a certain colour which frequently turns out to be singularly at variance with reality. For some reason or other, I had supposed Saratoga to be buried in a sort of elegant wilderness. I imagined a region of shady forest drives, with a bright, broad-terraced hotel gleaming here and there against a background of mysterious groves and glades. I had made a cruelly small allowance for the stern vulgarities of life—for the shops and sidewalks and loafers, the complex machinery of a city of pleasure. The fault was so wholly my own that it is quite without bitterness that I proceed to affirm that the Saratoga of experience is sadly different from this. I confess, however, that it has always seemed to me that one's visions, on the whole, gain more than they lose by being transmuted into fact. There is an essential indignity in indefiniteness; you cannot allow for accidents and details until you have seen them. They give more to the imagination than they receive from it. I frankly admit, therefore, that the Saratoga of reality is a much more satisfactory place than the all-too-primitive Elysium I had constructed. It is indeed, as I say, immensely different. There is a vast number of brick—nay, of asphalt—sidewalks, a great many shops, and a magnificent array of loafers. But what indeed are you to do at Saratoga—the morning draught having been achieved—unless you loaf? "Que faire en un gîte à moins que l'on ne songe?" Loafers being assumed, of course shops and sidewalks follow. The main avenue of Saratoga does not scruple to call itself Broadway. The untravelled reader may form a very accurate idea of it by recalling as distinctly as possible, not indeed the splendours of that famous thoroughfare, but the secondary charms of the Sixth Avenue. The place has what the French would call the "accent" of the Sixth Avenue. Its two main features are the two monster hotels which stand facing each other along a goodly portion of its course. One, I believe, is considered much better than the other—less of a monster and more of a refuge—but in appearance there is little choice between them. Both are immense brick structures, directly on the crowded, noisy street, with vast covered piazzas running along the façade, supported by great iron posts. The piazza of the Union Hotel, I have been repeatedly informed, is the largest "in the world." There are a number of objects in Saratoga, by the way, which in their respective kinds are the finest in the world. One of these is Mr. John Morrissey's casino. I bowed my head submissively to this statement, but privately I thought of the blue Mediterranean, and the little white promontory of Monaco, and the silver-gray verdure of olives, and the view across the outer sea toward the bosky cliffs of Italy. The Congress waters, too, it is well known, are excellent in the superlative degree; this I am perfectly willing to maintain.

The piazzas of these great hotels may very well be the

biggest of all piazzas. They have not architectural beauty; but they doubtless serve their purpose—that of affording sitting-space in the open air to an immense number of persons. They are, of course, quite the best places to observe the Saratoga world. In the evening, when the "boarders" have all come forth and seated themselves in groups, or have begun to stroll in (not always, I regret to say, to the sad detriment of the dramatic interest, bisexual) couples, the big heterogeneous scene affords a great deal of entertainment. Seeing it for the first time, the observer is likely to assure himself that he has neglected an important item in the sum of American manners. The rough brick wall of the house, illumined by a line of flaring gas-lights, forms a natural background to the crude, impermanent, discordant tone of the assembly. In the larger of the two hotels, a series of long windows open into an immense parlour—the largest, I suppose, in the world, and the most scantily furnished in proportion to its size. A few dozen rocking-chairs, an equal number of small tables, tripods to the eternal ice-pitcher, serve chiefly to emphasize the vacuous grandeur of the spot. On the piazza, in the outer multitude, ladies largely prevail, both by numbers and (you are not slow to perceive) by distinction of appearance. The good old times of Saratoga, I believe, as of the world in general, are rapidly passing away. The time was when it was the chosen resort of none but "nice people." At the present day, I hear it constantly affirmed, "the company is dreadfully mixed." What society may have been at Saratoga when its elements were thus simple and severe, I can only vaguely and mournfully conjecture. I confine myself to the dense, democratic, vulgar Saratoga of the current year. You are struck, to begin with, at the hotels, by the numerical superiority of the women; then, I think, by their personal superiority. It is incontestably the case that in appearance, in manner, in grace and completeness of aspect, American women surpass their husbands and brothers; the relation being reversed among some of the nations of Europe. Attached to the main entrance of the Union Hotel, and adjoining the ascent from the street to the piazza, is a "stoop" of mighty area, which, at most hours of the day and evening, is a favoured lounging-place of men. I should add, after the remark I have just made, that even in the appearance of the usual American male there seems to me to be a certain plastic intention. It is true that the lean, sallow, angular Yankee of tradition is dignified mainly by a look of decision, a hint of unimpassioned volition, the air of "smartness." This in some degree redeems him, but it fails to make him handsome. But in the average American of the present time, the typical leanness and sallowness are less than in his fathers, and the individual acuteness is at once equally marked and more frequently united with merit of form. Casting your eye over a group of your fellow-citizens in the portico of the Union Hotel, you will be inclined to admit that, taking the good with the bad, they are worthy sons of the great Republic. I have found, at any rate, a great deal of entertainment in watching them. They suggest to my fancy the swarming vastness—the multifarious possibilities and activities—of our young civilization. They come from the uttermost ends of the Union—from San Francisco, from New Orleans, from Alaska. As they sit with their white hats tilted forward, and their chairs tilted back, and their feet tilted up, and their cigars and toothpicks forming various angles with these various lines, I seem to see in their faces a tacit reference to the affairs of a continent. They are obviously persons of experience—of a somewhat narrow and monotonous experience certainly; an experience of which the diamonds and laces which their wives are exhibiting hard by are, perhaps, the most substantial and beautiful result; but, at any rate, they have *lived,* in every fibre of the will. For the time, they are lounging with the negro waiters, and the bootblacks, and the news-vendors; but it was not in lounging that they gained their hard wrinkles and the level impartial regard which they direct from beneath their hat-rims. They are not the mellow fruit of a society which has walked hand-in-hand with tradition and culture; they are hard nuts, which have grown and ripened as they could. When they talk among themselves, I seem to hear the cracking of the shells.

If the men are remarkable, the ladies are wonderful. Saratoga is famous, I believe, as the place of all places in America where women adorn themselves most, or as the place, at least, where the greatest amount of dressing may be seen by the greatest number of people. Your first impression is therefore of the—what shall I call it?—of the abundance of petticoats. Every woman you meet, young or old, is attired with a certain amount of richness, and with whatever good taste may be compatible with such a mode of life. You behold an interesting, indeed a quite momentous spectacle; the democratization of elegance. If I am to believe what I hear—in fact, I may say what I overhear—many of these sumptuous persons have enjoyed neither the advantages of a careful education nor the privileges of an introduction to society. She walks more or less of a queen, however, each uninitiated nobody. She often has, in dress, an admirable instinct of elegance and even of what the French call "chic." This instinct occasionally amounts to a sort of passion; the result then is wonderful. You look at the coarse brick walls, the rusty iron posts of the piazza, at the shuffling negro waiters, the great tawdry steamboat-cabin of a drawing-room—you see the tilted ill-dressed loungers on the steps—and you finally regret that a figure so exquisite should have so vulgar a setting. Your resentment, however, is speedily tempered by reflection. You feel the impertinence of your old reminiscences of English and French novels, and of the dreary social order in which privacy was the presiding genius and women arrayed themselves for the appreciation of the few. The crowd, the tavern-loungers, the surrounding ugliness and tumult and license, constitute the social medium of the young lady you are so inconsistent as to admire; she is dressed for publicity. The thought fills you with a kind of awe. The social order of tradition is far away indeed, and as for the transatlantic novels, you begin to doubt whether she is so amiably curious as to read even the silliest of them. To be dressed up to the eyes is obviously to give pledges to idleness. I have been forcibly struck with the apparent absence of any warmth and richness of detail in the lives of these wonderful ladies of the piazzas. We are freely accused of being an eminently wasteful people; and I know of few things which so largely warrant the accusation as the fact that these conspicuous *élégantes* adorn themselves, socially speaking, to so little purpose. To dress for every one is, practically, to dress for no one. There are few prettier sights than a charmingly-dressed woman, gracefully established in some shady spot, with a piece of needle-work or embroidery, or a book. Nothing very serious is accomplished, probably, but an æsthetic principle is recognized. The embroidery and the book are a tribute to culture, and I suppose they really figure somewhere out of the opening scenes of French comedies. But here at Saratoga, at any hour of morning or evening, you may see a hundred rustling beauties whose rustle is their sole occupation. One lady in particular there is, with whom it appears to be an inexorable fate that she shall be nothing more than dressed. Her apparel is tremendously modern, and my remarks would be much illumined if I had the learning necessary for describing it. I can only say that every evening for a fortnight she has revealed herself as a fresh creation. But she especially, as I say, has struck me as a person dressed beyond her life and her opportunities. I resent on her behalf —or on behalf at least of her finery—the extreme severity of her circumstances. What is she, after all, but a "regular boarder"? She ought to sit on the terrace of a stately castle, with a great baronial park shutting out the undressed world, and bandy quiet small-talk with an ambassador or a duke. My imagination is shocked when I behold her seated in gorgeous relief against the dusty clapboards of the hotel, with her beautiful hands folded in her silken lap, her head drooping slightly beneath the weight of her *chignon*, her lips parted in a vague contemplative gaze at Mr. Helmbold's well-known advertisement on the opposite fence, her husband beside her reading the New York *Herald*.

I have indeed observed cases of a sort of splendid social isolation here, which are not without a certain amount of pathos—people who know no one, who have money and finery and possessions, only no friends. Such at least is my inference, from the lonely grandeur with which I see them invested. Women, of course, are the most helpless victims of this cruel situation, although it must be said that they befriend each other with a generosity for which we hardly give them credit. I have seen women, for instance, at various "hops," approach their lonely sisters and invite them to waltz, and I have seen the fair invited surrender themselves eagerly to this humiliating embrace. Gentlemen at Saratoga are at a much higher premium than at European watering-places. It is an old story that in this country we have no "leisure-class"—the class from which the Saratogas of Europe recruit a large number of their male frequenters. A few months ago, I paid a visit to an English "bath," commemorated in various works of fiction, where, among many visible points of difference from American resorts, the most striking was the multitude of young men who had the whole day on their hands. While their sweethearts and sisters are waltzing together, our own young men are rolling up greenbacks in counting-houses and stores. I was recently reminded in another way, one evening, of the unlikeness of Saratoga to Cheltenham. Behind the biggest of the big hotels is a large planted yard, which it is the fashion at Saratoga to talk of as a "park," and which is perhaps believed to be the biggest in the world. At one end of it stands a great ballroom, approached by a range of wooden steps. It was late in the evening; the room, in spite of the intense heat, was blazing with light and the orchestra thundering a mighty waltz. A group of loungers, including myself, were hanging about to watch the ingress of the festally-minded. In the basement of the edifice, sunk beneath the ground, a noisy auctioneer, in his shirt and trousers, black in the face with heat and vociferation, was selling "pools" of the races to a dense group of frowsy betting-men. At the foot of the steps was stationed a man in a linen coat and straw hat, without waistcoat or necktie, to take the tickets of the ball-goers. As the latter failed to arrive in sufficient numbers, a musician came forth to the top of the steps and blew a loud summons on a horn. After this they began to straggle along. On this occasion, certainly, the company promised to be decidedly "mixed." The women, as usual, were much bedizened, though without any constant adhesion to the technicalities of full-dress. The men adhered to it neither in the letter nor the spirit. The possessor of a pair of satin-shod feet, twinkling beneath an uplifted volume of gauze and lace and flowers, tripped up the steps with her gloved hand on the sleeve of a railway "duster." Now and then two ladies arrived alone; generally a group of them approached under convoy of a single man. Children were freely scattered among their elders, and frequently a small boy would deliver his ticket and enter the glittering portal, beautifully unembarrassed. Of the children of Saratoga there would be wondrous things to relate. I believe that, in spite of their valuable aid, the festival of which I speak was rated rather a "fizzle." I see it advertised that they are soon to have, for their own peculiar benefit, a "Masquerade and Promenade Concert, beginning at 9 P.M." I observe that they usually open the "hops," and that it is only after their elders have borrowed confidence from the sight of their unfaltering paces that the latter dare to dance. You meet them far into the evening, roaming over the piazzas and corridors of the hotels—the little girls especially—lean, pale, formidable. Occasionally childhood confesses itself, even when maternity resists, and you see at eleven o'clock at night some poor little bedizened precocity collapsed in slumber in a lonely wayside chair. The part played by children in society here is only an additional instance of the wholesale equalization of the various social atoms which is the distinctive feature of collective Saratoga. A man in a "duster" at a ball is as good as a man in regulation-garments; a young woman dancing with another young woman is as good as a young woman dancing with a young man; a child of ten is as good as a woman of thirty; a double negative in conversation is rather better than a single.

An important feature in many a watering-place is the facility for leaving it a little behind you and tasting of the unmitigated country. You may wander to some shady hillside and sentimentalize upon the vanity of a high civilization. But at Saratoga civilization holds you fast. The most important feature of the place, perhaps, is the impossibility of carrying out any such pastoral dream. The surrounding country is a charming wilderness, but the roads are so abominably bad that walking and driving are alike unprofitable. Of course, however, if you are bent upon a walk, you will take a walk. There is a striking contrast between the concentrated prodigality of life in the immediate neighbourhood of the hotels and the pastoral solitudes into which a walk of half an hour may lead you. You have left the American citizen and his wife, the orchestras, the pools, the precocious infants, the cocktails, the importations from Worth, but a mile or two behind, but already the forest is primeval and the landscape is without figures. Nothing could be less manipulated than the country about Saratoga. The heavy roads are little more than sandy wheel-tracks; by the tangled wayside the blackberries wither unpicked. The horizon undulates with an air of having it all its own way. There are no white villages gleaming in the distance, no spires of churches, no salient details. It is all green, lonely, and vacant. If you wish to enjoy a detail, you must stop beneath a cluster of pines and listen to the murmur of the softly-troubled air, or follow upward the scaly straightness of their trunks to where the afternoon light gives it a colour. Here and there on a slope by the roadside stands a rough unpainted farmhouse, looking as if its dreary blackness were the result of its standing dark and lonely amid so many months—and such a wide expanse—of winter snow. It has turned black by contrast. The principal feature of the grassy unfurnished yard is the great wood-pile, telling grimly of the long reversion of the summer. For the time, however, it looks down contentedly enough over a goodly appanage of grain-fields and orchards, and I can fancy that it may be amusing to be a boy there. But to be a man, it must be quite what the lean, brown, serious farmers physiognomically hint it to be. You have, however, at the present season, for your additional beguilement, on the eastern horizon, the vision of the long bold chain of the Green Mountains, clad in that single coat of simple, candid blue which is the favourite garment of our American hills. As a visitor, too, you have for an afternoon's excursion your choice between a couple of lakes. Saratoga Lake, the larger and more distant of the two, is the goal of the regular afternoon drive. Above the shore is a well-appointed tavern—"Moon's" it is called by the voice of fame—where you may sit upon a broad piazza and partake of fried potatoes and "drinks"; the latter, if you happen to have come from poor dislicensed Boston, a peculiarly gratifying privilege. You enjoy the felicity sighed for by that wanton Italian lady of the anecdote, when, one summer evening, to the sound of music, she wished that to eat an ice were a sin. The other lake is small, and its shores are unadorned by any edifice but a boat-house, where you may hire a skiff and pull yourself out into the minnow-tickled, wood-circled oval. Here, floating in its darkened half, while you watch on the opposite shore the tree-stems, white and sharp in the declining sunlight, and their foliage whitening and whispering in the breeze, and you feel that this little solitude is part of a greater and more portentous solitude, you may recall certain passages of Ruskin, in which he dwells upon the needfulness of some human association, however remote, to make natural scenery fully impressive. You may recall that magnificent page in which he relates having tried with such fatal effect, in a battle-haunted valley of the Jura, to fancy himself in a nameless solitude of our own continent. You feel around you, with irresistible force, the eloquent silence of undedicated nature—the absence of serious associations, the nearness, indeed, of the vulgar and trivial associations of the least complete of all the cities of pleasure—you feel this, and you wonder what it is you so deeply and calmly enjoy. You make up your mind, possibly, that it is a great advantage to be able at once to enjoy Mr. Ruskin and to enjoy Mr. Ruskin's alarms. And hereupon you return to your hotel and read the New York papers on the plan of the French campaign and the Nathan murder.

Newport

1870

The season at Newport has an obstinate life. September has fairly begun, but as yet there is small visible diminution in the steady stream—the splendid, stupid stream—of carriages which rolls in the afternoon along the Avenue. There is, I think, a far more intimate fondness between Newport and its frequenters than that which in most American watering-places consecrates the somewhat mechanical relation between the visitors and the visited. This relation here is for the most part slightly sentimental. I am very far from professing a cynical contempt for the gaieties and vanities of Newport life: they are, as a spectacle, extremely amusing; they are full of a certain warmth of social colour which charms alike the eye and the fancy; they are worth observing, if only to conclude against them; they possess at least the dignity of all extreme and emphatic expressions of a social tendency; but they are not so untouched with Philistinism that I do not seem to overhear at times the still, small voice of this tender sense of the sweet, superior beauty of the natural things that surround them, pleading gently in their favour to the fastidious critic. I feel almost warranted in saying that here the background of life has sunk less in relative value and suffered less from the encroachments of pleasure-seeking man than the scenic dispositions of any other watering-place. For this, perhaps, we may thank rather the modest, incorruptible integrity of the Newport landscape than any very intelligent forbearance on the part of the summer colony. The beauty of this landscape is so subtle, so essential, so humble, so much a thing of character and expression, so little a thing of feature and pretension, that it cunningly eludes the grasp of the destroyer or the reformer, and triumphs in impalpable purity even when it seems to make concessions. I have sometimes wondered, in rational moods, why it is that Newport is so much appreciated by the votaries of idleness and pleasure. Its resources are few in number. It is extremely circumscribed. It has few drives, few walks, little variety of scenery. Its charms and its interest are confined to a narrow circle. It has of course the unlimited ocean, but seafaring idlers are not true Newporters, for any other sea would suit them as well. Last evening, it seemed to me, as I drove along the Avenue, that I guessed the answer to the riddle. The atmospheric tone, the careful selection of ingredients, your pleasant sense of a certain climatic ripeness—these are the real charm of Newport, and the secret of her supremacy. You are affected by the admirable art of the landscape, by seeing so much that is lovely and impressive achieved with such a frugality of means—with so little parade of the vast, the various, or the rare, with so narrow a range of colour and form. I could not help thinking, as I turned from the harmonies and purities which lay deepening on the breast of nature, with the various shades of twilight, to the heterogeneous procession in the Avenue, that, quite in their own line of effect, the usual performers in this exhibition might learn a few good lessons from the daily prospect of the great western expanse of rock and ocean in its relations with the declining sun. But this is asking too much. Many persons of course come to Newport simply because others come, and in this way the present brilliant colony has grown up. Let me not be suspected, when I speak of Newport, of the untasteful heresy of meaning primarily rocks and waves rather than ladies and gentlemen.

The ladies and gentlemen are in great force—the ladies, of course, especially. It is true everywhere, I suppose, that women are the animating element of "society"; but you feel this to be especially true as you pass along Bellevue Avenue. I doubt whether anywhere else so many women have a "good time" with so small a sacrifice of the luxury of self-respect. I heard a lady yesterday tell another, with a quiet ecstasy of tone, that she had been having a "most perfect time." This is the very poetry of pleasure. It is a part of our complacent tradition that in those foreign lands where women are supposed to be socially supreme, they maintain their empire by various clandestine and reprehensible arts. With us—we say it at Newport without bravado—they are both conspicuous and unsophisticated. You feel this most gratefully as you receive a confident bow from a pretty girl in her basket-phaeton. She is very young and very pretty, but she has a certain habitual assurance which is only a grace the more. She combines, you reflect with respectful tenderness, all that is possible in the way of modesty with all that is delightful in the way of facility. Shyness is certainly very pretty—when it is not very ugly; but shyness may often darken the bloom of genuine modesty, and a certain frankness and confidence may often incline it toward the light. Let us assume, then, that all the young ladies whom you may meet here are of the highest modern type. In the course of time they ripen into the delightful matrons who divide your admiration. It is easy to see that Newport must be a most agreeable sojourn for the male sex. The gentlemen, indeed, look wonderfully prosperous and well-conditioned. They gallop on shining horses or recline in a sort of coaxing Herculean submission beside the lovely mistress of a curricle. Young men—and young old men—I have occasion to observe, are far more numerous than at Saratoga, and of vastly superior quality. There is, indeed, in all things a striking difference in tone and aspect between these two great centres of pleasure. After Saratoga, Newport seems really substantial and civilized. Æsthetically speaking, you may remain at Newport with a fairly good conscience; at Saratoga you linger under passionate protest. At Newport life is public, if you will; at Saratoga it is absolutely common. The difference, in a word, is the difference between a group of undiscriminating hotels and a series of organized homes. Saratoga perhaps deserves our greater homage, as being characteristically democratic and American; let us, then, make Saratoga the heaven of our aspiration, but let us yet a while content ourselves with Newport as the lowly earth of our residence.

The villas and "cottages," the beautiful idle women, the beautiful idle men, the brilliant pleasure-fraught days and evenings, impart, perhaps, to Newport life a faintly European expression, in so far as they suggest the somewhat alien presence of leisure—"fine old Leisure," as George Eliot calls it. Nothing, it seems to me, however, can take place in America without straightway seeming very American; and, after a week at Newport, you begin to fancy that to live for amusement simply, beyond the noise of commerce or of care, is a distinctively national trait. Nowhere else in this country—nowhere, of course, within the range of our better civilization—does business seem so remote, so vague, and unreal. It is the only place in America in which enjoyment is organized. If there be any poetry in the ignorance of trade and turmoil and the hard processes of fortune, Newport may claim her share of it. She knows—or at least appears to know—for the most part nothing but results. Individuals here, of course, have private cares and burdens to preserve the balance and the dignity of life; but collective society conspires to forget everything that worries. It is a singular fact that a society that does nothing is decidedly more pictorial, more interesting to the eye of contemplation, than a society which is hard at work. Newport, in this way, is infinitely more fertile in combinations than Saratoga. There you feel that idleness is occasional, empirical. Most of the people you see are asking themselves, you imagine, whether the game is worth the candle and work is not better than such difficult play. But here, obviously, the habit of pleasure is formed, and (within the limits of a severe morality) many of the secrets of pleasure are known. Do what we will, on certain lines Europe is in advance of us yet. Newport lags altogether behind Trouville and Brighton in her exhibition of the unmentionable. All this is markedly absent from the picture, which is therefore signally destitute of the enhancing tints produced by the mysteries and fascinations of vice. But idleness *per se* is vicious, and of course you may imagine what you please. For my own part, I prefer to imagine nothing but the graceful and the pure; and with the help of such imaginings you may construct a very pretty sentimental undercurrent to the superficial movement of society. This I lately found very difficult to do at Saratoga. Sentiment there is pitifully shy and elusive. Here, the multiplied relations of men and women, under the permanent pressure of luxury and idleness, give it a very fair chance. Sentiment, indeed, of masterly force and interest, springs up in every soil, with a sovereign disregard of occasion. People love and hate and aspire with the greatest intensity when they have to make their time and opportunity. I should hardly come to Newport for the materials of a tragedy. Even in their own kind, the social elements are as yet too light and thin. But I can fancy finding here the motive of a drama which should depend more on smiles than tears. I can almost imagine, indeed, a transient observer of the Newport spectacle dreaming momentarily of a great American novel, in which the heroine might be infinitely realistic and yet neither a schoolmistress nor an outcast. I say intentionally the "transient" observer, because it is probable that here the suspicion only is friendly to dramatic point; the knowledge is hostile. The observer would discover, on a nearer view, I rather fear, that his possible heroines have too perfect a time.

This will remind the reader of what he must already have heard affirmed, that to speak of a place with abundance you must know it, but not too well. I suffer from knowing the natural elements of Newport too well to attempt to describe them. I have known them so long that I hardly know what I think of them. I have little more than a simple consciousness of enjoying them very much. Even this consciousness at times lies dumb and inert. I wonder at such times whether, to appeal fairly to the general human sense, the horizon has not too much of that mocking straightness which is such a misrepresentation of the real character of the sea—as if, forsooth, it were level. Life seems too short, space too narrow, to warrant you in giving an unqualified adhesion to a *paysage* which is two-thirds ocean. For the most part, however, I am willing to take the landscape as it stands, and to think that, without the water to make it precious, the land would be much less lovable. It is, in fact, a land exquisitely modified by marine influences. Indeed, in spite of all the evil it has done me, I could almost speak well of the ocean when I remember the charming tricks it plays with the Newport promontories.

The place consists, as the reader will know, of an ancient and honourable town, a goodly harbour, and a long, broad neck of land, stretching southward into the sea and forming the chief habitation of the summer colony. Along the greater part of its eastward length, this projecting coast is bordered with cliffs of no great height, and dotted with seaward-gazing villas. At the head of the promontory the villas enjoy a magnificent reach of prospect. The pure Atlantic—the old world westward tides—expire directly at their feet. Behind the line of villas runs the Avenue, with more villas yet—of which there is nothing at all to say but that those built recently are a hundred times prettier than those built fifteen years ago, and give one some hope of a revival of the architectural art. Some years ago, when I first knew Newport, the town proper was considered remarkably quaint. If an antique shabbiness that amounts almost to squalor is a pertinent element, as I believe it is, of this celebrated quality, the little main street at least—Thames Street by name—still deserves the praise. Here, in their crooked and dwarfish wooden mansions, are the shops that minister to the daily needs of the expanded city; and here of a summer morning, jolting over the cobble stones of the narrow roadway, you may see a hundred superfine ladies seeking with languid eagerness what they may buy—to "buy something," I believe, being a diurnal necessity of the conscientious American woman. This busy region gradually melts away into the grass-grown stillness of the Point, in the eyes of many persons the pleasantest quarter of Newport. It has superficially the advantage of being as yet uninvaded by fashion. When I first knew it, however, its peculiar charm was even more undisturbed than at present. The Point may be called the old residential, as distinguished from the commercial, town. It is meagre, shallow and scanty—a mere pinch of antiquity—but, so far as it goes, it retains an exquisite tone. It leaves the shops and the little wharves, and wanders close to the harbour, where the breeze-borne rattle of shifted sails and spars alone intrudes upon its stillness, till its mouldy-timbered quiet subsides into the low, tame rocks and beaches which edge the bay. Several matter-of-course modern houses have recently been erected on the water-side, absorbing the sober, primitive tenements which used to maintain the picturesque character of the place. They improve it, of course, as a residence, but they injure it as an unexpected corner. Enough of early architecture still remains, however, to suggest a multitude of thoughts as to the severe simplicity of the generation which produced it. The plain gray nudity of these little warped and shingled boxes seems to make it a hopeless task on their part to present any positive appearance at all. But here, as elsewhere, the magical Newport atmosphere wins half the battle. It aims at no mystery—it simply makes them scintillate in their bareness. Their homely notches and splinters twinkle till the mere friendliness of the thing makes a surface. Their steep gray roofs, barnacled with lichens, remind you of old barges, overturned on the beach to dry.

One of the more recent monuments of fashion is the long drive which follows the shore. The Avenue, where the Neck abruptly terminates, has been made to extend itself to the west, and to wander for a couple of miles over a lovely region of beach and lowly down and sandy meadow and salt brown sheep-grass. This region was formerly the most beautiful part of Newport—the least frequented and the most untamed by fashion. I by no means regret the creation of the new road, however. A walker may very soon isolate himself, and the occupants of carriages are exposed to a benefit quite superior to their power of injury. The peculiar charm of this great westward expanse is very difficult to define. It is in an especial degree the charm of Newport in general—the combined lowness of tone, as painters call it, in all the elements of *terra firma,* and the extraordinary elevation of tone in the air. For miles and miles you see at your feet, in mingled shades of yellow and gray, a desolate waste of moss-clad rock and sand-starved grass. At your left is nothing but the shine and surge of the ocean, and over your head that wonderful sky of Newport, which has such an unexpected resemblance to the sky of

Venice. In spite of the bare simplicity of this prospect, its beauty is far more a beauty of detail than that of the average American landscape. Descend into a hollow of the rocks, into one of the little warm climates, five feet square, which you may find there, beside the grateful ocean glare, and you will be struck quite as much by their fineness as by their roughness. From time to time, as you wander, you will meet a lonely, stunted tree, which is sure to be a charming piece of the individual grotesque. The region of which I speak is perhaps best seen in the late afternoon, from the high seat of a carriage on the Avenue. You seem to stand just outside the threshold of the west. At its opposite extremity sinks the sun, with such a splendour, perhaps, as I lately saw—a splendour of the deepest blue, more luminous and fiery than the usual redness of evening, and all streaked and barred with blown and drifted gold. The whole large interval, with its rocks and marshes and ponds, seems bedimmed with a kind of purple glaze. The near Atlantic fades and turns cold with that desolate look of the ocean when the day ceases to care for it. In the foreground, a short distance from the road, an old orchard uplifts its tangled stems and branches against the violet mists of the west. It seems strangely grotesque and enchanted. No ancient olive-grove of Italy or Provence was ever more hoarily romantic. This is what people commonly behold on the last homeward bend of the drive. For such of them as are happy enough to occupy one of the villas on the cliffs, the beauty of the day has even yet not expired. The present summer has been emphatically the summer of moonlights. Not the nights, however, but the long days, in these agreeable homes, are what especially appeal to my fancy. Here you find a solution of the insoluble problem—to combine an abundance of society with an abundance of solitude. In their charming broad-windowed drawing-rooms, on their great seaward piazzas, within sight of the serious Atlantic horizon, which is so familiar to the eye and so mysterious to the heart, caressed by the gentle breeze which makes all but simple, social, delightful *now* and *here* seem unreal and untasteful—the sweet fruit of the lotus grows more than ever succulent and magical. How sensible they ought to be, the denizens of these pleasant places, of their peculiar felicity and distinction! How it should purify their temper and refine their tastes! How delicate, how wise, how discriminating they should become! What excellent manners—what enlightened opinions—their situation should produce! How it should purge them of vulgarity! Happy *villeggianti* of Newport!

Quebec

1871

I

A traveller who combines a taste for old towns with a love of letters ought not, I suppose, to pass through "the most picturesque city in America" without making an attempt to commemorate his impressions. His first impression will certainly have been that not America, but Europe, should have the credit of Quebec. I came, some days since, by a dreary night-journey, to Point Levi, opposite the town, and as we rattled toward our goal in the faint raw dawn, and, already attentive to "effects," I began to consult the misty window-panes and descried through the moving glass little but crude, monotonous woods, suggestive of nothing that I had ever heard of in song or story, I felt that the land would have much to do to give itself a romantic air. And, in fact, the feat is achieved with almost magical suddenness. The old world rises in the midst of the new in the manner of a change of scene on the stage. The St. Lawrence shines at your left, large as a harbour-mouth, gray with smoke and masts, and edged on its hither verge by a bustling water-side *faubourg* which looks French or English, or anything not local that you please; and beyond it, over against you, on its rocky promontory, sits the ancient town, belted with its hoary wall and crowned with its granite citadel. Now that I have been here a while I find myself wondering how the city would strike one if the imagination had not been bribed beforehand. The place, after all, is of the soil on which it stands; yet it appeals to you so cunningly with its little stock of transatlantic wares that you overlook its flaws and lapses, and swallow it whole. Fancy lent a willing hand the morning I arrived, and zealously retouched the picture. The very sky seemed to have been brushed in like the sky in an English water-colour, the light to filter down through an atmosphere more dense and more conscious. You cross a ferry, disembark at the foot of the rock on unmistakably foreign soil, and then begin to climb into the city proper—the city *intra muros*. These walls, to the American vision, are of course the sovereign fact of Quebec; you take off your hat to them as you clatter through the gate. They are neither very high nor, after all, very hoary. Our clear American air is hostile to those mellow deposits and incrustations which enrich the venerable surfaces of Europe. Still, they are walls; till but a short time ago they quite encircled the town; they are garnished with little slits for musketry and big embrasures for cannon; they offer here and there to the strolling bourgeoisie a stretch of grassy rampart; and they make the whole place definite and personal.

Before you reach the gates, however, you will have been reminded at a dozen points that you have come abroad. What is the essential difference of tone between street-life in an old civilisation and in a new? It seems something subtler and deeper than mere external accidents—than foreign architecture, than foreign pinks, greens, and yellows plastering the house-fronts, than the names of the saints on the corners, than all the pleasant crookedness, narrowness and duskiness, the quaint economised spaces, the multifarious detail, the brown French faces, the ruddy English ones. It seems to be the general fact of detail itself—the hint in the air of a slow, accidental accretion, in obedience to needs more timidly considered and more sparingly gratified than the pressing necessities of American progress. But apart from the metaphysics of the question, Quebec has a great many pleasant little ripe spots and amenities. You note the small, boxlike houses in rugged stone or in stucco, each painted with uncompromising *naïveté* in some bright hue of the owner's fond choice; you note with joy, with envy, with momentary self-effacement, as a New Yorker, as a Bostonian, the innumerable calashes and cabs which contend for your selection; and you observe when you arrive at the hotel, that this is a blank and gloomy inn, of true provincial aspect, with slender promise of the "American plan." Perhaps, even the clerk at the office will have the courtesy of the ages of leisure. I confess that, in my case, he was terribly modern, so that I was compelled to resort for a lodging to a private house near by, where I enjoy a transitory glimpse of the *vie intime* of Quebec. I fancied, when I came in, that it would be a compensation for worse quarters to possess the little Canadian vignette I enjoy from my windows. Certain shabby Yankee sheds, indeed, encumber the foreground, but they are so near that I can overlook them. Beyond is a piece of garden, attached to nothing less than a convent of the cloistered nuns of St. Ursula. The convent chapel rises inside it, crowned with what seemed to me, in view of the circumstances, a real little *clocher de France*. The "circumstances," I confess, are simply a couple of stout French poplars. I call them French because they are alive and happy; whereas, if they had been American they would have died of a want of appreciation, like their brothers in the "States." I do not say that the little convent-belfry, roofed and coated as it is with quaint scales of tin, would, by itself, produce any very deep illusion; or that the whispering poplars, *per se,* would transport me to the Gallic mother-land; but poplars and belfry together constitute an "effect"—strike a musical note in the scale of association. I look fondly even at the little casements which command this prospect, for they too are an old-world heritage. They open sidewise, in two wings, and are screwed together by that bothersome little iron handle over which we have fumbled so often in European inns.

If the windows tell of French dominion, of course larger matters testify with greater eloquence. In a place so small as Quebec, the bloom of novelty of course rubs off; but when first I walked abroad I fancied myself again in a French seaside town where I once spent a year, in common with a large number of economically disposed English. The French element offers the groundwork, and the English colony wears, for the most part, that half-genteel and migratory air which stamps the exiled and provincial British. They look as if they were still *en voyage*—still in search of low prices—the men in woollen shirts and Scotch bonnets; the ladies with a certain look of being equipped for dangers and difficulties. Your very first steps will be likely to lead you to the market-place, which is a genuine bit of Europeanism. One side of it is occupied by a huge edifice of yellow plaster, with stone facings painted in blue, and a manner of *porte-cochère,* leading into a veritable court—originally, I believe, a college of the early Jesuits, now a place of military stores. On the other stands the French cathedral, with an ample stone façade, a bulky stone tower, and a high-piled, tin-scaled belfry; not architectural, of course, nor imposing, but with a certain gray maturity, and, as regards the belfry, a quite adequate quaintness. Round about are shops and houses, touching which, I think, it is no mere fancy that they might, as they stand, look down into some dull and rather dirty *place* in France. The stalls and booths in the centre—tended by genuine peasants of tradition, brown-faced old Frenchwomen, with hard wrinkles and short petticoats, and white caps beneath their broad-brimmed hats, and more than one price, as I think you'll find—these, and the stationed caleches and cabriolets complete a passably fashionable French picture. It is a proof of how nearly the old market-women resemble their originals across the sea that you rather resentfully miss one or two of the proper features of the type—the sabots for the feet and the donkey for the load. Of course you go into the cathedral, and how forcibly that swing of the door, as you doff your hat in the cooler air, recalls the old tourist strayings and pryings beneath other skies! You find a big garish church, with a cold high light, a promiscuity of stucco and gilding, and a mild odour of the seventeenth century. It is, perhaps, a shade or so more sensibly Catholic than it would be with ourselves; but, in fine, it has pews and a boarded floor, and the few paintings are rather pale in their badness, and you are forced to admit that the old-world tone which sustains itself so comfortably elsewhere falters most where most is asked of it.

Among the other lions of Quebec—notably in the Citadel—you find Protestant England supreme. A robust trooper of her Majesty, with a pair of very tight trousers and a very small cap, takes charge of you at the entrance of the fortifications, and conducts you through all kinds of incomprehensible defences. I cannot speak of the place as an engineer, but only as a tourist, and the tourist is chiefly concerned with the view. This is altogether superb, and if Quebec is not the most picturesque city in America, this is no fault of its incomparable site. Perched on its mountain of rock, washed by a river as free and ample as an ocean-gulf, sweeping from its embattled crest, the villages, the forests, the blue undulations of the imperial province of which it is warden—as it has managed from our scanty annals to squeeze out a past, you pray in the name of all that's majestic that it may have a future. I may add that, to the mind of the reflective visitor, these idle ramparts and silent courts present other visions than that of the mighty course of the river and its anchorage for navies. They evoke a shadowy image of that great English power, the arches of whose empire were once built strong on foreign soil; and as you stand where they are highest and look abroad upon a land of alien speech, you seem to hear the echoed names of other strongholds and provinces—Gibraltar, Malta, India. Whether these arches are crumbling now, I do not pretend to say; but the last regular troops (in number lately much diminished) are just about to be withdrawn from Quebec, and in the private circles to which I have been admitted I hear sad forebodings of what society will lose by the departure of the "military." This single word is eloquent; it reveals a social order distinctly affiliated, in spite of remoteness, to the society reproduced for the pacific American in novels in which the hero is a captain of the army or navy, and of which the scene is therefore necessarily laid in countries provided with these branches of the public service. Another opportunity for some such reflections, worthy of a historian or an essayist, as those I have hinted at, is afforded you on the Plains of Abraham, to which you probably adjourn directly from the Citadel—another, but I am bound to say, in my opinion, a less inspiring one. A battlefield remains a battlefield, whatever may be done to it; but the scene of Wolfe's victory has been profaned by the erection of a vulgar prison, and this memento of human infirmities does much to efface the meagre column which, with its neat inscription, "Here died Wolfe, victorious," stands there as a symbol of exceptional virtue.

II

To express the historical interest of the place completely, I should dwell on the light provincial—French provincial—aspect of some of the little residential streets. Some of the houses have the staleness of complexion which Balzac loved to describe. They are chiefly built of stone or brick, with a stoutness and separateness of structure which stands in some degree in stead of architecture. I know not that, externally, they have any greater charm than that they belong to that category of dwellings which in our own cities were long since pulled down to make room for brown-stone fronts. I know not, indeed, that I can express better the picturesque merit of Quebec than by saying that it has no fronts of this luxurious and horrible substance. The greater number of houses are built of rough-hewn squares of some more vulgar mineral, painted with frank chocolate or buff, and adorned with blinds of a cruder green than we admire. As you pass the low windows of these abodes, you perceive the walls to be of extraordinary thickness; the embrasure is of great depth; Quebec was built for winter. Door-plates are frequent, and you observe that the tenants are of the Gallic persuasion. Here and there, before a door, stands a comely private equipage—a fact agreeably suggestive of a low scale of prices; for evidently in Quebec one need not be a millionaire to keep a carriage, and one may make a figure on moderate means. The great number of private carriages visible in the streets is another item, by the way, among the Europeanisms of the place; and not, as I may say, as regards the simple fact that they exist, but as regards the fact that they are considered needful for women, for young persons, for gentility. What does it do with itself, this gentility, keeping a gig or not, you wonder, as you stroll past its little multicoloured mansions. You strive almost vainly to picture the life of this French society, locked up in its small dead capital, isolated on a heedless continent, and gradually consuming its principal, as one may say—its vital stock of memories, traditions, superstitions. Its evenings must be as dull as the evenings described by Balzac in his *Vie de Province;* but has it the same ways and means of dulness? Does it play loto and "boston" in the long winter nights, and arrange marriages between its sons and daughters, whose education it has confided to abbés and abbesses? I have met in the streets here little old Frenchmen who look as if they had stepped out of Balzac —bristling with the habits of a class, wrinkled with old-world expressions. Something assures one that Quebec must be a city of gossip; for evidently it is not a city of culture. A glance at the few booksellers' windows gives evidence of this. A few Catholic statuettes and prints, two or three Catholic publications, a festoon or so of rosaries, a volume of Lamartine, a supply of ink and matches, form the principal stock.

In the lower class of the French population there is a much livelier vitality. They are a genuine peasantry; you very soon observe it, as you drive along the pleasant country-roads. Just what it is that makes a peasantry, it is, perhaps, not easy to determine; but whatever it is, these good people have it—in their simple, unsharpened faces, in their narrow patois, in their ignorance and naïveté, and their evident good terms with the tin-spired parish church, standing there as bright and clean with ungrudged paint and varnish as a Nürnberg toy. One of them spoke to me with righteous contempt of the French of France—"They are worth nothing; they are bad Catholics." These are good Catholics, and I doubt whether anywhere Catholicism wears a brighter face and maintains more docility at the cost of less misery. It is, perhaps, not Longfellow's *Evangeline* for chapter and verse, but it is a tolerable prose transcript. There is no visible squalor, there are no rags and no curses, but there is a most agreeable tinge of gentleness, thrift, and piety. I am assured that the country-people are in the last degree mild and peaceable; surely, such neatness and thrift, without the irritability of the French genius —it is true the genius too is absent—is a very pleasant type of character. Without being ready to proclaim, with an enthusiastic friend, that the roadside scenery is more French than France, I may say that, in its way, it is quite as picturesque as anything within the city. There is an air of completeness and maturity in the landscape which suggests an old country. The roads, to begin with, are decidedly better than our own, and the cottages and farmhouses would need only a bit of thatch and a few red tiles here and there to enable them to figure creditably by the waysides of Normandy or Brittany. The road to Montmorency, on which tourists most congregate, is also, I think, the prettiest. The rows of poplars, the heavy stone cottages, seamed and cracked with time, in many cases, and daubed in coarse, bright hues, the little bourgeois villas, rising middle-aged at the end of short vistas, the sunburnt women in the fields, the old men in woollen stockings and red nightcaps, the long-kirtled curé nodding to doffed hats, the more or less bovine stare which greets you from cottage-doors, are all so many touches of a local colour reflected from over the sea. What especially strikes one, however, is the peculiar tone of the light and the atmospheric effects—the chilly whites and grays, the steely reflections, the melancholy brightness of a frigid zone. Winter here gives a stamp to the year, and seems to leave even through spring and summer a kind of scintillating trail of his presence. To me, I confess it is terrible, and I fancy I see constantly in the brilliant sky the hoary genius of the climate brooding grimly over his dominion.

The falls of Montmorency, which you reach by the pleasant avenue I speak of, are great, I believe, among the falls of the earth. They are certainly very fine, even in the attenuated shape to which they are reduced at the present season. I doubt whether you obtain anywhere in simpler and more powerful form the very essence of a cataract—the wild, fierce, suicidal plunge of a living, sounding flood. A little platform, lodged in the cliff, enables you to contemplate it with almost shameful convenience; here you may stand at your leisure and spin analogies, more or less striking, on the very edge of the white abyss. The leap of the water begins directly at your feet, and your eye trifles dizzily with the long, perpendicular shaft of foam, and tries, in the eternal crash, to effect some vague notation of its successive stages of sound and fury; but the vaporous sheet, for ever dropping, lapses from beneath the eye, and leaves the vision distracted in mid-space; and the vision, in search of a resting-place, sinks in a flurry to the infamous saw-mill which defaces the very base of the torrent. The falls of Montmorency are obviously one of the greatest of the beauties of nature, "falls" are to me the least satisfying. A mountain, a precipice, a river, a forest, a plain, I can enjoy at my ease; they are natural, normal, self-assured: they make no appeal; they imply no human admiration, no petty human cranings and shrinkings, head-swimmings and similes. A cataract, of course, is essentially violent. You are certain, moreover, to have to approach it through a turnstile, and to enjoy it from some terribly cockneyfied little booth. The spectacle at Montmorency appears to be the private property of a negro innkeeper, who "runs" it evidently with great pecuniary profit. A day or two since I went so far as to be glad to leave it behind, and drive some five miles farther along the road, to a village rejoicing in the pretty name of Château-Richer. The village is so pretty that you count on finding there the elderly manor which might have baptized it. But, of course, in such pictorial efforts as this Quebec breaks down; one must not ask too much of it. You enjoy from here, however, a revelation of the noble position of the city. The river, finding room in mid-stream for the long island of Orleans, opens out below you with a peculiar freedom and serenity, and leads the eye far down to where an azure mountain gazes up the channel and responds to the dark headland of Quebec. I noted, here and there, as I went, an extremely sketchable effect. Between the road and the river stand a succession of ancient peasant-dwellings, with their back-windows looking toward the stream. Glancing, as I passed, into the apertures that face the road, I saw, as through a picture-frame, their dark, rich-toned interiors, played into by the late river light and making an admirable series of mellow *tableaux de genre*. The little curtained alcoves, the big household beds, and presses, and dressers, the black-mouthed chimney-pieces, the crucifixes, the old women at their spinning-wheels, the little heads at the supper-table, around the big French loaf, outlined with a rim of light, were all as warmly, as richly composed, as French, as Dutch, as worthy of the brush, as anything in the countries to which artists resort for subjects.

I suppose no patriotic American can look at all these things, however idly, without reflecting on the ultimate possibility of their becoming absorbed into his own huge state. Whenever, sooner or later, the change is wrought, the sentimental tourist will keenly feel that a long stride has been taken, rough-shod, from the past to the present. The largest appetite in modern civilisation will have swallowed the largest morsel. What the change may bring of comfort or of grief to the Canadians themselves, will be for them to say; but, in the breast of this sentimental tourist of ours, it will produce little but regret. The foreign elements of eastern Canada, at least, are extremely interesting; and it is of good profit to us Americans to have near us, and of easy access, an ample something which is not our expansive selves. Here we find a hundred mementoes of an older civilisation than our own, of different manners, of social forces once mighty, and still glowing with a sort of autumnal warmth. The old-world needs which created the dark-walled cities of France and Italy seem to reverberate faintly in the steep and narrow and Catholic streets of Quebec. The little houses speak to the fancy by rather inexpensive arts; the ramparts are endued with a sort of silvery innocence; but the historic sense, conscious of a general solidarity in the picturesque, ekes out the romance and deepens the colouring.

Niagara

1871

My journey hitherward by a morning's sail from Toronto across Lake Ontario, seemed to me, as regards a certain dull vacuity in this episode of travel, a kind of calculated preparation for the uproar of Niagara—a pause or hush on the threshold of a great impression; and this, too, in spite of the reverent attention I was mindful to bestow on the first seen, in my experience, of the great lakes. It has the merit, from the shore, of producing a slight ambiguity of vision. It is the sea, and yet just not the sea. The huge expanse, the landless line of the horizon, suggest the ocean; while an indefinable shortness of pulse, a kind of fresh-water gentleness of tone, seem to contradict the idea. What meets the eye is on the scale of the ocean, but you feel somehow that the lake is a thing of smaller spirit. Lake-navigation, therefore, seems to me not especially entertaining. The scene tends to offer, as one may say, a sort of marine-effect missed. It has the blankness and vacancy of the sea, without that vast essential swell which, amid the belting brine, so often saves the situation to the eye. I was occupied, as we crossed, in wondering whether this dull reduction of the main contained that which could properly be termed "scenery." At the mouth of the Niagara River, however, after a sail of three hours, scenery really begins, and very soon crowds upon you in force. The steamer puts into the narrow channel of the stream, and heads upward between high embankments. From this point, I think, you really enter into relations with Niagara. Little by little the elements become a picture, rich with the shadow of coming events. You have a foretaste of the great spectacle of colour which you enjoy at the Falls. The even cliffs of red-brown earth are crusted and spotted with autumnal orange and crimson, and, laden with this gorgeous decay, they plunge sheer into the deep-dyed green of the river. As you proceed, the river begins to tell its tale—at first in broken syllables of foam and flurry, and then, as it were, in rushing, flashing sentences and passionate ejaculations. Onwards from Lewiston, where you are transferred from the boat to the train, you see it from the edge of the American cliff, far beneath you, now superbly unnavigable. You have a lively sense of something happening ahead; the river, as a man near me said, has evidently been in a row. The cliffs here are imménse; they form a *vomitorium* worthy of the living floods whose exit they protect. This is the first act of the drama of Niagara; for it is, I believe, one of the commonplaces of description that you instinctively convert it into a series of "situations." At the station pertaining to the railway suspension-bridge, you see in mid-air, beyond an interval of murky confusion produced at once by the farther bridge, the smoke of the trains, and the thickened atmosphere of the peopled bank, a huge far-flashing sheet which glares through the distance as a monstrous absorbent and irradiant of light. And here, in the interest of the picturesque, let me note that this obstructive bridge tends in a way to enhance the first glimpse of the cataract. Its long black span, falling dead along the shining brow of the Falls, seems shivered and smitten by their fierce effulgence, and trembles across the field of vision like some enormous mote in a light too brilliant. A moment later, as the train proceeds, you plunge into the village, and the cataract, save as a vague ground-tone to this trivial interlude, is, like so many other goals of æsthetic pilgrimage, temporarily postponed to the hotel.

With this postponement comes, I think, an immediate decline of expectation; for there is every appearance that the spectacle you have come so far to see is to be choked in the horribly vulgar shops and booths and catchpenny artifices which have pushed and elbowed to within the very spray of the Falls, and ply their importunities in shrill competition with its thunder. You see a multitude of hotels and taverns and stores, glaring with white paint, bedizened with placards and advertisements, and decorated by groups of those gentlemen who flourish most rankly on the soil of New York and in the vicinage of hotels; who carry their hands in their pockets, wear their hats always and every way, and, although of a stationary habit, yet spurn the earth with their heels. A side-glimpse of the Falls, however, calls out your philosophy; you reflect that this may be regarded as one of those sordid foregrounds which Turner liked to use, and which may be effective as a foil; you hurry to where the roar grows louder, and, I was going to say, you escape from the village. In fact, however, you don't escape from it; it is constantly at your elbow, just to the right or the left of the line of contemplation. It would be paying Niagara a poor compliment to say that, practically, she does not hurl away this chaffering by-play from her edge; but as you value the integrity of your impression, you are bound to affirm that it suffers appreciable abatement from such sources. You wonder, as you stroll about, whether it is altogether an unrighteous dream that with the slow progress of taste and the possible or impossible growth of some larger comprehension of beauty and fitness, the public conscience may not tend to confer upon such sovereign phases of nature something of the inviolability and privacy which we are slow to bestow, indeed, upon fame, but which we do not grudge at least to art. We place a great picture, a great statue, in a museum: we erect a great monument in the centre of our largest square, and if we can suppose ourselves nowadays to build a cathedral, we should certainly isolate it as much as possible and expose it to no ignoble contact. We cannot enclose Niagara with walls and a roof, nor girdle it with a palisade; but the sentimental tourist may muse upon the contingency of its being guarded by the negative homage of empty spaces and absent barracks and decent forbearance. The actual abuse of the scene belongs evidently to that immense class of iniquities which are destined to grow very much worse in order to grow a very little better. The good humour engendered by the main spectacle bids you suffer it to run its course.

Though hereabouts so much is great, distances are small, and a ramble of two or three hours enables you to gaze hither and thither from a dozen standpoints. The one you are likely to choose first is that on the Canada cliff, a little way above the suspension-bridge. The great Fall faces you, enshrined in its own surging incense. The common feeling just here, I believe, is one of disappointment at its want of height; the whole thing appears to many people somewhat smaller than its fame. My own sense, I confess, was absolutely gratified from the first; and, indeed, I was not struck with anything being tall or short, but with everything being perfect. You are, moreover, at some distance, and you feel that with the lessening interval you will not be cheated of your chance to be dizzied with mere dimensions. Already you see the world-famous green, baffling painters, baffling poets, shining on the lip of the precipice; the more so, of course, for the clouds of silver and snow into which it speedily resolves itself. The whole picture before you is admirably simple. The Horseshoe glares and boils and smokes from the centre to the right, drumming itself into powder and thunder; in the centre the dark pedestal of Goat Island divides the double flood; to the left booms in vaporous dimness the minor battery of the American Fall; while on a level with the eye, above the still crest of either cataract, appear the white faces of the hithermost rapids. The circle of weltering froth at the base of the Horseshoe, emerging from the dead white vapours—absolute white, as moonless midnight is absolute black—which muffle impenetrably the crash of the river upon the lower bed, melts slowly into the darker shades of green. It seems in itself a drama of thrilling interest, this blanched survival and recovery of the stream. It stretches away like a tired swimmer, struggling from the snowy scum and the silver drift, and passing slowly from an eddying foam-sheet, touched with green lights, to a cold verd-antique, streaked and marbled with trails and wild arabesques of foam. This is the beginning of that air of recent distress which marks the river as you meet it at the lake. It shifts along, tremendously conscious, relieved, disengaged, knowing the worst is over, with its dignity injured but its volume undiminished, the most stately, the least turbid of torrents. Its movement, its sweep and stride, are as admirable as its colour, but as little as its colour to be made a matter of words. These things are but part of a spectacle in which nothing is imperfect. As you draw nearer and nearer, on the Canada cliff, to the right arm of the Horseshoe, the mass begins in all conscience to be large enough. You are able at last to stand on the very verge of the shelf from which the leap is taken, bathing your boot-toes, if you like, in the side-ooze of the glassy curve. I may say, in parenthesis, that the importunities one suffers here, amid the central din of the cataract, from hackmen and photographers and vendors of gimcracks, are simply hideous and infamous. The road is lined with little drinking-shops and warehouses, and from these retreats their occupants dart forth upon the hapless traveller with their competitive attractions. You purchase release at last by the fury of your indifference, and stand there gazing your fill at the most beautiful object in the world.

The perfect taste of it is the great characteristic. It is not in the least monstrous; it is thoroughly artistic and, as the phrase is, thought out. In the matter of line it beats Michael Angelo. One may seem at first to say the least, but the careful observer will admit that one says the most, in saying that it *pleases*—pleases even a spectator who was not ashamed to write the other day that he didn't care for cataracts. There are, however, so many more things to say about it—its multitudinous features crowd so upon the vision as one looks—that it seems absurd to begin to analyze. The main feature, perhaps, is the incomparable loveliness of the immense line of the shelf and its lateral abutments. It neither falters, nor breaks nor stiffens, but maintains from wing to wing the lightness of its semicircle. This perfect curve melts into the sheet that seems at once to drop from it and sustain it. The famous green loses nothing, as you may imagine, on a nearer view. A green more vividly cool and pure it is impossible to conceive. It is to the vulgar greens of earth what the blue of a summer sky is to artificial dyes, and is, in fact, as sacred, as remote, as impalpable as that. You can fancy it the parent-green, the head-spring of colour to all the verdant water-caves and all the clear, sub-fluvial haunts and bowers of naiads and mermen in all the streams of the earth. The lower half of the watery wall is shrouded in the steam of the boiling gulf—a veil never rent nor lifted. At its heart this eternal cloud seems fixed and still with excess of motion—still and intensely white; but, as it rolls and climbs against its lucent cliff, it tosses little whiffs and fumes and pants of snowy smoke, which betray the convulsions we never behold. In the middle of the curve, the depth of the recess, the converging walls are ground into a dust of foam, which rises in a tall column, and fills the upper air with its hovering drift. Its summit far overtops the crest of the cataract, and, as you look down along the rapids above, you see it hanging over the averted gulf like some far-flowing signal of danger. Of these things some vulgar verbal hint may be attempted; but what words can render the rarest charm of all—the clear-cut brow of the Fall, the very act and figure of the leap, the rounded passage of the horizontal to the perpendicular? To say it is simple is to make a phrase about it. Nothing was ever more successfully executed. It is carved as sharp as an emerald, as one must say and say again. It arrives, it pauses, it plunges; it comes and goes for ever; it melts and shifts and changes, all with the sound as of millions of bass-voices; and yet its outline never varies, never moves with a different pulse. It is as gentle as the pouring of wine from a flagon—of melody from the lip of a singer. From the little grove beside the American Fall you catch this extraordinary profile better than you are able to do at the Horseshoe. If the line of beauty had vanished from the earth elsewhere, it would survive on the brow of Niagara. It is impossible to insist too strongly on the grace of the thing, as seen from the Canada cliff. The genius who invented it was certainly the first author of the idea that order, proportion and symmetry are the conditions of perfect beauty. He applied his faith among the watching and listening forests, long before the Greeks proclaimed theirs in the measurements of the Parthenon. Even the roll of the white batteries at the base seems fixed and poised and ordered, and in the vague middle zone of difference between the flood as it falls and the mist as it rises you imagine a mystical meaning—the passage of body to soul, of matter to spirit, of human to divine.

Goat Island, of which every one has heard, is the menagerie of lions, and the spot where your single stone—or, in plain prose, your half-dollar—kills most birds. This broad insular strip, which performs the excellent office of withholding the American shore from immediate contact with the flood, has been left very much to itself, and here you may ramble, for the most part, in undiverted contemplation. The island is owned, I believe, by a family of co-heirs, who have the good taste to keep it quiet. More than once, however, as I have been told, they have been offered a "big price" for the privilege of building an hotel upon this sacred soil. They have been wise, but, after all, they are human, and the offer may be made once too often. Before this fatal day dawns, why should not the State buy up the precious acres, as California has done the Yosemite? It is the opinion of a sentimental tourist that no price would be too great to pay. Otherwise, the only hope for their integrity is in the possibility of a shrewd prevision on the part of the gentlemen who know how to keep hotels that the music of the dinner-band would be injured by the roar of the cataract. You approach from Goat Island the left abutment of the Horseshoe. The little tower which, with the classic rainbow, figures in all "views" of the scene, is planted at a dozen feet from the shore, directly on the shoulder of the Fall. This little tower, I think, deserves a compliment. One might have said beforehand that it would never do, but, as it stands, it makes rather a good point. It serves as a unit of appreciation of the scale of things, and from its spray-blackened summit it admits you to an almost downward peep into the green gulf. More here, even, than on the Canada shore, you perceive the unlimited *wateriness* of the whole spectacle. Its liquid masses take on at moments the likeness of walls and pillars and columns, and, to present any vivid picture of them, we are compelled to talk freely of emerald and crystal, of silver and marble. But really, all the simplicity of the Falls, and half their grandeur, reside in their unmitigated fluidity, which excludes all rocky staging and earthy commixture. It is water piled on water, pinned on water, hinging and hanging on water, breaking, crashing, whitening in shocks altogether watery. And yet for all this no solid was ever so solid as that sculptured shoulder of the Horseshoe. From this little tower, or, better still, from various points farther along the island-shore, even to look is to be immersed. Before you stretches the huge expanse of the upper river, with its belittled cliffs, now mere black lines of forest, dull as with the sadness of gazing at perpetual trouble, eternal danger. Anything more horribly desolate than this boundless livid welter of the rapids it is impossible to conceive, and you very soon begin to pay it the tribute of your own suddenly-assumed suspense, in the impulse to people it with human forms. On this theme you can work out endless analogies. Yes, they are alive, every fear-blanched billow and eddy of them—alive and frenzied with the sense of their doom. They see below them that nameless pause of the arrested current, and the high-tossed drift of sound and spray which rises up lamenting, like the ghosts of their brothers who have been dashed to pieces. They shriek, they sob, they clasp their white hands and toss their long hair; they cling and clutch and wrestle, and, above all, they appear to *bite*. Especially tragical is the air they have of being forced backward, with averted faces, to their fate. Every pulse of the flood is like the grim stride of a giant, wading huge-kneed to his purpose, with the white teeth of a victim fastened in his neck. The outermost of three small islands, interconnected by short bridges, at the extremity of this shore, places one in singularly intimate relation with this portentous flurry. To say that hereabouts the water leaps and plunges and rears and dives, that its uproar makes even one's own ideas about it inaudible, and its current sweeps those ideas to perdition, is to give a very pale account of the universal agitation.

The great spectacle may be called complete only when you have gone down the river some four miles, on the American side, to the so-called rapids of the Whirlpool. Here the unhappy stream tremendously renews its anguish. Two approaches have been contrived on the cliff—one to the rapids proper, the other, farther below, to the scene of the sudden bend. The first consists of a little wooden cage, of the "elevator" pattern, which slides up and down a gigantic perpendicular shaft of horrible flimsiness. But a couple of the usual little brides, staggering beneath the weight of gorgeous cashmeres, entered the conveyance with their respective consorts at the same time with myself; and, as it thus carried Hymen and his fortunes, we survived the adventure. You obtain from below—that is, on the shore of the river—a specimen of the noblest cliff-scenery. The green embankment at the base of the sheer red wall is by itself a very fair example of what they call in the Rocky Mountains a foothill; and from this continuous pedestal erects itself a bristling palisade of earth. As it stands, Gustave Doré might have drawn it. He would have sketched with especial ardour certain parasitical shrubs and boskages—lone and dizzy witnesses of autumn; certain outward-peering wens and warts and other perpendicular excrescences of rock; and, above all, near the summit, the fantastic figures of sundry audacious minor cliffs, grafted upon the greater by a mere lateral attachment and based in the empty air, with great slim trees rooted on their verges, like the tower of the Palazzo Vecchio at Florence. The actual whirlpool is a third of a mile farther down the river, and is best seen from the cliff above. From this point of view, it seems to me by all odds the finest of the secondary episodes of the drama of Niagara, and one on which a scribbling tourist, ineffectively playing at showman, may be content to ring down his curtain. The channel at this point turns away to the right, at a clean right-angle, and the river, arriving from the rapids just above with stupendous velocity, meets the hollow elbow of the Canada shore. The movement with which it betrays its surprise and bewilderment —the sudden issueless maze of waters—is, I think, after the Horseshoe Fall, the very finest thing in its progress. It breaks into no small rage; the offending cliffs receive no drop of spray; for the flood moves in a body and wastes no vulgar side-spurts; but you see it shaken to its innermost bowels and panting hugely, as if smothered in its excessive volume. Pressed back upon its centre, the current creates a sort of pivot, from which it eddies, groping for exit in vast slow circles, delicately and irregularly outlined in foam. The Canada shore, shaggy and gaudy with late September foliage, closes about it like the rising shelves of an amphitheatre, and deepens by contrast the strong blue-green of the stream. This slow-revolving surface—it seems in places perfectly still—resembles nothing so much as some ancient palace-pavement, cracked and scratched by the butts of legionary spears and the gold-stiffened hem of the garments of kings.

Part II

The Passionate Pilgrim

England and London

1872—1897

Editor's Note

James first visited England as a baby in the first year of his life. It was not until he was twenty-six, in 1869, that he made his first independent discovery of the country with which his future life was to become so closely identified, and not until 1872 that he began to record his impressions in the long series of essays he was to devote to English towns, villages, countrysides, relics, customs, and manners. They began to appear in The Nation in 1872, and continued intermittently for another thirty years in American journals and magazines and in his book collections. Four of them—"Chester," "Lichfield and Warwick," "North Devon," "Wells and Salisbury"—were included in Transatlantic Sketches in 1875; these reappeared with some revision in Foreign Parts in 1883; eight more, dating from 1877 to 1879, were included in Portraits of Places in 1883 ("An English Easter," "London at Midsummer," "Two Excursions," "In Warwickshire," "Abbeys and Castles," "English Vignettes," "An English New Year," "An English Winter Watering-Place"); the long essay on "London," first printed in The Century Magazine in December, 1888, was included in Essays in London and Elsewhere in 1893; and in 1905 James assembled the whole body of his English essays with some further revisions in his volume English Hours, where he added the paper on "Browning in Westminster Abbey" already included in Essays in London, "Old Suffolk" from Harper's Weekly, September 25, 1897, and a final essay, "Winchelsea, Rye, and 'Denis Duval'," from Scribner's Magazine, January, 1901, which formed his tribute to the Sussex coastal towns and to Rye, the old Cinque Port in which he had discovered Lamb House in 1896 and where he had taken up his last settled residence in England in the old red brick house he came to love beyond any of his other English homes.

The English essays chosen here are all taken from the text of English Hours (1905). James's impressions and experiences in England are recorded in a great number of his letters from 1879 onward, and in many of his novels and tales, especially from the time of "A Passionate Pilgrim" in 1871, where his own first emotion of discovery and homage is dramatized. The Portrait of a Lady, The Princess Casamassima, The Tragic Muse, The Spoils of Poynton, The Awkward Age, The Sacred Fount, and The Golden Bowl are among the longer novels that evoke the place spirit of London and England most richly, and one of the two novels he left unfinished at his death, The Sense of the Past, was to revive the early theme of the passionate pilgrim from America who seeks to identify himself with England and her past. James's long and close relations with England and the English led him to devote his most acute attention, as observer, admirer, analyst, and critic, to English scenes, society, history, and institutions. The role England plays in his fiction, letters, and essays rivals only that of America, and surpasses even the lifelong enthusiasm he devoted to France and Italy.

Of the essays chosen for inclusion here, "Chester," "Abbeys and Castles," "Old Suffolk," and "London" are printed complete. The passages on "Wells" and "Salisbury" were originally combined as a single essay; "Warwick" is taken *from "Lichfield and Warwick"; "Rochester and Canterbury" from "An English Easter"; "Oxford" from "Two Excursions"; "Cambridge" from "English Vignettes." The details of their dating and original publication are given in the Bibliography, and all texts follow James's final revisions in* English Hours.

Chester

1872

If the Atlantic voyage be counted, as it certainly may, even with the ocean in a fairly good humour, an emphatic zero in the sum of one's better experience, the American traveller arriving at this venerable town finds himself transported, without a sensible gradation, from the edge of the new world to the very heart of the old. It is almost a misfortune perhaps that Chester lies so close to the threshold of England; for it is so rare and complete a specimen of an antique town that the later-coming wonders of its sisters in renown, —of Shrewsbury, Coventry, and York—suffer a trifle by comparison, and the tourist's appetite for the picturesque just loses its finer edge. Yet the first impressions of an observant American in England—of our old friend the sentimental tourist—stir up within him such a cloud of sensibility that while the charm is still unbroken he may perhaps as well dispose mentally of the greater as of the less. I have been playing at first impressions for the second time, and have won the game against a cynical adversary. I have been strolling and restrolling along the ancient wall—so perfect in its antiquity—which locks this dense little city in its stony circle, with a certain friend who has been treating me to a bitter lament on the decay of his relish for the picturesque. "I have turned the corner of youth," is his ceaseless plaint; "I suspected it, but now I know it—now that my heart beats but once where it beat a dozen times before, and that where I found sermons in stones and pictures in meadows, delicious revelations and intimations ineffable, I find nothing but the hard, heavy prose of British civilisation." But little by little I have grown used to my friend's sad monody, and indeed feel half indebted to it as a warning against cheap infatuations.

I defied him, at any rate, to argue successfully against the effect of the brave little walls of Chester. There could be no better example of that phenomenon so delightfully frequent in England—an ancient property or institution lovingly readopted and consecrated to some modern amenity. The good Cestrians may boast of their walls without a shadow of that mental reservation on grounds of modern ease which is so often the tax paid by the romantic; and I can easily imagine that, though most modern towns contrive to get on comfortably without this stony girdle, these people should have come to regard theirs as a prime necessity. For through it, surely, they may know their city more intimately than their unbuckled neighbours—survey it, feel it, rejoice in it as many times a day as they please. The civic consciousness, sunning itself thus on the city's rim and glancing at the little swarming towered and gabled town within, and then at the blue undulations of the near Welsh border, may easily deepen to delicious complacency. The wall enfolds the place in a continuous ring, which, passing through innumerable picturesque vicissitudes, often threatens to snap, but never fairly breaks the link; so that, starting at any point, an hour's easy stroll will bring you back to your station. I have quite lost my heart to this charming creation, and there are so many things to be said about it that I hardly know where to begin. The great fact, I suppose, is that it contains a Roman substructure, rests for much of its course on foundations laid by that race of master-builders. But in spite of this sturdy origin, much of which is buried in the well-trodden soil of the ages, it is the gentlest and least offensive of ramparts; it completes its long irregular curve without a frown or menace in all its disembattled stretch. The earthy deposit of time has indeed in some places climbed so high about its base that it amounts to no more than a causeway of modest dimensions. It has everywhere, however, a rugged outer parapet and a broad hollow flagging, wide enough for two strollers abreast. Thus equipped, it wanders through its adventurous circuit; now sloping, now bending, now broadening into a terrace, now narrowing into an alley, now swelling into an arch, now dipping into steps, now passing some thorn-screened garden, and now reminding you that it was once a more serious matter than all this by the extrusion of a rugged, ivy-smothered tower.

Its final hoary humility is enhanced, to your mind, by the freedom with which you may approach it from any point in the town. Every few steps, as you go, you see some little court or alley boring toward it through the close-pressed houses. It is full of that delightful element of the crooked, the accidental, the unforeseen, which, to American eyes, accustomed to our eternal straight lines and right angles, is the striking feature of European street scenery. An American strolling in the Chester street finds a perfect feast of crookedness—of those random corners, projections, and recesses, odd domestic interspaces charmingly saved or lost, those innumerable architectural surprises and caprices and fantasies which lead to such refreshing exercise a vision benumbed by brown-stone fronts. An American is born to the idea that on his walks abroad it is perpetual level wall ahead of him, and such a revelation as he finds here of infinite accident and infinite effect gives a wholly novel zest to the use of his eyes. It produces too the reflection—a superficial and fallacious one perhaps—that amid all this cunning chiaroscuro of its *mise en scène* life must have more of a certain homely entertainment. It is at least no fallacy to say that childhood—or the later memory of childhood—must borrow from such a background a kind of anecdotical wealth. We all know how in the retrospect of later moods the incidents of early youth "compose," visibly, each as an individual picture, with a magic for which the greatest painters have no corresponding art. There is a vivid reflection of this magic in some of the early pages of Dickens's *Copperfield* and of George Eliot's *Mill on the Floss,* the writers having had the happiness of growing up among old, old things. Two or three of the phases of this rambling wall belong especially to the class of things fondly remembered. In one place it skirts the edge of the cathedral graveyard and sweeps beneath the great square tower and behind the sacred east window of the choir.

Of the cathedral there is more to say; but just the spot I speak of is the best standpoint for feeling how fine an influence in the architectural line—where theoretically, at least, influences are great—is the massive tower of an English abbey, dominating the homes of men; and for watching the eddying flight of swallows make vaster still to the eye the high calm fields of stonework. At another point two battered and crumbling towers, decaying in their winding-sheets of ivy, make a prodigiously designed diversion. One inserted in the body of the wall and the other connected with it by a short, crumbling ridge of masonry, they contribute to a positive jumble of local colour. A shaded mall wanders at the foot of the rampart; beside this passes a narrow canal, with locks and barges and burly watermen in smocks and breeches; while the venerable pair of towers, with their old red sandstone sides peeping through the gaps in their green mantles, rest on the soft grass of one of those odd fragments of public garden, a crooked strip of ground turned to social account, which one meets at every turn, apparently, in England—a tribute to the needs of the "masses." *Stat magni nominis umbra.* The quotation is doubly pertinent here, for this little garden-strip is adorned with mossy fragments of Roman stonework, bits of pavement, altars, baths, disinterred in the local soil. England is the land of small economies, and the present rarely fails to find good use for the odds and ends of the past. These two hoary shells of masonry are therefore converted into "museums," receptacles for the dustiest and shabbiest of tawdry back-parlour curiosities. Here preside a couple of those grotesque creatures, *à la* Dickens, whom one finds squeezed into every cranny of English civilisation, scraping a thin subsistence like mites in a mouldy cheese.

Next after its wall—possibly even before it—Chester values its Rows, an architectural idiosyncrasy which must be seen to be appreciated. They are a sort of gothic edition of the blessed arcades and porticoes of Italy, and consist, roughly speaking, of a running public passage tunnelled through the second story of the houses. The low basement is thus directly on the drive-way, to which a flight of steps descends, at frequent intervals, from this superincumbent verandah. The upper portion of the houses projects to the outer line of the gallery, where they are propped with pillars and posts and parapets. The shop-fronts face along the arcade and admit you to little caverns of traffic, more or less dusky according to their opportunities for illumination in the rear. If the romantic be measured by its hostility to our modern notions of convenience, Chester is probably the most romantic city in the world. This arrangement is endlessly rich in opportunities for amusing effect, but the full charm of the architecture of which it is so essential a part must be observed from the street below. Chester is still an antique town, and mediæval England sits bravely under her gables. Every third house is a "specimen"—gabled and latticed, timbered and carved, and wearing its years more or less lightly. These ancient dwellings present every shade and degree of historical colour and expression. Some are dark with neglect and deformity, and the horizontal slit admitting light into the lurking Row seems to collapse on its dislocated props like a pair of toothless old jaws. Others stand there square-shouldered and sturdy, with their beams painted and straightened, their plaster whitewashed, their carvings polished, and the low casement covering the breadth of the frontage adorned with curtains and flower-pots. It is noticeable that the actual townsfolk have bravely accepted the situation bequeathed by the past, and the large number of rich and intelligent restorations of the old façades makes an effective jumble of their piety and their policy. These elaborate and ingenious repairs attest a highly informed consciousness of the pictorial value of the city. I indeed suspect much of this revived innocence of having recovered a freshness that never can have been, of having been restored with usurious interest. About the genuine antiques there would be properly a great deal to say, for they are really a theme for the philosopher; but the theme is too heavy for my pen, and I can give them but the passing tribute of a sigh. They are cruelly quaint, dreadfully expressive. Fix one of them with your gaze and it seems fairly to reek with mortality. Every stain and crevice seems to syllable some human record—a record of lives airless and unlighted. I have been trying hard to fancy them animated by the children of "Merry England," but I am quite unable to think of them save as peopled by the victims of dismal old-world pains and fears. Human life, surely, packed away behind those impenetrable lattices of lead and bottle-glass, just above which the black outer beam marks the suffocating nearness of the ceiling, can have expanded into scant freedom and bloomed into small sweetness.

Nothing has struck me more in my strolls along the Rows than the fact that the most zealous observation can keep but uneven pace with the fine differences in national manners. Some of the most sensible of these differences are yet so subtle and indefinable that one must give up the attempt to express them, though the omission leave but a rough sketch. As you pass with the bustling current from shop to shop you feel local custom and tradition—another tone of things—pressing on you from every side. The tone of things is somehow heavier than with us; manners and modes are more absolute and positive; they seem to swarm and to thicken the atmosphere about you. Morally and physically it is a denser air than ours. We seem loosely hung together at home as compared with the English, every man of whom is a tight fit in his place. It is not an inferential but a palpable fact that England is a crowded country. There is stillness and space—grassy, oak-studded space—at Eaton Hall, where the Marquis of Westminster dwells (or I believe can afford to humour his notion of not dwelling), but there is a crowd and a hubbub in Chester. Wherever you go the population has overflowed. You stroll on the walls at eventide and you hardly find elbow-room. You haunt the cathedral shades and a dozen sauntering mortals temper your solitude. You glance up an alley or side street and discover populous windows and doorsteps. You roll along country roads and find countless humble pedestrians dotting the green waysides. The English landscape is always a "landscape with figures." And everywhere you go you are accompanied by a vague consciousness of the British child hovering about your knees and coatskirts, naked, grimy, and portentous. You reflect with a sort of physical relief on Australia, Canada, India. Where there are many men, of course, there are many needs; which helps to justify to the philosophic stranger the vast number and the irresistible coquetry of the little shops which adorn these low-browed

Rows. The shop-fronts have always seemed to me the most elegant things in England; and I waste more time than I should care to confess to in covetous contemplation of the vast, clear panes behind which the nether integuments of gentlemen are daintily suspended from glittering brass rods. The manners of the dealers in these comfortable wares seldom fail to confirm your agreeable impression. You are thanked with effusion for expending twopence—a fact of deep significance to the truly analytic mind, and which always seems to me a vague reverberation from certain of Miss Edgeworth's novels, perused in childhood. When you think of the small profits, the small jealousies, the long waiting and the narrow margin for evil days implied by this redundancy of shops and shopmen, you hear afresh the steady rumble of that deep keynote of English manners, overscored so often, and with such sweet beguilement, by finer harmonies, but never extinguished—the economic struggle for existence.

The Rows are as "scenic" as one could wish, and it is a pity that before the birth of their modern consciousness there was no English Balzac to introduce them into a realistic romance with a psychological commentary. But the cathedral is better still, modestly as it stands on the roll of English abbeys. It is of moderate dimensions and rather meagre in form and ornament; but to an American it expresses and answers for the type, producing thereby the proper vibrations. Among these is a certain irresistible regret that so much of its hoary substance should give place to the fine, fresh-coloured masonry with which Mr. Gilbert Scott, ruthless renovator, is so intelligently investing it. The red sandstone of the primitive structure, darkened and devoured by time, survives at many points in frowning mockery of the imputed need of tinkering. The great tower, however,—completely restored,—rises high enough to seem to belong, as cathedral towers should, to the far-off air that vibrates with the chimes and the swallows, and to square serenely, east and west and south and north, its embossed and fluted sides. English cathedrals, within, are apt at first to look pale and naked; but after a while, if the proportions be fair and the spaces largely distributed, when you perceive the light beating softly down from the cold clerestory and your eye measures caressingly the tallness of columns and the hollowness of arches, and lingers on the old genteel inscriptions of mural marbles and brasses; and, above all, when you become conscious of that sweet, cool mustiness in the air which seems to haunt these places as the very climate of Episcopacy, you may grow to feel that they are less the empty shells of a departed faith than the abodes of a faith which may still affirm a presence and awaken echoes. Catholicism has gone, but Anglicanism has the next best music. So at least it seemed to me, a Sunday or two since, as I sat in the choir at Chester awaiting a discourse from Canon Kingsley. The Anglican service had never seemed to my profane sense so much an affair of magnificent intonations and cadences—of pompous effects of resonance and melody. The vast oaken architecture of the stalls among which we nestled—somewhat stiffly and with a due apprehension of wounded ribs and knees—climbing vainly against the dizzier reach of the columns; the beautiful English voices of certain officiating canons, the little rosy "king's scholars" sitting ranged beneath the pulpit, in white-winged surplices, which made their heads, above the pew-edges, look like rows of sleepy cherubs: every element in the scene gave it a great spectacular beauty. They suggested too what is suggested in England at every turn, that conservatism here has all the charm and leaves dissent and democracy and other vulgar variations nothing but their bald logic. Conservatism has the cathedrals, the colleges, the castles, the gardens, the traditions, the associations, the fine names, the better manners, the poetry; Dissent has the dusky brick chapels in provincial by-streets, the names out of Dickens, the uncertain tenure of the *h,* and the poor *mens sibi conscia recti.* Differences which in other countries are slight and varying, almost metaphysical, as one may say, are marked in England by a gulf. Nowhere else does the degree of one's respectability involve such solid consequences, and I am sure I don't wonder that the sacramental word which with us (and, in such correlatives as they possess, more or less among the continental races) is pronounced lightly and facetiously and as a quotation from the Philistines, is uttered here with a perfectly grave face. To have the courage of one's mere convictions is in short to have a prodigious deal of courage, and I think one must need as much to be a Dissenter as one needs patience not to be a duke. Perhaps the Dissenters (to limit the question to them) manage to stay out of the church by letting it all hang on the sermon. Canon Kingsley's discourse was one more example of the familiar truth—not without its significance to minds zealous for the good old fashion of "making an effort,"—that there is an odd link between large forms and small emanations. The sermon, beneath that triply consecrated vault, should have had a builded majesty. It had not; and I confess that a tender memory of ancient obligations to the author of *Westward Ho!* and *Hypatia* forbids my saying more of it. An American, I think, is not incapable of taking a secret satisfaction in an incongruity of this kind. He finds with relief that even mortals reared as in the ring of a perpetual circus are only mortals. His constant sense of the beautiful scenic properties of English life is apt to beget a habit of melancholy reference to the dead-blank wall which forms the background of our own life-drama; and from doubting in this fantastic humour whether we have even that modest value in the scale of beauty that he has sometimes fondly hoped, he lapses into a moody scepticism as to our place in the scale of "importance," and finds himself wondering vaguely whether this be not a richer race as well as a lovelier land. That of course will never do; so that when after being escorted down the beautiful choir in what, from the American point of view, is an almost gorgeous ecclesiastical march, by the Dean in a white robe trimmed with scarlet and black-robed sacristans carrying silver wands, the officiating canon mounts into a splendid canopied and pinnacled pulpit of gothic stonework and proves —not an "acting" Jeremy Taylor, our poor sentimental tourist begins to hold up his head again and to reflect that so far as we *have* opportunities we mostly rise to them. I am not sure indeed that in the excess of his reaction he is not tempted to accuse his English neighbours of being impenetrable and uninspired, to affirm that they do not half discern their good fortune, and that it takes passionate pilgrims, vague aliens, and other disinherited persons to appreciate the "points" of this admirable country.

Wells

1872

The pleasantest thing in life is doubtless ever the pleasantness that has found one off one's guard—though if I was off my guard in arriving at Wells it could only have been by the effect of a frivolous want of information. I knew in a general way that this ancient little town had a great cathedral to produce, but I was far from suspecting the intensity of the impression that awaited me. The immense predominance of the Minster towers, as you see them from the approaching train over the clustered houses at their feet, gives you indeed an intimation of its character, suggests that the city is nothing if not sanctified; but I can wish the traveller no better fortune than to stroll forth in the early evening with as large a reserve of ignorance as my own, and treat himself to an hour of discoveries. I was lodged on the edge of the Cathedral lawn and had only to pass beneath one of the three crumbling Priory gates which enclose it, and cross the vast grassy oval, to stand before a minster-front which ranks among the first three or four in England. Wells Cathedral is extremely fortunate in being approached by this wide green level, on which the spectator may loiter and stroll to and fro and shift his standpoint to his heart's content. The spectator who does not hesitate to avail himself of his privilege of unlimited fastidiousness might indeed pronounce it too isolated for perfect picturesqueness—too uncontrasted with the profane architecture of the human homes for which it pleads to the skies. But Wells is in fact not a city with a cathedral for central feature; it is a cathedral with a little city gathered at the base and forming hardly more than an extension of the spacious close. You feel everywhere the presence of the beautiful church; the place seems always to savour of a Sunday afternoon; and you imagine every house tenanted by a canon, a prebendary, or a precentor, with "backs" providing for choristers and vergers.

The great façade is remarkable not so much for its expanse as for its elaborate elegance. It consists of two great truncated towers, divided by a broad centre bearing, beside its rich fretwork of statues, three narrow lancet windows. The statues on this vast front are the great boast of the cathedral. They number, with the lateral figures of the towers, no less than three hundred; it seems densely embroidered by the chisel. They are disposed, in successive niches, along six main vertical shafts; the central windows are framed and divided by narrower shafts, and the wall above them rises into a pinnacled screen traversed by two superb horizontal rows. Add to these a close-running cornice of images along the line corresponding with the summit of the aisles and the tiers which complete the decoration of the towers on either side, and you have an immense system of images governed by a quaint theological order and most impressive in its completeness. Many of the little high-lodged effigies are mutilated, and not a few of the niches are empty, but the injury of time is not sufficient to diminish the noble serenity of the building. The injury of time is indeed being actively repaired, for the front is partly masked by a slender scaffolding. The props and platforms are of the most delicate structure, and look in fact as if they were meant to facilitate no more ponderous labour than a fitting-on of noses to disfeatured bishops and a rearrangement of the mantle-folds of strait-laced queens discomposed by the centuries. The main beauty of Wells Cathedral, to my mind, is not its more or less visible wealth of detail, but its singularly charming tone of colour. An even, sober, mouse-like grey invests it from summit to base, deepening nowhere to the melancholy black of your truly romantic gothic, but showing as yet none of the spotty brightness of renovation. It is a wonderful fact that the great towers, from their lofty outlook, see never a factory chimney—those cloud-compelling spires which so often break the charm of the softest English horizons; and the general atmosphere of Wells seemed to me, for some reason, peculiarly luminous and sweet. The cathedral has never been discoloured by the moral malaria of a city with an independent secular life. As you turn back from its portal and glance at the open lawn before it, edged by the mild grey seventeenth-century deanery and the other dwellings, hardly less stately, which seem to reflect in their comfortable fronts the rich respectability of the church, and then up again at the beautiful clear-hued pile, you may fancy it less a temple for man's needs than a monument of his pride—less a fold for the flock than for the shepherds; a visible token that, besides the actual assortment of heavenly thrones, there is constantly on hand a "full line" of cushioned cathedral stalls. Within the cathedral this impression is not diminished. The interior is vast and massive, but it lacks incident—the incident of monuments, sepulchres, and chapels—and it is too brilliantly lighted for picturesque, as distinguished from strictly architectural, interest. Under this latter head it has, I believe, great importance. For myself, I can think of it only as I saw it from my place in the choir during afternoon service of a hot Sunday. The Bishop sat facing me, enthroned in a stately gothic alcove and clad in his crimson band, his lawn sleeves and his lavender gloves; the canons, in their degree, with still other priestly forms, reclined comfortably in the carven stalls, and the scanty congregation fringed the broad aisle. But though scanty, the congregation was select; it was unexceptionably black-coated, bonneted and gloved. It savoured intensely in short of that inexorable gentility which the English put on with their Sunday bonnets and beavers, and which fills me —as a mere taster of produced tastes—with a sort of fond reactionary remembrance of those animated bundles of rags which one sees kneeling in the churches of Italy. But even here, as taster of tastes, I found my account. You always do if you throw yourself confidently enough, in England, on the chapter of accidents. Before me and beside me sat a row of the comeliest young men, clad in black gowns and wearing on their shoulders long hoods trimmed with white fur. Who and what they were I know not, for I preferred not to learn, lest by chance they should not be so mediæval as they looked.

My fancy found its account even better in the singular quaintness of the little precinct known as the Vicars' Close. It directly adjoins the Cathedral Green, and you enter it beneath one of the solid old gate-houses which form so striking an element in the ecclesiastical furniture of Wells. It consists of a narrow, oblong court, bordered on each side with thirteen small dwellings and terminating in a ruinous little chapel. Here formerly dwelt a congregation of minor priests, established in the thirteenth century to do curates' work for the canons. The little houses are very much modernised; but they retain their tall chimneys, with carven tablets in the face, their antique compactness and neatness, and a certain little sanctified air as of cells in a cloister. The place is adorably of another world and time, and, approaching it as I did in the first dimness of twilight, it looked to me, in its exaggerated perspective, like one of those conventional streets represented on the stage, down whose impossible vista the heroes and confidants of romantic comedies come swaggering arm-in-arm and hold amorous converse with heroines perched at second-story windows. But though the Vicars' Close is a curious affair enough, the great boast of Wells is its episcopal Palace. The Palace loses nothing from being seen for the first time in the kindly twilight, and from being approached with an uncautioned mind. To reach it (unless you go from within the cathedral by the cloisters), you pass out of the Green by another ancient gateway into the market-place, and thence back again through its own peculiar portal. My own first glimpse of it had all the felicity of a *coup de théâtre*. I saw within the dark archway an enclosure bedimmed at once with the shadows of trees and heightened with the glitter of water. The picture was worthy of this agreeable promise. Its main feature is the little grey-walled island on which the Palace stands, rising in feudal fashion out of a broad, clear moat, flanked with round towers and approached by a proper drawbridge. Along the outer side of the moat is a short walk beneath a row of picturesquely stunted elms; swans and ducks disport themselves in the current and ripple the bright shadows of the overclambering plants from the episcopal gardens and masses of wall-flower lodged on the hoary battlements. On the evening of my visit the haymakers were at work on a great sloping field in the rear of the Palace, and the sweet perfume of the tumbled grass in the dusky air seemed all that was wanting to fix the scene for ever in the memory. Beyond the moat and within the grey walls dwells my lord Bishop, in the finest seat of all his order. The mansion dates from the thirteenth century; but, stately dwelling though it is, it occupies but a subordinate place in its own grounds. Their great ornament, picturesquely speaking, is the massive ruin of a banqueting-hall erected by a free-living mediæval bishop and more or less demolished at the Reformation. With its still perfect towers and beautiful shapely windows, hung with those green tapestries so stoutly woven by the English climate, it is a relic worthy of being locked away behind an embattled wall. I have among my impressions of Wells, besides this picture of the moated Palace, half a dozen memories of the romantic sort, which I lack space to transcribe. The clearest impression perhaps is that of the beautiful church of St. Cuthbert, of the same date as the cathedral, and in very much the same style of elegant, temperate early English. It wears one of the high-soaring towers for which Somersetshire is justly celebrated, as you may see from the window of the train in rolling past its almost topheavy hamlets. The beautiful old church, surrounded with its green graveyard, and large enough to be impressive, without being too large (a great merit, to my sense) to be easily compassed by a deplorably unarchitectural eye, wore a native English expression to which certain humble figures in the foreground gave additional point. On the edge of the churchyard was a low-gabled house, before which four old men were gossiping in the eventide. Into the front of the house was inserted an antique alcove in stone, divided into three shallow little seats, two of which were occupied by extraordinary specimens of decrepitude. One of these ancient paupers had a huge protuberant forehead, and sat with a pensive air, his head gathered painfully upon his twisted shoulders and his legs resting across his crutch. The other was rubicund, blear-eyed, and frightfully besmeared with snuff. Their voices were so feeble and senile that I could scarcely understand them, and only just managed to make out the answer to my enquiry of who and what they were—"We 're Still's Almhouse, sir."

One of the lions, almost, of Wells (whence it is but five miles distant) is the ruin of the famous Abbey of Glastonbury, on which Henry VIII, in the language of our day, came down so heavily. The ancient splendour of the architecture survives but in scattered and scanty fragments, among influences of a rather inharmonious sort. It was cattle-market in the little town as I passed up the main street, and a savour of hoofs and hide seemed to accompany me through the easy labyrinth of the old arches and piers. These occupy a large back yard, close behind the street, to which you are most prosaically admitted by a young woman who keeps a wicket and sells tickets. The continuity of tradition is not altogether broken, however, for the little street of Glastonbury has rather an old-time aspect, and one of the houses at least must have seen the last of the abbots ride abroad on his mule. The little inn is a capital bit of character, and as I waited for the 'bus under its low dark archway (in something of the mood, possibly, in which a train was once waited for at Coventry), and watched the barmaid flirting her way to and fro out of the heavy-browed kitchen and among the lounging young appraisers of colts and steers and barmaids, I might have imagined that the merry England of the Tudors had not utterly passed away. A beautiful England this must have been as well, if it contained many such abbeys as Glastonbury. Such of the ruined columns and portals and windows as still remain are of admirable design and finish. The doorways are rich in marginal ornament—ornament within ornament, as it often is; for the dainty weeds and wild flowers overlace the antique tracery with their bright arabesques and deepen the grey of the stonework as it brightens their bloom. The thousand flowers which grow among English ruins deserve a chapter to themselves. I owe them, as an observer, a heavy debt of satisfaction, but I am too little of a botanist to pay them in their own coin. It has often seemed to me in England that the purest enjoyment of architecture was to be had among the ruins of great buildings.

In the perfect building one is rarely sure that the impression is simply architectural: it is more or less pictorial and romantic; it depends partly upon association and partly upon various accessories and details which, however they may be wrought into harmony with the architectural idea, are not part of its essence and spirit. But in so far as beauty of structure is beauty of line and curve, balance and harmony of masses and dimensions, I have seldom relished it as deeply as on the grassy nave of some crumbling church, before lonely columns and empty windows where the wild flowers were a cornice and the sailing clouds a roof. The arts certainly hang together in what they do for us. These hoary relics of Glastonbury reminded me in their broken eloquence of one of the other great ruins of the world—the Last Supper of Leonardo. A beautiful shadow, in each case, is all that remains; but that shadow is the soul of the artist.

From "Wells and Salisbury" (1872)

Salisbury

1872

Salisbury Cathedral, to which I made a pilgrimage on leaving Wells, is the very reverse of a ruin, and you take your pleasure there on very different grounds from those I have just attempted to define. It is perhaps the best-known typical church in the world, thanks to its shapely spire; but the spire is so simply and obviously fair that when you have respectfully made a note of it you have anticipated æsthetic analysis. I had seen it before and admired it heartily, and perhaps I should have done as well to let my admiration rest. I confess that on repeated inspection it grew to seem to me the least bit *banal,* or even *bête,* since I am talking French, and I began to consider whether it does not belong to the same range of art as the Apollo Belvedere or the Venus de' Medici. I am inclined to think that if I had to live within sight of a cathedral and encounter it in my daily comings and goings, I should grow less weary of the rugged black front of Exeter than of the sweet perfection of Salisbury. There are people by temperament easily sated with beauties specifically fair, and the effect of Salisbury Cathedral architecturally is equivalent to that of flaxen hair and blue eyes physiognomically. The other lions of Salisbury, Stonehenge and Wilton House, I revisited with undiminished interest. Stonehenge is rather a hackneyed shrine of pilgrimage. At the time of my former visit a picnic-party was making libations of beer on the dreadful altar-sites. But the mighty mystery of the place has not yet been stared out of countenance; and as on this occasion there were no picnickers we were left to drink deep of all its ambiguities and intensities. It stands as lonely in history as it does on the great plain whose many-tinted green waves, as they roll away from it, seem to symbolise the ebb of the long centuries which have left it so portentously unexplained. You may put a hundred questions to these rough-hewn giants as they bend in grim contemplation of their fallen companions; but your curiosity falls dead in the vast sunny stillness that enshrouds them, and the strange monument, with all its unspoken memories, becomes simply a heart-stirring picture in a land of pictures. It is indeed immensely vague and immensely deep. At a distance you see it standing in a shallow dell of the plain, looking hardly larger than a group of ten-pins on a bowling-green. I can fancy sitting all a summer's day watching its shadows shorten and lengthen again, and drawing a delicious contrast between the world's duration and the feeble span of individual experience. There is something in Stonehenge almost reassuring to the nerves; if you are disposed to feel that the life of man has rather a thin surface, and that we soon get to the bottom of things, the immemorial grey pillars may serve to represent for you the pathless vaults beneath the house of history. Salisbury is indeed rich in antiquities. Wilton House, a delightful old residence of the Earls of Pembroke, contains a noble collection of Greek and Roman marbles. These are ranged round a charming cloister occupying the centre of the house, which is exhibited in the most liberal fashion. Out of the cloister opens a series of drawing-rooms hung with family portraits, chiefly by

Vandyck, all of superlative merit. Among them hangs supreme, as the Vandyck *par excellence,* the famous and magnificent group of the whole Pembroke family of James the First's time. This splendid work has every pictorial merit —design, colour, elegance, force, and finish, and I have been vainly wondering to this hour what it needs to be the finest piece of portraiture, as it surely is one of the most ambitious, in the world. What it lacks, characteristically, in a certain uncompromising veracity, it recovers in the beautiful dignity of its position—unmoved from the stately house in which its author sojourned and wrought, familiar to the descendants of its noble originals.

From "Wells and Salisbury" (1872)

Warwick

1872

To walk in quest of any object that one has more or less tenderly dreamed of, to find your way, to steal upon it softly, to see at last, if it be church or castle, the tower-tops peeping above elms or beeches—to push forward with a rush, and emerge and pause and draw that first long breath which is the compromise between so many sensations: this is a pleasure left to the tourist even after the broad glare of photography has dissipated so many of the sweet mysteries of travel; even in a season when he is fatally apt to meet a dozen fellow-pilgrims returning from the shrine, each as big a fool, so to speak, as he ever was, or to overtake a dozen more telegraphing their impressions down the line as they arrive. Such a pleasure I lately enjoyed quite in its perfection, in a walk to Haddon Hall, along a meadow-path by the Wye, in this interminable English twilight which I am never weary of admiring watch in hand. Haddon Hall lies among Derbyshire hills, in a region infested, I was about to write, by Americans. But I achieved my own sly pilgrimage in perfect solitude; and as I descried the grey walls among the rook-haunted elms I felt not like a dusty tourist, but like a successful adventurer.

I have certainly had, as a dusty tourist, few more charming moments than some—such as any one, I suppose, is free to have—that I passed on a little ruined grey bridge which spans, with its single narrow arch, a trickling stream at the base of the eminence from which those walls and trees look down. The twilight deepened, the ragged battlements and the low, broad oriels glanced duskily from the foliage, the rooks wheeled and clamoured in the glowing sky; and if there had been a ghost on the premises I certainly ought to have seen it. In fact I did see it, as we see ghosts nowadays. I felt the incommunicable spirit of the scene with the last, the right intensity. The old life, the old manners, the old figures seemed present again. The great *coup de théâtre* of the young woman who shows you the Hall—it is rather languidly done on her part—is to point out a little dusky door opening from a turret to a back terrace as the aperture through which Dorothy Vernon eloped with Lord John Manners. I was ignorant of this episode, for I was not to enter the place till the morrow, and I am still unversed in the history of the actors. But as I stood in the luminous dusk weaving the romance of the spot, I recognised the inevitability of a Dorothy Vernon and quite understood a Lord John. It was of course on just such an evening that the romantic event came off, and by listening with the proper credulity I might surely hear on the flags of the castle-court ghostly footfalls and feel in their movement the old heartbeats. The only footfall I can conscientiously swear to, however, is the far from spectral tread of the damsel who led me through the mansion in the prosier light of the next morning. Haddon Hall, I believe, is one of the sights in which it is the fashion to be "disappointed;" a fact explained in a great measure by the absence of a formal approach to the house, which shows its low, grey front to every trudger on the high-road. But the charm of the spot is so much less that of grandeur than that of melancholy, that it is rather deepened than diminished by this attitude of obvious survival and decay. And for that matter, when you have entered the steep little outer court through the huge thickness of the low gateway, the present seems effectually walled out and the past walled in, even as a dead man in a sepulchre. It is very dead, of a fine June morning, the genius of Haddon Hall; and the silent courts and chambers, with their hues of ashen grey and faded brown, seem as time-bleached as the dry bones of any mouldering mortality. The comparison is odd, but Haddon Hall reminded me perversely of some of the larger houses at Pompeii. The private life of the past is revealed in each case with very much the same distinctness and on a scale small enough not to stagger the imagination. This old dwelling indeed has so little of the mass and expanse of the classic feudal castle that it almost suggests one of those miniature models of great buildings which lurk in dusty corners of museums. But it is large enough to be delectably complete and to contain an infinite store of the poetry of grass-grown courts looked into by wide, jutting windows and climbed out of by crooked stone stairways mounting against the walls to little high-placed doors. The "tone" of Haddon Hall, of all its walls and towers and stonework, is the grey of unpolished silver, and the reader who has been in England need hardly be reminded of the sweet accord—to eye and mind alike—existing between all stony surfaces covered with the pale corrosions of time and the deep living green of the strong ivy which seems to feed on their slow decay. Of this effect and of a hundred others—from those that belong to low-browed, stone-paved empty rooms where life was warm and atmospheres thick, to those one may note where the dark tower stairway emerges at last, on a level with the highest beech-tops, against the cracked and sun-baked parapet which flaunted the castle standard over the castle woods—of every form of sad desuetude and picturesque decay Haddon Hall contains some delightful example. Its finest point is undoubtedly a certain court from which a stately flight of steps ascends to the terrace where that daughter of the Vernons whom I have mentioned took such happy thought for our requiring, as the phrase is, a reference. These steps, with the terrace, its balustrade topped with great ivy-muffled knobs of stone and its high background of massed woods, form the ideal *mise en scène* for portions of Shakespeare's comedies. "It's exactly Elizabethan," said my companion. Here the Countess Olivia may have listened to the fantastic Malvolio, or Beatrix, superbest of flirts, have come to summon Benedick to dinner.

The glories of Chatsworth, which lies but a few miles from Haddon, serve as a marked offset to its more delicate merits, just as they are supposed to gain, I believe, in the tourist's eyes, by contrast with its charming, its almost Italian shabbiness. But the glories of Chatsworth, incontestable as they are, were so effectually eclipsed to my mind, a couple of days later, that in future, when I think of an English mansion, I shall think only of Warwick, and when I think of an English park, only of Blenheim. Your run by train through the gentle Warwickshire land does much to prepare you for the great spectacle of the castle, which seems hardly more than a sort of massive symbol and synthesis of the broad prosperity and peace and leisure diffused over this great pastoral expanse. The Warwickshire meadows are to common English scenery what this is to that of the rest of the world. For mile upon mile you can see nothing but broad sloping pastures of velvet turf, overbrowsed by sheep of the most fantastic shagginess and garnished with hedges out of the trailing luxury of whose verdure great ivy-tangled oaks and elms arise with a kind of architectural regularity. The landscape indeed sins by excess of nutritive suggestion; it savours of larder and manger; it is too ovine, too bovine, it is almost asinine; and if you were to believe what you see before you this rugged globe would be a sort of boneless ball covered with some such plush-like integument as might be figured by the down on the cheek of a peach. But a great thought keeps you company as you go and gives character to the scenery. Warwickshire—you say it over and over—was Shakespeare's country. Those who think that a great genius is something supremely ripe and healthy and human may find comfort in the fact. It helps greatly to enliven my own vague conception of Shakespeare's temperament, with which I find it no great shock to be obliged to associate ideas of mutton and beef. There is something as final, as disillusioned of the romantic horrors of rock and forest, as deeply attuned to human needs in the Warwickshire pastures as there is in the underlying morality of the poet.

With human needs in general Warwick Castle may be in no great accord, but few places are more gratifying to the sentimental tourist. It is the only great residence he may have coveted as a home. The fire that we heard so much of last winter in America appears to have consumed but an inconsiderable and easily spared portion of the house, and the great towers rise over the great trees and the town with the same grand air as before. Picturesquely, Warwick gains from not being sequestered, after the common fashion, in acres of park. The village street winds about the garden walls, though its hum expires before it has had time to scale them. There can be no better example of the way in which stone walls, if they do not of necessity make a prison, may on occasions make a palace, than the prodigious privacy maintained thus about a mansion whose windows and towers form the main feature of a bustling town. At Warwick the past joins hands so stoutly with the present that you can hardly say where one begins and the other ends, and you rather miss the various crannies and gaps of what I just now called the Italian shabbiness of Haddon.

There is a Cæsar's tower and a Guy's tower and half a dozen more, but they are so well-conditioned in their ponderous antiquity that you are at loss whether to consider them parts of an old house revived or of a new house picturesquely superannuated. Such as they are, however, plunging into the grassed and gravelled courts from which their battlements look really feudal, and into gardens large enough for all delight and too small, as they should be, to be amazing; and with ranges between them of great apartments at whose hugely recessed windows you may turn from Vandyck and Rembrandt to glance down the cliff-like pile into the Avon, washing the base like a lordly moat, with its bridge, and its trees and its memories, they mark the very model of a great hereditary dwelling—one which amply satisfies the imagination without irritating the democratic conscience. The pictures at Warwick reminded me afresh of an old conclusion on this matter; that the best fortune for good pictures is not to be crowded into public collections—not even into the relative privacy of Salons Carrés and Tribunes—but to hang in largely-spaced half-dozens on the walls of fine houses. Here the historical atmosphere, as one may call it, is almost a compensation for the often imperfect light. If this be true of most pictures it is especially so of the works of Vandyck, whom you think of, wherever you may find him, as having, with that thorough good-breeding which is the stamp of his manner, taken account in his painting of the local conditions and predestined his picture to just the spot where it hangs. This is in fact an illusion as regards the Vandycks at Warwick, for none of them represent members of the house. The very finest perhaps after the great melancholy, picturesque Charles I—death, or at least the presentiment of death on the pale horse—is a portrait from the Brignole palace at Genoa; a beautiful noble matron in black, with her little son and heir. The last Vandycks I had seen were the noble company this lady had left behind her in the Genoese palace, and as I looked at her I thought of her mighty change of circumstance. Here she sits in the mild light of midmost England; there you could almost fancy her blinking in the great glare sent up from the Mediterranean. Intensity for intensity—intensity of situation constituted—I hardly know which to choose.

From "Lichfield and Warwick" (1872)

Rochester and Canterbury

1877

At Rochester I stopped for the sake of its castle, which I espied from the railway train as it perched on a grassy bank beside the widening Medway. There were other beguilements as well; the place has a small cathedral, and, leaving the creators of Falstaff and of the tale-telling Pilgrims out of the question, one had read about it in Dickens, whose house of Gadshill was a couple of miles from the town. All this Kentish country, between London and Dover, figures indeed repeatedly in Dickens; he expresses to a certain extent, for our later age, the spirit of the land. I found this to be quite the case at Rochester. I had occasion to go into a little shop kept by a talkative old woman who had a photograph of Gadshill lying on her counter. This led to my asking her whether the illustrious master of the house had often, to her old-time vision, made his appearance in the town. "Oh, bless you, sir," she said, "we every one of us knew him to speak to. He was in this very shop on the Tuesday with a party of foreigners—as he was dead in his bed on the Friday." (I should remark that I probably do not repeat the days of the week as she gave them.) "He 'ad on his black velvet suit, and it always made him look so 'andsome. I said to my 'usband, 'I *do* think Charles Dickens looks so nice in that black velvet suit.' But he said he couldn't see as he looked any way particular. He was in this very shop on the Tuesday, with a party of foreigners." Rochester consists of little more than one long street, stretching away from the castle and the river toward neighbouring Chatham, and edged with low brick houses, of intensely provincial aspect, most of which have some small, dull smugness or quaintness of gable or window. Nearly opposite to the shop of the old lady with the snubby husband is a little dwelling with an inscribed slab set into its face, which must often have provoked a smile in the great master of the comic. The slab relates that in the year 1579 Richard Watts here established a charity which should furnish "six poor travellers, not rogues or proctors," one night's lodging and entertainment gratis, and fourpence in the morning to go on their way withal, and that in memory of his "munificence" the stone has lately been renewed. The inn at Rochester had small hospitality, and I felt strongly tempted to knock at the door of Mr. Watts's asylum, under plea of being neither a rogue nor a proctor. The poor traveller who avails himself of the testamentary fourpence may easily resume his journey as far as Chatham without breaking his treasure. Is not this the place where little Davy Copperfield slept under a cannon on his journey from London to Dover to join his aunt Miss Trotwood? The two towns are really but one, which forms an interminable crooked thoroughfare, lighted up in the dusk, as I measured it up and down, with the red coats of the vespertinal soldier quartered at the various barracks of Chatham.

The cathedral of Rochester is small and plain, hidden away in rather an awkward corner, without a verdant close to set it off. It is dwarfed and effaced by the great square Norman keep of the adjacent castle. But within it is very charming, especially beyond the detestable wall, the vice of almost all the English cathedrals, which shuts in the choir and breaks the sacred perspective of the aisle. Here, as at Canterbury, you ascend a high range of steps, to pass through the small door in the wall. When I speak slightingly, by the way, of the outside of Rochester cathedral, I intend my faint praise in a relative sense. If we were so happy as to have this secondary pile within reach in America we should go barefoot to see it; but here it stands in the great shadow of Canterbury, and that makes it humble. I remember, however, an old priory gateway which leads you to the church, out of the main street; I remember a kind of haunted-looking deanery, if that be the technical name, at the base of the eastern walls; I remember a fluted tower that took the afternoon light and let the rooks and the swallows come circling and clamouring around it. Better still than these things, I remember the ivy-muffled squareness of the castle, a very noble and imposing ruin. The old walled precinct has been converted into a little public garden, with flowers and benches and a pavilion for a band, and the place was not empty, as such places in England never are. The result is agreeable, but I believe the process was barbarous, involving the destruction and dispersion of many interesting portions of the ruin. I lingered there for a long time, looking in the fading light at what was left. This rugged pile of Norman masonry will be left when a great many solid things have departed; it mocks, ever so monotonously, at destruction, at decay. Its walls are fantastically thick; their great time-bleached expanses and all their rounded roughnesses, their strange mixture of softness and grimness, have an undefinable fascination for the eye. English ruins always come out peculiarly when the day begins to fail. Weather-bleached, as I say they are, they turn even paler in the twilight and grow consciously solemn and spectral. I have seen many a mouldering castle, but I remember in no single mass of ruin more of the helpless, bereaved, amputated look.

It is not the absence of a close that damages Canterbury; the cathedral stands amid grass and trees, with a cultivated margin all round it, and is placed in such a way that, as you pass out from under the gate-house you appreciate immediately its grand feature—its extraordinary and magnificent length. None of the English cathedrals seems to sit more gravely apart, to desire more to be shut up to itself. It is a long walk, beneath the walls, from the gateway of the close to the farther end of the last chapel. Of all that there is to observe in this upward-gazing stroll I can give no detailed account; I can, in my fear to pretend to dabble in the esoteric constructional question—often so combined with an absence of other felt relations—speak only of the picture, the mere builded *scène*. This is altogether delightful. None of the rivals of Canterbury has a more complicated and elaborate architecture, a more perplexing intermixture of periods, a more charming jumble of Norman arches and English points and perpendiculars. What makes the side-view superb, moreover, is the double transepts, which produce the finest agglomeration of gables and buttresses. It is as if two great churches had joined forces toward the middle—one giving its nave and the other its choir, and each keeping its own great cross-aisles. Astride of the roof, between them, sits a huge gothic tower, which is one of the latest portions of the building, though it looks like one of the earliest, so tempered and tinted, so thumb-marked and rubbed smooth is it, by the handling of the ages and the breath of the elements. Like the rest of the structure it has a magnificent colour—a sort of rich dull yellow, a sort of personal accent of tone that is neither brown nor grey. This is particularly appreciable from the cloisters on the further side of the church—the side, I mean, away from the town and the open garden-sweep I spoke of; the side that looks toward a damp old clerical house, lurking behind a brown archway through which you see young ladies in Gainsborough hats playing something on a patch of velvet turf; the side, in short, that is somehow intermingled with a green quadrangle—a quadrangle serving as a playground to a King's School and adorned externally with a very precious and picturesque old fragment of Norman staircase. This cloister is not "kept up;" it is very dusky and mouldy and dilapidated, and of course very sketchable. The old black arches and capitals are various and handsome, and in the centre are tumbled together a group of crooked gravestones, themselves almost buried in the deep soft grass. Out of the cloister opens the chapter-house, which is not kept up either, but which is none the less a magnificent structure; a noble, lofty hall, with a beautiful wooden roof, simply arched like that of a tunnel, without columns or brackets. The place is now given up to dust and echoes; but it looks more like a banqueting-hall than a council-room of priests, and as you sit on the old wooden bench, which, raised on two or three steps, runs round the base of the four walls, you may gaze up and make out the faint ghostly traces of decorative paint and gold upon the brown ceiling. A little patch of this has been restored "to give an idea." From one of the angles of the cloister you are recommended by the verger to take a view of the great tower, which indeed detaches itself with tremendous effect. You see it base itself upon the roof as broadly as if it were striking roots in earth, and then pile itself away to a height which seems to make the very swallows dizzy as they drop from the topmost shelf. Within the cathedral you hear a great deal, of course, about poor great Thomas A'Becket, and the special sensation of the place is to stand on the spot where he was murdered and look down at a small fragmentary slab which the verger points out to you as a bit of the pavement that caught the blood-drops of the struggle. It was late in the afternoon when I first entered the church; there had been a service in the choir, but that was well over, and I had the place to myself. The verger, who had some pushing-about of benches to attend to, turned me into the locked gates and left me to wander through the side-aisles of the choir and into the great chapel beyond it. I say I had the place to myself; but it would be more decent to affirm that I shared it, in particular, with another gentleman. This personage was stretched upon a couch of stone, beneath a quaint old canopy of wood; his hands were crossed upon his breast, and his pointed toes rested upon a little griffin or leopard. He was a very handsome fellow and the image of a gallant knight. His name was Edward Plantagenet, and his sobriquet was the Black Prince. "*De la mort ne pensai-je mye,*" he says in the beautiful inscription embossed upon the bronze base of his image; and I too, as I stood there, lost the sense of death in a momentary impression of personal nearness to him. One had been further off, after all, from other famous knights. In this same chapel, for many a year, stood the shrine of St. Thomas of Canterbury, one of the richest and most potent in Christendom. The pavement which lay before it has kept its place, but Henry VIII swept away everything else in his famous short cut to reform. Becket was originally buried in the crypt of the church; his ashes lay there for fifty years, and it was only little by little that his martyrdom was made a "draw." Then he was transplanted into the Lady Chapel; every grain of his dust became a priceless relic, and the pavement was hallowed by the knees of pilgrims. It was on this errand of course that Chaucer's story-telling cavalcade came to Canterbury. I made my way down into the crypt, which is a magnificent maze of low, dark arches and pillars, and groped about till I found the place where the frightened monks had first shuffled the inanimate victim of Moreville and Fitzurse out of the reach of further desecration. While I stood there a violent thunderstorm broke over the cathedral; great rumbling gusts and rain-drifts came sweeping through the open sides of the crypt and, mingling with the darkness which seemed to deepen and flash in corners and with the potent mouldy smell, made me feel as if I had descended into the very bowels of history. I emerged again, but the rain had settled down and spoiled the evening, and I splashed back to my inn and sat, in an uncomfortable chair by the coffee-room fire, reading Dean Stanley's agreeable *Memorials of Canterbury* and wondering over the musty appointments and meagre resources of so many English hostels. This establishment had entitled itself (in compliment to the Black Prince, I suppose) the "Fleur-de-Lis." The name was very pretty (I had been foolish enough to let it attract me to the inn), but the lily was sadly deflowered.

From "An English Easter" (1877)

Abbeys and Castles

1877

It is a frequent perception with the stranger in England that the beauty and interest of the country are private property and that to get access to them a key is always needed. The key may be large or it may be small, but it must be something that will turn a lock. Of the things that contribute to the happiness of an American observer in these tantalising conditions, I can think of very few that do not come under this definition of private property. When I have mentioned the hedgerows and the churches I have almost exhausted the list. You can enjoy a hedgerow from the public road, and I suppose that even if you are a Dissenter you may enjoy a Norman abbey from the street. If therefore you talk of anything beautiful in England, the presumption will be that it is private; and indeed such is my admiration of this delightful country that I feel inclined to say that if you talk of anything private the presumption will be that it is beautiful. This is something of a dilemma. When the observer permits himself to commemorate charming impressions he is in danger of giving to the world the fruits of friendship and hospitality. When on the other hand he withholds his impression he lets something admirable slip away without having marked its passage, without having done it proper honour. He ends by mingling discretion with enthusiasm, and he says to himself that it is not treating a country ill to talk of its treasures when the mention of each has tacit reference to some kindness conferred.

The impressions I have in mind in writing these lines were gathered in a part of England of which I had not before had even a traveller's glimpse, but as to which, after a day or two, I found myself quite ready to agree with a friend who lived there and who knew and loved it well, when he said very frankly, "I do believe it is the loveliest corner of the world!" This was not a dictum to quarrel about, and while I was in the neighbourhood I was quite of his opinion. I felt I might easily come to care for it very much as he cared for it; I had a glimpse of the kind of romantic passion such a country may inspire. It is a capital example of that density of feature which is the great characteristic of English scenery. There are no waste details; everything in the landscape is something particular—has a history, has played a part, has a value to the imagination. It is a region of hills and blue undulations, and, though none of the hills are high, all of them are interesting,—interesting as such things are interesting in an old, small country, by a kind of exquisite modulation, something suggesting that outline and colouring have been retouched and refined by the hand of time. Independently of its castles and abbeys, the definite relics of the ages, such a landscape seems charged and interfused. It has, has always had, human relations and is intimately conscious of them. That little speech about the loveliness of his county, or of his own part of his county, was made to me by my companion as we walked up the grassy slope of a hill, or "edge," as it is called there, from the crest of which we seemed in an instant to look away over most of the remainder of England. Certainly one would have grown to love such a view as that quite in the same way as to love some magnificent yet sensitive friend. The "edge" plunged down suddenly, as if the corresponding slope on the other side had been excavated, and you might follow the long ridge for the space of an afternoon's walk with this vast, charming prospect before your eyes. Looking across an English county into the next but one is a very pretty entertainment, the county seeming by no means so small as might be supposed. How can a county seem small in which, from such a vantage-point as the one I speak of, you see, as a darker patch across the lighter green, the great territory of one of the greatest representatives of territorial greatness? These things constitute immensities, and beyond them are blue undulations of varying tone, and then another bosky province which furnishes forth, as you are told, the residential and other umbrage of another magnate. And to right and left of these, in wooded expanses, lie other domains of equal consequence. It was therefore not the smallness but the vastness of the country that struck me, and I was not at all in the mood of a certain American who once, in my hearing, burst out laughing at an English answer to my enquiry as to whether my interlocutor often saw Mr. B——. "Oh no," the answer had been, "we never see him: he lives away off in the West." It was the western part of his county our friend meant, and my American humourist found matter for infinite jest in his meaning. "I should as soon think," he remarked, "of talking of my own west or east foot."

I do not think, even, that my sensibility to the charm of this delightful region—for its hillside prospect of old red farmhouses lighting up the dark-green bottoms, of gables and chimney-tops of great houses peeping above miles of woodland, and, in the vague places of the horizon, of far-away towns and sites that one had always heard of—was conditioned upon having "property" in the neighbourhood, so that the little girls in the town should suddenly drop curtsies to me in the street; though that too would certainly have been pleasant. At the same time having a little property would without doubt have made the attachment stronger. People who wander about the world without money in their pockets indulge in dreams—dreams of the things they would buy if their pockets were workable. These dreams are very apt to have relation to a good estate in any neighbourhood in which the wanderer may happen to find himself. For myself, I have never been in a country so unattractive that I didn't find myself "drawn" to its most exemplary mansion. In New England and other portions of the United States I have felt my heart go out to the Greek temple, the small Parthenon, in white-painted wood; in Italy I have made imaginary proposals for the yellow-walled villa with statues on the roof. My fancy, in England, has seldom fluttered so high as the very best house, but it has again and again hovered about one of the quiet places, unknown to fame, which are locally spoken of as merely "good." There was one in especial, in the neighbourhood I allude to, as to which the dream of having impossibly acquired it from an embarrassed owner kept melting into the vision of "moving in" on the morrow. I saw this place unfortunately, to small advantage; I saw it in the rain, but I am glad fine weather didn't meddle with the affair, for the irritation of envy might in this case have poisoned the impression. It was a long, wet Sunday, and the waters were deep. I had been in the house all day, for the weather can best be described by my saying that it had been deemed to exonerate us from church. But in the afternoon, the prospective interval between lunch and tea assuming formidable proportions, my host took me a walk, and in the course of our walk he led me into a park which he described as "the paradise of a small English country-gentleman." It was indeed a modern Eden, and the trees might have been trees of knowledge. They were of high antiquity and magnificent girth and stature; they were strewn over the grassy levels in extraordinary profusion, and scattered upon and down the slopes in a fashion than which I have seen nothing more felicitous since I last looked at the chestnuts above the Lake of Como. The point was that the property was small, but that one could perceive nowhere any limit. Shortly before we turned into the park the rain had renewed itself, so that we were awkwardly wet and muddy; but, being near the house, my companion proposed to leave his card in a neighbourly way. The house was most agreeable; it stood on a kind of terrace, in the middle of a lawn and garden, and the terrace overhung one of the most copious rivers in England, as well as looking across to those blue undulations of which I have already spoken. On the terrace also was a piece of ornamental water, and there was a small iron paling to divide the lawn from the park. All this I beheld in the rain. My companion gave his card to the butler with the remark that we were too much bespattered to come in, and we turned away to complete our circuit. As we turned away I became acutely conscious of what I should have been tempted to call the cruelty of this proceeding. My imagination gauged the whole position. It was a blank, a blighted Sunday afternoon—no one could come. The house was charming, the terrace delightful, the oaks magnificent, the view most interesting. But the whole thing confessed to the blankness if not to the dulness. In the house was a drawing-room, and in the drawing-room was—by which I meant *must be*—an English lady, a perfectly harmonious figure. There was nothing fatuous in believing that on this rainy Sunday afternoon it would not please her to be told that two gentlemen had walked across the country to her door only to go through the ceremony of leaving a card. Therefore, when, before we had gone many yards, I heard the butler hurrying after us, I felt how just my sentiment of the situation had been. Of course we went back, and I carried my muddy boots into the drawing-room—just the drawing-room I had imagined—where I found—I will not say just the lady I had imagined, but a lady even more in keeping. Indeed there were two ladies, one of whom was staying in the house. In whatever company you find yourself in England, you may always be sure that some one present is "staying," and you come in due time to feel the abysses within the word. The large windows of the drawing-room I speak of looked away over the river to the blurred and blotted hills, where the rain was drizzling and drifting. It was very quiet, as I say; there was an air of large leisure. If one wanted to do anything here, there was evidently plenty of time—and indeed of every other appliance—to do it. The two ladies talked about "town:" that is what people talk about in the country. If I were disposed I might represent them as talking with a positive pathos of yearning. At all events I asked myself how it could be that one should live in this charming place and trouble one's head about what was going on in London in July. Then we had fine strong tea and bread and butter.

I returned to the habitation of my friend—for I too was guilty of "staying"—through an old Norman portal, massively arched and quaintly sculptured, across whose hollow threshold the eye of fancy might see the ghosts of monks and the shadows of abbots pass noiselessly to and fro. This aperture admits you to a beautiful ambulatory of the thirteenth century—a long stone gallery or cloister, repeated in two stories, with the interstices of its traceries now glazed, but with its long, low, narrow, charming vista still perfect and picturesque, with its flags worn away by monkish sandals and with huge round-arched doorways opening from its inner side into great rooms roofed like cathedrals. These rooms are furnished with narrow windows, of almost defensive aspect, set in embrasures three feet deep and ornamented with little grotesque mediæval faces. To see one of the small monkish masks grinning at you while you dress and undress, or while you look up in the intervals of inspiration from your letter-writing, is a mere detail in the entertainment of living in a *ci-devant* priory. This entertainment is inexhaustible; for every step you take in such a house confronts you in one way or another with the remote past. You devour the documentary, you inhale the historic. Adjoining the house is a beautiful ruin, part of the walls and windows and bases of the piers of the magnificent church administered by the predecessor of your host, the mitred abbot. These relics are very desultory, but they are still abundant, and they testify to the great scale and the stately beauty of the abbey. You may lie upon the grass at the base of an ivied fragment, measure the girth of the great stumps of the central columns, half-smothered in soft creepers, and think how strange it is that in this quiet hollow, in the midst of lonely hills, so exquisite and elaborate a work of art should have risen. It is but an hour's walk to another great ruin, which has held together more completely. There the central tower stands erect to half its altitude and the round arches and massive pillars of the nave make a perfect vista on the unencumbered turf. You get an impression that when Catholic England was in her prime great abbeys were as thick as milestones. By native amateurs even now the region is called "wild," though to American eyes it seems almost suburban in its smoothness and finish. There is a noiseless little railway running through the valley, and there is an ancient little town at the abbey gates—a town indeed with no great din of vehicles, but with goodly brick houses, with a dozen "publics," with tidy, whitewashed cottages, and with little girls, as I have said, bobbing curtsies in the street. Yet even now, if one had wound one's way into the valley by the railroad, it would be rather a surprise to find a great architectural display in a setting so peaceful and pastoral. How impressive then must the beautiful church have been in the days of its prosperity, when the pilgrim came down to it from the grassy hillside and its bells made the stillness sensible! The abbey was in those days a great affair; it sprawled, as my companion said, all over the place. As you walk away from it you think you have got to the end of its geography, but you encounter it still in the shape of a rugged outhouse enriched with an early-English arch, of an ancient well hidden in a kind of sculptured cavern. It is noticeable that even if you are a traveller from a land where there are no early-English—and indeed few late-English—arches, and where the well-covers are, at their hoariest, of fresh-looking shingles, you grow used with little delay to all this antiquity. Anything very old seems extremely natural; there is nothing we suffer to get so near us as the tokens of the remote. It is not too much to say that after spending twenty-four hours in a house that is six hundred years old you seem yourself to have lived in it six hundred years. You seem yourself to have hollowed the flags with your tread and to have polished the oak with your touch. You walk along the little stone gallery where the monks used to pace, looking out of the gothic window-places at their beautiful church, and you pause at the big, round, rugged doorway that admits you to what is now the drawing-room. The massive step by which you ascend to the threshold is a trifle crooked, as it should be; the lintels are cracked and worn by the myriad-fingered years. This strikes your casual glance. You look up and down the miniature cloister before you pass in; it seems wonderfully old and queer. Then you turn into the drawing-room, where you find modern conversation and late publications and the prospect of dinner. The new life and the old have melted together; there is no dividing-line. In the drawing-room wall is a queer funnel-shaped hole, with the broad end inward, like a small casemate. You ask what it is, but people have forgotten. It is something of the monks; it is a mere detail. After dinner you are told that there is of course a ghost, a grey friar who is seen in the dusky hours at the end of passages. Sometimes the servants see him; they afterwards go surreptitiously to sleep in the village. Then, when you take your chamber-candle and go wandering bedward by a short cut through empty rooms, you are conscious of an attitude toward the grey friar which you hardly know whether to read as a fond hope or as a great fear.

A friend of mine, an American, who knew this country, had told me not to fail, while I was in the neighbourhood, to go to Stokesay and two or three other places. "Edward IV and Elizabeth," he said, "are still hanging about there." So admonished, I made a point of going at least to Stokesay, and I saw quite what my friend meant. Edward IV and Elizabeth indeed are still to be met almost anywhere in the county; as regards domestic architecture few parts of England are still more vividly old-English. I have rarely had, for a couple of hours, the sensation of dropping back personally into the past so straight as while I lay on the grass beside the well in the little sunny court of this small castle and lazily appreciated the still definite details of mediæval life. The place is a capital example of a small *gentilhommière* of the thirteenth century. It has a good deep moat, now filled with wild verdure, and a curious gate-house of a much later period—the period when the defensive attitude had been wellnigh abandoned. This gate-house, which is not in the least in the style of the habitation, but gabled and heavily timbered, with quaint cross-beams protruding from surfaces of coarse white plaster, is a very effective anomaly in regard to the little grey fortress on the other side of the court. I call this a fortress, but it is a fortress which might easily have been taken, and it must have assumed its present shape at a time when people had ceased to peer through narrow slits at possible besiegers. There are slits in the outer walls for such peering, but they are noticeably broad and not particularly oblique, and might easily have been applied to the uses of a peaceful parley. This is part of the charm of the place; human life there must have lost an earlier grimness; it was lived in by people who were beginning to believe in good intentions. They must have lived very much together; that is one of the most obvious reflections in the court of a mediæval dwelling. The court was not always grassy and empty, as it is now, with only a couple of gentlemen in search of impressions lying at their length, one of them handling a wine-flask that colours the clear water drawn from the well into a couple of tumblers by a decent, rosy, smiling, talking old woman who has come bustling out of the gate-house and who has a large, dropsical, innocent husband standing about on crutches in the sun and making no sign when you ask after his health. This poor man has reached that ultimate depth of human simplicity at which even a chance to talk about one's ailments is not appreciated. But the civil old woman talks for every one, even for an artist who has come out of one of the rooms, where I see him afterward reproducing its mouldering repose. The rooms are all unoccupied and in a state of extreme decay, though the castle is, as yet, far from being a ruin. From one of the windows I see a young lady sitting under a tree, across a meadow, with her knees up, dipping something into her mouth. It is indubitably a camel's hair paint-brush; the young lady is inevitably sketching. These are the only besiegers to which the place is exposed now, and they can do no great harm, as I doubt whether the young lady's aim is very good. We wandered about the empty interior, thinking it a pity such things should fall to pieces. There is a beautiful great hall—great, that is, for a small castle (it would be extremely handsome in a modern house)—with tall, ecclesiastical-looking windows, and a long staircase at one end, which climbs against the wall into a spacious bedroom. You may still apprehend very well the main lines of that simpler life; and it must be said that, simpler though it was, it was apparently by no means destitute of many of our own conveniences. The chamber at the top of the staircase ascending from the hall is charming still, with its irregular shape, its low-browed ceiling, its cupboards in the walls, its deep bay window formed of a series of small lattices. You can fancy people stepping out from it upon the platform of the staircase, whose rugged wooden logs, by way of steps, and solid, deeply-guttered hand-rail, still remain. They looked down into the hall, where, I take it, there was always a congregation of retainers, much lounging and waiting and passing to and fro, with a door open into the court. The court, as I said just now, was not the grassy, æsthetic spot which you may find it at present of a summer's day; there were beasts tethered in it, and hustling men-at-arms, and the earth was trampled into puddles. But my lord or my lady, looking down from the chamber-door, commanded the position and, no doubt, issued their orders accordingly. The sight of the groups on the floor beneath, the calling up and down, the oaken tables spread and the brazier in the middle—all this seemed present again; and it was not difficult to pursue the historic vision through the rest of the building—through the portion which connected the great hall with the tower (where the confederate of the sketching young lady without had set up the peaceful three-legged engine of his craft); through the dusky, roughly circular rooms of the tower itself, and up the corkscrew staircase of the same to that most charming part of every old castle, where visions must leap away off the battlements to elude you—the bright, dizzy platform at the tower-top, the place where the castle-standard hung and the vigilant inmates surveyed the approaches. Here, always, you really overtake the impression of the place—here, in the sunny stillness, it seems to pause, panting a little, and give itself up.

It was not only at Stokesay that I lingered a while on the summit of the keep to enjoy the complete impression so overtaken. I spent such another half-hour at Ludlow, which is a much grander and more famous monument. Ludlow, however, is a ruin—the most impressive and magnificent of ruins. The charming old town and the admirable castle form a capital object of pilgrimage. Ludlow is an excellent example of a small English provincial town that has not been soiled and disfigured by industry; it exhibits no tall chimneys and smoke-streamers, no attendant purlieus and slums. The little city is perched upon a hill near which the goodly Severn wanders, and it has a remarkable air of civic dignity. Its streets are wide and clean, empty and a little grass-grown, and bordered with spacious, mildly-ornamental brick houses which look as if there had been more going on in them in the first decade of the century than there is in the present, but which can still nevertheless hold up their heads and keep their window-panes clear, their knockers brilliant, and their door-steps whitened. The place seems to say that some hundred years ago it was the centre of a large provincial society and that this society was very "good" of its kind. It must have transported itself to Ludlow for the season—in rumbling coaches and heavy curricles—and there entertained itself in decent emulation of that more majestic capital which a choice of railway lines had not as yet placed within its immediate reach. It had balls at the assembly rooms; it had Mrs. Siddons to play; it had Catalani to sing. Miss Burney's and Miss Austen's heroines might perfectly well have had their first love-affair there; a journey to Ludlow would certainly have been a great event to Fanny Price or Emma Woodhouse, or even to those more romantically-connected young ladies Evelina and Cecilia. It is a place on which a provincial aristocracy has left so sensible a stamp as to enable you to measure both the grand manners and the small ways. It is a very interesting array of houses of the period after the poetry of domestic architecture had begun to wane and before the vulgarity had come—a fine familiar classic prose. Such places, such houses, such relics and intimations, carry us back to the near antiquity of that pre-Victorian England which it is still easy for a stranger to picture with a certain vividness, thanks to the partial survival of many of its characteristics. It is still easier for a stranger who has dwelt a time in England to form an idea of the tone, the habits, the aspect of the social life before its classic insularity had begun to wane, as all observers agree that it did about thirty years ago. It is true that the mental operation in this matter reduces itself to our imaging some of the things which form the peculiar national notes as infinitely exaggerated: the rigidly aristocratic constitution of society, the unæsthetic temper of the people, the small public fund of convenience, of elegance. Let an old gentleman of conservative tastes, who can remember the century's youth, talk to you at a club *temporis acti*—tell you wherein it is that from his own point of view London, as a residence for a gentleman, has done nothing but fall off for the last forty years. You will listen, of course, with an air of decent sympathy, but privately you will say to yourself how difficult a place of sojourn London must have been in those days for the traveller from other countries—how little cosmopolitan, how bound, in a thousand ways, with narrowness of custom. What was true of the great city at that time was of course doubly true of the provinces; and a community of the type of Ludlow must have been a kind of focus of insular propriety. Even then, however, the irritated alien would have had the magnificent ruins of the castle to dream himself back into good humour in. They would effectually have transported him beyond all waning or waxing Philistinisms.

Old Suffolk

1897

I am not sure that before entering the county of Suffolk in the early part of August, I had been conscious of any personal relation to it save my share in what we all inevitably feel for a province enshrining the birthplace of a Copperfield. The opening lines in David's history offered in this particular an easy perch to my young imagination; and to recall them to-day, though with a memory long unrefreshed, is to wonder once more at the depth to which early impressions strike down. This one in especial indeed has been the privilege of those millions of readers who owe to Dickens the glow of the prime response to the romantic, that first bite of the apple of knowledge which leaves a taste for ever on the tongue. The great initiators give such a colour to mere names that the things they represent have often, before contact, been a lively part of experience. It is hard therefore for an undefended victim of this kind of emotion to measure, when contact arrives, the quantity of picture already stored up, to point to the nucleus of the gallery or trace the history of the acquaintance. It is true that for the divine plant of sensibility in youth the watering need never have been lavish. It flowered, at all events, at the right moment, in a certain case, into the branching image of Blunderstone—which, by the way, I am sorry to see figure as "Blunderston" in gazetteers of recent date and more than questionable tact. Dickens took his Rookery exactly where he found it, and simply fixed it for ever; he left the cradle of the Copperfields the benefit of its delightful name; or I should say better perhaps, left the delightful name and the obscure nook the benefit of an association ineffaceable: all of which makes me the more ashamed not as yet to have found the right afternoon—it would have in truth to be abnormally long—for a pious pilgrimage to the distracting little church where, on David's sleepy Sundays, one used to lose one's self with the sketchy Phiz. One of the reasons of this omission, so profane on a prior view, is doubtless that everything, in England, in old-time corners, has the connecting touch and the quality of illustration, and that, in a particularly golden August, with an impression in every bush, the immediate vision, wherever one meets it, easily attaches and suffices. Another must have been, I confess, the somewhat depressed memory of a visit paid a few years since to the ancient home of the Peggottys, supposedly so "sympathetic," but with little left, to-day, as the event then proved, of the glamour it had worn to the fancy. Great Yarmouth, it will be remembered, was a convenient drive from Blunderstone; but Great Yarmouth, with its mile of cockneyfied sea-front and its overflow of nigger minstrelsy, now strikes the wrong note so continuously that I, for my part, became conscious, on the spot, of a chill to the spirit of research.

This time, therefore, I have allowed that spirit its ease; and I may perhaps intelligibly make the point I desire if I contrive to express somehow that I have found myself, most of the month, none the less abundantly occupied in reading a fuller sense into the lingering sound given out, for a candid mind, by my superscription and watching whatever it may stand for gradually flush with a stronger infusion. It takes, in England, for that matter, no wonderful corner of the land to make the fiddle-string vibrate. The old usual rural things do this enough, and a part of the charm of one's exposure to them is that they ask one to rise to no heroics. What is the charm, after all, but just the abyss of the familiar? The peopled fancy, the haunted memory are themselves what pay the bill. The game can accordingly be played with delightful economy, a thrift involving the cost of little more than a good bicycle. The bicycle indeed, since I fall back on that admission, may perhaps, without difficulty, be too good for the roads. Those of the more devious kind often engender hereabouts, like the Aristotelian tragedy, pity and terror; but almost equally with others they lead, on many a chance, to the ruddiest, greenest hamlets. What this comes to is saying that I have had, for many a day, the sweet sense of living, æsthetically, at really high pressure without, as it were, drawing on the great fund. By the great fund I mean the public show, the show for admission to which you are charged and overcharged, made to taste of the tree of possible disappointment. The beauty of old Suffolk in general, and above all of the desperate depth of it from which I write, is that these things whisk you straight out of conceivable relation to that last danger.

I defy any one, at desolate, exquisite Dunwich, to be disappointed in anything. The minor key is struck here with a felicity that leaves no sigh to be breathed, no loss to be suffered; a month of the place is a real education to the patient, the inner vision. The explanation of this is, appreciably, that the conditions give you to deal with not, in the manner of some quiet countries, what is meagre and thin, but what has literally, in a large degree, ceased to be at all. Dunwich is not even the ghost of its dead self; almost all you can say of it is that it consists of the mere letters of its old name. The coast, up and down, for miles, has been, for more centuries than I presume to count, gnawed away by the sea. All the grossness of its positive life is now at the bottom of the German Ocean, which moves for ever, like a ruminating beast, an insatiable, indefatigable lip. Few things are so melancholy—and so redeemed from mere ugliness by sadness—as this long, artificial straightness that the monster has impartially maintained. If at low tide you walk on the shore, the cliffs, of little height, show you a defence picked as bare as a bone; and you can say nothing kinder of the general humility and general sweetness of the land than that this sawlike action gives it, for the fancy, an interest, a sort of mystery, that more than makes up for what it may have surrendered. It stretched, within historic times, out into towns and promontories for which there is now no more to show than the empty eye-holes of a skull; and half the effect of the whole thing, half the secret of the impression, and what I may really call, I think, the source of the distinction, is this very visibility of the mutilation. Such at any rate is the case for a mind that can properly brood. There is a presence in what is missing—there is history in there being so little. It is so little, to-day, that every item of the handful counts.

The biggest items are of course the two ruins, the great church and its tall tower, now quite on the verge of the cliff, and the crumbled, ivied wall of the immense cincture of the Priory. These things have parted with almost every grace, but they still keep up the work that they have been engaged in for centuries and that cannot better be described than as the adding of mystery to mystery. This accumulation, at present prodigious, is, to the brooding mind, unconscious as the shrunken little Dunwich of to-day may be of it, the beginning and the end of the matter. I hasten to add that it is to the brooding mind only, and from it, that I speak. The mystery sounds for ever in the hard, straight tide, and hangs, through the long, still summer days and over the low, diked fields, in the soft, thick light. We play with it as with the answerless question, the question of the spirit and attitude, never again to be recovered, of the little city submerged. For it *was* a city, the main port of Suffolk, as even its poor relics show; with a fleet of its own on the North Sea, and a big religious house on the hill. We wonder what were then the apparent conditions of security, and on what rough calculation a community could so build itself out to meet its fate. It keeps one easy company here to-day to think of the whole business as a magnificent mistake. But Mr. Swinburne, in verses of an extraordinary poetic eloquence, quite brave enough for whatever there may have been, glances in the right direction much further than I can do. Read moreover, for other glances, the *Letters of Edward FitzGerald*, Suffolk worthy and whimsical subject, who, living hard by at Woodbridge, haunted these regions during most of his life, and has left, in delightful pages, at the service of the emulous visitor, the echo of every odd, quaint air they could draw from his cracked, sweet instrument. He has paid his tribute, I seem to remember, to the particular delicate flower—the pale Dunwich rose—that blooms on the walls of the Priory. The emulous visitor, only yesterday, on the most vulgar of vehicles—which, however, he is quite aware he must choose between using and abusing—followed, in the mellow afternoon, one of these faint hints across the land and as far as the old, old town of Aldeburgh, the birthplace and the commemorated *Borough* of the poet Crabbe.

FitzGerald, devoted to Crabbe, was apparently not less so to this small break in the wide, low, heathery bareness that brings the sweet Suffolk commons—rare purple and gold when I arrived—nearly to the edge of the sea. We don't, none the less, always gather the particular impression we bravely go forth to seek. We doubtless gather another indeed that will serve as well any such turn as here may wait for it; so that if it was somehow not easy to work FitzGerald into the small gentility of the sea-front, the little "marina," as of a fourth-rate watering-place, that has elbowed away, evidently in recent years, the old handful of character, one could at least, to make up for that, fall back either on the general sense of the happy trickery of genius or on the special beauty of the mixture, in the singer of Omar Khayyam, that, giving him such a place for a setting, could yet feed his fancy so full. Crabbe, at Aldeburgh, for that matter, is perhaps even more wonderful—in the light, I mean, of what is left of the place by one's conjuring away the little modern vulgar accumulation. What is left is just the stony beach and the big gales and the cluster of fishermen's huts and the small, wide, short street of decent, homely, shoppy houses. These are the private emotions of the historic sense—glimpses in which we recover for an hour, or rather perhaps, with an intensity, but for the glimmer of a minute, the conditions that, grimly enough, could engender masterpieces, or at all events classics. What a mere pinch of manners and customs in the midst of winds and waves! Yet if it was a feature of these to return a member to Parliament, what wonder that, up to the Reform Bill, dead Dunwich should have returned two?

The glimpses I speak of are, in all directions, the constant company of the afternoon "spin." Beginning, modestly enough, at Dunwich itself, they end, for intensity, as far inland as you have time to go; far enough—this is the great point—to have shown you, in their quiet vividness of type, a placid series of the things into which you may most read the old story of what is softest in the English complexity. I scarce know what murmur has been for weeks in my ears if it be not that of the constant word that, as a recall of the story, may serve to be put under the vignette. And yet this word is in its last form nothing more eloquent than the mere admonition to be pleased. Well, so you are, even as I was yesterday at Wesselton with the characteristic "value" that expressed itself, however shyly, in the dear old red inn at which I halted for the queer restorative—I thus discharge my debt to it—of a bottle of lemonade with a "dash." The dash was only of beer, but the refreshment was immense. So even was that of the sight of a dim, draped, sphinx-like figure that loomed, at the end of a polished passage, out of a little dusky back parlour which had a windowful of the choked light of a small green garden—a figure proving to be an old woman desirous to dilate on all the years she had sat there with rheumatism "most cruel." So, inveterately—and in these cases without the after-taste—is that of the pretty little park gates you pass to skirt the walls and hedges beyond which the great affair, the greatest of all, the deep, still home, sits in the midst of its acres and strikes you all the more for being, precisely, so unrenowned. It is the charming repeated lesson that the amenity of the famous seats in this country is nothing to that of the lost and buried ones. This impression in particular may bring you round again harmoniously to Dunwich and above all perhaps to where the Priory, laid, as I may say, flat on its back, rests its large outline on what was once the high ground, with the inevitable "big" house, beyond and a little above, folded, for privacy, in a neat, impenetrable wood. Here as elsewhere the cluster offers without complication just the signs of the type. At the base of the hill are the dozen cottages to which the village has been reduced, and one of which contains, to my hearing, though by no means, alas, to his own, a very ancient man who will count for you on his fingers, till they fail, the grand acres that, in his day, he has seen go the way of the rest. He likes to figure that he ploughed of old where only the sea ploughs now. Dunwich, however, will still last his time; and that of as many others as—to repeat my hint—may yet be drawn here (though not, I hope, on the instance of these prudent lines) to judge for themselves into how many meanings a few elements can compose. One never need be bored, after all, when "composition" really rules. It rules in the way the brown hamlet really disposes itself, and the grey square tower of the church, in just the right relation, peeps out of trees that remind me exactly of those which, in the frontispieces of Birket Foster, offered to my childish credulity the very essence of England. Let me put it directly for old Suffolk that this credulity finds itself here, at the end of time, more than ever justified. Let me put it perhaps also that the very essence of England has a way of presenting itself with completeness in almost any fortuitous combination of rural objects at all, so that, wherever you may be, you get, reduced and simplified, the whole of the scale. The big house and its woods are always at hand; with a "party" always, in the intervals of shooting, to bring down to the rustic sports that keep up the tradition of the village green. The russet, low-browed inn, the "ale-house" of Shakespeare, the immemorial fountain of beer, looking over that expanse, swings, with an old-time story-telling creak, the sign of the Marquis of Carabas. The pretty girls, within sight of it, alight from the Marquis's wagonette; the young men with the one eye-glass and the new hat sit beside them on the benches supplied for their sole accommodation, and thanks to which the meditator on manners has, a little, the image, gathered from faded fictions by female hands, of the company brought over, for the triumph of the heroine, to the hunt or the county ball. And it is always Hodge and Gaffer that, at bottom, *font les frais*—always the mild children of the glebe on whom, in the last resort, the complex superstructure rests.

The discovery, in the twilight of time, of the merits, as a building-site, of Hodge's broad bent back remains surely one of the most sagacious strokes of the race from which the squire and the parson were to be evolved. He is there in force—at the rustic sports—in force or in feebleness, with Mrs. Hodge and the Miss Hodges, who participate with a silent glee in the chase, over fields where their shadows are long, of a pig with a greased tail. He pulls his forelock in the tent in which, after the pig is caught, the rewards of valour are dispensed by the squire's lady, and if he be in favour for respectability and not behind with rent, he penetrates later to the lawn within the wood, where he is awaited by a band of music and a collation of beer, buns, and tobacco.

I mention these things as some of the light notes, but the picture is never too empty for a stronger one not to sound. The strongest, at Dunwich, is indeed one that, without in the least falsifying the scale, counts immensely for filling in. The palm in the rustic sports is for the bluejackets; as, in England, of course, nothing is easier than for the village green to alternate with the element that Britannia still more admirably rules. I had often dreamed that the ideal refuge for a man of letters was a cottage so placed on the coast as to be circled, as it were, by the protecting arm of the Admiralty. I remember to have heard it said in the old country—in New York and Boston—that the best place to live in is next to an enginehouse, and it is on this analogy that, at Dunwich, I have looked for ministering peace in near neighbourhood to one of those stations of the coastguard that, round all the edge of England, at short intervals, on rock and sand and heath, make, with shining whitewash and tar, clean as a great state is at least theoretically clean, each its own little image of the reach of the empire. It is in each case an image that, for one reason and another, you respond to with a sort of thrill; and the thing becomes as concrete as you can wish on your discovering in the three or four individual members of the simple staff of the establishment all sorts of educated decency and many sorts of beguilement to intercourse. Prime among the latter, in truth, is the great yarn-spinning gift. It differs from man to man, but here and there it glows like a cut ruby. May the last darkness close before I cease to care for sea-folk!—though this, I hasten to add, is not the private predilection at which, in these incoherent notes, I proposed most to glance. Let me have mentioned it merely as a sign that the fault is all my own if, this summer, the arm of the Admiralty has not, in the full measure of my theory, represented the protection under which the long literary morning may know—abyss of delusion!—nothing but itself.

This essay, though dated 1879 in the London edition of English Hours *(1905) and "Dunwich, August 31, 1879" in the American edition (1905), was first printed in* Harper's Weekly, *September 25, 1897. The latter date is given for it here.*

Oxford

1877

It seemed to me such a piece of good fortune to have been asked down to Oxford at Commemoration by a gentleman implicated in the remarkable ceremony which goes on under that name, who kindly offered me the hospitality of his college, that I scarcely stayed even to thank him—I simply went and awaited him. I had had a glimpse of Oxford in former years, but I had never slept in a low-browed room looking out on a grassy quadrangle and opposite a mediæval clock-tower. This satisfaction was vouchsafed me on the night of my arrival; I was made free of the rooms of an absent undergraduate. I sat in his deep armchairs; I burned his candles and read his books, and I hereby thank him as effusively as possible. Before going to bed I took a turn through the streets and renewed in the silent darkness that impression of the charm imparted to them by the quiet college-fronts which I had gathered in former years. The college-fronts were now quieter than ever, the streets were empty, and the old scholastic city was sleeping in the warm starlight. The undergraduates had retired in large numbers, encouraged in this impulse by the collegiate authorities, who deprecate their presence at Commemoration. However many young gownsmen may be sent away, there yet always remain a collection sufficient to represent the sound of many voices. There can be no better indication of the resources of Oxford in a spectacular way than this fact that the first step toward preparing an impressive ceremony is to get rid of as many as possible of the actors.

In the morning I breakfasted with a young American who, in common with a number of his countrymen, had come hither to seek stimulus for a finer strain of study. I know not whether he would have reckoned as such stimulus the conversation of a couple of those ingenuous youths, sons of the soil, whose society I always find charming; but it added, from my own point of view, in respect to the place, to the element of intensity of character. After the entertainment was over, I repaired, in company with a crowd of ladies and elderly people, interspersed with gownsmen, to the hoary rotunda of the Sheldonian theatre, which every visitor to Oxford will remember from its curious cincture of clumsily carven heads of warriors and sages perched upon stone posts. The interior of this edifice is the scene of the classic hooting, stamping, and cat-calling by which the undergraduates confer the last consecration upon the distinguished gentlemen who come up for the honorary degree of D.C.L. It is with the design of attenuating as much as possible this volume of sound that the heads of colleges, on the close of the term, a few days before Commemoration, speed their too demonstrative disciples upon the homeward way. As I have already hinted, however, the contingent of irreverence was on this occasion quite large enough to preserve the type of the racket. This made the scene a very singular one. An American of course, with his fondness for antiquity, his relish for picturesqueness, his "emotional" attitude at historic shrines, takes Oxford much more seriously than its sometimes unwilling familiars can be expected to do. These people are not always upon the high horse; they are not always in a state of fine vibration. Nevertheless there is a certain maximum of disaccord with their beautiful circumstances which the ecstatic outsider vaguely expects them not to transcend. No effort of the intellect beforehand would enable him to imagine one of those silver-grey temples of learning converted into a semblance of the Bowery Theatre when the Bowery Theatre is being trifled with.

The Sheldonian edifice, like everything at Oxford, is more or less monumental. There is a double tier of galleries, with sculptured pulpits protruding from them; there are full-length portraits of kings and worthies; there is a general air of antiquity and dignity, which, on the occasion of which I speak, was enhanced by the presence of certain ancient scholars seated in crimson robes in high-backed chairs. Formerly, I believe, the undergraduates were placed apart—packed together in a corner of one of the galleries. But now they are scattered among the general spectators, a large number of whom are ladies. They muster in especial force, however, on the floor of the theatre, which has been cleared of its benches. Here the dense mass is at last severed in twain by the entrance of the prospective D.C.L.'s walking in single file, clad in crimson gowns, preceded by mace-bearers and accompanied by the Regius professor of Civil Law, who presents them individually to the Vice-Chancellor of the University, in a Latin speech which is of course a glowing eulogy. The five gentlemen to whom this distinction had been offered in 1877 were not among those whom fame has trumpeted most loudly; but there was something "as pretty as a picture" in their standing in their honourable robes, with heads modestly bent, while the orator, as effectively draped, recited their titles sonorously to the venerable dignitary in the high-backed chair. Each of them, when the little speech is ended, ascends the steps leading to the chair; the Vice-Chancellor bends forward and shakes his hand, and the new D.C.L. goes and sits in the blushing row of his fellow doctors. The impressiveness of all this is much diminished by the boisterous conduct of the "students," who superabound in extravagant applause, in impertinent interrogation, and in lively disparagement of the orator's Latinity. Of the scene that precedes the episode I have just described I have given no account; vivid portrayal of it is not easy. Like the return from the Derby it is a carnival of "chaff;" and it is a singular fact that the scholastic festival should have forcibly reminded me of the great popular "lark." In each case it is the same race enjoying a certain definitely chartered license; in the young votaries of a liberal education and the London rabble on the Epsom road it is the same perfect good humour, the same muscular jocosity.

After the presentation of the doctors came a series of those collegiate exercises which have a generic resemblance all the world over: a reading of Latin verses and English essays, a spouting of prize poems and Greek paraphrases. The prize poem alone was somewhat attentively listened to; the other things were received with an infinite variety of critical ejaculation. But after all, I reflected, as the ceremony drew to a close, the romping element is more characteristic than it seems; it is at bottom only another expression of the venerable and historic side of Oxford. It is tolerated because it is traditional; it is possible because it is classical. Looked at in this light it became romantically continuous with the human past that everything else referred to.

I was not obliged to find ingenious pretexts for thinking well of another ceremony of which I was witness after we adjourned from the Sheldonian theatre. This was a lunch-party at the particular college in which I should find it the highest privilege to reside and which I may not further specify. Perhaps indeed I may go so far as to say that the reason for my dreaming of this privilege is that it is deemed by persons of a reforming turn the best-appointed abuse in a nest of abuses. A commission for the expurgation of the universities has lately been appointed by Parliament to look into it—a commission armed with a gigantic broom, which is to sweep away all the fine old ivied and cobwebbed improprieties. Pending these righteous changes, one would like while one is about it—about, that is, this business of admiring Oxford—to attach one's self to the abuse, to bury one's nostrils in the rose before it is plucked. At the college in question there are no undergraduates. I found it agreeable to reflect that those grey-green cloisters had sent no delegates to the slangy congregation I had just quitted. This delightful spot exists for the satisfaction of a small society of Fellows who, having no dreary instruction to administer, no noisy hobbledehoys to govern, no obligations but toward their own culture, no care save for learning as learning and truth as truth, are presumably the happiest and most charming people in the world. The party invited to lunch assembled first in the library of the college, a cool, grey hall, of very great length and height, with vast wall-spaces of rich-looking book-titles and statues of noble scholars set in the midst. Had the charming Fellows ever anything more disagreeable to do than to finger these precious volumes and then to stroll about together in the grassy courts, in learned comradeship, discussing their precious contents? Nothing, apparently, unless it were to give a lunch at Commemoration in the dining-hall of the college. When lunch was ready there was a very pretty procession to go to it. Learned gentlemen in crimson gowns, ladies in bright finery, paired slowly off and marched in a stately diagonal across the fine, smooth lawn of the quadrangle, in a corner of which they passed through a hospitable door. But here we cross the threshold of privacy; I remained on the further side of it during the rest of the day. But I brought back with me certain memories, of which, if I were not at the end of my space, I should attempt a discreet adumbration: memories of a fête champêtre in the beautiful gardens of one of the other colleges—charming lawns and spreading trees, music of Grenadier Guards, ices in striped marquees, mild flirtation of youthful gownsmen and bemuslined maidens; memories, too, of quiet dinner in common-room, a decorous, excellent repast; old portraits on the walls and great windows open upon the ancient court, where the afternoon light was fading in the stillness; superior talk upon current topics, and over all the peculiar air of Oxford—the air of liberty to care for the things of the mind assured and secured by machinery which is in itself a satisfaction to sense.

From "Two Excursions" (1877)

Cambridge

1879

If Oxford were not the finest thing in England the case would be clearer for Cambridge. It was clear enough there, for that matter, to my imagination, for thirty-six hours. To the barbaric mind, ambitious of culture, Oxford is the usual image of the happy reconciliation between research and acceptance. It typifies to an American the union of science and sense—of aspiration and ease. A German university gives a greater impression of science and an English country-house or an Italian villa a greater impression of idle enjoyment; but in these cases, on one side, knowledge is too rugged, and on the other satisfaction is too trivial. Oxford lends sweetness to labour and dignity to leisure. When I say Oxford I mean Cambridge, for a stray savage is not the least obliged to know the difference, and it suddenly strikes me as being both very pedantic and very good-natured in him to pretend to know it. What institution is more majestic than Trinity College? what can affect more a stray savage than the hospitality of such an institution? The first quadrangle is of immense extent, and the buildings that surround it, with their long, rich fronts of time-deepened grey, are the stateliest in the world. In the centre of the court are two or three acres of close-shaven lawn, out of the midst of which rises a grand gothic fountain, where the serving-men fill up their buckets. There are towers and battlements and statues, and besides these things there are cloisters and gardens and bridges. There are charming rooms in a kind of stately gate-tower, and the rooms, occupying the thickness of the building, have windows looking out on one side over the magnificent quadrangle, with half a mile or so of decorated architecture, and on the other into deep-bosomed trees. And in the rooms is the best company conceivable—distinguished men who are thoroughly conversible, intimately affable. I spent a beautiful Sunday morning walking about the place with one of these gentlemen and attempting to *débrouiller* its charms. These are a very complicated tangle, and I do not pretend, in memory, to keep the colleges apart. There are none the less half a dozen points that make ineffaceable pictures. Six or eight of the colleges stand in a row, turning their backs to the river; and hereupon ensues the loveliest confusion of gothic windows and ancient trees, of grassy banks and mossy balustrades, of sun-chequered avenues and groves, of lawns and gardens and terraces, of single-arched bridges spanning the little stream, which is small and shallow and looks as if it had been turned on for ornamental purposes. The thin-flowing Cam appears to exist simply as an occasion for these brave little bridges—the beautiful covered gallery of John's or the slightly collapsing arch of Clare. In the way of college-courts and quiet scholastic porticoes, of grey-walled gardens and ivied nooks of study, in all the pictorial accidents of a great English university, Cambridge is delightfully and inexhaustibly rich. I looked at these one by one and said to myself always that the last was the best. If I were called upon, however, to mention the prettiest corner of the world, I should draw out a thoughtful sigh and point the way to the garden of

Trinity Hall. My companion, who was very competent to judge (but who spoke indeed with the partiality of a son of the house), declared, as he ushered me into it, that it was, to his mind, the most beautiful *small* garden in Europe. I freely accepted, and I promptly repeat, an affirmation so magnanimously conditioned. The little garden at Trinity Hall is narrow and crooked; it leans upon the river, from which a low parapet, all muffled in ivy, divides it; it has an ancient wall adorned with a thousand matted creepers on one side, and on the other a group of extraordinary horse-chestnuts. The trees are of prodigious size; they occupy half the garden, and are remarkable for the fact that their giant limbs strike down into the earth, take root again and emulate, as they rise, the majesty of the parent stem. The manner in which this magnificent group of horse-chestnuts sprawls about over the grass, out into the middle of the lawn, is one of the most heart-shaking features of the garden of Trinity Hall. Of course the single object at Cambridge that makes the most abiding impression is the famous chapel of King's College—the most beautiful chapel in England. The effect it attempts to produce within is all in the sphere of the sublime. The attempt succeeds, and the success is attained by a design so light and elegant that at first it almost defeats itself. The sublime usually has more of a frown and straddle, and it is not until after you have looked about you for ten minutes that you perceive the chapel to be saved from being the prettiest church in England by the accident of its being one of the noblest. It is a cathedral without aisles or columns or transepts, but (as a compensation) with such a beautiful slimness of clustered tracery soaring along the walls and spreading, bending, and commingling in the roof, that its simplicity seems only a richness the more. I stood there for a quarter of an hour on a Sunday morning; there was no service, but in the choir behind the great screen which divides the chapel in half the young choristers were rehearsing for the afternoon. The beautiful boy voices rose together and touched the splendid vault; they hung there, expanding and resounding, and then, like a rocket that spends itself, they faded and melted toward the end of the building. It was positively a choir of angels.

From "English Vignettes" (1879)

London

1888

I

There is a certain evening that I count as virtually a first impression,—the end of a wet, black Sunday, twenty years ago, about the first of March. There had been an earlier vision, but it had turned to grey, like faded ink, and the occasion I speak of was a fresh beginning. No doubt I had mystic prescience of how fond of the murky modern Babylon I was one day to become; certain it is that as I look back I find every small circumstance of those hours of approach and arrival still as vivid as if the solemnity of an opening era had breathed upon it. The sense of approach was already almost intolerably strong at Liverpool, where, as I remember, the perception of the English character of everything was as acute as a surprise, though it could only be a surprise without a shock. It was expectation exquisitely gratified, superabundantly confirmed. There was a kind of wonder indeed that England should be as English as, for my entertainment, she took the trouble to be; but the wonder would have been greater, and all the pleasure absent, if the sensation had not been violent. It seems to sit there again like a visiting presence, as it sat opposite to me at breakfast at a small table in a window of the old coffee-room of the Adelphi Hotel—the unextended (as it then was), the unimproved, the unblushingly local Adelphi. Liverpool is not a romantic city, but that smoky Saturday returns to me as a supreme success, measured by its association with the kind of emotion in the hope of which, for the most part, we betake ourselves to far countries.

It assumed this character at an early hour—or rather, indeed, twenty-four hours before—with the sight, as one looked across the wintry ocean, of the strange, dark, lonely freshness of the coast of Ireland. Better still, before we could come up to the city, were the black steamers knocking about in the yellow Mersey, under a sky so low that they seemed to touch it with their funnels, and in the thickest, windiest light. Spring was already in the air, in the town; there was no rain, but there was still less sun—one wondered what had become, on this side of the world, of the big white splotch in the heavens; and the grey mildness, shading away into black at every pretext, appeared in itself a promise. This was how it hung about me, between the window and the fire, in the coffee-room of the hotel—late in the morning for breakfast, as we had been long disembarking. The other passengers had dispersed, knowingly catching trains for London (we had only been a handful); I had the place to myself, and I felt as if I had an exclusive property in the impression. I prolonged it, I sacrificed to it, and it is perfectly recoverable now, with the very taste of the national muffin, the creak of the waiter's shoes as he came and went (could anything be so English as his intensely professional back? it revealed a country of tradition), and the rustle of the newspaper I was too excited to read.

I continued to sacrifice for the rest of the day; it didn't seem to me a sentient thing, as yet, to enquire into the means of getting away. My curiosity must indeed have languished, for I found myself on the morrow in the slowest of Sunday trains, pottering up to London with an interruptedness which might have been tedious without the conversation of an old gentleman who shared the carriage with me and to whom my alien as well as comparatively youthful character had betrayed itself. He instructed me as to the sights of London and impressed upon me that nothing was more worthy of my attention than the great cathedral of St. Paul. "Have you seen St. Peter's in Rome? St. Peter's is more highly embellished, you know; but you may depend upon it that St. Paul's is the better building of the two." The impression I began with speaking of was, strictly, that of the drive from Euston, after dark, to Morley's Hotel in Trafalgar Square. It was not lovely—it was in fact rather horrible; but as I move again through dusky, tortuous miles, in the greasy four-wheeler to which my luggage had compelled me to commit myself, I recognise the first step in an initiation of which the subsequent stages were to abound in pleasant things. It is a kind of humiliation in a great city not to know where you are going, and Morley's Hotel was then, to my imagination, only a vague ruddy spot in the general immensity. The immensity was the great fact, and that was a charm; the miles of housetops and viaducts, the complication of junctions and signals through which the train made its way to the station had already given me the scale. The weather had turned to wet, and we went deeper and deeper into the Sunday night. The sheep in the fields, on the way from Liverpool, had shown in their demeanour a certain consciousness of the day; but this momentous cab-drive was an introduction to the rigidities of custom. The low black houses were as inanimate as so many rows of coal-scuttles, save where at frequent corners, from a gin-shop, there was a flare of light more brutal still than the darkness. The custom of gin—that was equally rigid, and in this first impression the public-houses counted for much.

Morley's Hotel proved indeed to be a ruddy spot; brilliant, in my recollection, is the coffee-room fire, the hospitable mahogany, the sense that in the stupendous city this, at any rate for the hour, was a shelter and a point of view. My remembrance of the rest of the evening—I was probably very tired—is mainly a remembrance of a vast four-poster. My little bedroom-candle, set in its deep basin, caused this monument to project a huge shadow and to make me think, I scarce knew why, of "The Ingoldsby Legends." If at a tolerably early hour the next day I found myself approaching St. Paul's, it was not wholly in obedience to the old gentleman in the railway-carriage: I had an errand in the City, and the City was doubtless prodigious. But what I mainly recall is the romantic consciousness of passing under the Temple Bar, and the way two lines of *Henry Esmond* repeated themselves in my mind as I drew near the masterpiece of Sir Christopher Wren. "The stout, red-faced woman" whom Esmond had seen tearing after the staghounds over the slopes at Windsor was not a bit like the effigy "which turns its stony back upon St. Paul's and faces the coaches struggling up Ludgate Hill." As I looked at Queen Anne over the apron of my hansom—she struck me as very small and dirty, and the vehicle ascended the mild incline without an effort—it was a thrilling thought that the statue had been familiar to the hero of the incomparable novel. All history appeared to live again, and the continuity of things to vibrate through my mind.

To this hour, as I pass along the Strand, I take again the walk I took there that afternoon. I love the place to-day, and that was the commencement of my passion. It appeared to me to present phenomena, and to contain objects of every kind, of an inexhaustible interest; in particular it struck me as desirable and even indispensable that I should purchase most of the articles in most of the shops. My eyes rest with a certain tenderness on the places where I resisted and on those where I succumbed. The fragrance of Mr. Rimmel's establishment is again in my nostrils; I see the slim young lady (I hear her pronunciation) who waited upon me there. Sacred to me to-day is the particular aroma of the hair-wash that I bought of her. I pause before the granite portico of Exeter Hall (it was unexpectedly narrow and wedge-like), and it evokes a cloud of associations which are none the less impressive because they are vague; coming from I don't know where—from *Punch*, from Thackeray, from volumes of the *Illustrated London News* turned over in childhood; seeming connected with Mrs. Beecher Stowe and *Uncle Tom's Cabin*. Memorable is a rush I made into a glover's at Charing Cross—the one you pass, going eastward, just before you turn into the station; that, however, now that I think of it, must have been in the morning, as soon as I issued from the hotel. Keen within me was a sense of the importance of deflowering, of despoiling the shop.

A day or two later, in the afternoon, I found myself staring at my fire, in a lodging of which I had taken possession on foreseeing that I should spend some weeks in London. I had just come in, and, having attended to the distribution of my luggage, sat down to consider my habitation. It was on the ground floor, and the fading daylight reached it in a sadly damaged condition. It struck me as stuffy and unsocial, with its mouldy smell and its decoration of lithographs and wax-flowers—an impersonal black hole in the huge general blackness. The uproar of Piccadilly hummed away at the end of the street, and the rattle of a heartless hansom passed close to my ears. A sudden horror of the whole place came over me, like a tiger-pounce of homesickness which had been watching its moment. London was hideous, vicious, cruel, and above all overwhelming; whether or no she was "careful of the type," she was as indifferent as Nature herself to the single life. In the course of an hour I should have to go out to my dinner, which was not supplied on the premises, and that effort assumed the form of a desperate and dangerous quest. It appeared to me that I would rather remain dinnerless, would rather even starve, than sally forth into the infernal town, where the natural fate of an obscure stranger would be to be trampled to death in Piccadilly and have his carcass thrown into the Thames. I did not starve, however, and I eventually attached myself by a hundred human links to the dreadful, delightful city. That momentary vision of its smeared face and stony heart has remained memorable to me, but I am happy to say that I can easily summon up others.

II

It is, no doubt, not the taste of every one, but for the real London-lover the mere immensity of the place is a large part of its savour. A small London would be an abomination, as it fortunately is an impossibility, for the idea and the name are beyond everything an expression of extent and number. Practically, of course, one lives in a quarter, in a plot; but in imagination and by a constant mental act of reference the accommodated haunter enjoys the whole—and it is only of him that I deem it worth while to speak. He fancies himself, as they say, for being a particle in so unequalled an aggregation; and its immeasurable circumference, even though unvisited and lost in smoke, gives him the sense of a social, an intellectual margin. There is a luxury in the knowledge that he may come and go without being noticed, even when his comings and goings have no nefarious end. I don't mean by this that the tongue of London is not a very active member; the tongue of London would indeed be worthy of a chapter by itself. But the eyes which at least in some measure feed its activity are fortunately for the common advantage solicited at any moment by a thousand different objects. If the place is big, everything it contains is certainly not so; but this may at least be said—that if small questions play a part there, they play it without illusions about its importance. There are too many questions, small or great; and each day, as it arrives, leads its children, like a kind of mendicant mother, by the hand. Therefore perhaps the most general characteristic is the absence of insistence. Habits and inclinations flourish and fall, but intensity is never one of them. The spirit of the great city is not analytic, and, as they come up, subjects rarely receive at its hands a treatment drearily earnest or tastelessly thorough. There are not many—of those of which London disposes with the assurance begotten of its large experience—that wouldn't lend themselves to a tenderer manipulation elsewhere. It takes a very great affair, a turn of the Irish screw or a divorce case lasting many days, to be fully threshed out. The mind of Mayfair, when it aspires to show what it really can do, lives in the hope of a new divorce case, and an indulgent providence—London is positively in certain ways the spoiled child of the world—abundantly recognises this particular aptitude and humours the whim.

The compensation is that material does arise; that there is a great variety, if not morbid subtlety; and that the whole of the procession of events and topics passes across your stage. For the moment I am speaking of the inspiration there may be in the sense of far frontiers; the London-lover loses himself in this swelling consciousness, delights in the idea that the town which encloses him is after all only a paved country, a state by itself. This is his condition of mind quite as much if he be an adoptive as if he be a matter-of-course son. I am by no means sure even that he need be of Anglo-Saxon race and have inherited the birthright of English speech; though, on the other hand, I make no doubt that these advantages minister greatly to closeness of allegiance. The great city spreads her dusky mantle over innumerable races and creeds, and I believe there is scarcely a known form of worship that has not some temple there (have I not attended at the Church of Humanity, in Lamb's Conduit, in company with an American lady, a vague old gentleman, and several seamstresses?) or any communion of men that has not some club or guild. London is indeed an epitome of the round world, and just as it is a commonplace to say that there is nothing one can't "get" there, so it is equally true that there is nothing one may not study at first hand.

One doesn't test these truths every day, but they form part of the air one breathes (and welcome, says the London-hater,—for there be such perverse reasoners,—to the pestilent compound). They colour the thick, dim distances which in my opinion are the most romantic town-vistas in the world; they mingle with the troubled light to which the straight, ungarnished aperture in one's dull, undistinctive house-front affords a passage and which makes an interior of friendly corners, mysterious tones, and unbetrayed ingenuities, as well as with the low, magnificent medium of the sky, where the smoke and fog and the weather in general, the strangely undefined hour of the day and season of the year, the emanations of industries and the reflection of furnaces, the red gleams and blurs that may or may not be of sunset—as you never see any *source* of radiance, you can't in the least tell—all hang together in a confusion, a complication, a shifting but irremoveable canopy. They form the undertone of the deep, perpetual voice of the place. One remembers them when one's loyalty is on the defensive; when it is a question of introducing as many striking features as possible into the list of fine reasons one has sometimes to draw up, that eloquent catalogue with which one confronts the hostile indictment—the array of *other* reasons which may easily be as long as one's arm. According to these other reasons it plausibly and conclusively stands that, as a place to be happy in, London will never do. I don't say it is necessary to meet so absurd an allegation except for one's personal complacency. If indifference, in so gorged an organism, is still livelier than curiosity, you may avail yourself of your own share in it simply to feel that since such and such a person doesn't care for real richness, so much the worse for such and such a person. But once in a while the best believer recognises the impulse to set his religion in order, to sweep the temple of his thoughts and trim the sacred lamp. It is at such hours as this that he reflects with elation that the British capital is the particular spot in the world which communicates the greatest sense of life.

III

The reader will perceive that I do not shrink even from the extreme concession of speaking of our capital as British, and this in a shameless connection with the question of loyalty on the part of an adoptive son. For I hasten to explain that if half the source of one's interest in it comes from feeling that it is the property and even the home of the human race,—Hawthorne, that best of Americans, says so somewhere, and places it in this sense side by side with Rome,—one's appreciation of it is really a large sympathy, a comprehensive love of humanity. For the sake of such a charity as this one may stretch one's allegiance; and the most alien of the cockneyfied, though he may bristle with every protest at the intimation that England has set its stamp upon him, is free to admit with conscious pride that he has submitted to Londonisation. It is a real stroke of luck for a particular country that the capital of the human race happens to be British. Surely every other people would have it theirs if they could. Whether the English deserve to hold it any longer might be an interesting field of enquiry; but as they have not yet let it slip, the writer of these lines professes without scruple that the arrangement is to his personal taste. For, after all, if the sense of life is greatest there, it is a sense of the life of people of our consecrated English speech. It is the headquarters of that strangely elastic tongue; and I make this remark with a full sense of the terrible way in which the idiom is misused by the populace in general, than whom it has been given to few races to impart to conversation less of the charm of tone. For a man of letters who endeavours to cultivate, however modestly, the medium of Shakespeare and Milton, of Hawthorne and Emerson, who cherishes the notion of what it has achieved and what it may even yet achieve, London must ever have a great illustrative and suggestive value, and indeed a kind of sanctity. It is the single place in which most readers, most possible lovers, are gathered together; it is the most inclusive public and the largest social incarnation of the language, of the tradition. Such a personage may well let it go for this, and leave the German and the Greek to speak for themselves, to express the grounds of *their* predilection, presumably very different.

When a social product is so vast and various, it may be approached on a thousand different sides, and liked and disliked for a thousand different reasons. The reasons of Piccadilly are not those of Camden Town, nor are the curiosities and discouragements of Kilburn the same as those of Westminster and Lambeth. The reasons of Piccadilly—I mean the friendly ones—are those of which, as a general thing, the rooted visitor remains most conscious; but it must be confessed that even these, for the most part, do not lie upon the surface. The absence of style, or rather of the intention of style, is certainly the most general characteristic of the face of London. To cross to Paris under this impression is to find one's self surrounded with far other standards. There everything reminds you that the idea of beautiful and stately arrangement has never been out of fashion, that the art of composition has always been at work or at play. Avenues and squares, gardens and quays, have been distributed for effect, and to-day the splendid city reaps the accumulation of all this ingenuity. The result is not in every quarter interesting, and there is a tiresome monotony of the "fine" and the symmetrical, above all, of the deathly passion for making things "to match." On the other hand the whole air of the place is architectural. On the banks of the Thames it is a tremendous chapter of accidents—the London-lover has to confess to the existence of miles upon miles of the dreariest, stodgiest commonness. Thousands of acres are covered by low black houses of the cheapest construction, without ornament, without grace, without character or even identity. In fact there are many, even in the best quarters, in all the region of Mayfair and Belgravia, of so paltry and inconvenient, especially of so diminutive a type (those that are let in lodgings—such poor lodgings as they make—may serve as an example), that you wonder what peculiarly limited domestic need they were constructed to meet. The great misfortune of London to the eye (it is true that this remark applies much less to the City), is the want of elevation. There is no architectural impression without a certain degree of height, and the London street-vista has none of that sort of pride.

All the same, if there be not the intention, there is at least the accident, of style, which, if one looks at it in a friendly way, appears to proceed from three sources. One of these is simply the general greatness, and the manner in which that makes a difference for the better in any particular spot; so that, though you may often perceive yourself to be in a shabby corner, it never occurs to you that this is the end of it. Another is the atmosphere, with its magnificent mystifications, which flatters and superfuses, makes everything brown, rich, dim, vague, magnifies distances and minimises details, confirms the inference of vastness by suggesting that, as the great city makes everything, it makes its own system of weather and its own optical laws. The last is the congregation of the parks, which constitute an ornament not elsewhere to be matched, and give the place a superiority that none of its uglinesses overcome. They spread themselves with such a luxury of space in the centre of the town that they form a part of the impression of any walk, of almost any view, and, with an audacity altogether their own, make a pastoral landscape under the smoky sky. There is no mood of the rich London climate that is not becoming to them—I have seen them look delightfully romantic, like parks in novels, in the wettest winter—and there is scarcely a mood of the appreciative resident to which they have not something to say. The high things of London, which here and there peep over them, only make the spaces vaster by reminding you that you are, after all, not in Kent or Yorkshire; and these things, whatever they be—rows of "eligible" dwellings, towers of churches, domes of institutions—take such an effective grey-blue tint that a clever water-colourist would seem to have put them in for pictorial reasons.

The view from the bridge over the Serpentine has an extraordinary nobleness, and it has often seemed to me that the Londoner, twitted with his low standard, may point to it with every confidence. In all the town-scenery of Europe there can be few things so fine; the only reproach it is open to is that it begs the question by seeming—in spite of its being the pride of five millions of people—not to belong to a town at all. The towers of Notre Dame, as they rise in Paris from the island that divides the Seine, present themselves no more impressively than those of Westminster as you see them looking doubly far beyond the shining stretch of Hyde Park water. Equally delectable is the large river-like manner in which the Serpentine opens away between its wooded shores. Just after you have crossed the bridge (whose very banisters, old and ornamental, of yellowish-brown stone, I am particularly fond of), you enjoy on your left, through the gate of Kensington Gardens as you go towards Bayswater, an altogether enchanting vista—a footpath over the grass, which loses itself beneath the scattered oaks and elms exactly as if the place were a "chase." There could be nothing less like London in general than this particular morsel, and yet it takes London, of all cities, to give you such an impression of the country.

IV

It takes London to put you in the way of a purely rustic walk from Notting Hill to Whitehall. You may traverse this immense distance—a most comprehensive diagonal—altogether on soft, fine turf, amid the song of birds, the bleat of lambs, the ripple of ponds, the rustle of admirable trees. Frequently have I wished that, for the sake of such a daily luxury and of exercise made romantic, I were a Government clerk living, in snug domestic conditions, in a Pembridge villa,—let me suppose,—and having my matutinal desk in Westminster. I should turn into Kensington Gardens at their northwest limit, and I should have my choice of a hundred pleasant paths to the gates of Hyde Park. In Hyde Park I should follow the water-side, or the Row, or any other fancy of the occasion; liking best, perhaps, after all, the Row in its morning mood, with the mist hanging over the dark-red course, and the scattered early riders taking an identity as the soundless gallop brings them nearer. I am free to admit that in the Season, at the conventional hours, the Row becomes a weariness (save perhaps just for a glimpse once a year, to remind one's self how much it is like Du Maurier); the preoccupied citizen eschews it and leaves it for the most part to the gaping barbarian. I speak of it now from the point of view of the pedestrian; but for the rider as well it is at its best when he passes either too early or too late. Then, if he be not bent on comparing it to its disadvantage with the bluer and boskier alleys of the Bois de Boulogne, it will not be spoiled by the fact that, with its surface that looks like tan, its barriers like those of the ring on which the clown stands to hold up the hoop to the young lady, its empty benches and chairs, its occasional orange-peel, its mounted policemen patrolling at intervals like expectant supernumeraries, it offers points of real contact with a circus whose lamps are out. The sky that bends over it is frequently not a bad imitation of the dingy tent of such an establishment. The ghosts of past cavalcades seem to haunt the foggy arena, and somehow they are better company than the mashers and elongated beauties of current seasons. It is not without interest to remember that most of the salient figures of English society during the present century—and English society means, or rather has hitherto meant, in a large degree, English history—have bobbed in the saddle between Apsley House and Queen's Gate. You may call the roll if you care to, and the air will be thick with dumb voices and dead names, like that of some Roman amphitheatre.

It is doubtless a signal proof of being a London-lover *quand même* that one should undertake an apology for so bungled an attempt at a great public place as Hyde Park Corner. It is certain that the improvements and embellishments recently enacted there have only served to call further attention to the poverty of the elements and to the fact that this poverty is terribly illustrative of general conditions. The place is the beating heart of the great West End, yet its main features are a shabby, stuccoed hospital, the low park-gates, in their neat but unimposing frame, the drawing-room windows of Apsley House and of the commonplace frontages on the little terrace beside it; to which must be added, of course, the only item in the whole prospect that is in the least monumental—the arch spanning the private road beside the gardens of Buckingham Palace. This structure is now bereaved of the rueful effigy which used to surmount it—the Iron Duke in the guise of a tin soldier—and has not been enriched by the transaction as much as might have been expected.[1] There is a fine view of Piccadilly and Knightsbridge, and of the noble mansions, as the house-agents call them, of Grosvenor Place, together with a sense of generous space beyond the vulgar little railing of the Green Park; but, except for the impression that there would be room for something better, there is nothing in all this that speaks to the imagination: almost as much as the grimy desert of Trafalgar Square the prospect conveys the idea of an opportunity wasted.

None the less has it on a fine day in spring an expressiveness of which I shall not pretend to explain the source further than by saying that the flood of life and luxury is immeasurably great there. The edifices are mean, but the social stream itself is monumental, and to an observer not purely stolid there is more excitement and suggestion than I can give a reason for in the long, distributed waves of traffic, with the steady policemen marking their rhythm, which roll together and apart for so many hours. Then the great, dim city becomes bright and kind, the pall of smoke turns into a veil of haze carelessly worn, the air is coloured and almost scented by the presence of the biggest society in the world, and most of the things that meet the eye—or

[1] The monument in the middle of the square, with Sir Edgar Boehm's four fine soldiers, had not been set up when these words were written.

perhaps I should say more of them, for the most in London is, no doubt, ever the realm of the dingy—present themselves as "well appointed." Everything shines more or less, from the window-panes to the dog-collars. So it all looks, with its myriad variations and qualifications, to one who surveys it over the apron of a hansom, while that vehicle of vantage, better than any box at the opera, spurts and slackens with the current.

It is not in a hansom, however, that we have figured our punctual young man, whom we must not desert as he fares to the southeast, and who has only to cross Hyde Park Corner to find his way all grassy again. I have a weakness for the convenient, familiar, treeless, or almost treeless, expanse of the Green Park and the friendly part it plays as a kind of encouragement to Piccadilly. I am so fond of Piccadilly that I am grateful to any one or anything that does it a service, and nothing is more worthy of appreciation than the southward look it is permitted to enjoy just after it passes Devonshire House—a sweep of horizon which it would be difficult to match among other haunts of men, and thanks to which, of a summer's day, you may spy, beyond the browsed pastures of the foreground and middle distance, beyond the cold chimneys of Buckingham Palace and the towers of Westminster and the swarming river-side and all the southern parishes, the hard modern twinkle of the roof of the Crystal Palace.

If the Green Park is familiar, there is still less of the exclusive in its pendant, as one may call it,—for it literally hangs from the other, down the hill,—the remnant of the former garden of the queer, shabby old palace whose black, inelegant face stares up St. James's Street. This popular resort has a great deal of character, but I am free to confess that much of its character comes from its nearness to the Westminster slums. It is a park of intimacy, and perhaps the most democratic corner of London, in spite of its being in the royal and military quarter and close to all kinds of stateliness. There are few hours of the day when a thousand smutty children are not sprawling over it, and the unemployed lie thick on the grass and cover the benches with a brotherhood of greasy corduroys. If the London parks are the drawing-rooms and clubs of the poor,—that is of those poor (I admit it cuts down the number) who live near enough to them to reach them,—these particular grass-plots and alleys may be said to constitute the very *salon* of the slums.

I know not why, being such a region of greatness,—great towers, great names, great memories; at the foot of the Abbey, the Parliament, the fine fragment of Whitehall, with the quarters of the sovereign right and left,—but the edge of Westminster evokes as many associations of misery as of empire. The neighbourhood has been much purified of late, but it still contains a collection of specimens—though it is far from unique in this—of the low, black element. The air always seems to me heavy and thick, and here more than elsewhere one hears old England—the panting, smoke-stained Titan of Matthew Arnold's fine poem—draw her deep breath with effort. In fact one is nearer to her heroic lungs, if those organs are figured by the great pinnacled and fretted talking-house on the edge of the river. But this same dense and conscious air plays such everlasting tricks to the eye that the Foreign Office, as you see it from the bridge, often looks romantic, and the sheet of water it overhangs poetic—suggests an Indian palace bathing its feet in the Ganges. If our pedestrian achieves such a comparison as this he has nothing left but to go on to his work—which he will find close at hand. He will have come the whole way from the far northwest on the green—which is what was to be demonstrated.

V

I feel as if I were taking a tone almost of boastfulness, and no doubt the best way to consider the matter is simply to say—without going into the treachery of reasons—that, for one's self, one likes this part or the other. Yet this course would not be unattended with danger, inasmuch as at the end of a few such professions we might find ourselves committed to a tolerance of much that is deplorable. London is so clumsy and so brutal, and has gathered together so many of the darkest sides of life, that it is almost ridiculous to talk of her as a lover talks of his mistress, and almost frivolous to appear to ignore her disfigurements and cruelties. She is like a mighty ogress who devours human flesh; but to me it is a mitigating circumstance—though it may not seem so to every one—that the ogress herself is human. It is not in wantonness that she fills her maw, but to keep herself alive and do her tremendous work. She has no time for fine discriminations, but after all she is as good-natured as she is huge, and the more you stand up to her, as the phrase is, the better she takes the joke of it. It is mainly when you fall on your face before her that she gobbles you up. She heeds little what she takes, so long as she has her stint, and the smallest push to the right or the left will divert her wavering bulk from one form of prey to another. It is not to be denied that the heart tends to grow hard in her company; but she is a capital antidote to the morbid, and to live with her successfully is an education of the temper, a consecration of one's private philosophy. She gives one a surface for which in a rough world one can never be too thankful. She may take away reputations, but she forms character. She teaches her victims not to "mind," and the great danger for them is perhaps that they shall learn the lesson too well.

It is sometimes a wonder to ascertain what they do mind, the best seasoned of her children. Many of them assist, without winking, at the most unfathomable dramas, and the common speech of others denotes a familiarity with the horrible. It is her theory that she both produces and appreciates the exquisite; but if you catch her in flagrant repudiation of both responsibilities and confront her with the shortcoming, she gives you a look, with a shrug of her colossal shoulders, which establishes a private relation with you for evermore. She seems to say: "Do you really take me so seriously as that, you dear, devoted, voluntary dupe, and don't you know what an immeasurable humbug I am?" You reply that you shall know it henceforth; but your tone is good-natured, with a touch of the cynicism that she herself has taught you; for you are aware that if she makes herself out better than she is, she also makes herself out much worse. She is immensely democratic, and that, no doubt, is part of the manner in which she is salutary to the individual; she teaches him his "place" by an incomparable discipline, but deprives him of complaint by letting him see that she has exactly the same lash for every other back. When he has swallowed the lesson he may enjoy the rude but unfailing justice by which, under her eye, reputations and positions elsewhere esteemed great are reduced to the relative. There are so many reputations, so many positions, that supereminence breaks down, and it is difficult to be so rare that London can't match you. It is a part of her good-nature and one of her clumsy coquetries to pretend sometimes that she hasn't your equivalent, as when she takes it into her head to hunt the lion or form a ring round a celebrity. But this artifice is so very transparent that the lion must be very candid or the celebrity very obscure to be taken by it. The business is altogether subjective, as the philosophers say, and the great city is primarily looking after herself. Celebrities are convenient—they are one of the things that people are asked to "meet"—and lion-cutlets, put upon ice, will nourish a family through periods of dearth.

This is what I mean by calling London democratic. You may be in it, of course, without being of it; but from the moment you *are* of it—and on this point your own sense will soon enough enlighten you—you belong to a body in which a general equality prevails. However exalted, however able, however rich, however renowned you may be, there are too many people at least as much so for your own idiosyncrasies to count. I think it is only by being beautiful that you may really prevail very much; for the loveliness of woman it has long been noticeable that London will go most out of her way. It is when she hunts that particular lion that she becomes most dangerous; then there are really moments when you would believe, for all the world, that she is thinking of what she can give, not of what she can get. Lovely ladies, before this, have paid for believing it, and will continue to pay in days to come. On the whole the people who are least deceived are perhaps those who have permitted themselves to believe, in their own interest, that poverty is not a disgrace. It is certainly not considered so in London, and indeed you can scarcely say where—in virtue of diffusion—it would more naturally be exempt. The possession of money is, of course, immensely an advantage, but that is a very different thing from a disqualification in the lack of it.

Good-natured in so many things in spite of her cynical tongue, and easy-going in spite of her tremendous pace, there is nothing in which the large indulgence of the town is more shown than in the liberal way she looks at obligations of hospitality and the margin she allows in these and cognate matters. She wants above all to be amused; she keeps her books loosely, doesn't stand on small questions of a chop for a chop, and if there be any chance of people's proving a diversion, doesn't know or remember or care whether they have "called." She forgets even if she herself have called. In matters of ceremony she takes and gives a long rope, wasting no time in phrases and circumvallations. It is no doubt incontestable that one result of her inability to stand upon trifles and consider details is that she has been obliged in some ways to lower rather portentously the standard of her manners. She cultivates the abrupt—for even when she asks you to dine a month ahead the invitation goes off like the crack of a pistol—and approaches her ends not exactly *par quatre chemins*. She doesn't pretend to attach importance to the lesson conveyed in Matthew Arnold's poem of "The Sick King in Bokhara," that,

> Though we snatch what we desire,
> We may not snatch it eagerly.

London snatches it more than eagerly if that be the only way she can get it. Good manners are a succession of details, and I don't mean to say that she doesn't attend to them when she has time. She has it, however, but seldom —*que voulez-vous?* Perhaps the matter of note-writing is as good an example as another of what certain of the elder traditions inevitably have become in her hands. She lives by notes—they are her very heart-beats; but those that bear her signatures are as disjointed as the ravings of delirium, and have nothing but a postage-stamp in common with the epistolary art.

VI

If she doesn't go into particulars it may seem a very presumptuous act to have attempted to do so on her behalf, and the reader will doubtless think I have been punished by having egregiously failed in my enumeration. Indeed nothing could well be more difficult than to add up the items—the column would be altogether too long. One may have dreamed of turning the glow—if glow it be—of one's lantern on each successive facet of the jewel; but, after all, it may be success enough if a confusion of brightness be the result. One has not the alternative of speaking of London as a whole, for the simple reason that there is no such thing as the whole. It is immeasurable—its embracing arms never meet. Rather it is a collection of many wholes, and of which of them is it most important to speak? Inevitably there must be a choice, and I know of none more scientific than simply to leave out what we may have to apologise for. The uglinesses, the "rookeries," the brutalities, the night-aspect of many of the streets, the gin-shops and the hour when they are cleared out before closing—there are many elements of this kind which have to be counted out before a genial summary can be made.

And yet I should not go so far as to say that it is a condition of such geniality to close one's eyes upon the immense misery; on the contrary, I think it is partly because we are irremediably conscious of that dark gulf that the most general appeal of the great city remains exactly what it is, the largest chapter of human accidents. I have no idea of what the future evolution of the strangely mingled monster may be; whether the poor will improve away the rich, or the rich will expropriate the poor, or they will all continue to dwell together on their present imperfect terms of intercourse. Certain it is, at any rate, that the impression of suffering is a part of the general vibration; it is one of the things that mingle with all the others to make the sound that is supremely dear to the consistent London-lover—the rumble of the tremendous human mill. This is the note which, in all its modulations, haunts and fascinates and inspires him. And whether or no he may succeed in keeping the misery out of the picture, he will freely confess that the latter is not spoiled for him by some of its duskiest shades. We are far from liking London well enough till we like its defects: the dense darkness of much of its winter, the soot on the chimney-pots and everywhere else, the early lamplight, the brown blur of the houses, the splashing of hansoms in Oxford Street or the Strand on December afternoons.

There is still something that recalls to me the enchantment of children—the anticipation of Christmas, the delight of a holiday walk—in the way the shop-fronts shine into the fog. It makes each of them seem a little world of light and warmth, and I can still waste time in looking at them with dirty Bloomsbury on one side and dirtier Soho on the other. There are winter effects, not intrinsically sweet, it would appear, which somehow, in absence, touch the chords of memory and even the fount of tears; as for instance the front of the British Museum on a black afternoon, or the portico, when the weather is vile, of one of the big square clubs in Pall Mall. I can give no adequate account of the subtle poetry of such reminiscences; it depends upon associations of which we have often lost the thread. The wide colonnade of the Museum, its symmetrical wings, the high iron fence in its granite setting, the sense of the misty halls within, where all the treasures lie—these things loom patiently through atmospheric layers which instead of making them dreary impart to them something of a cheer of red lights in a storm. I think the romance of a winter afternoon in London arises partly from the fact that, when it is not altogether smothered, the general lamplight takes this hue of hospitality. Such is the colour of the interior glow of the clubs in Pall Mall, which I positively like best when the fog loiters upon their monumental staircases.

In saying just now that these retreats may easily be, for the exile, part of the phantasmagoria of homesickness, I by no means alluded simply to their solemn outsides. If they are still more solemn within, that does not make them any less dear, in retrospect at least, to a visitor much bent upon liking his London to the end. What is the solemnity but a tribute to your nerves, and the stillness but a refined proof of the intensity of life? To produce such results as these the balance of many tastes must be struck, and that is only possible in a very high civilisation. If I seem to intimate that this last abstract term must be the cheer of him who has lonely possession of a foggy library, without even the excitement of watching for some one to put down the magazine he wants, I am willing to let the supposition pass, for the appreciation of a London club at one of the empty seasons is nothing but the strong expression of a preference for the great city—by no means so unsociable as it may superficially appear—at periods of relative abandonment. The London year is studded with holidays, blessed little islands of comparative leisure—intervals of absence for good society. Then the wonderful English faculty for "going out of town for a little change" comes into illimitable play, and families transport their nurseries and their bath-tubs to those rural scenes which form the real substratum of the national life. Such moments as these are the paradise of the genuine London-lover, for he then finds himself face to face with the object of his passion; he can give himself up to an intercourse which at other times is obstructed by his rivals. Then every one he knows is out of town, and the exhilarating sense of the presence of every one he doesn't know becomes by so much the deeper.

This is why I pronounce his satisfaction not an unsociable, but a positively affectionate emotion. It is the mood in which he most measures the immense humanity of the place and in which its limits recede farthest into a dimness peopled with possible illustrations. For his acquaintance, however numerous it may be, is finite; whereas the other, the unvisited London, is infinite. It is one of his pleasures to think of the experiments and excursions he may make in it, even when these adventures don't particularly come off.

The friendly fog seems to protect and enrich them—to add both to the mystery and security, so that it is most in the winter months that the imagination weaves such delights. They reach their climax perhaps during the strictly social desolation of Christmas week, when the country-houses are crowded at the expense of the capital. Then it is that I am most haunted with the London of Dickens, feel most as if it were still recoverable, still exhaling its queerness in patches perceptible to the appreciative. Then the big fires blaze in the lone twilight of the clubs, and the new books on the tables say, "Now at last you have time to read me," and the afternoon tea and toast, and the torpid old gentleman who wakes up from a doze to order potash-water, appear to make the assurance good. It is not a small matter either, to a man of letters, that this is the best time for writing, and that during the lamplit days the white page he tries to blacken becomes, on his table, in the circle of the lamp, with the screen of the climate folding him in, more vivid and absorbent. Those to whom it is forbidden to sit up to work in the small hours may, between November and March, enjoy a semblance of this luxury in the morning. The weather makes a kind of sedentary midnight and muffles the possible interruptions. It is bad for the eyesight, but excellent for the image.

VII

Of course it is too much to say that all the satisfaction of life in London comes from literally living there, for it is not a paradox that a great deal of it consists in getting away. It is almost easier to leave it than not to, and much of its richness and interest proceeds from its ramifications, the fact that all England is in a suburban relation to it. Such an affair it is in comparison to get away from Paris or to get into it. London melts by wide, ugly zones into the green country, and becomes pretty insidiously, inadvertently—without stopping to change. It is the spoiling perhaps of the country, but it is the making of the insatiable town, and if one is a helpless and shameless cockney that is all one is obliged to look at. Anything is excusable which enlarges one's civic consciousness. It ministers immensely to that of the London-lover that, thanks to the tremendous system of coming and going, to the active, hospitable habits of the people, to the elaboration of the railway-service, the frequency and rapidity of trains, and last, though not least, to the fact that much of the loveliest scenery in England lies within a radius of fifty miles—thanks to all this he has the rural picturesque at his door and may cultivate unlimited vagueness as to the line of division between centre and circumference. It is perfectly open to him to consider the remainder of the United Kingdom, or the British empire in general, or even, if he be an American, the total of the English-speaking territories of the globe, as the mere margin, the fitted girdle.

Is it for this reason—because I like to think how great we all are together in the light of heaven and the face of the rest of the world, with the bond of our glorious tongue, in which we labour to write articles and books for each other's candid perusal, how great we all are and how great is the great city which we may unite fraternally to regard as the capital of our race—is it for this that I have a singular kindness for the London railway-stations, that I like them æsthetically, that they interest and fascinate me, and that I view them with complacency even when I wish neither to depart nor to arrive? They remind me of all our reciprocities and activities, our energies and curiosities, and our being all distinguished together from other people by our great common stamp of perpetual motion, our passion for seas and deserts and the other side of the globe, the secret of the impression of strength—I don't say of social roundness and finish—that we produce in any collection of Anglo-Saxon types. If in the beloved foggy season I delight in the spectacle of Paddington, Euston, or Waterloo,—I confess I prefer the grave northern stations,—I am prepared to defend myself against the charge of puerility; for what I seek and what I find in these vulgar scenes is at bottom simply so much evidence of our larger way of looking at life. The exhibition of variety of type is in general one of the bribes by which London induces you to condone her abominations, and the railway-platform is a kind of compendium of that variety. I think that nowhere so much as in London do people wear—to the eye of observation—definite signs of the sort of people they may be. If you like above all things to know the sort, you hail this fact with joy; you recognise that if the English are immensely distinct from other people, they are also socially—and that brings with it, in England, a train of moral and intellectual consequences—extremely distinct from each other. You may see them all together, with the rich colouring of their differences, in the fine flare of one of Mr. W. H. Smith's bookstalls—a feature not to be omitted in any enumeration of the charms of Paddington and Euston. It is a focus of warmth and light in the vast smoky cavern; it gives the idea that literature is a thing of splendour, of a dazzling essence, of infinite gas-lit red and gold. A glamour hangs over the glittering booth, and a tantalising air of clever new things. How brilliant must the books all be, how veracious and courteous the fresh, pure journals! Of a Saturday afternoon, as you wait in your corner of the compartment for the starting of the train, the window makes a frame for the glowing picture. I say of a Saturday afternoon, because that is the most characteristic time—it speaks most of the constant circulation and in particular of the quick jump, by express, just before dinner, for the Sunday, into the hall of the country-house and the forms of closer friendliness, the prolonged talks, the familiarising walks which London excludes.

There is the emptiness of summer as well, when you may have the town to yourself, and I would discourse of it—counting the summer from the first of August—were it not that I fear to seem ungracious in insisting so much on the negative phases. In truth they become positive in another manner, and I have an endearing recollection of certain happy accidents attached to the only period when London life may be said to admit of accident. It is the most luxurious existence in the world, but of that especial luxury—the unexpected, the extemporized—it has in general too little. In a very tight crowd you can't scratch your leg, and in London the social pressure is so great that it is difficult to deflect from the perpendicular or to move otherwise than with the mass. There is too little of the loose change of time; every half-hour has its preappointed use, written down month by month in a little book. As I intimated, however, the pages of this volume exhibit from August to November an attractive blankness; they represent the season during which you may taste of that highest kind of inspiration, the inspiration of the moment.

This is doubtless what a gentleman had in mind who once said to me, in regard to the vast resources of London and its having something for every taste, "Oh, yes; when you are bored or want a little change you can take the boat down to Blackwall." I have never had occasion yet to resort to this particular remedy. Perhaps it's a proof that I have never been bored. Why Blackwall? I indeed asked myself at the time; nor have I yet ascertained what distractions the mysterious name represents. My interlocutor probably used it generically, as a free, comprehensive allusion to the charms of the river at large. Here the London-lover goes with him all the way, and indeed the Thames is altogether such a wonderful affair that he feels he has distributed his picture very clumsily not to have put it in the very forefront. Take it up or take it down, it is equally an adjunct of London life, an expression of London manners.

From Westminster to the sea its uses are commercial, but none the less pictorial for that; while in the other direction—taking it properly a little further up—they are personal, social, athletic, idyllic. In its recreative character it is absolutely unique. I know of no other classic stream that is so splashed about for the mere fun of it. There is something almost droll and at the same time almost touching in the way that on the smallest pretext of holiday or fine weather the mighty population takes to the boats. They bump each other in the narrow, charming channel; between Oxford and Richmond they make an uninterrupted procession. Nothing is more suggestive of the personal energy of the people and their eagerness to take, in the way of exercise and adventure, whatever they can get. I hasten to add that what they get on the Thames is exquisite, in spite of the smallness of the scale and the contrast between the numbers and the space. In a word, if the river is the busiest suburb of London, it is also by far the prettiest. That term applies to it less of course from the bridges down, but it is only because in this part of its career it deserves a larger praise. To be consistent, I like it best when it is all dyed and disfigured with the town, and you look from bridge to bridge—they seem wonderfully big and dim—over the brown, greasy current, the barges and the penny-steamers, the black, sordid, heterogeneous shores. This prospect, of which so many of the elements are ignoble, etches itself to the eye of the lover of "bits" with a power that is worthy perhaps of a better cause.

The way that with her magnificent opportunity London has neglected to achieve a river-front is of course the best possible proof that she has rarely, in the past, been in the architectural mood which at present shows somewhat inexpensive signs of settling upon her. Here and there a fine fragment apologises for the failure which it doesn't remedy. Somerset House stands up higher perhaps than anything else on its granite pedestal, and the palace of Westminster reclines—it can hardly be said to stand—on the big parliamentary bench of its terrace. The Embankment, which is admirable if not particularly interesting, does what it can, and the mannered houses of Chelsea stare across at Battersea Park like eighteenth-century ladies surveying a horrid wilderness. On the other hand, the Charing Cross railway-station, placed where it is, is a national crime; Milbank prison is a worse act of violence than any it was erected to punish, and the water-side generally a shameless renunciation of effect. We acknowledge, however, that its very cynicism is expressive; so that if one were to choose again—short of there being a London Louvre—between the usual English irresponsibility in such matters and some particular flight of conscience, one would perhaps do as well to let the case stand. We know what it is, the stretch from Chelsea to Wapping, but we know not what it might be. It doesn't prevent my being always more or less thrilled, of a summer afternoon, by the journey on a penny-steamer to Greenwich.

VIII

But why do I talk of Greenwich and remind myself of one of the unexecuted vignettes with which it had been my plan that these desultory and, I fear, somewhat incoherent remarks should be studded? They will present to the reader no vignettes but those which the artist who has kindly consented to associate himself with my vagaries may be so good as to bestow upon them. Why should I speak of Hampstead, as the question of summer afternoons just threatened to lead me to do after I should have exhausted the subject of Greenwich, which I may not even touch? Why should I be so arbitrary when I have cheated myself out of the space privately intended for a series of vivid and ingenious sketches of the particular physiognomy of the respective quarters of the town? I had dreamed of doing them all, with their idiosyncrasies and the signs by which you shall know them. It is my pleasure to have learned these signs—a deeply interesting branch of observation—but I must renounce the display of my lore.

I have not the conscience to talk about Hampstead, and what a pleasant thing it is to ascend the long hill which overhangs, as it were, St. John's Wood and begins at the Swiss Cottage—you must mount from there, it must be confessed, as you can—and pick up a friend at a house of friendship on the top, and stroll with him on the rusty Heath, and skirt the garden walls of the old square Georgian houses which survive from the time when, near as it is to-day to London, the place was a kind of provincial centre, with Joanna Baillie for its muse, and take the way by the Three Spaniards—I would never miss that—and look down at the smoky city or across at the Scotch firs and the red sunset. It would never do to make a tangent in that direction when I have left Kensington unsung and Bloomsbury unattempted, and have said never a word about the mighty eastward region—the queer corners, the dark secrets, the rich survivals and mementoes of the City. I particularly regret having sacrificed Kensington, the once-delightful, the Thackerayan, with its literary vestiges, its quiet, pompous red palace, its square of Queen Anne, its house of Lady Castlewood, its Greyhound tavern, where Henry Esmond lodged.

But I can reconcile myself to this when I reflect that I have also sacrificed the Season, which doubtless, from an elegant point of view, ought to have been the central *mor-*

ceau in the panorama. I have noted that the London-lover loves everything in the place, but I have not cut myself off from saying that his sympathy has degrees, or from remarking that the sentiment of the author of these pages has never gone all the way with the dense movement of the British carnival. That is really the word for the period from Easter to midsummer; it is a fine, decorous, expensive, Protestant carnival, in which the masks are not of velvet or silk, but of wonderful deceptive flesh and blood, the material of the most beautiful complexions in the world. Holding that the great interest of London is the sense the place gives us of multitudinous life, it is doubtless an inconsequence not to care most for the phase of greatest intensity. But there is life and life, and the rush and crush of these weeks of fashion is after all but a tolerably mechanical expression of human forces. Nobody would deny that it is a more universal, brilliant, spectacular one than can be seen anywhere else; and it is not a defect that these forces often take the form of women extremely beautiful. I risk the declaration that the London season brings together year by year an unequalled collection of handsome persons. I say nothing of the ugly ones; beauty has at the best been allotted to a small minority, and it is never, at the most, anywhere, but a question of the number by which that minority is least insignificant.

There are moments when one can almost forgive the follies of June for the sake of the smile which the sceptical old city puts on for the time and which, as I noted in an earlier passage of this disquisition, fairly breaks into laughter where she is tickled by the vortex of Hyde Park Corner. Most perhaps does she seem to smile at the end of the summer days, when the light lingers and lingers, though the shadows lengthen and the mists redden and the belated riders, with dinners to dress for, hurry away from the trampled arena of the Park. The population at that hour surges mainly westward and sees the dust of the day's long racket turned into a dull golden haze. There is something that has doubtless often, at this particular moment, touched the fancy even of the bored and the *blasés* in such an emanation of hospitality, of waiting dinners, of the festal idea, of the whole spectacle of the West End preparing herself for an evening six parties deep. The scale on which she entertains is stupendous, and her invitations and "reminders" are as thick as the leaves of the forest.

For half an hour, from eight to nine, every pair of wheels presents the portrait of a diner-out. To consider only the rattling hansoms, the white neckties and "dressed" heads which greet you from over the apron in a quick, interminable succession, conveys the overwhelming impression of a complicated world. Who are they all, and where are they all going, and whence have they come, and what smoking kitchens and gaping portals and marshalled flunkies are prepared to receive them, from the southernmost limits of a loosely interpreted, an almost transpontine Belgravia, to the hyperborean confines of St. John's Wood? There are broughams standing at every door, and carpets laid down for the footfall of the issuing if not the entering reveller. The pavements are empty now, in the fading light, in the big sallow squares and the stuccoed streets of gentility, save for the groups of small children holding others that are smaller—Ameliar-Ann intrusted with Sarah Jane—who collect, wherever the strip of carpet lies, to see the fine ladies pass from the carriage or the house. The West End is dotted with these pathetic little gazing groups; it is the party of the poor—*their* Season and way of dining out, and a happy illustration of "the sympathy that prevails between classes." The watchers, I should add, are by no means all children, but the lean mature also, and I am sure these wayside joys are one of the reasons of an inconvenience much deplored—the tendency of the country poor to flock to London. They who dine only occasionally or never at all have plenty of time to contemplate those with whom the custom has more amplitude. However, it was not my intention to conclude these remarks in a melancholy strain, and goodness knows that the diners are a prodigious company. It is as moralistic as I shall venture to be if I drop a very soft sigh on the paper as I confirm that truth. Are they all illuminated spirits and is their conversation the ripest in the world? This is not to be expected, nor should I ever suppose it to be desired that an agreeable society should fail to offer frequent opportunity for intellectual rest. Such a shortcoming is not one of the sins of the London world in general, nor would it be just to complain of that world, on any side, on grounds of deficiency. It is not what London fails to do that strikes the observer, but the general fact that she does everything in excess. Excess is her highest reproach, and it is her incurable misfortune that there is really too much of her. She overwhelms you by quantity and number—she ends by making human life, by making civilisation, appear cheap to you. Wherever you go, to parties, exhibitions, concerts, "private views," meetings, solitudes, there are already more people than enough on the field. How it makes you understand the high walls with which so much of English life is surrounded, and the priceless blessing of a park in the country, where there is nothing animated but rabbits and pheasants and, for the worst, the importunate nightingales! And as the monster grows and grows for ever, she departs more and more—it must be acknowledged—from the ideal of a convenient society, a society in which intimacy is possible, in which the associated meet often and sound and select and measure and inspire each other, and relations and combinations have time to form themselves. The substitute for this, in London, is the momentary concussion of a million of atoms. It is the difference between seeing a great deal of a few and seeing a little of every one.

"When did you come–are you 'going on?'" and it is over; there is no time even for the answer. This may seem a perfidious arraignment, and I should not make it were I not prepared, or rather were I not eager, to add two qualifications. One of these is that, cumbrously vast as the place may be, I would not have had it smaller by a hair's-breadth or have missed one of the fine and fruitful impatiences with which it inspires you and which are at bottom a heartier tribute, I think, than any great city receives. The other is that out of its richness and its inexhaustible good-humour it belies the next hour any generalisation you may have been so simple as to make about it.

Part III

The Cosmopolite

Paris and France

1876—1884

Editor's Note

France, like England, was rediscovered for himself by James when he made his first adult trip to Europe in 1869–70, but his acquaintance with that country was one of the earliest of his conscious experiences. His memoir A Small Boy and Others *of 1913 tells of the schooldays he shared with his brother William in Paris and Boulogne-sur-Mer;* Notes of a Son and Brother (*1914*) *continues the account into his later boyhood. His first published story, "A Tragedy of Error"* (The Continental Monthly, *February, 1864*)*, had a French setting. A good many other early tales were set in Paris or other French backgrounds.* The American (*1877*) *was the first novel to be laid wholly in France; and in the future such novels as* The Princess Casamassima, The Tragic Muse, *and notably* The Ambassadors *were to draw heavily on all that France, Paris, and their civilization meant to James and on what they counted for in his literary, intellectual, and personal development.*

Paris was the city of his first European literary schooling and contacts. His letters of 1869–70 and particularly of 1875–76 reveal what the city of Flaubert, Daudet, Mérimée, Maupassant, Zola, the Goncourts, and the expatriate Turgenev, and of the salons of Madame Viardot and Madame de Blocqueville, meant to him in those years. When he published his first book of literary studies, French Poets and Novelists, in 1878, it was an account of what Musset, Gautier, Baudelaire, Balzac, George Sand, Flaubert, Turgenev, Mérimée, and the Théâtre Français had taught him, the judgments and decisions they enforced in him, at that crucial stage of his formation as a writer. In 1875–76 he contributed a series of twenty sketches on Parisian life, art, theater, society, and politics to the New York Tribune.

Transatlantic Sketches, in 1875, included little on France (only a slight report on "The Parisian Stage"), but Portraits of Places in 1883 contained the essays on "Occasional Paris," "Rheims" (from "Rheims and Laon"), and "Chartres" included here, as well as three others on "Rouen," "Etretat," and "From Normandy to the Pyrenees." In 1884 James devoted a full volume to A Little Tour in France, based on a series of essays he wrote for The Atlantic Monthly in 1883–84 about a journey he made through Touraine, Provence, and eastern France in the autumn of 1882. Here, he said in his introduction, he hoped to make his "small personal effort" to "shake off" the "taste for Paris" which had too long led Americans to take "the wondrous capital, and the wondrous capital alone, for their object." Spurred by his devotion to Balzac, he visited Tours; went on to the châteaux of the Loire—Blois, Chambord, Amboise, Chenonceaux, Azay-le-Rideau, Langeais, Loches; then to Bourges, Le Mans, Angers, Nantes, La Rochelle, and Poitiers; then south into Provence by way of Angoulême, Toulouse, Carcassonne, Narbonne, Montpellier, the Pont du Gard, Aigues-Mortes, and Nîmes; thus to the Tarascon of Daudet's romances of Tartarin (one of which James translated in 1890) and to Arles, Les Baux, Avignon, Villeneuve-Lès-Avignon, Vaucluse, Orange, and Macon; and so back to Paris by way of Bourg-en-Bresse, Beaune, and Dijon. Of these essays the group on the châteaux makes a series that strongly invited inclusion here, but since James is likely to *be more warmly inspired by cities than by châteaux, they have been omitted in favor of the essays on ten cities that appeared in* Portraits of Places *and* A Little Tour, *the texts from the former book being taken from its 1883 edition and those of the latter from the revised edition which James published in 1900.*

Occasional Paris

1877

It is hard to say exactly what is the profit of comparing one race with another, and weighing in opposed groups the manners and customs of neighbouring countries; but it is certain that as we move about the world we constantly indulge in this exercise. This is especially the case if we happen to be infected with the baleful spirit of the cosmopolite—that uncomfortable consequence of seeing many lands and feeling at home in none. To be a cosmopolite is not, I think, an ideal; the ideal should be to be a concentrated patriot. Being a cosmopolite is an accident, but one must make the best of it. If you have lived about, as the phrase is, you have lost that sense of the absoluteness and the sanctity of the habits of your fellow-patriots which once made you so happy in the midst of them. You have seen that there are a great many *patriae* in the world, and that each of these is filled with excellent people for whom the local idiosyncrasies are the only thing that is not rather barbarous. There comes a time when one set of customs, wherever it may be found, grows to seem to you about as provincial as another; and then I suppose it may be said of you that you have become a cosmopolite. You have formed the habit of comparing, of looking for points of difference and of resemblance, for present and absent advantages, for the virtues that go with certain defects, and the defects that go with certain virtues. If this is poor work compared with the active practice, in the sphere to which a discriminating Providence has assigned you, of the duties of a tax-payer, an elector, a juryman or a diner-out, there is nevertheless something to be said for it. It is good to think well of mankind, and this, on the whole, a cosmopolite does. If you limit your generalisations to the sphere I mentioned just now, there is a danger that your occasional fits of pessimism may be too sweeping. When you are out of humour the whole country suffers, because at such moments one is never discriminating, and it costs you very little bad logic to lump your fellow-citizens together. But if you are living about, as I say, certain differences impose themselves. The worst you can say of the human race is, for instance, that the Germans are a detestable people. They do not represent the human race for you, as in your native town your fellow-citizens do, and your unflattering judgment has a flattering reverse. If the Germans are detestable, you are mentally saying, there are those admirable French, or those charming Americans, or those interesting English. (Of course it is simply by accident that I couple the German name here with the unfavourable adjective. The epithets may be transposed at will.) Nothing can well be more different from anything else than the English from the French, so that, if you are acquainted with both nations, it may be said that on any special point your agreeable impression of the one implies a censorious attitude toward the other, and *vice versâ*. This has rather a shocking sound; it makes the cosmopolite appear invidious and narrow-minded. But I hasten to add that there seems no real reason why even the most delicate conscience should take alarm. The consequence of the cosmopolite spirit is to initiate you into the merits of all peoples; to convince you that national virtues are numerous, though they may be very different, and to make downright preference really very hard. I have, for instance, every disposition to think better of the English race than of any other except my own. There are things which make it natural I should; there are inducements, provocations, temptations, almost bribes. There have been moments when I have almost burned my ships behind me, and declared that, as it simplified matters greatly to pin one's faith to a chosen people, I would henceforth cease to trouble my head about the lights and shades of the foreign character. I am convinced that if I had taken this reckless engagement, I should greatly have regretted it. You may find a room very comfortable to sit in with the window open, and not like it at all when the window has been shut. If one were to give up the privilege of comparing the English with other people, one would very soon, in a moment of reaction, make once for all (and most unjustly) such a comparison as would leave the English nowhere. Compare then, I say, as often as the occasion presents itself. The result as regards any particular people, and as regards the human race at large, may be pronounced agreeable, and the process is both instructive and entertaining.

So the author of these observations finds it on returning to Paris after living for upwards of a year in London. He finds himself comparing, and the results of comparison are several disjointed reflections, of which it may be profitable to make a note. Certainly Paris is a very old story, and London is a still older one; and there is no great reason why a journey across the channel and back should quicken one's perspicacity to an unprecedented degree. I therefore will not pretend to have been looking at Paris with new eyes, or to have gathered on the banks of the Seine a harvest of extraordinary impressions. I will only pretend that a good many old impressions have recovered their freshness, and that there is a sort of renovated entertainment in looking at the most brilliant city in the world with eyes attuned to a different pitch. Never, in fact, have those qualities of brightness and gaiety that are half the stock-in-trade of the city by the Seine seemed to me more uncontestable. The autumn is but half over, and Paris is, in common parlance, empty. The private houses are closed, the lions have returned to the jungle, the Champs Elysées are not at all "mondains." But I have never seen Paris more Parisian, in the pleasantest sense of the word; better humoured, more open-windowed, more naturally entertaining. A radiant September helps the case; but doubtless the matter is, as I hinted above, in a large degree "subjective." For when one comes to the point there is nothing very particular just now for Paris to rub her hands about. The Exhibition of 1878 is looming up as large as a mighty mass of buildings on the Trocadéro can make it. These buildings are very magnificent and fantastical; they hang over the Seine, in their sudden immensity and glittering newness, like a palace in a fairy-tale. But the trouble is that most people appear to regard the Exhibition as in fact a fairy-tale. They speak of the wonderful structures on the Champ de Mars and the Trocadéro as a predestined monument to the folly of a group of gentlemen destitute of a sense of the opportune. The moment certainly does not seem very well chosen for inviting the world to come to Paris to amuse itself. The world is too much occupied with graver cares—with reciprocal cannonading and chopping, with cutting of throats and burning of homes, with murder of infants and mutilation of mothers, with warding off famine and civil war, with lamenting the failure of its resources, the dulness of trade, the emptiness of its pockets. Rome is burning altogether too fast for even its most irresponsible spirits to find any great satisfaction in fiddling. But even if there is (as there very well may be) a certain scepticism at headquarters as to the accomplishment of this graceful design, there is no apparent hesitation, and everything is going forward as rapidly as if mankind were breathless with expectation. That familiar figure, the Parisian *ouvrier*, with his white, chalky blouse, his attenuated person, his clever face, is more familiar than ever, and I suppose, finding plenty of work to his hand, is for the time in a comparatively rational state of mind. He swarms in thousands, not only in the region of the Exhibition, but along the great thoroughfare—the Avenue de l'Opéra—which has just been opened in the interior of Paris.

This is an extremely Parisian creation, and as it is really a great convenience—it will save a great many steps and twists and turns—I suppose it should be spoken of with gratitude and admiration. But I confess that to my sense it belongs primarily to that order of benefits which during the twenty years of the Empire gradually deprived the streets of Paris of nine-tenths of their ancient individuality. The deadly monotony of the Paris that M. Haussmann called into being—its huge, blank, pompous, featureless sameness—sometimes comes over the wandering stranger with a force that leads him to devote the author of these miles of architectural commonplace to execration. The new street is quite on the imperial system; it must make the late Napoleon III smile with beatific satisfaction as he looks down upon it from the Bonapartist corner of Paradise. It stretches straight away from the pompous façade of the Opéra to the doors of the Théâtre Français, and it must be admitted that there is something fine in the vista that is closed at one end by the great sculptured and gilded mass of the former building. But it smells of the modern asphalt; it is lined with great white houses that are adorned with machine-made arabesques, and each of which is so exact a copy of all the rest that even the little white porcelain number on a blue ground, which looks exactly alike all the other numbers, hardly constitutes an identity. Presently there will be a long succession of milliners' and chocolate-makers' shops in the basement of this homogeneous row, and the pretty bonnets and bonbonnières in the shining windows will have their ribbons knotted with a *chic* that you must come to Paris to see. Then there will be little glazed sentry-boxes at regular intervals along the curbstone, in which churlish old women will sit selling half a dozen copies of each of the newspapers; and over the hardened bitumen the young Parisian of our day will constantly circulate, looking rather pallid and wearing very large shirt-cuffs. And the new avenue will be a great success, for it will place in symmetrical communication two of the most important establishments in France—the temple of French music and the temple of French comedy.

I said just now that no two things could well be more unlike than England and France; and though the remark is not original, I uttered it with the spontaneity that it must have on the lips of a traveller who, having left either country, has just disembarked in the other. It is of course by this time a very trite observation, but it will continue to be made so long as Boulogne remains the same lively antithesis of Folkestone. An American, conscious of the family-likeness diffused over his own huge continent, never quite unlearns his surprise at finding that so little of either of these two almost contiguous towns has rubbed off upon the other. He is surprised at certain English people feeling so far away from France, and at all French people feeling so far away from England. I travelled from Boulogne the other day in the same railway-carriage with a couple of amiable and ingenuous young Britons, who had come over to spend ten days in Paris. It was their first landing in France; they had never yet quitted their native island; and in the course of a little conversation that I had with them I was struck with the scantiness of their information in regard to French manners and customs. They were very intelligent lads; they were apparently fresh from a university; but in respect to the interesting country they were about to enter, their minds were almost a blank. If the conductor, appearing at the carriage door to ask for our tickets, had had the leg of a frog sticking out of his pocket, I think their only very definite preconception would have been confirmed. I parted with them at the Paris station, and I have no doubt that they very soon began to make precious discoveries; and I have alluded to them not in the least to throw ridicule upon their "insularity"—which indeed, being accompanied with great modesty, I thought a very pretty spectacle—but because having become, since my last visit to France, a little insular myself, I was more conscious of the emotions that attend on an arrival.

The brightness always seems to begin while you are still out in the channel, when you fairly begin to see the French coast. You pass into a region of intenser light—a zone of clearness and colour. These properties brighten and deepen as you approach the land, and when you fairly stand upon that good Boulognese quay, among the blue and red douaniers and soldiers, the small ugly men in cerulean blouses, the charming fishwives, with their folded kerchiefs and their crisp cap-frills, their short striped petticoats, their tightly-drawn stockings, and their little clicking sabots—when you look about you at the smokeless air, at the pink and yellow houses, at the white-fronted café, close at hand, with its bright blue letters, its mirrors and marble-topped tables, its white-aproned, alert, undignified waiter, grasping a huge coffee-pot by a long handle—when you perceive all these things you feel the additional savour that foreignness gives to the picturesque; or feel rather, I should say, that simple foreignness may itself make the picturesque; for certainly the elements in the picture I have just sketched are not especially exquisite. No matter; you are amused, and your amusement continues—being sensibly stimulated by a visit to the buffet at the railway-station, which is better than the refreshment-room at Folkestone. It is a pleasure to have people offering you soup again, of their own movement; it is a pleasure to find a little pint of Bordeaux standing naturally before your plate; it is a pleasure to have a napkin; it is a pleasure, above all, to take up one of the good long sticks of French bread—as bread is called the staff of life, the French bake it literally in the shape of staves—and break off a loose, crisp, crusty morsel.

There are impressions, certainly, that imperil your good-humour. No honest Anglo-Saxon can like a French railway-station; and I was on the point of adding that no honest Anglo-Saxon can like a French railway-official. But I will not go so far as that; for after all I cannot remember any great harm that such a functionary has ever done me—except in locking me up as a malefactor. It is necessary to say, however, that the honest Anglo-Saxon, in a French railway-station, is in a state of chronic irritation—an irritation arising from his sense of the injurious effect upon the genial French nature of the possession of an administrative uniform. I believe that the consciousness of brass buttons on his coat and stripes on his trousers has spoiled many a modest and amiable Frenchman, and the sight of these aggressive insignia always stirs within me a moral protest. I repeat that my aversion to them is partly theoretic, for I have found, as a general thing, that an inquiry civilly made extracts a civil answer from even the most official-looking personage. But I have also found that such a personage's measure of the civility due to him is inordinately large; if he places himself in any degree at your service, it is apparently from the sense that true greatness can afford to unbend. You are constantly reminded that you must not presume. In England these intimations never proceed from one's "inferiors." In France the "administration" is the first thing that touches you; in a little while you get used to it, but you feel somehow that, in the process, you have lost the flower of your self-respect. Of course you are under some obligation to it. It has taken you off the steamer at Boulogne;[1] made you tell your name to a gentleman with a sword, stationed at the farther end of the plank—not a drawn sword, it is true, but still, at the best, a very nasty weapon; marshalled you into the railway-station; assigned you to a carriage—I was going to say to a seat; transported you to Paris, marshalled you again out of the train, and under a sort of military surveillance, into an enclosure containing a number of human sheep-pens, in one of which it has imprisoned you for some half-hour. I am always on the point, in these places, of asking one of my gaolers if I may not be allowed to walk about on parole. The administration at any rate has finally taken you out of your pen, and, through the medium of a functionary who "inscribes" you in a little book, transferred you to a cab selected by a logic of its own. In doing all this it has certainly done a great deal for you; but somehow its good offices have made you feel sombre and resentful. The other day, on arriving from London, while I was waiting for my luggage, I saw several of the porters who convey travellers' impedimenta to the cab come up and deliver over the coin they had just received for this service to a functionary posted *ad hoc* in a corner, and armed with a little book in which he noted down these remittances. The *pour-boires* are apparently thrown into a common fund and divided among the guild of porters. The system is doubtless an excellent one, excellently carried out; but the sight of the poor round-shouldered man of burdens dropping his coin into the hand of the official arithmetician was to my fancy but another

[1] The text of *Portraits of Places* (1883 [1884]) has Folkestone here; it should obviously be Boulogne.

reminder that the individual, as an individual, loses by all that the administration assumes.

After living a while in England you observe the individual in Paris with quickened attention; and I think it must be said that at first he makes an indifferent figure. You are struck with the race being physically and personally a poorer one than that great family of largely-modelled, fresh-coloured people you have left upon the other side of the channel. I remember that in going to England a year ago and disembarking of a dismal, sleety Sunday evening at Folkestone, the first thing that struck me was the good looks of the railway porters—their broad shoulders, their big brown beards, their well-cut features. In like manner, landing lately at Boulogne of a brilliant Sunday morning, it was impossible not to think the little men in numbered caps who were gesticulating and chattering in one's path, rather ugly fellows. In arriving from other countries one is struck with a certain want of dignity in the French face. I do not know, however, whether this is anything worse than the fact that the French face is expressive; for it may be said that, in a certain sense, to express anything is to compromise with one's dignity, which likes to be understood without taking trouble. As regards the lower classes, at any rate, the impression I speak of always passes away; you perceive that the good looks of the French working-people are to be found in their look of intelligence. These people, in Paris, strike me afresh as the cleverest, the most perceptive, and intellectually speaking, the most human of their kind. The Paris *ouvrier,* with his democratic blouse, his expressive, demonstrative, agreeable eye, his meagre limbs, his irregular, pointed features, his sallow complexion, his face at once fatigued and animated, his light, nervous organisation, is a figure that I always encounter again with pleasure. In some cases he looks depraved and perverted, but at his worst he looks refined, he is full of vivacity of perception, of something that one can appeal to.

It takes some courage to say this, perhaps, after reading *L'Assommoir;* but in M. Emile Zola's extraordinary novel one must make the part, as the French say, of the horrible uncleanness of the author's imagination. *L'Assommoir,* I have been told, has had great success in the lower walks of Parisian life; and if this fact is not creditable to the delicacy of M. Zola's humble readers, it proves a good deal in favour of their intelligence. With all its grossness the book in question is essentially a literary performance; you must be tolerably clever to appreciate it. It is highly appreciated, I believe, by the young ladies who live in the region of the Latin Quarter—those young ladies who thirty years ago were called grisettes, and now are called I don't know what. They know long passages by heart; they repeat them with infinite gusto. "Ce louchon d'Augustine"—the horrible little girl with a squint, who is always playing nasty tricks and dodging slaps and projectiles in Gervaise's shop, is their particular favourite; and it must be admitted that "ce louchon d'Augustine" is, as regards reality, a wonderful creation.

If Parisians, both small and great, have more of the intellectual stamp than the people one sees in London, it is striking, on the other hand, that the people of the better sort in Paris look very much less "respectable." I did not know till I came back to Paris how used I had grown to the English *cachet;* but I immediately found myself missing it. You miss it in the men much more than in the women; for the well-to-do Frenchwoman of the lower orders, as one sees her in public, in the streets and in shops, is always a delightfully comfortable and creditable person. I must confess to the highest admiration for her, an admiration that increases with acquaintance. She, at least, is essentially respectable; the neatness, compactness, and sobriety of her dress, the decision of her movement and accent suggest the civic and domestic virtues—order, thrift, frugality, the moral necessity of making a good appearance. It is, I think, an old story that to the stranger in France the women seem greatly superior to the men. Their superiority, in fact, appears to be conceded; for wherever you turn you meet them in the forefront of action. You meet them, indeed, too often; you pronounce them at times obtrusive. It is annoying when you go to order your boots or your shirts, to have to make known your desires to even the most neat-waisted female attendant; for the limitations to the feminine intellect are, though few in number, distinct, and women are not able to understand certain masculine needs. Mr. Worth makes ladies' dresses; but I am sure there will never be a fashionable tailoress. There are, however, points at which, from the commercial point of view, feminine assistance is invaluable. For insisting upon the merits of an article that has failed to satisfy you, talking you over, and making you take it; for defending a disputed bill, for paying the necessary compliments or supplying the necessary impertinence—for all these things the neat-waisted sex has peculiar and precious faculties. In the commercial class in Paris the man always appeals to the woman; the woman always steps forward. The woman always proposes the conditions of a bargain. Go about and look for furnished rooms, you always encounter a concierge and his wife. When you ask the price of the rooms, the woman takes the words out of her husband's mouth, if indeed he have not first turned to her with a questioning look. She takes you in hand; she proposes conditions; she thinks of things he would not have thought of.

What I meant just now by my allusion to the absence of the "respectable" in the appearance of the Parisian population was that the men do not look like gentlemen, as so many Englishmen do. The average Frenchman that one encounters in public is of so different a type from the average Englishman that you can easily believe that to the end of time the two will not understand each other. The Frenchman has always, comparatively speaking, a Bohemian, empirical look; the expression of his face, its colouring, its movement, have not been toned down to the neutral complexion of that breeding for which in English speech we reserve the epithet of "good." He is at once more artificial and more natural; the former where the Englishman is positive, the latter where the Englishman is negative. He takes off his hat with a flourish to a friend, but the Englishman never bows. He ties a knot in the end of a napkin and thrusts it into his shirt-collar, so that, as he sits at breakfast, the napkin may serve the office of a pinafore. Such an operation as that seems to the Englishman as *naïf* as the flourishing of one's hat is pretentious.

I sometimes go to breakfast at a café on the Boulevard, which I formerly used to frequent with considerable regularity. Coming back there the other day, I found exactly the same group of habitués at their little tables, and I mentally exclaimed as I looked at them over my newspaper, upon their unlikeness to the gentlemen who confront you in the same attitude at a London club. Who are they? what are they? On these points I have no information; but the stranger's imagination does not seem to see a majestic social order massing itself behind them as it usually does in London. He goes so far as to suspect that what is behind them is not adapted for exhibition; whereas your Englishmen, whatever may be the defects of their personal character, or the irregularities of their conduct, are pressed upon from the rear by an immense body of private proprieties and comforts, of domestic conventions and theological observances. But it is agreeable all the same to come back to a café of which you have formerly been an habitué. Adolphe or Edouard, in his long white apron and his large patent-leather slippers, has a perfect recollection of "les habitudes de Monsieur." He remembers the table you preferred, the wine you drank, the newspaper you read. He greets you with the friendliest of smiles, and remarks that it is a long time since he has had the pleasure of seeing Monsieur. There is something in this simple remark very touching to a heart that has suffered from that incorruptible dumbness of the British domestic. But in Paris such a heart finds consolation at every step; it is reminded of that most classic quality of the French nature—its sociability; a sociability which operates here as it never does in England, from below upward. Your waiter utters a greeting because, after all, something human within him prompts him; his instinct bids him say something, and his taste recommends that it be agreeable. The obvious reflection is that a waiter must not say too much, even for the sake of being human. But in France the people always like to make the little extra remark, to throw in something above the simply necessary. I stop before a little man who is selling newspapers at a street-corner, and ask him for the *Journal des Débats*. His answer deserves to be literally given: "Je ne l'ai plus, Monsieur; mais je pourrai vous donner quelquechose à peu près dans le même genre—la *République Française*." Even a person of his humble condition must have had a lurking sense of the comicality of offering anything as an equivalent for the "genre" of the venerable, classic, academic *Débats*. But my friend could not bear to give me a naked, monosyllabic refusal.

There are two things that the returning observer is likely to do with as little delay as possible. One is to dine at some *cabaret* of which he retains a friendly memory; another is to betake himself to the Théâtre Français. It is early in the season; there are no new pieces; but I have taken great pleasure in seeing some of the old ones. I lost no time in going to see Mademoiselle Sarah Bernhardt in *Andro-*

maque. *Andromaque* is not a novelty, but Mademoiselle Sarah Bernhardt has a perennial freshness. The play has been revived, to enable her to represent not the great part, the injured and passionate Hermione, but that of the doleful funereal widow of Hector. This part is a poor one; it is narrow and monotonous, and offers few brilliant opportunities. But the actress knows how to make opportunities, and she has here a very sufficient one for crossing her thin white arms over her nebulous black robes, and sighing forth in silver accents her dolorous rhymes. Her rendering of the part is one more proof of her singular intelligence—of the fineness of her artistic nature. As there is not a great deal to be done with it in the way of declamation, she has made the most of its plastic side. She understands the art of motion and attitude as no one else does, and her extraordinary personal grace never fails her. Her Andromaque has postures of the most poetic picturesqueness—something that suggests the broken stem and drooping head of a flower that had been rudely plucked. She bends over her classic confidant like the figure of Bereavement on a bas-relief, and she has a marvellous manner of lifting and throwing back her delicate arms, locking them together, and passing them behind her hanging head.

The *Demi-Monde* of M. Dumas *fils* is not a novelty either; but I quite agree with M. Francisque Sarcey that it is on the whole, in form, the first comedy of our day. I have seen it several times, but I never see it without being forcibly struck with its merits. For the drama of our time it must always remain the model. The interest of the story, the quiet art with which it is unfolded, the naturalness and soberness of the means that are used, and by which great effects are produced, the brilliancy and richness of the dialogue—all these things make it a singularly perfect and interesting work. Of course it is admirably well played at the Théâtre Français. Madame d'Ange was originally a part of too great amplitude for Mademoiselle Croizette; but she is gradually filling it out and taking possession of it; she begins to give a sense of the "calme infernal," which George Sand somewhere mentions as the leading attribute of the character. As for Delaunay, he does nothing better, more vividly and gallantly, than Olivier de Jalin. When I say gallantry I say it with qualification; for what a very queer fellow is this M. de Jalin! In seeing the *Demi-Monde* again I was more than ever struck with the oddity of its morality and with the way that the ideal of fine conduct differs in different nations. The *Demi-Monde* is the history of the eager, the almost heroic, effort of a clever and superior woman, who has been guilty of what the French call "faults," to pass from the irregular and equivocal circle to which these faults have consigned her into what is distinctively termed "good society." The only way in which the passage can be effected is by her marrying an honourable man; and to induce an honourable man to marry her, she must suppress the more discreditable facts of her career. Taking her for an honest woman, Raymond de Nanjac falls in love with her, and honestly proposes to make her his wife. But Raymond de Nanjac has contracted an intimate friendship with Olivier de Jalin, and the action of the play is more especially De Jalin's attempt—a successful one—to rescue his friend from the ignominy of a union with Suzanne d'Ange. Jalin knows a great deal about her, for the simple reason that he has been her lover. Their relations have been most harmonious, but from the moment that Suzanne sets her cap at Nanjac, Olivier declares war. Suzanne struggles hard to keep possession of her suitor, who is very much in love with her, and Olivier spares no pains to detach him. It is the means that Olivier uses that excite the wonderment of the Anglo-Saxon spectator. He takes the ground that in such a cause all means are fair, and when, at the climax of the play, he tells a thumping lie in order to make

Madame d'Ange compromise herself, expose herself, he is pronounced by the author "le plus honnête homme que je connaisse." Madame d'Ange, as I have said, is a superior woman; the interest of the play is in her being a superior woman. Olivier has been her lover; he himself is one of the reasons why she may not marry Nanjac; he has given her a push along the downward path. But it is curious how little this is held by the author to disqualify him from fighting the battle in which she is so much the weaker combatant. An English-speaking audience is more "moral" than a French, more easily scandalised; and yet it is a singular fact that if the *Demi-Monde* were represented before an English-speaking audience, its sympathies would certainly not go with M. de Jalin. It would pronounce him rather a coward. Is it because such an audience, although it has not nearly such a pretty collection of pedestals to place under the feet of the charming sex, has, after all, in default of this degree of gallantry, a tenderness more fundamental? Madame d'Ange has stained herself, and it is doubtless not at all proper that such ladies should be led to the altar by honourable young men. The point is not that the English-speaking audience would be disposed to condone Madame d'Ange's irregularities, but that it would remain perfectly cold before the spectacle of her ex-lover's masterly campaign against her, and quite fail to think it positively admirable, or to regard the fib by which he finally clinches his victory as a proof of exceptional honesty. The ideal of our own audience would be expressed in some such words as, "I say, that's not fair game. Can't you let the poor woman alone?"

Chartres

1876

The spring, in Paris, since it has fairly begun, has been enchanting. The sun and the moon have been blazing in emulation, and the difference between the blue sky of day and of night has been as slight as possible. There are no clouds in the sky, but there are little thin green clouds, little puffs of raw, tender verdure, entangled among the branches of the trees. All the world is in the streets; the chairs and tables which have stood empty all winter before the doors of the cafés are at a premium; the theatres have become intolerably close; the puppet-shows in the Champs Elysées are the only form of dramatic entertainment which seems consistent with the season. By way of doing honour, at a small cost, to this ethereal mildness, I went out the other day to the ancient town of Chartres, where I spent several hours, which I cannot consent to pass over as if nothing had happened. It is the experience of the writer of these lines, who likes nothing so much as moving about to see the world, that if one has been for a longer time than usual resident and stationary, there is a kind of overgrown entertainment in taking the train, even for a suburban goal; and that if one takes it on a charming April day, when there is a sense, almost an odour, of change in the air, the innocent pleasure is as nearly as possible complete. My accessibility to emotions of this kind amounts to an infirmity, and the effect of it was to send me down to Chartres in a shamelessly optimistic state of mind. I was so prepared to be entertained and pleased with everything that it is only a mercy that the cathedral happens really to be a fine building. If it had not been, I should still have admired it inordinately, at the risk of falling into heaven knows what æsthetic heresy. But I am almost ashamed to say how soon my entertainment began. It began, I think, with my hailing a little open carriage on the Boulevard and causing myself to be driven to the Gare de l'Ouest—far away across the river, up the Rue Bonaparte, of art-student memories, and along the big, straight Rue de Rennes to the Boulevard Montparnasse. Of course, at this rate, by the time I reached Chartres—the journey is of a couple of hours—I had almost drained the cup of pleasure. But it was replenished at the station, at the buffet, from the pungent bottle of wine I drank with my breakfast. Here, by the way, is another excellent excuse for being delighted with any day's excursion in France—that wherever you are, you may breakfast to your taste. There may, indeed, if the station is very small, be no buffet; but if there is a buffet, you may be sure that civilisation—in the persons of a sympathetic young woman in a well-made black dress, and a rapid, zealous, grateful waiter—presides at it. It was quite the least, as the French say, that after my breakfast I should have thought the cathedral, as I saw it from the top of the steep hill on which the town stands, rising high above the clustered houses and seeming to make of their red-roofed agglomeration a mere pedestal for its immense beauty, promised remarkably well. You see it so as you emerge from the station, and then, as you climb slowly into town, you lose sight of it. You perceive Chartres to be a rather shabby little *ville de province,* with a few sunny, empty open *places,* and crooked shady streets, in which two or three times you lose your way, until at last, after more than once catching a glimpse, high above some slit between the houses, of the clear gray towers shining against the blue sky, you push forward again, risk another short cut, turn another interposing corner, and stand before the goal of your pilgrimage.

I spent a long time looking at this monument. I revolved around it, like a moth around a candle; I went away and I came back; I chose twenty different standpoints; I observed it during the different hours of the day, and saw it in the moonlight as well as the sunshine. I gained, in a word, a certain sense of familiarity with it; and yet I despair of giving any coherent account of it. Like most French cathedrals, it rises straight out of the street, and is destitute of that setting of turf and trees and deaneries and canonries which contribute so largely to the impressiveness of the great English churches. Thirty years ago a row of old houses was glued to its base and made their back walls of its sculptured sides. These have been plucked away, and, relatively speaking, the church is fairly isolated. But the little square that surrounds it is deplorably narrow, and you flatten your back against the opposite houses in the vain attempt to stand off and survey the towers. The proper way to look at them would be to go up in a balloon and hang poised, face to face with them, in the blue air. There is, however, perhaps an advantage in being forced to stand so directly under them, for this position gives you an overwhelming impression of their height. I have seen, I suppose, churches as beautiful as this one, but I do not remember ever to have been so fascinated by superpositions and vertical effects. The endless upward reach of the great west front, the clear, silvery tone of its surface, the way three or four magnificent features are made to occupy its serene expanse, its simplicity, majesty, and dignity—these things crowd upon one's sense with a force that makes the act of vision seem for the moment almost all of life. The impressions produced by architecture lend themselves as little to interpretation by another medium as those produced by music. Certainly there is an inexpressible harmony in the façade of Chartres.

The doors are rather low, as those of the English cathedrals are apt to be, but (standing three together) are set in a deep framework of sculpture—rows of arching grooves, filled with admirable little images, standing with their heels on each other's heads. The church, as it now exists, except the northern tower, dates from the middle of the thirteenth century, and these closely-packed figures are full of the grotesqueness of the period. Above the triple portals is a vast round-topped window, in three divisions, of the grandest dimensions and the stateliest effect. Above this window is a circular aperture of huge circumference, with a double row of sculptured spokes radiating from its centre and looking on its lofty field of stone as expansive and symbolic as if it were the wheel of Time itself. Higher still is a little gallery with a delicate balustrade, supported on a beautiful cornice and stretching across the front from tower to tower; and above this is a range of niched statues of kings—fifteen, I believe, in number. Above the statues is a gable, with an image of the Virgin and Child on its front, and another of Christ on its apex. In the relation of all these parts there is such a high felicity that while on the one side the eye rests on a great many large blanks there is no approach on the other to poverty. The little gallery that I have spoken of, beneath the statues of the kings, had for me a peculiar charm. Useless, at its tremendous altitude, for other purposes, it seemed intended for the little images to step down and walk about upon. When the great façade begins to glow in the late afternoon light, you can imagine them strolling up and down their long balcony in couples, pausing with their elbows on the balustrade, resting their stony chins in their hands, and looking out, with their little blank eyes, on the great view of the old French monarchy they once ruled, and which now has passed away. The two great towers of the cathedral are among the noblest of their kind. They rise in solid simplicity to a height as great as the eye often troubles itself to travel, and then suddenly they begin to execute a magnificent series of feats in architectural gymnastics. This is especially true of the northern spire, which is a late creation, dating from the sixteenth century. The other is relatively quiet; but its companion is a sort of tapering bouquet of sculptured stone. Statues and buttresses, gargoyles, arabesques and crockets pile themselves in successive stages, until the eye loses the sense of everything but a sort of architectural lacework. The pride of Chartres, after its front, is the two portals of its transepts—great dusky porches, in three divisions, covered with more images than I have time to talk about. Wherever you look, along the sides of the church, a time-worn image is niched or perched. The face of each flying buttress is garnished with one, with the features quite melted away.

The inside of the cathedral corresponds in vastness and grandeur to the outside—it is the perfection of gothic in its prime. But I looked at it rapidly, the place was so intolerably cold. It seemed to answer one's query of what becomes of the winter when the spring chases it away. The winter hereabouts has sought an asylum in Chartres cathedral, where it has found plenty of room and may reside in a state of excellent preservation until it can safely venture abroad again. I supposed I had been in cold churches before, but the delusion had been an injustice to the temperature of Chartres. The nave was full of the little padded chairs of the local bourgeoisie, whose faith, I hope for their comfort, is of the good old red-hot complexion. In a higher temperature I should have done more justice to the magnificent old glass of the windows—which glowed through the icy dusk like the purple and orange of a winter sunset—and to the immense sculptured external casing of the choir. This latter is an extraordinary piece of work. It is a high gothic screen, shutting in the choir, and covered with elaborate bas-reliefs of the sixteenth and seventeenth centuries, representing scenes from the life of Christ and of the Virgin. Some of the figures are admirable, and the effect of the whole great semicircular wall, chiselled like a silver bowl, is superb. There is also a crypt of high antiquity and, I believe, great interest, to be seen; but my teeth chattered a respectful negative to the sacristan who offered to guide me to it. It was so agreeable to stand in the warm outer air again, that I spent the rest of the day in it.

Although, besides its cathedral, Chartres has no very rare architectural treasures, the place is pictorial, in a shabby, third-rate, poverty-stricken degree, and my observations were not unremunerative. There is a little church of Saint-Aignan, of the sixteenth century, with an elegant, decayed façade, and a small tower beside it, lower than its own roof, to which it is joined, in unequal twinship, by a single long buttress. Standing there with its crumbling Renaissance doorway, in a kind of grass-grown alcove, it reminded me of certain monuments that the tourist encounters in small Italian towns. Most of the streets of Chartres are crooked lanes, winding over the face of the steep hill, the summit of the hill being occupied by half a dozen little open squares, which seem like reservoirs of the dulness and stillness that flow through the place. In the midst of one of them rises an old dirty brick obelisk, commemorating the glories of the young General Marceau, of the first Republic—"Soldier at 16, general at 23, he died at 27." Such memorials, when one comes upon them unexpectedly, produce in the mind a series of circular waves of feeling, like a splash in a quiet pond. Chartres gives us an impression of extreme antiquity, but it is an antiquity that has gone down in the world. I saw very few of those stately little hôtels, with pilastered fronts, which look so well in the silent streets of provincial towns. The houses are mostly low, small, and of sordid aspect, and though many of them have overhanging upper stories, and steep, battered gables, they are rather wanting in character. I was struck, as an American always is in small French and English towns, with the immense number of shops, and their brilliant appearance, which seems so out of proportion to any visible body of consumers. At Chartres the shopkeepers must all feed upon each other, for, whoever buys, the whole population sells. This population appeared to consist mainly of several hundred brown old peasant women, in the seventies and eighties, with their faces cross-hatched with wrinkles and their quaint white coifs drawn tightly over their weather-blasted eye-brows. Labour-stricken grandams, all the world over, are the opposite of lovely, for the toil that wrestles for its daily bread, morsel by morsel, is not beautifying; but I thought I had never seen the possibilities of female ugliness so variously embodied as in the crones of Chartres. Some of them were leading small children by the hand—little red-cheeked girls, in the close black caps and black pinafores of humble French infancy—a costume which makes French children always look like orphans. Others were guiding along the flinty lanes the steps of small donkeys, some of them fastened into little carts, some with well-laden backs. These were the only quadrupeds I perceived at Chartres. Neither horse nor carriage did I behold, save at the station the omnibuses of the rival inns—the "Grand Monarque" and the "Duc de Chartres"—which glare at each other across the Grande Place. A friend of mine told me that a few years ago, passing through Chartres, he went by night to call upon a gentleman who lived there. During his visit it came on to rain violently, and when the hour for his departure arrived the rain had made the streets impassable. There was no vehicle to be had, and my friend was resigning himself to a soaking. "You can be taken of course in the sedan-chair," said his host with dignity. The sedan-chair was produced, a couple of serving-men grasped the handles, my friend stepped into it, and went swinging back—through the last century—to the "Grand Monarque." This little anecdote, I imagine, still paints Chartres socially.

Before dinner I took a walk on the planted promenade which encircles the town—the Tour-de-ville it is called—much of which is extremely picturesque. Chartres has lost her walls as a whole, but here and there they survive, and play a desultory part in holding the town together. In one place the rampart is really magnificent—smooth, strong and lofty, curtained with ivy, and supporting on its summit an old convent and its garden. Only one of the city-gates remains—a narrow arch of the fourteenth century, flanked by two admirable round towers, and preceded by a fosse. If you stoop a little, as you stand outside, the arch of this hoary old gate makes a capital setting for the picture of the interior of the town, and, on the inner hill-top, against the sky, the large gray mass of the cathedral. The ditch is full, and to right and to left it flows along the base of the mouldering wall, through which the shabby backs of houses extrude, and which is garnished with little wooden galleries, lavatories of the town's soiled linen. These little galleries are filled with washerwomen, who crane over and dip their many-coloured rags into the yellow stream. The old patched and interrupted wall, the ditch with its weedy edges, the spots of colour, the white-capped laundresses in their little wooden cages—one lingers to look at it all.

Rheims

1877

It was a very little tour, but the charm of the three or four old towns and monuments that it embraced, the beauty of the brilliant October, the pleasure of reminding one's self how much of the interest, strength and dignity of France is to be found outside of that huge pretentious caravansary called Paris (a reminder often needed), these things deserve to be noted. I went down to Rheims to see the famous cathedral, and to reach Rheims I travelled through the early morning hours along the charming valley of the Marne. The Marne is a pretty little green river, the vegetation upon whose banks, otherwise unadorned, had begun to blush with the early frosts in a manner that suggested the autumnal tints of American scenery. The trees and bushes were scarlet and orange; the light was splendid and a trifle harsh; I could have fancied myself immersed in an American "fall," if at intervals some gray old large-towered church had not lifted a sculptured front above a railway-station, to dispel the fond illusion. One of these church-fronts (I saw it only from the train) is particularly impressive; the little cathedral of Meaux, of which the great Bossuet was bishop, and along whose frigid nave he set his eloquence rolling with an impetus which it has not wholly lost to this day. It was entertaining, moreover, to enter the country of champagne; for Rheims is in the ancient province whose later fame is syllabled the world over in popping corks. A land of vineyards is not usually accounted sketchable; but the country about Epernay seemed to me to have a charm of its own. It stretched away in soft undulations that were pricked all over with little stakes muffled in leaves. The effect at a distance was that of vast surfaces, long, subdued billows, of pincushion; and yet it was very pretty. The deep blue sky was over the scene; the undulations were half in sun and half in shade; and here and there, among their myriad bristles, were groups of vintagers, who, though they are in reality, doubtless, a prosaic and mercenary body of labourers, yet assumed, to a fancy that glanced at them in the cursory manner permitted by the passage of the train, the appearance of joyous and disinterested votaries of Bacchus. The blouses of the men, the white caps of the women, were gleaming in the sunshine; they moved about crookedly among the tiny vine-poles. I thought them full of a charming suggestiveness. Of all the delightful gifts of France to the world, this was one of the most agreeable—the keen, living liquid in which the finest flower of sociability is usually dipped. It came from these sunny places; this little maze of curling-sticks supplied the world with half the world's gaiety. I call it little only in relation to the immense number of bottles with gilded necks in which this gaiety is annually stored up. The acreage of the champagne seemed to me, in fact, large; the bristling slopes went rolling away to new horizons in a manner that was positively reassuring. Making the handsomest allowance for the wine manufactured from baser elements, it was apparent that this big corner of a province represents a very large number of bottles.

As you draw near to Rheims the vineyards become

sparser, and finally disappear, a fact not to be regretted, for there is something incongruous in the juxtaposition of champagne and gothic architecture. It may be said, too, that for the proper appreciation of a structure like the cathedral of Rheims you have need of all your head. As, after my arrival, I sat in my window at the inn, gazing up at the great façade, I found something dizzying in the mere climbing and soaring of one's astonished vision; and later, when I came to wander about in the upper regions of the church, and to peep down through the rugged lacework of the towers at the little streets and the small spots of public places, I found myself musing upon the beauty of soberness. My window at the Lion d'Or was like a proscenium-box at the play; to admire the cathedral at my leisure I had only to perch myself in the casement with a good opera-glass. I sat there for a long time watching the great architectural drama. A drama I may call it, for no church-front that I have seen is more animated, more richly figured. The density of the sculptures, the immense scale of the images, detract, perhaps, at first, in a certain sense, from the impressiveness of the cathedral of Rheims; the absence of large surfaces, of ascending lines, deceives you as to the elevation of the front, and the dimensions of some of the upper statues bring them unduly near the eye. But little by little you perceive that this great figured and storied screen has a mass proportionate to its detail, and that it is the grandest part of a structure which, as a whole, is one of the noblest works of man's hands. Most people remember to have seen some print or some photograph of this heavily-charged façade of Rheims, which is usually put forward as the great example of the union of the purity and the possible richness of gothic. I must first have seen some such print in my earliest years, for I have always thought of Rheims as the typical gothic cathedral. I had vague associations with it; it seemed to me that I had already stood there in the little over-whelmed *place*. One's literary associations with Rheims are indeed very vivid and impressive; they begin with the picture of the steel-clad Maid passing under the deeply-sculptured portal with a banner in her hand which she has no need to lower, and while she stands amid the incense and the chants, the glitter of arms and the glow of coloured lights, asking leave of the young king whom she has crowned to turn away and tend her flocks. And after that there is the sense of all the kings of France having travelled down to Rheims in their splendour to be consecrated; the great groups on the front of the church must have looked down on groups almost as stately—groups full of colour and movement—assembled in the square. (The square of Rheims, it must be confessed, is rather shabby. It is singular that the august ceremony of the *sacre* should not have left its mark upon the disposition of the houses, should not have kept them at a respectful distance. Louis XIV, smoothing his plumage before he entered the church, can hardly have had space to swing the train of his coronation-robe.) But when in driving into the town I reached the small precinct, such as it is, and saw the cathedral lift its spireless towers above the long rows of its carven saints, the huge wheel of its window, the three great caverns of its portals, with the high acute pediments above each arch, and the sides abutting outward like the beginning of a pyramid; when I looked at all this I felt that I had carried it in my mind from my earliest years, and that the stately vision had been implanted there by some forgotten glimpse of an old-fashioned water-colour sketch, in which the sky was washed in with expressive splashes, the remoter parts of the church tinted with a fascinating blueness, and the foundations represented as encumbered with little gabled and cross-timbered houses, inhabited by women in red petticoats and curious caps.

I shall not attempt any regular enumeration of the great

details of the façade of Rheims; I cannot profess even to have fully apprehended them. They are a glorious company, and here and there, on its high-hung pedestal, one of the figures detaches itself with peculiar effectiveness. Over the central portal sits the Virgin Mary, meekly submitting her head to the ponderous crown which her Son prepares to place upon it. The attitude and movement of Christ are full of a kind of splendid politeness. The three great doorways are in themselves a museum of imagery, disposed in each case in five close tiers, the statues in each of the tiers packed perpendicularly against their comrades. The effect of these great hollowed and chiselled recesses is extremely striking; they are a proper vestibule to the dusky richness of the interior. The cathedral of Rheims, more fortunate than many of its companions, appears not to have suffered from the iconoclasts of the Revolution; I noticed no absent heads nor broken noses. It is very true that these members may have had adventures to which they do not, as it were, allude. But, like many of its companions, it is so pressed upon by neighbouring houses that it is not easy to get a general view of the sides and the rear. You may walk round it, and note your walk as a long one; you may observe that the choir of the church travels back almost into another quarter of the city; you may see the far-spreading mass lose itself for a while in parasitic obstructions, and then emerge again with all its buttresses flying; but you miss that wide margin of space and light which should enable it to present itself as a consistent picture. Pictures have their frames, and poems have their margins; a great work of art, such as a gothic cathedral, should at least have elbow-room. You may, however, stroll beneath the walls of Rheims, along a narrow, dark street, and look up at the mighty structure and see its higher parts foreshortened into all kinds of delusive proportions. There is a grand entertainment in the view of the church which you obtain from the farthermost point to which you may recede from it in the rear, keeping it still within sight. I have never seen a cathedral so magnificently buttressed. The buttresses of Rheims are all double; they have a tremendous spring, and are supported upon pedestals surmounted by immense crocketed canopies containing statues of wide-winged angels. A great balustrade of gothic arches connects these canopies one with another, and along this balustrade are perched strange figures of sitting beasts, unicorns and mermaids, griffins and monstrous owls. Huge, terrible gargoyles hang far over into the street, and doubtless some of them have a detail which I afterwards noticed at Laon. The gargoyle represents a grotesque beast—a creature partaking at once of the shape of a bird, a fish, and a quadruped. At Laon, on either side of the main entrance, a long-bellied monster cranes forth into the air with the head of a hippopotamus; and under its belly crouches a little man, hardly less grotesque, making up a rueful grimace and playing some ineffectual trick upon his terrible companion. One of these little figures has plunged a sword, up to the hilt, into the belly of the monster above him, so that when he draws it forth there will be a leak in the great stone gutter; another has suspended himself to a rope that is knotted round the neck of the gargoyle, and is trying in the same manner to interrupt its functions by pulling the cord as tight as possible. There was sure to be a spirit of life in an architectural conception that could range from the combination of clustering towers and opposing fronts to this infinitely minute play of humour.

There is no great play of humour in the interior of Rheims, but there is a great deal of beauty and solemnity. This interior is a spectacle that excites the sensibility, as our forefathers used to say; but it is not an easy matter to describe. It is no description of it to say that it is four hundred and sixty-six feet in length, and that the roof is one hundred and twenty-four feet above the pavement; nor is there any very vivid portraiture in the statement that if there is no coloured glass in the lower windows, there is, *per contra,* a great deal of the most gorgeous and most ancient in the upper ones. The long sweep of the nave, from the threshold to the point where the coloured light-shafts of the choir lose themselves in the gray distance, is a triumph of perpendicular perspective. The white light in the lower part of Rheims really contributes to the picturesqueness of the interior. It makes the gloom above look richer still, and throws that part of the roof which rests upon the gigantic piers of the transepts into mysterious remoteness. I wandered about for a long time; I sat first in one place and then in another; I attached myself to that most fascinating part of every great church, the angle at which the nave and transept divide. It was the better to observe this interesting point, I think, that I passed into the side gate of the choir—the gate that stood ajar in the tall gilded railing. I sat down on a stool near the threshold; I leaned back against the side of one of the stalls; the church was empty, and I lost myself in the large perfection of the place. I lost myself, but the beadle found me; he stood before me, and with a silent, imperious gesture, motioned me to depart. I risked an argumentative glance, whereupon he signified his displeasure, repeated his gesture, and pointed to an old gentleman with a red cape, who had come into the choir softly, without my seeing him, and had seated himself in one of the stalls. This old gentleman seemed plunged in pious thoughts; I was not, after all, very near him, and he did not look as if I disturbed him. A canon is at any time, I imagine, a more merciful man than a beadle. But of course I obeyed the beadle, and eliminated myself from this peculiarly sacred precinct. I found another chair, and I fell to admiring the cathedral again. But this time I think it was with a difference—a difference which may serve as an excuse for the triviality of my anecdote. Sundry other old gentlemen in red capes emerged from the sacristy and went into the choir; presently, when there were half a dozen, they began to chant, and I perceived that the impending vespers had been the reason of my expulsion. This was highly proper, and I forgave the beadle; but I was not so happy as before, for my thoughts had passed out of the architectural channel into—what shall I say?—into the political. Here they found nothing so sweet to feed upon. It was the 5th of October; ten days later the elections for the new Chamber were to take place—the Chamber which was to replace the Assembly dissolved on the 16th of May by Marshal MacMahon, on a charge of "latent" radicalism. Stranger though one was, it was impossible not to be much interested in the triumph of the republican cause; it was impossible not to sympathise with this supreme effort of a brilliant and generous people to learn the lesson of national self-control and self-government. It was impossible, by the same token, not to have noted and detested the alacrity with which the Catholic party had rallied to the reactionary cause, and the unction with which the clergy had converted itself into the go-betweens of Bonapartism. The clergy was giving daily evidence of its devotion to arbitrary rule and to every iniquity that shelters itself behind the mask of "authority." These had been frequent and irritating reflections; they lurked in the folds of one's morning paper. They came back to me in the midst of that tranquil grandeur of Rheims, as I listened to the droning of the old gentlemen in the red capes. Some of the canons, it was painful to observe, had not been punctual; they came hurrying out of the sacristy after the service had begun. They looked like amiable and venerable men; their chanting and droning, as it spread itself under the great arches, was not disagreeable to listen to; I could certainly bear them no grudge. But their presence there was distracting and vexatious; it had spoiled my enjoyment of their church, in which I doubtless had no business. It had set me thinking of the activity and vivacity of the great organisation to which they belonged, and of all the odious things it would have done before the 15th of October. To what base uses do we come at last! It was this same organisation that had erected the magnificent structure around and above me, and which had then seemed an image of generosity and benignant power. Such an edifice might at times make one feel tenderly sentimental toward the Catholic church—make one remember how many of the great achievements of the past we owe to her. To lapse gently into this state of mind seems indeed always, while one strolls about a great cathedral, a proper recognition of its hospitality; but now I had lapsed gently out of it, and it was one of the exasperating elements of the situation that I felt, in a manner, called upon to decide how far such a lapse was unbecoming. I found myself even extending the question a little, and picturing to myself that conflict which must often occur at such a moment as the present—which is actually going on, doubtless, in many thousands of minds—between the actively, practically liberal instinct and what one may call the historic, æsthetic sense, the sense upon which old cathedrals lay a certain palpable obligation. How far should a lover of old cathedrals let his hands be tied by the sanctity of their traditions? How far should he let his imagination bribe him, as it were, from action? This of course is a question for each man to answer for himself; but as I sat listening to the drowsy old canons of Rheims, I was visited, I scarcely know why, by a kind of revelation of the anti-Catholic passion, as it must burn to-day in the breasts of certain radicals. I felt that such persons must be intent upon war to the death; how that must seem the most sacred of all duties. Can anything, in the line of action, for a votary of the radical creed, be more sacred? I asked myself; and can any instruments be too trenchant? I raised my eyes again to the dusky splendour of the upper aisles and measured their enchanting perspective, and it was with a sense of doing them full justice that I gave my fictive liberal my good wishes.

This little operation restored my equanimity, so that I climbed several hundred steps and wandered lightly over the roof of the cathedral. Climbing into cathedral-towers and gaping at the size of the statues that look small from the street has always seemed to me a rather brutal pastime; it is not the proper way to treat a beautiful building; it is like holding one's nose so close to a picture that one sees only the grain of the canvas. But when once I had emerged into the upper wilderness of Rheims the discourse of a very urbane and appreciative old bell-ringer, whom I found lurking behind some gigantic excrescence, gave an æsthetic complexion to what would otherwise have been a rather vulgar fest of gymnastics. It was very well to see what a great cathedral is made of, and in these high places of the immensity of Rheims I found the matter very impressively illustrated. I wandered for half an hour over endless expanses of roof, along the edge of sculptured abysses, through hugely-timbered attics and chambers that were in themselves as high as churches. I stood knee-high to strange images, of unsuspected proportions, and I followed the topmost staircase of one of the towers, which curls upward like the groove of a corkscrew, and gives you at the summit a hint of how a sailor feels at the masthead. The ascent was worth making to learn the fulness of beauty of the church, the solidity and perfection, the mightiness of arch and buttress, the latent ingenuity of detail. At the angles of the balustrade which ornaments the roof of the choir are perched a series of huge sitting eagles, which from below, as you look up at them, produce a great effect. They are immense, grim-looking birds, and the sculptor has given to each of them a pair of very neatly carved human legs, terminating in talons. Why did he give them human legs? Why did he indulge in this ridiculous conceit? I am unable to say, but the conceit afforded me pleasure. It seemed to tell of an imagination always at play, fond of the unexpected and delighting in its labour.

From "Rheims and Laon" (1878)

Tours

1882

I

I am ashamed to begin with saying that Touraine is the garden of France; that remark has long ago lost its bloom. The town of Tours, however, has something sweet and bright, which suggests that it is surrounded by a land of fruits. It is a very agreeable little city; few towns of its size are more ripe, more complete, or, I should suppose, in better humor with themselves and less disposed to envy the responsibilities of bigger places. It is truly the capital of its smiling province; a region of easy abundance, of good living, of genial, comfortable, optimistic, rather indolent opinions. Balzac says in one of his tales that the real Tourangeau will not make an effort, or displace himself even, to go in search of a pleasure; and it is not difficult to understand the sources of this amiable cynicism. He must have a vague conviction that he can only lose by almost any change. Fortune has been kind to him: he lives in a temperate, reasonable, sociable climate, on the banks of a river which, it is true, sometimes floods the country around it, but of which the ravages appear to be so easily repaired that its aggressions may perhaps be regarded (in a region where so many good things are certain) merely as an occasion for healthy suspense. He is surrounded by fine old traditions, religious, social, architectural, culinary; and he may have the satisfaction of feeling that he is French to the core. No part of his admirable country is more characteristically national. Normandy is Normandy, Burgundy is Burgundy, Provence is Provence; but Touraine is essentially France. It is the land of Rabelais, of Descartes, of Balzac, of good books and good company, as well as good dinners and good houses. George Sand has somewhere a charming passage about the mildness, the convenient quality, of the physical conditions of central France—"son climat souple et chaud, ses pluies abondantes et courtes." In the autumn of 1882 the rains perhaps were less short than abundant; but when the days were fine it was impossible that anything in the way of weather could be more charming. The vineyards and orchards looked rich in the fresh, gay light; cultivation was everywhere, but everywhere it seemed to be easy. There was no visible poverty; thrift and success presented themselves as matters of good taste. The white caps of the women glittered in the sunshine, and their well-made sabots clicked cheerfully on the hard, clean roads. Touraine is a land of old châteaux,—a gallery of architectural specimens and of large hereditary properties. The peasantry have less of the luxury of ownership than in most other parts of France; though they have enough of it to give them quite their share of that shrewdly conservative look which, in the little chaffering *place* of the market-town, the stranger observes so often in the wrinkled brown masks that surmount the agricultural blouse. This is, moreover, the heart of the old French monarchy; and as that monarchy was splendid and picturesque, a reflection of the splendor still glitters in the current of the Loire. Some of the most striking events of French history have occurred on the banks of that river, and the soil it waters bloomed for a while with the flowering of the Renaissance. The Loire gives a great "style" to a landscape of which the features are not, as the phrase is, prominent, and carries the eye to distances even more poetic than the green horizons of Touraine. It is a very fitful stream, and is sometimes observed to run thin and expose all the crudities of its channel,—a great defect certainly in a river which is so much depended upon to give an air to the place it waters. But I speak of it as I saw it last; full, tranquil, powerful, bending in large slow curves, and sending back half the light of the sky. Nothing can be finer than the view of its course which you get from the battlements and terraces of Amboise. As I looked down on it from that elevation one lovely Sunday morning through a mild glitter of autumn sunshine, it seemed the very model of a generous, beneficent stream. The most charming part of Tours is naturally the shaded quay that overlooks it, and looks across too at the friendly faubourg of Saint Symphorien and at the terraced heights which rise above this. Indeed, throughout Touraine it is half the charm of the Loire that you can travel beside it. The great dyke which protects it, or protects the country from it, from Blois to Angers, is an admirable road; and on the other side as well the highway constantly keeps it company. A wide river, as you follow a wide road, is excellent company; it brightens and shortens the way.

The inns at Tours are in another quarter, and one of them, which is midway between the town and the station, is very good. It is worth mentioning for the fact that every one belonging to it is extraordinarily polite—so unnaturally polite as at first to excite your suspicion that the hotel has some hidden vice, so that the waiters and chambermaids are trying to pacify you in advance. There was one waiter in especial who was the most accomplished social being I have ever encountered; from morning till night he kept up an inarticulate murmur of urbanity, like the hum of a spinning-top. I may add that I discovered no dark secrets at the Hôtel de l'Univers; for it is not a secret to any traveler to-day that the obligation to partake of a lukewarm dinner in an overheated room is as imperative as it is detestable. For the rest, at Tours, there is a certain Rue Royale which has pretensions to the monumental; it was constructed a hundred years ago, and the houses, all alike, have on a moderate scale a pompous eighteenth-century look. It connects the Palais de Justice, the most important secular building in the town, with the long bridge which spans the Loire—the spacious, solid bridge pronounced by Balzac, in *Le Curé de Tours,* "one of the finest monuments of French architecture." The Palais de Justice was the seat of the Government of Léon Gambetta in the autumn of 1870, after the dictator had been obliged to retire in his balloon from Paris and before the Assembly was constituted at Bordeaux. The Germans occupied Tours during that terrible winter; it is astonishing, the number of places the Germans occupied. It is hardly too much to say that wherever one goes in certain parts of France, one encounters two great historic facts: one is the Revolution; the other is the German invasion. The traces of the Revolution remain in a hundred scars and bruises and mutilations, but the visible marks of the war of 1870 have passed away. The country is so rich, so living, that she has been able to dress her wounds, to hold up her head, to smile again; so that the shadow of that darkness has ceased to rest upon her. But what you do not see you still may hear; and one remembers with a certain shudder that only a few short years ago this province, so intimately French, was under the heel of a foreign foe. To be intimately French was apparently not a safeguard; for so successful an invader it could only be a challenge. Peace and plenty, however, have succeeded that episode; and among the gardens and vineyards of Touraine it seems only a legend the more in a country of legends.

It was not, all the same, for the sake of this checkered story that I mentioned the Palais de Justice and the Rue Royale. The most interesting fact, to my mind, about the high-street of Tours was that as you walk toward the bridge on the right hand *trottoir* you can look up at the house, on the other side of the way, in which Honoré de Balzac first saw the light. That violent and complicated genius was a child of the good-humored and succulent Touraine. There is something anomalous in this fact, though, if one thinks about it a little, one may discover certain correspondences between his character and that of his native province. Strenuous, laborious, constantly infelicitous in spite of his great successes, he suggests at times a very different set of influences. But he had his jovial, full-feeding side,—the side that comes out in the *Contes Drolatiques,* which are the romantic and epicurean chronicle of the old manors and abbeys of this region. And he was moreover the product of a soil into which a great deal of history had been trodden. Balzac was genuinely as well as affectedly monarchical, and he was saturated with a sense of the past. Number 39 Rue Royale—of which the basement, like all the basements in the Rue Royale, is occupied by a shop—is not shown to the public; and I know not whether tradition designates the chamber in which the author of *Le Lys dans la Vallée* opened his eyes into a world in which he was to see and to imagine such extraordinary things. If this were the case I would willingly have crossed its threshold; not for the sake of any relic of the great novelist which it may possibly contain, nor even for that of any mystic virtue which may be supposed to reside within its walls, but simply because to look at those four modest walls can hardly fail to give one a strong impression of the force of human endeavor. Balzac, in the maturity of his vision, took in more of human life than any one, since Shakespeare, who has attempted to tell us stories about it; and the very small scene on which his consciousness dawned is one end of the immense scale that he traversed. I confess it shocked me a little to find that he was born in a house "in a row,"—a house, moreover, which at the date of his birth must have been only about twenty years old. All that is contradictory. If the tenement selected for this honor could not be ancient and embrowned, it should at least have been detached.

There is a charming description in his little tale of *La Grenadière* of the view of the opposite side of the Loire as you have it from the square at the end of the Rue Royale, —a square that has some pretensions to grandeur, overlooked as it is by the Hôtel de Ville and the Musée, a pair of edifices which directly contemplate the river, and ornamented with marble images of François Rabelais and René Descartes. The former, erected a few years since, is a very honorable production; the pedestal of the latter could, as a matter of course, only be inscribed with the *Cogito ergo Sum*. The two statues mark the two opposite poles to which the wondrous French mind has traveled; and if there were an effigy of Balzac at Tours it ought to stand midway between them. Not that he by any means always struck the happy mean between the sensible and the metaphysical; but one may say of him that half of his genius looks in one direction and half in the other. The side that turns toward François Rabelais would be, on the whole, the side that takes the sun. But there is no statue of Balzac at Tours; there is only in one of the chambers of the melancholy museum a rather clever, coarse bust. The description in *La Grenadière* of which I just spoke is too long to quote; neither have I space for any one of the brilliant attempts at landscape-painting which are woven into the shimmering texture of *Le Lys dans la Vallée*. The little manor of Clochegourde, the residence of Madame de Mortsauf, the heroine of that extraordinary work, was within a moderate walk of Tours, and the picture in the novel is presumably a copy from an original which it would be possible to-day to discover. I did not, however, even make the attempt. There are so many châteaux in Touraine commemorated in history that it would take one too far to look up those which have been commemorated in fiction. The most I did was to endeavor to identify the former residence of Mademoiselle Gamard, the sinister old maid of *Le Curé de Tours*. This terrible woman occupied a small house in the rear of the cathedral, where I spent a whole morning in wondering rather stupidly which house it could be. To reach the cathedral from the little *place* where we stopped just now to look across at the Grenadière, without, it must be confessed, very vividly seeing it, you follow the quay to the right and pass out of sight of the charming *côteau* which, from beyond the river, faces the town—a soft agglomeration of gardens, vineyards, scattered villas, gables and turrets of slate-roofed châteaux, terraces with gray balustrades, moss-grown walls draped in scarlet Virginia-creeper. You turn into the town again beside a great military barrack which is ornamented with a rugged mediæval tower, a relic of the ancient fortifications, known to the Tourangeaux of to-day as the Tour de Guise. The young Prince of Joinville, son of that Duke of Guise who was murdered by the order of Henry II at Blois, was, after the death of his father confined here for more than two years, but made his escape one summer evening in 1591, under the nose of his keepers, with a gallant audacity which has attached the memory of the exploit to his sullen-looking prison. Tours has a garrison of five regiments, and the little red-legged soldiers light up the town. You see them stroll upon the clean, uncommercial quay, where there are no signs of navigation, not even by oar, no barrels nor bales, no loading nor unloading, no masts against the sky nor booming of steam in the air. The most active business that goes on there is that patient and fruitless angling in which the French, as the votaries of art for art, excel all other people. The little soldiers, weighed down by the contents of their enormous pockets, pass with respect from one of these masters of the rod to the other, as he sits soaking an indefinite bait in the large indifferent stream. After you turn your back to the quay you have only to go a little way before you reach the cathedral.

II

Tours: The Cathedral

It is a very beautiful church of the second order of importance, with a charming mouse-colored complexion and a pair of fantastic towers. There is a commodious little square in front of it, from which you may look up at its very ornamental face; but for purposes of frank admiration the sides and the rear are perhaps not sufficiently detached. The cathedral of Tours, which is dedicated to Saint Gatianus, took a long time to build. Begun in 1170, it was finished only in the first half of the sixteenth century; but the ages and the weather have interfused so well the tone of the different parts that it presents, at first at least, no striking incongruities, and looks even exceptionally harmonious and complete. There are many grander cathedrals, but there are probably few more pleasing; and this effect of delicacy and grace is at its best towards the close of a quiet afternoon, when the densely decorated towers, rising above the little Place de l'Archevêché, lift their curious lanterns into the slanting light and offer a multitudinous perch to troops of circling pigeons. The whole front, at such a time, has an appearance of great richness, although the niches which surround the three high doors (with recesses deep enough for several circles of sculpture) and indent the four great buttresses that ascend beside the huge rose-window, carry no figures beneath their little chiseled canopies. The blast of the great Revolution blew down most of the statues in France, and the wind has never set very strongly towards putting them up again. The embossed and crocketed cupolas which crown the towers of Saint Gatien are not very pure in taste; but, like a good many impurities, they have a certain character. The interior has a stately slimness with which no fault is to be found and which in the choir, rich in early glass and surrounded by a broad passage, becomes very bold and noble. Its principal treasure perhaps is the charming little tomb of the two children (who died young) of Charles VIII and Anne of Brittany, in white marble embossed with symbolic dolphins and exquisite arabesques. The little boy and girl lie side by side on a slab of black marble, and a pair of small kneeling angels, both at their head and at their feet, watch over them. Nothing could be more elegant than this monument, which is the work of Michel Colomb, one of the earlier glories of the French Renaissance; it is really a lesson in good taste. Originally placed in the great abbey-church of Saint Martin, which was for so many ages the holy place of Tours, it happily survived the devastation to which that edifice, already sadly shattered by the wars of religion and successive profanations, finally succumbed in 1797. In 1815 the tomb found an asylum in a quiet corner of the cathedral.

I ought perhaps to be ashamed to acknowledge that I found the profane name of Balzac capable of adding an interest even to this venerable sanctuary. Those who have read the terrible little story of *Le Curé de Tours* will perhaps remember that, as I have already mentioned, the simple and childlike old Abbé Birotteau, victim of the infernal machinations of the Abbé Troubert and Mademoiselle Gamard, had his quarters in the house of that lady (she had a specialty of letting lodgings to priests), which stood on the north side of the cathedral, so close under its walls that the supporting pillar of one of the great flying buttresses was planted in the spinster's garden. If you wander round behind the church in search of this more than historic habitation you will have occasion to see that the side and rear of Saint Gatien make a delectable and curious figure. A narrow lane passes beside the high wall which conceals from sight the palace of the archbishop and beneath the flying buttresses, the far-projecting gargoyles, and the fine south porch of the church. It terminates in a little dead grass-grown square entitled the Place Grégoire de Tours. All this part of the exterior of the cathedral is very brown, ancient, Gothic, grotesque; Balzac calls the whole place "a desert of stone." A battered and gabled wing or out-house (as it appears to be) of the hidden palace, with a queer old stone pulpit jutting out from it, looks down on this melancholy spot, on the other side of which is a seminary for young priests, one of whom issues from a door in a quiet corner, and, holding it open a moment behind him, shows a glimpse of a sunny garden, where you may fancy other black young figures strolling up and down. Mademoiselle Gamard's house, where she took her two abbés to board, and basely conspired with one against the other, is still further round the cathedral. You cannot quite put your hand upon it to-day, for the dwelling of which you say to yourself that it must have been Mademoiselle Gamard's does not fulfill all the conditions mentioned in Balzac's description. The edifice in question, however, fulfills conditions enough; in particular, its little court offers hospitality to the big buttress of the church. Another buttress, corresponding with this (the two, between them, sustain the gable of the north transept), is planted in the small cloister, of which the door on the further side of the little soundless Rue de la Psalette, where nothing seems ever to pass, opens opposite to that of Mademoiselle Gamard. There is a very genial old sacristan, who introduced me to this cloister from the church. It is very small and solitary, and much mutilated; but it nestles with a kind of wasted friendliness beneath the big walls of the cathedral. Its lower arcades have been closed, and it has a small plot of garden in the middle, with fruit-trees which I should imagine to be too much overshadowed. In one corner is a remarkably picturesque turret, the cage of a winding staircase which ascends (no great distance) to an upper gallery, where an old priest, the *chanoine-gardien* of the church, was walking to and fro with his breviary. The turret, the gallery, and even the chanoine-gardien, belonged, that sweet September morning, to the class of objects that are dear to painters in water-colors.

The first three essays in this section —"Occasional Paris," "Chartres," and "Rheims"—are dated as James dates them in Portraits of Places *(1883 [1884]). The above essays on "Tours" and those following, first published in* The Atlantic Monthly *in 1883–84, and included in* A Little Tour in France *(1885 [1884]), are dated 1882 because that was the year of James's autumn tour in France.*

Toulouse

1882

I

There is much entertainment in the journey through the wide, smiling garden of Gascony; I speak of it as I took it in going from Bordeaux to Toulouse. It is the south, quite the south, and had for the present narrator its full measure of the charm he is always determined to find in countries that may even by courtesy be said to appertain to the sun. It was, moreover, the happy and genial view of these mild latitudes, which, goodness knows, often have a dreariness of their own; a land teeming with corn and wine, and speaking everywhere (that is, everywhere the phylloxera had not laid it waste) of wealth and plenty. The road runs constantly near the Garonne, touching now and then its slow, brown, rather sullen stream, a sullenness that incloses great dangers and disasters. The traces of the horrible floods of 1875 have disappeared, and the land smiles placidly enough while it waits for another immersion. Toulouse, at the period I speak of, was up to its middle (and in places above it) in water, and looks still as if it had been thoroughly soaked—as if it had faded and shriveled with a long steeping. The fields and copses, of course, are more forgiving. The railway line follows as well the charming Canal du Midi, which is as pretty as a river, barring the straightness, and here and there occupies the foreground, beneath a screen of dense, tall trees, while the Garonne takes a larger and more irregular course a little way beyond it. People who are fond of canals—and, speaking from the pictorial standpoint, I hold the taste to be most legitimate—will delight in this admirable specimen of the class, which has a very interesting history, not to be narrated here. On the other side of the road (the left), all the way, runs a long, low line of hills, or rather one continuous hill, or perpetual cliff, with a straight top, in the shape of a ledge of rock, which might pass for a ruined wall. I am afraid the reader will lose patience with my habit of constantly referring to the landscape of Italy as if that were the measure of the beauty of every other. Yet I am still more afraid that I cannot apologize for it and must leave it in its culpable nakedness. It is an idle habit; but the reader will long since have discovered that this was an idle journey, and that I give my impressions as they came to me. It came to me then that in all this view there was something transalpine, with a greater smartness and freshness and much less elegance and languor. This impression was occasionally deepened by the appearance, on the long eminence of which I speak, of a village, a church, a château, that seemed to look down at the plain from over the ruined wall. The perpetual vines, the bright-faced, flat-roofed houses, covered with tiles, the softness and sweetness of the light and air, recalled the prosier portions of the Lombard plain. Toulouse itself has a little of this Italian expression, but not enough to give a color to its dark, dirty, crooked streets, which are irregular without being eccentric, and which, if it were not for the superb church of Saint-Sernin, would be quite destitute of monuments.

I have already alluded to the way in which the names

of certain places impose themselves on the mind, and I must add that of Toulouse to the list of expressive appellations. It certainly evokes a vision—suggests something highly *méridional*. But the city, it must be confessed, is less pictorial than the word, in spite of the Place du Capitole, in spite of the quay of the Garonne, in spite of the curious cloister of the old museum. What justifies the images that are latent in the word is not the aspect, but the history, of the town. The hotel to which the well-advised traveler will repair stands in a corner of the Place du Capitole, which is the heart and centre of Toulouse, and which bears a vague and inexpensive resemblance to Piazza Castello at Turin. The Capitol, with a wide modern face, occupies one side, and, like the palace at Turin, looks across at a high arcade, under which the hotels, the principal shops, and the lounging citizens are gathered. The shops are probably better than the Turinese, but the people are not so good. Stunted, shabby, rather vitiated looking, they have none of the personal richness of the sturdy Piedmontese; and I will take this occasion to remark that in the course of a journey of several weeks in the French provinces I rarely encountered a well-dressed male. Can it be possible that republics are unfavorable to a certain attention to one's boots and one's beard? I risk this somewhat futile inquiry because the proportion of neat coats and trousers seemed to be about the same in France and in my native land. It was notably lower than in England and in Italy, and even warranted the supposition that most good provincials have their chin shaven and their boots blacked but once a week. I hasten to add, lest my observation should apear to be of a sadly superficial character, that the manners and conversation of these gentlemen bore (whenever I had occasion to appreciate them) no relation to the state of their chin and their boots. They were almost always marked by an extreme amenity. At Toulouse there was the strongest temptation to speak to people simply for the entertainment of hearing them reply with that curious, that fascinating accent of the Languedoc, which appears to abound in final consonants and leads the Toulousians to say *bien-g* and *maison-g* like Englishmen learning French. It is as if they talked with their teeth rather than with their tongue. I find in my note-book a phrase in regard to Toulouse which is perhaps a little ill-natured, but which I will transcribe as it stands: "The oddity is that the place should be both animated and dull. A big, brown-skinned population, clattering about in a flat, tortuous town, which produces nothing whatever that I can discover. Except the church of Saint-Sernin and the fine old court of the Hôtel d'Assézat, Toulouse has no architecture; the houses are for the most part of brick, of a grayish-red color, and have no particular style. The brickwork of the place is in fact very poor—inferior to that of the North Italian towns, and quite wanting in the wealth of tone which this homely material takes on in general in the climates of dampness and greenness." And then my note-book goes on to narrate a little visit to the Capitol, which was soon made, as the building was in course of repair and half the rooms were closed.

II

Toulouse: The Capitol

The history of Toulouse is detestable, saturated with blood and perfidy; and the ancient custom of the Floral Games, grafted upon all sorts of internecine traditions, seems, with its false pastoralism, its mock chivalry, its display of fine feelings, to set off rather than to mitigate these horrors. The society was founded in the fourteenth century, and it has held annual meetings ever since—meetings at which poems in the fine old *langue d'oc* are declaimed and a blushing laureate is chosen. This business takes place in the Capitol, before the chief magistrate of the town, who is known as the *capitoul,* and of all the pretty women as well—a class very numerous at Toulouse. It is unusual to present a finer person than that of the portress who pretended to show me the apartments in which the Floral Games are held; a big, brown, expansive woman, still in the prime of life, with a speaking eye, an extraordinary assurance, and a pair of magenta stockings, which were inserted into the neatest and most polished little black sabots, and which, as she clattered up the stairs before me, lavishly displaying them, made her look like the heroine of an *opéra-bouffe.* Her talk was all in *n*'s, *g*'s and *d*'s, and in mute *e*'s strongly accented, as *autré, thêâtré, splendidé*—the last being an epithet she applied to everything the Capitol contained, and especially to a horrible picture representing the famous Clémence Isaure, the reputed foundress of the poetical contest, presiding on one of these occasions. I wondered whether Clémence Isaure had been anything like this terrible Toulousaine of to-day, who would have been a capital figure-head for a floral game. The lady in whose honor the picture I have just mentioned was painted is a somewhat mythical personage, and she is not to be found in the *Biographie Universelle.* She is, however, a very graceful myth; and if she never existed her statue at least does—a shapeless effigy transferred to the Capitol from the so-called tomb of Clémence in the old church of La Daurade. The great hall in which the Floral Games are held was encumbered with scaffoldings, and I was unable to admire the long series of busts of the bards who have won prizes and the portraits of all the capitouls of Toulouse. As a compensation I was introduced to a big bookcase filled with the poems that have been crowned since the days of the troubadours (a portentous collection), and the big butcher's knife with which, according to the legend,

Henry, Duke of Montmorency, who had conspired against the great cardinal with Gaston of Orleans and Mary de' Medici, was, in 1632, beheaded on this spot by the order of Richelieu. With these objects the interest of the Capitol was exhausted. The building indeed has not the grandeur of its name, which is a sort of promise that the visitor will find some sensible embodiment of the old Roman tradition that once flourished in this part of France. It is inferior in impressiveness to the other three famous Capitols of the modern world—that of Rome (if I may call the present structure modern) and those of Washington and Albany!

The only Roman remains at Toulouse are to be found in the museum—a very interesting establishment, which I was condemned to see as imperfectly as I had seen the Capitol. It was being rearranged; and the gallery of paintings, which is the least interesting feature, was the only part that was not upside-down. The pictures are mainly of the modern French school, and I remember nothing but a powerful though disagreeable specimen of Henner, who paints the human body, and paints it so well, with a brush dipped in blackness; and, placed among the paintings, a bronze replica of the charming young David of Mercié. These things have been set out in the church of an old monastery, long since suppressed, and the rest of the collection occupies the cloisters. These are two in number—a small one, which you enter first from the street, and a very vast and elegant one beyond it, which with its light gothic arches and slim columns (of the fourteenth century), its broad walk, its little garden with old tombs and statues in the centre, is by far the most picturesque, the most sketchable, spot in Toulouse. It must be doubly so when the Roman busts, inscriptions, slabs, and sarcophagi are ranged along the walls; it must indeed (to compare small things with great, and as the judicious Murray remarks) bear a certain resemblance to the Campo Santo at Pisa. But these things are absent now; the cloister is a litter of confusion, and its treasures have been stowed away confusedly in sundry inaccessible rooms. The custodian attempted to console me by telling me that when they are exhibited again it will be on a scientific basis and with an order and regularity of which they were formerly innocent. But I was not consoled. I wanted simply the spectacle, the picture, and I didn't care in the least for the classification. Old Roman fragments exposed to light in the open air, under a southern sky, in a quadrangle round a garden, have an immortal charm simply in their general effect; and the charm is all the greater when the soil of the very place has yielded them up.

III

Toulouse: Saint-Sernin

My real consolation was an hour I spent in Saint-Sernin, one of the noblest churches in southern France, and easily the first among those of Toulouse. This great structure, a masterpiece of twelfth-century romanesque and dedicated to Saint Saturninus—the Toulousians have abbreviated—is, I think, alone worth a journey to Toulouse. What makes it so is the extraordinary seriousness of its interior; no other term occurs to me as expressing so well the character of its clear gray nave. As a general thing I favor little the fashion of attributing moral qualities to buildings; I shrink from talking about tender cornices and sincere campanili; but one feels that one can scarce get on without imputing some sort of morality to Saint-Sernin. As it stands to-day the church has been completely restored by Viollet-le-Duc. The exterior is of brick and has little charm save that of a tower of four rows of arches, narrowing together as they ascend. The nave is of great length and height, the barrel roof of stone, the effect of the round arches and pillars in the triforium especially fine. There are two low aisles on either side. The choir is very deep and narrow; it seems to close together and looks as if it were meant for intensely earnest rites. The transepts are most noble, especially the arches of the second tier. The whole church is narrow for its length and is singularly complete and homogeneous. As I say all this I feel that I quite fail to give an impression of its manly gravity, its strong proportions, or of the lonesome look of its renovated stones, as I sat there while the October twilight gathered. It is a real work of art, a high conception. The crypt, into which I was eventually led captive by an importunate sacristan, is quite another affair, though indeed I suppose it may also be spoken of as a work of art. It is a rich museum of relics, and contains the head of Saint Thomas Aquinas wrapped up in a napkin and exhibited in a glass case. The sacristan took a lamp and guided me about, presenting me to one saintly remnant after another. The impression was grotesque, but some of the objects were contained in curious old cases of beaten silver and brass; these things, at least, which looked as if they had been transmitted from the early church, were venerable. There was, however, a kind of wholesale sanctity about the place which overshot the mark; it pretends to be one of the holiest spots in the world. The effect is spoiled by the way the sacristans hang about and offer to take you into it for ten sous—I was accosted by two and escaped from another—and by the familiar manner in which you pop in and out. This episode rather broke the charm of Saint-Sernin, so that I took my departure and went in search of the cathedral. It was scarcely worth finding, and struck me as an odd, dislocated fragment. The front consists only of a portal, beside which a tall brick tower of a later period has been erected. The nave was wrapped in dimness, with a few scattered lamps. I could only distinguish an immense vault, like a high cavern, without aisles. Here and there in the gloom was a kneeling figure; the whole place was mysterious and lopsided. The choir was curtained off; it appeared not to correspond with the nave—that is, not to have the same axis. The only other ecclesiastical impression I gathered at Toulouse came to me in the church of La Daurade, of which the front, on the quay by the Garonne, was closed with scaffoldings; so that one entered it from behind, where it is completely masked by houses, through a door which has at first no traceable connection with it. It is a vast, high, modernized, heavily decorated church, dimly lighted at all times, I should suppose, and enriched by the shades of evening at the time I looked into it. I perceived that it consisted mainly of a large square, beneath a dome, in the centre of which a single person—a lady—was praying with the utmost absorption. The manner of access to the church interposed such an obstacle to the outer profanities that I had a sense of intruding and presently withdrew, carrying with me a picture of the vast, still interior, the gilded roof gleaming in the twilight and the solitary worshiper. What was she praying for, and was she not almost afraid to remain there alone?

For the rest the picturesque at Toulouse consists principally of the walk beside the Garonne, which is spanned, to the faubourg of Saint-Cyprien, by a stout brick bridge. This hapless suburb, the baseness of whose site is noticeable, lay for days under the water at the time of the last inundations. The Garonne had almost mounted to the roofs of the houses, and the place continues to present a blighted, frightened look. Two or three persons with whom I had some conversation spoke of that time as a memory of horror. I have not done with my Italian comparisons; I shall never have done with them. I am therefore free to say that in the way in which Toulouse looks out on the Garonne there was something that reminded me vaguely of the way in which Pisa looks out on the Arno. The red-faced houses —all of brick—along the quay have a mixture of brightness and shabbiness, as well as the fashion of the open *loggia* in the top story. The river, with another bridge or two, might be the Arno, and the buildings on the other side of it—a hospital, a suppressed convent—dip their feet into it with real southern cynicism. I have spoken of the old Hôtel d'Assézat as the best house at Toulouse; with the exception of the cloister of the museum it is the only "bit" I remember. It has fallen from the state of a noble residence of the sixteenth century to that of a warehouse and a set of offices; but a certain dignity lingers in its melancholy court, which is divided from the street by a gateway that is still imposing and in which a clambering vine and a red Virginia-creeper were suspended to the rusty walls of brick and stone.

The most interesting house at Toulouse is far from being the most striking. At the door of No. 50 Rue des Filatiers, a featureless, solid structure, was found hanging, one autumn evening, the body of the young Marc-Antoine Calas, whose ill-inspired suicide was to be the first act of a tragedy so horrible. The fanaticism aroused in the townsfolk by this incident; the execution by torture of Jean Calas, accused as a Protestant of having hanged his son, who had gone over to the Church of Rome; the ruin of the family; the claustration of the daugthers; the flight of the widow to Switzerland; her introduction to Voltaire; the excited zeal of that incomparable partisan and the passionate persistence with which, from year to year, he pursued a reversal of judgment till at last he obtained it and devoted the tribunal of Toulouse to execration and the name of the victims to lasting wonder and pity—these things form part of one of the most interesting and touching episodes of the social history of the eighteenth century. The story has the fatal progression, the dark rigor, of one of the tragic dramas of the Greeks. Jean Calas, advanced in life, blameless, bewildered, protesting his innocence, had been broken on the wheel; and the sight of his decent dwelling, which brought home to me all that had been suffered there, spoiled for me, for half an hour, the impression of Toulouse.

Carcassonne

1882

I

I spent but a few hours at Carcassonne; but those hours had a rounded felicity, and I cannot do better than transcribe from my note-book the little record made at the moment. Vitiated as it may be by crudity and incoherency, it has at any rate the freshness of a great emotion. This is the best quality that a reader may hope to extract from a narrative in which "useful information" and technical lore even of the most general sort are completely absent. For Carcassonne is moving, beyond a doubt; and the traveler who in the course of a little tour in France may have felt himself urged, in melancholy moments, to say that on the whole the disappointments are as numerous as the satisfactions, must admit that there can be nothing better than this.

The country after you leave Toulouse continues to be charming; the more so that it merges its flatness in the distant Cévennes on one side, and on the other, far away on your right, in the richer range of the Pyrenees. Olives and cypresses, pergolas and vines, terraces on the roofs of houses, soft, iridescent mountains, a warm yellow light—

what more could the difficult tourist want? He left his luggage at the station, warily determined to look at the inn before committing himself to it. It was so evident (even to a cursory glance) that it might easily have been much better that he simply took his way to the town, with the whole of a superb afternoon before him. When I say the town, I mean the towns; there being two at Carcassonne, perfectly distinct, and each with excellent claims to the title. They have settled the matter between them, however, and the elder, the shrine of pilgrimage, to which the other is but a stepping-stone, or even, as I may say, a humble door-mat, takes the name of the Cité. You see nothing of the Cité from the station; it is masked by the agglomeration of the *ville-basse,* which is relatively (but only relatively) new. A wonderful avenue of acacias leads to it from the station—leads past it, rather, and conducts you to a little high-backed bridge over the Aude, beyond which, detached and erect, a distinct mediæval silhouette, the Cité presents itself. Like a rival shop on the invidious side of a street, it has "no connection" with the establishment across the way, although the two places are united (if old Carcassonne may be said to be united to anything) by a vague little rustic faubourg. Perched on its solid pedestal, the perfect detachment of the Cité is what first strikes you. To take leave, without delay, of the *ville-basse,* I may say that the splendid acacias I have mentioned flung a summerish dusk over the place, in which a few scattered remains of stout walls and big bastions looked venerable and picturesque. A little boulevard winds round the town, planted with trees and garnished with more benches than I ever saw provided by a soft-hearted municipality. This precinct had a warm, lazy, dusty, southern look, as if the people sat out-of-doors a great deal and wandered about in the stillness of summer nights. The figure of the elder town at these hours must be ghostly enough on its neighboring hill.

Even by day it has the air of a vignette of Gustave Doré, a couplet of Victor Hugo. It is almost too perfect—as if it were an enormous model placed on a big green table at a museum. A steep, paved way, grass-grown like all roads where vehicles never pass, stretches up to it in the sun. It has a double enceinte, complete outer walls and complete inner (these, elaborately fortified, are the more curious); and this congregation of ramparts, towers, bastions, battlements, barbicans, is as fantastic and romantic as you please. The approach I mention here leads to the gate that looks toward Toulouse—the Porte de l'Aude. There is a second, on the other side, called, I believe, the Porte Narbonnaise, a magnificent gate, flanked with towers thick and tall, defended by elaborate outworks; and these two apertures alone admit you to the place—putting aside a small sallyport, protected by a great bastion, on the quarter that looks toward the Pyrenees.

As a votary, always, in the first instance, of a general impression, I walked all round the outer enceinte—a process on the very face of it entertaining. I took to the right of the Porte de l'Aude, without entering it, where the old moat has been filled in. The filling-in of the moat has created a grassy level at the foot of the big gray towers, which, rising at frequent intervals, stretch their stiff curtain of stone from point to point, the curtain drops without a fold upon the quiet grass, which was dotted here and there with a humble native dozing away the golden afternoon. The natives of the elder Carcassonne are all humble; for the core of the Cité has shrunken and decayed, and there is little life among the ruins. A few tenacious laborers who work in the neighboring fields or in the *ville-basse,* and sundry octogenarians of both sexes who are dying where they have lived and contribute much to the pictorial effect—these are the principal inhabitants. The process of converting the place from an irresponsible old town into a conscious "specimen" has of course been attended with eliminations; the population has, as a general thing, been restored away. I should lose no time in saying that restoration is the great mark of the Cité. M. Viollet-le-Duc has worked his will upon it, put it into perfect order, revived the fortifications in every detail. I do not pretend to judge the performance, carried out on a scale and in a spirit which really impose themselves on the imagination. Few architects have had such a chance, and M. Viollet-le-Duc must have been the envy of the whole restoring fraternity. The image of a more crumbling Carcassonne rises in the mind, and there is no doubt that forty years ago the place was more affecting. On the other hand, as we see it to-day it is a wonderful evocation; and if there is a great deal of new in the old, there is plenty of old in the new. The repaired crenellations, the inserted patches of the walls of the outer circle sufficiently express this commixture. My walk brought me into full view of the Pyrenees, which, now that the sun had begun to sink and the shadows to grow long, had a wonderful violet glow. The platform at the base of the walls has a greater width on this side, and it made the scene more complete. Two or three old crones had crawled out of the Porte Narbonnaise to examine the advancing visitor; and a very ancient peasant, lying there with his back against a tower, was tending half a dozen lean sheep. A poor man in a very old blouse, crippled and with crutches lying beside him, had been brought out and placed on a stool, where he enjoyed the afternoon as best he might. He looked so ill and so patient that I spoke to him; found that his legs were paralyzed and he was quite helpless. He had formerly been seven years in the army and had made the campaign of Mexico with Bazaine. Born in the old Cité, he had come back there to end his days. It seemed strange, as he sat there with those romantic walls behind him and the great picture of the Pyrenees in front, to think that he had been across the seas to the far-away new world, had made part of a famous expedition, and was now a cripple at the gate of the mediæval city where he had played as a child. All this struck me as a great deal of history for so modest a figure—a poor little figure that could only just unclose its palm for a small silver coin.

He was not the only acquaintance I made at Carcassonne. I had not pursued my circuit of the walls much further when I encountered a person of quite another type, of whom I asked some question which had just then presented itself, and who proved to be the very genius of the spot. He was a sociable son of the *ville-basse,* a gentleman, and, as I afterwards learned, an employé at the prefecture —a person, in short, much esteemed at Carcassonne. (I may say all this, as he will never read these pages.) He had been ill for a month, and in the company of his little dog was taking his first airing; in his own phrase he was *amoureux-fou de la Cité*—he could lose no time in coming back to it. He talked of it indeed as a lover, and, giving me for half an hour the advantage of his company, showed me all the points of the place. (I speak here always of the outer enceinte; you penetrate to the inner—which is the specialty of Carcassonne, and the great curiosity—only by application at the lodge of the regular custodian, a remarkable functionary, who, half an hour later, when I had been introduced to him by my friend the amateur, marched me over the fortifications with a tremendous accompaniment of dates and technical terms.) My companion pointed out to me in particular the traces of different periods in the structure of the walls. There is a portentous amount of history embedded in them, beginning with Romans and Visigoths; here and there are marks of old breaches hastily repaired. We passed into the town—into that part of it not included in the citadel. It is the queerest and most fragmentary little place in the world, as everything save the fortifications is being suffered to crumble away in order that the spirit of M. Viollet-le-Duc alone may pervade it and it may subsist simply as a magnificent shell. As the leases of the wretched little houses fall in, the ground is cleared of them; and a mumbling old woman approached me in the course of my circuit, inviting me to condole with her on the disappearance of so many of the hovels which in the last few hundred years (since the collapse of Carcassonne as a stronghold) had attached themselves to the base of the walls, in the space between the two circles. These habitations, constructed of materials taken from the ruins, nestled there snugly enough. This intermediate space had therefore become a kind of street, which has crumbled in turn, as the fortress has grown up again. There are other streets beside, very diminutive and vague, where you pick your way over heaps of rubbish and become conscious of unexpected faces looking at you out of windows as detached as the cherubic heads. The most definite thing in the place was the little café, where the waiters, I think, must be the ghosts of the old Visigoths; the most definite, that is, after the little château and the little cathedral. Everything in the Cité is little; you can walk round the walls in twenty minutes. On the drawbridge of the château, which, with a picturesque old face, flanking towers, and a dry moat, is to-day simply a bare *caserne*, lounged half a dozen soldiers, unusually small. Nothing could be more odd than to see these objects inclosed in a receptacle which has much of the appearance of an enormous toy. The Cité and its population vaguely reminded me of an immense Noah's ark.

II

Carcassonne dates from the Roman occupation of Gaul. The place commanded one of the great roads into Spain, and in the fourth century Romans and Franks ousted each other from such a point of vantage. In the year 436 Theodoric, King of the Visigoths, superseded both these parties; and it was during his occupation that the inner enceinte was raised upon the ruins of the Roman fortifications. Most of the Visigoth towers that are still erect are seated upon Roman substructions, which appear to have been formed hastily, probably at the moment of the Frankish invasion. The authors of these solid defenses, though occasionally disturbed, held Carcassonne and the neighboring country, in which they had established their kingdom of Septimania, till the year 713, when they were expelled by the Moors of Spain, who ushered in an unillumined period of four centuries, of which no traces remain. These facts I derive from a source no more recondite than a pamphlet by M. Viollet-le-Duc—a very luminous description of the fortifications, which you may buy from the accomplished custodian. The writer makes a jump to the year 1209, when Carcassonne, then forming part of the realm of the viscounts of Béziers and infected by the Albigensian heresy, was besieged, in the name of the Pope, by the terrible Simon de Montfort and his army of crusaders. Simon was accustomed to success, and the town succumbed in the course of a fortnight. Thirty-one years later, having passed into the hands of the King of France, it was again besieged by the young Raymond de Trincavel, the last of the viscounts of Béziers; and of this siege M. Viollet-le-Duc gives a long and minute account, which the visitor who has a head for such things may follow, with the brochure in hand, on the fortifications themselves. The young Raymond de Trincavel, baffled and repulsed, retired at the end of twenty-four days. Saint Louis and Philip the Bold, in the thirteenth century, multiplied the defenses of Carcassonne, which was one of the bulwarks of their kingdom on the Spanish quarter; and from this time forth, being regarded as impregnable, the place had nothing to fear. It was not even attacked; and when in 1355

Edward the Black Prince marched into it the inhabitants had opened the gates to the conqueror before whom all Languedoc was prostrate. I am not one of those who, as I said just now, have a head for such things, and having extracted these few facts had made all the use of M. Viollet-le-Duc's pamphlet of which I was capable.

I have mentioned that my obliging friend the *amoureux-fou* handed me over to the doorkeeper of the citadel. I should add that I was at first committed to the wife of this functionary, a stout peasant-woman, who took a key down from a nail, conducted me to a postern door, and ushered me into the presence of her husband. Having just begun his rounds with a party of four persons, he was not many steps in advance. I added myself perforce to this party, which was not brilliantly composed, except that two of its members were gendarmes in full toggery, who announced in the course of our tour that they had been stationed for a year at Carcassonne and had never before had the curiosity to come up to the Cité. There was something brilliant certainly in that. The *gardien* was an extraordinarily typical little Frenchman, who struck me even more forcibly than the wonders of the inner enceinte; and as I am bound to assume, at whatever cost to my literary vanity, that there is not the slightest danger of his reading these remarks, I may treat him as public property. With his diminutive stature and his perpendicular spirit, his flushed face, expressive, protuberant eyes, high, peremptory voice, extreme volubility, lucidity and neatness of utterance, he reminded me of the gentry who figure in the revolutions of his native land. If he was not a fierce little Jacobin he ought to have been, for I am sure there were many men of his pattern on the Committee of Public Safety. He knew absolutely what he was about, understood the place thoroughly, and constantly reminded his audience of what he himself had done in the way of excavations and reparations.

He described himself as the brother of the architect of the work actually going forward (that which has been done since the death of M. Viollet-le-Duc, I suppose he meant), and this fact was more illustrative than all the others. It reminded me, as one is reminded at every turn, of the democratic conditions of French life: a man of the people, with a wife *en bonnet,* extremely intelligent, full of special knowledge, and yet remaining essentially of the people, and showing his intelligence with a kind of ferocity, of defiance. Such a personage helps one to understand the red radicalism of France, the revolutions, the barricades, the sinister passion for theories. (I do not, of course, take upon myself to say that the individual I describe—who can know nothing of the liberties I am taking with him—is actually devoted to these ideals; I only mean that many such devotees must have his qualities.) In just the *nuance* that I have tried to indicate here it is a terrible pattern of man. Permeated in a high degree by civilization, it is yet untouched by the desire which one finds in the Englishman, in proportion as he rises in the world, to approximate to the figure of the gentleman. On the other hand, a *netteté,* a faculty of exposition, such as the English gentleman is rarely either blessed or cursed with.

This brilliant, this suggestive warden of Carcassonne marched us about for an hour, haranguing, explaining, illustrating as he went; it was a complete little lecture, such as might have been delivered at the Lowell Institute, on the manner in which a first-rate *place forte* used to be attacked and defended. Our peregrinations made it very clear that Carcassonne was impregnable; it is impossible to imagine without having seen them such refinements of immurement, such ingenuities of resistance. We passed along the battlements and *chemins de ronde,* ascended and descended towers, crawled under arches, peered out of loopholes, lowered ourselves into dungeons, halted in all sorts of tight places while the purpose of something or other was described to us. It was very curious, very interesting; above all it was very pictorial and involved perpetual peeps into the little crooked, crumbling, sunny, grassy, empty Cité. In places, as you stand upon it, the great towered and embattled enceinte produces an illusion; it looks as if it were still equipped and defended. One vivid challenge, at any rate, it flings down before you; it calls upon you to make up your mind on the matter of restoration. For myself I have no hesitation; I prefer in every case the ruined, however ruined, to the reconstructed, however splendid. What is left is more precious than what is added; the one is history, the other is fiction; and I like the former the better of the two—it is so much more romantic. One is positive, so far as it goes; the other fills up the void with things more dead than the void itself, inasmuch as they have never had life. After that I am free to say that the restoration of Carcassonne is a splendid achievement. The little custodian dismissed us at last, after having, as usual, inducted us into the inevitable repository of photographs. These photographs are a great nuisance all over the Midi. They are exceedingly bad for the most part; and the worst—those in the form of the hideous little *album-panorama*—are thrust upon you at every turn. They are a kind of tax that you must pay; the best way is to pay to be let off. It was not to be denied that there was a relief in separating from our accomplished guide, whose manner of imparting information reminded me of the energetic process by which I had seen mineral waters bottled. All this while the afternoon had grown more lovely; the sunset had deepened, the horizon of hills grown purple; the mass of the Canigou became more delicate, yet more distinct. The day had so far faded that the interior of the little cathedral was wrapped in twilight, into which the glowing windows projected something of their color. This church has high beauty and value, but

I will spare the reader a presentation of details which I myself had no opportunity to master. It consists of a romanesque nave, of the end of the eleventh century, and a Gothic choir and transepts of the beginning of the fourteenth; and, shut up in its citadel like a precious casket in a cabinet, it seems—or seemed at that hour—to have a sort of double sanctity. After leaving it and passing out of the two circles of walls, I treated myself, in the most infatuated manner, to another walk round the Cité. It is certainly this general impression that is most striking—the impression from outside, where the whole place detaches itself at once from the landscape. In the warm southern dusk it looked more than ever like a city in a fairy tale. To make the thing perfect, a white young moon, in its first quarter, came out and hung just over the dark silhouette. It was hard to come away—to incommode one's self for anything so vulgar as a railway train; I would gladly have spent the evening in revolving round the walls of Carcassonne. But I had in a measure engaged to proceed to Narbonne, and there was a certain magic in that name which gave me strength—Narbonne, the richest city in Roman Gaul.

Montpellier

1882

Cette, with its glistening houses white,
  Curves with the curving beach away
To where the lighthouse beacons bright,
    Far in the bay.

That stanza of Matthew Arnold's, which I happened to remember, gave a certain importance to the half-hour I spent in the buffet of the station at Cette while I waited for the train to Montpellier. I had left Narbonne in the afternoon, and by the time I reached Cette the darkness had descended. I therefore missed the sight of the glistening houses, and had to console myself with that of the beacon in the bay, as well as with a *bouillon* of which I partook at the buffet aforesaid; for, since the morning, I had not ventured to return to the *table d'hôte* at Narbonne. The Hôtel Nevet, at Montpellier, which I reached an hour later, has an ancient renown all over the south of France—advertises itself, I believe, as *le plus vaste du midi*. It seemed to me the model of a good provincial inn; a big rambling, creaking establishment, with brown, labyrinthine corridors, a queer old open-air vestibule, into which the diligence, in the *bon temps*, used to penetrate, and an hospitality more expressive than that of the new caravansaries. It dates from the days when Montpellier was still accounted a fine winter residence for people with weak lungs; and this rather melancholy tradition, together with the former celebrity of the school of medicine still existing there, but from which the glory has departed, helps to account for its combination of high antiquity and vast proportions. The old hotels were usually more concentrated; but the school of medicine passed for one of the attractions of Montpellier. Long before Mentone was discovered or Colorado invented, British invalids traveled down through France in the post-chaise or the public coach, to spend their winters in the wonderful place which boasted both a climate and a faculty. The air is mild, no doubt, but there are refinements of mildness which were not then suspected and which in a more analytic age have carried the annual wave far beyond Montpellier. The place is charming all the same; and it served the purpose of John Locke, who made a long stay there, between 1675 and 1679, and became acquainted with a noble fellow-visitor, Lord Pembroke, to whom he dedicated the famous Essay. There are places that please without your being able to say wherefore, and Montpellier is one of the number. It has some charming views, from the great promenade of the Peyrou; but its position is not strikingly fine. Beyond this it contains a good museum and the long façades of its school, but these are its only definite treasures. Its cathedral struck me as quite the weakest I had seen, and I remember no other monument that made up for it. The place has neither the gayety of a modern nor the solemnity of an ancient town, and it is agreeable as certain women are agreeable who are neither beautiful nor clever. An Italian would remark that it is sympathetic; a German would admit that it is *gemüthlich.* I spent two days there, mostly in the rain, and even under these circumstances I carried away a kindly impression. I think the

Hôtel Nevet had something to do with it, and the sentiment of relief with which, in a quiet, even a luxurious, room that looked out on a garden, I reflected that I had washed my hands of Narbonne. The phylloxera has destroyed the vines in the country that surrounds Montpellier, and at that moment I was capable of rejoicing in the thought that I should not breakfast with vintners.

The gem of the place is the Musée Fabre, one of the best collections of paintings in a provincial city. François Fabre, a native of Montpellier, died there in 1837, after having spent a considerable part of his life in Italy, where he had collected a good many valuable pictures and some very poor ones, the latter class including several from his own hand. He was the hero of a remarkable episode, having succeeded no less a person than Vittorio Alfieri in the affections of no less a person than Louise de Stolberg, Countess of Albany, widow of no less a person than Charles Edward Stuart, the second pretender to the British crown. Surely no woman ever was associated sentimentally with three figures more diverse—a disqualified sovereign, an Italian dramatist, and a bad French painter. The productions of M. Fabre, who followed in the steps of David, bear the stamp of a cold mediocrity; there is not much to be said even for the portrait of the genial countess (her life has been written by M. Saint-Réné-Taillandier, who depicts her as delightful), which hangs in Florence, in the gallery of the Uffizzi, and makes a pendant to a likeness of Alfieri by the same author. Stendhal, in his *Mémoires d'un Touriste*, says that this work of art represents her as a cook who has pretty hands. I am delighted to have an opportunity of quoting Stendhal, whose two volumes of the *Mémoires d'un Touriste* every traveler in France should carry in his portmanteau. I have had this opportunity more than once, for I have met him at Tours, at Nantes, at Bourges; and everywhere he is suggestive. But he has the defect that he is never pictorial, that he never by any chance makes an image, and that his style is perversely colorless, for a man so fond of contemplation. His taste is often singularly false; it is the taste of the early years of the present century, the period that produced clocks surmounted with sentimental "subjects." Stendhal does not admire these clocks, but he almost does. He admires Domenichino and Guercino, he prizes the Bolognese school of painters because they "spoke to the soul." He is a votary of the new classic, is fond of tall, square, regular buildings, and thinks Nantes, for instance, full of the "air noble." It was a pleasure to me to reflect that five-and-forty years ago he had alighted in that city, at the very inn in which I spent a night and which looks down on the Place Graslin and the theatre. The hotel that was the best in 1837 appears to be the best to-day. On the subject of Touraine Stendhal is extremely refreshing; he finds the scenery meagre and much overrated, and proclaims his opinion with perfect frankness. He does, however, scant justice to the banks of the Loire; his want of appreciation of the picturesque—want of the sketcher's sense—causes him to miss half the charm of a landscape which is nothing if not "quiet," as a painter would say, and of which the felicities reveal themselves only to waiting eyes. He even despises the Indre, the river of Madame Sand. The *Mémoires d'un Touriste* are written in the character of a commercial traveler, and the author has nothing to say about Chenonceaux or Chambord, or indeed about any of the châteaux of that part of France; his system being to talk only of the large towns, where he may be supposed to find a market for his goods. It was his ambition to pass for an ironmonger. But in the large towns he is usually excellent company, though as discursive as Sterne and strangely indifferent, for a man of imagination, to those superficial aspects of things which the poor pages now before the reader are mainly an attempt to render. It is his conviction that Alfieri, at Florence, bored the Countess of Albany terribly; and he adds that the famous Gallophobe died of jealousy of the little painter from Montpellier. The Countess of Albany left her property to Fabre; and I suppose some of the pieces in the museum of his native town used to hang in the sunny saloons of that fine old palace on the Arno which is still pointed out to the stranger in Florence as the residence of Alfieri.

The institution has had other benefactors, notably a certain M. Bruyas, who has enriched it with an extraordinary number of portraits of himself. As these, however, are by different hands, some of them distinguished, we may suppose that it was less the model than the artists to whom M. Bruyas wished to give publicity. Easily first are two large specimens of David Teniers, which are incomparable for brilliancy and a glowing perfection of execution. I have a weakness for this singular genius, who combined the delicate with the groveling, and I have rarely seen richer examples. Scarcely less valuable is a Gerard Dow which hangs near them, though it must rank lower as having kept less of its freshness. This Gerard Dow did me good, for a master is a master, whatever he may paint. It represents a woman paring carrots, while a boy before her exhibits a mousetrap in which he has caught a frightened victim. The goodwife has spread a cloth on the top of a big barrel which serves her as a table, and on this brown, greasy napkin, of which the texture is wonderfully rendered, lie the raw vegetables she is preparing for domestic consumption. Beside the barrel is a large caldron lined with copper, with a rim of brass. The way these things are painted brings tears to the eyes; but they give the measure of the Musée Fabre, where two specimens of Teniers and a Gerard Dow are the jewels. The Italian pictures are of small value; but there is a work by Sir Joshua Reynolds, said to be the only one in France—an infant Samuel in prayer, apparently a repetition of the picture in England which inspired the little plaster image, disseminated in Protestant lands, that we used to admire in our childhood. Sir Joshua, somehow, was an eminently Protestant painter; no one can forget that, who in the National Gallery in London has looked at the picture in which he represents several young ladies as nymphs, voluminously draped, hanging garlands over a statue—a picture suffused indefinably with the Anglican spirit and exasperating to a member of one of the Latin races. It is an odd chance therefore that has led him into that part of France where Protestants have been least *bien vus*. This is the country of the dragonnades of Louis XIV and of the pastors of the desert. From the garden of the Peyrou, at Montpellier, you may see the hills of the Cévennes, to which they of the religion fled for safety and out of which they were hunted and harried.

I have only to add, in regard to the Musée Fabre, that it contains the portrait of its founder—a little, pursy, fat-faced, elderly man, whose countenance contains few indications of the power that makes distinguished victims. He is, however, just such a personage as the mind's eye sees walking on the terrace of the Peyrou of an October afternoon in the early years of the century; a plump figure in a chocolate-colored coat and a *culotte* that exhibits a good leg—a culotte provided with a watch-fob from which a heavy seal is suspended. This Peyrou (to come to it at last) is a wonderful place, especially to be found in a little provincial city. France is certainly the country of towns that aim at completeness; more than in other lands they contain stately features as a matter of course. We should never have ceased to hear about the Peyrou if fortune had placed it at a Shrewsbury or a Buffalo. It is true that the place enjoys a certain celebrity at home, which it amply deserves, moreover; for nothing could be more impressive and monumental. It consists of an "elevated platform," as Murray says,

—an immense terrace laid out, in the highest part of the town, as a garden, and commanding in all directions a view which in clear weather must be of the finest. I strolled there in the intervals of showers and saw only the nearer beauties —a great pompous arch of triumph in honor of Louis XIV (which is not, properly speaking, in the garden, but faces it, straddling across the *place* by which you approach it from the town), an equestrian statue of that monarch set aloft in the middle of the terrace, and a very exalted and complicated fountain, which forms a background to the picture. This fountain gushes from a kind of hydraulic temple, or *château d'eau,* to which you ascend by broad flights of steps, and which is fed by a splendid aqueduct, stretched in the most ornamental and unexpected manner across the neighboring valley. All this work dates from the middle of the last century. The combination of features—the triumphal arch, or gate; the wide fair terrace, with its beautiful view; the statue of the grand monarch; the big architectural fountain, which would not surprise one at Rome, but does surprise one at Montpellier; and, to complete the effect, the extraordinary aqueduct, charmingly foreshortened—all this is worthy of a capital, of a little court-city. The whole place, with its repeated steps, its balustrades, its massive and plentiful stonework, is full of the air of the last century—*sent bien son dix-huitième siècle;* none the less so, I am afraid, that, as I read in my faithful Murray, after the revocation of the Edict of Nantes the block, the stake, the wheel had been erected here for the benefit of the desperate Camisards.

Avignon

1882

I had been twice at Avignon before, and, yet I was not satisfied. I probably am satisfied now; nevertheless, I enjoyed my third visit. I shall not soon forget the first, on which a particular emotion set an indelible stamp. I was creeping northward, in 1870, after four months spent, for the first time, in Italy. It was the middle of January, and I had found myself unexpectedly forced to return to England for the rest of the winter. It was an insufferable disappointment; I was wretched and broken-hearted. Italy appeared to me at that time so much better than anything else in the world, that to rise from table in the middle of the feast was a prospect of being hungry for the rest of my days. I had heard a great deal of praise of the south of France; but the south of France was a poor consolation. In this state of mind I arrived at Avignon, which under a bright, hard winter sun was tingling—fairly spinning—with the *mistral*. I find in my journal of the other day a reference to the acuteness of my reluctance in January, 1870. France, after Italy, appeared in the language of the latter country, *poco simpatica;* and I thought it necessary, for reasons now inconceivable, to read the *Figaro*, which was filled with descriptions of the horrible Troppmann, the murderer of the *famille* Kink. Troppmann, Kink, *le crime de Pantin*—the very names that figured in this episode seemed to wave me back. Had I abandoned the sonorous south to associate with vocables so base?

It was very cold the other day at Avignon; for though there was no mistral, it was raining as it rains in Provence, and the dampness had a terrible chill in it. As I sat by my fire late at night—for in genial Avignon, in October, I had to have a fire—it came back to me that eleven years before I had at that same hour sat by a fire in that same room, and, writing to a friend to whom I was not afraid to appear extravagant, had made a vow that at some happier period of the future I would avenge myself on the *ci-devant* city of the Popes by taking it in a contrary sense. I suppose that I redeemed my vow on the occasion of my second visit better than on my third; for then I was on my way to Italy, and that vengeance, of course, was complete. The only drawback was that I was in such a hurry to get to Ventimiglia (where the Italian custom-house was to be the sign of my triumph), that I scarcely took time to make it clear to myself at Avignon that this was better than reading the *Figaro*. I hurried on almost too fast to enjoy the consciousness of moving southward. On this last occasion I was unfortunately destitute of that happy faith. Avignon was my southernmost limit; after which I was to turn round and proceed back to England. But in the interval I had been a great deal in Italy, and that made all the difference.

I had plenty of time to think of this, for the rain kept me practically housed for the first twenty-four hours. It had been raining in these regions for a month, and people had begun to look askance at the Rhone, though as yet the volume of the river was not exorbitant. The only excursion possible, while the torrent descended, was a kind of horizontal dive, accompanied with infinite splashing, to the little *musée* of the town, which is within a moderate walk of the hotel. I had a memory of it from my first visit; it had appeared to me more pictorial than its pictures. I found that recollection had flattered it a little, and that it is neither better nor worse than most provincial museums. It has the usual musty chill in the air, the usual grass-grown forecourt, in which a few lumpish Roman fragments are disposed, the usual red tiles on the floor, and the usual specimens of the more livid schools on the walls. I rang up the *gardien,* who arrived with a bunch of keys, wiping his mouth; he unlocked doors for me, opened shutters, and while (to my distress, as if the things had been worth lingering over) he shuffled about after me, he announced the names of the pictures before which I stopped in a voice that reverberated through the melancholy halls, and seemed to make the authorship shameful when it was obscure, and grotesque when it pretended to be great. Then there were intervals of silence, while I stared absent-mindedly, at haphazard, at some indistinguishable canvas, and the only sound was the downpour of the rain on the skylights. The museum of Avignon derives a certain dignity from its Roman fragments. The town has no Roman monuments to show; in this respect, beside its brilliant neighbors, Arles and Nîmes, it is a blank. But a great many small objects have been found in its soil—pottery, glass, bronzes, lamps, vessels and ornaments of gold and silver. The glass is especially charming—small vessels of the most delicate shape and substance, many of them perfectly preserved. These diminutive, intimate things bring one near to the old Roman life; they seem like pearls strung upon the slender thread that swings across the gulf of time. A little glass cup that Roman lips have touched says more to us than the great vessel of an arena. There are two small silver *casseroles,* with chiseled handles, in the museum of Avignon, that struck me as among the most charming survivals of antiquity.

I did wrong, just above, to speak of my attack on this establishment as the only recreation I took that first wet day; for I remember a terribly moist visit to the former palace of the Popes, which could have taken place only in the same tempestuous hours. It is true that I scarcely know why I should have gone out to see the Papal palace in the rain, for I had been over it twice before, and even then had not found the interest of the place so complete as it ought to be; the fact nevertheless remains that this last occasion is much associated with an umbrella, which was not superfluous even in some of the chambers and corridors of the gigantic pile. It had already seemed to me the dreariest of all historical buildings, and my final visit confirmed the impression. The place is as intricate as it is vast, and as desolate as it is dirty. The imagination has, for some reason or other, to make more than the effort usual in such cases to restore and repeople it. The fact, indeed, is simply that the palace has been so incalculably abused and altered. The alterations have been so numerous that, though I have duly conned the enumerations, supplied in guide-books, of the principal perversions, I do not pretend to carry any of them in my head. The huge bare mass, without ornament, without grace, despoiled of its battlements and defaced with sordid modern windows, covering the Rocher des Doms, and looking down over the Rhone and the broken bridge of Saint-Bénazet (which stops in such a sketchable manner in mid-stream), and across at the lonely tower of Philippe le Bel and the ruined wall of Villeneuve, makes at a distance, in spite of its poverty, a great figure, the effect of which is carried out by the tower of the church beside it (crowned though the latter be, in a top-heavy fashion, with an immense modern image of the Virgin) and by the thick, dark foliage of the garden laid out on a still higher portion of the eminence. This garden recalls faintly and a trifle perversely the grounds of the Pincian at Rome. I know not whether it is the shadow of the Papal name, present in both places, combined with a vague analogy between the churches—which, approached in each case by a flight of steps, seemed to defend the precinct—but each time I have seen the Promenade des Doms it has carried my thoughts to the wider and loftier terrace from which you look away at the Tiber and Saint Peter's.

As you stand before the Papal palace, and especially as you enter it, you are struck with its being a very dull monument. History enough was enacted here: the great schism lasted from 1305 to 1370, during which seven Popes, all Frenchmen, carried on the court of Avignon on principles that have not commended themselves to the esteem of posterity. But history has been whitewashed away, and the scandals of that period have mingled with the dust of dilapidations and repairs. The building has for many years been occupied as a barrack for regiments of the line, and the main characteristics of a barrack—an extreme nudity and a very queer smell—prevail throughout its endless compartments. Nothing could have been more cruelly dismal than the appearance it presented at the time of this third visit of mine. A regiment, changing quarters, had departed the day before, and another was expected to arrive (from Algeria) on the morrow. The place had been left in the befouled and belittered condition which marks the passage of the military after they have broken camp, and it would offer but a melancholy welcome to the regiment that was about to take possession. Enormous windows had been left carelessly open all over the building, and the rain and wind were beating into empty rooms and passages; making draughts which purified, perhaps, but which scarcely cheered. For an arrival it was horrible. A handful of soldiers had remained behind. In one of the big vaulted rooms several of them were lying on their wretched beds, in the dim light, in the cold, in the damp, with the bleak bare walls before them, and their overcoats, spread over them, pulled up to their noses. I pitied them immensely, though they may have felt less wretched than they looked. I thought not of the old profligacies and crimes, not of the funnel-shaped torture-chamber (which, after exciting the shudder of generations, has been ascertained now, I believe, to have been a mediæval bakehouse), not of the tower of the *glacière* and the horrors perpetrated here in the Revolution, but of the military burden of young France. One wonders how young France endures it, and one is forced to believe that the French conscript has, in addition to his notorious good-humor, greater toughness than is commonly supposed by those who consider only the more relaxing influences of French civilization. I hope he finds occasional compensation for such moments as I saw those damp young peasants passing on the mattresses of their hideous barrack, without anything around to remind them that they were in the most civilized of countries. The only traces of former splendor now visible in the Papal pile are the walls and vaults of two small chapels, painted in fresco, so battered and effaced as to be scarcely distinguishable, by Simone Memmi. It offers of course a peculiarly good field for restoration, and I believe the government intend to take it in hand. I mention this fact without a sigh, for they cannot well make it less interesting than it is at present.

Arles

1882

I

There are two shabby old inns at Arles which compete closely for your custom. I mean by this that if you elect to go to the Hôtel du Forum, the Hôtel du Nord, which is placed exactly beside it (at a right angle) watches your arrival with ill-concealed disapproval; and if you take the chances of its neighbor, the Hôtel du Forum seems to glare at you invidiously from all its windows and doors. I forget which of these establishments I selected; whichever it was, I wished very much that it had been the other. The two stand together on the Place des Hommes, a little public square of Arles, which somehow quite misses its effect. As a city, indeed, Arles quite misses its effect in every way; and if it is a charming place, as I think it is, I can hardly tell the reason why. The straight-nosed Arlésiennes account for it in some degree; and the remainder may be charged to the ruins of the arena and the theatre. Beyond this, I remember with affection the ill-proportioned little Place des Hommes; not at all monumental, and given over to puddles and to shabby cafés. I recall with tenderness the tortuous and featureless streets, which looked like the streets of a village and were paved with villainous little sharp stones, making all exercise penitential. Consecrated by association is even a tiresome walk that I took the evening I arrived, with the purpose of obtaining a view of the Rhone. I had been to Arles before, years ago, and it seemed to me that I remembered finding on the banks of the stream some sort of picture. I think that on the evening of which I speak there was a watery moon, which it seemed to me would light up the past as well as the present. But I found no picture, and I scarcely found the Rhone at all. I lost my way, and there was not a creature in the streets to whom I could appeal. Nothing could be more provincial than the situation of Arles at ten o'clock at night. At last I arrived at a kind of embankment, where I could see the great mud-colored stream slipping along in the soundless darkness. It had come on to rain, I know not what had happened to the moon, and the whole place was anything but gay. It was not what I had looked for; what I had looked for was in the irrecoverable past. I groped my way back to the inn over the infernal *cailloux,* feeling like a discomfited Dogberry. I remember now that this hotel was the one (whichever that may be) which has the fragment of a Gallo-Roman portico inserted into one of its angles. I had chosen it for the sake of this exceptional ornament. It was damp and dark, and the floors felt gritty to the feet; it was an establishment at which the dreadful *gras-double* might have appeared at the *table d'hôte,* as it had done at Narbonne. Nevertheless, I was glad to get back to it; and nevertheless, too—and this is the moral of my simple anecdote—my pointless little walk (I don't speak of the pavement) suffuses itself, as I look back upon it, with a romantic tone. And in relation to the inn, I suppose I had better mention that I am well aware of the inconsistency of a person who dislikes the modern caravansary and yet grumbles when he finds a hotel of the superannuated sort. One ought to choose, it would seem, and make the best of either alternative. The two old taverns at Arles are quite unimproved; such as they must have been in the infancy of the modern world, when Stendhal passed that way and the lumbering diligence deposited him in the Place des Hommes, such in every detail they are to-day. *Vieilles auberges de France*, one ought to enjoy their gritty floors and greasy window-panes. Let it be put on record, therefore, that I have been, I won't say less comfortable, but at least less happy, at better inns.

To be really historic, I should have mentioned that before going to look for the Rhone I had spent part of the evening on the opposite side of the little place, and that I indulged in this recreation for two definite reasons. One of these was that I had an opportunity of gossiping at a café with a conversable young Englishman whom I had met in the afternoon at Tarascon and more remotely, in other years, in London; the other was that there sat enthroned behind the counter a splendid mature Arlésienne, whom my companion and I agreed that it was a rare privilege to contemplate. There is no rule of good manners or morals which makes it improper, at a café, to fix one's eyes upon the *dame de comptoir;* the lady is, in the nature of things, a part of your *consommation.* We were therefore free to admire without restriction the handsomest person I had ever seen give change for a five-franc piece. She was a large quiet woman who would never see forty again; of an intensely feminine type, yet wonderfully rich and robust, and full of a certain physical nobleness. Though she was not really old, she was antique, and she was very grave, even a little sad. She had the dignity of a Roman empress, and she handled coppers as if they had been stamped with the head of Cæsar. I have seen washerwomen in the Trastevere who were perhaps as handsome as she; but even the head-dress of the Roman contadina contributes less to the dignity of the person born to wear it than the sweet and stately Arlesian cap, which sits at once aloft and on the back of the head; which is accompanied with a wide black bow covering a considerable part of the crown; and which, finally, accommodates itself indescribably well to the manner in which the tresses of the front are pushed behind the ears.

This admirable dispenser of lumps of sugar has distracted me a little; for I am still not sufficiently historical. Before going to the café I had dined, and before dining I had found time to go and look at the arena. Then it was that I discovered that Arles has no general physiognomy and, except the delightful little church of Saint Trophimus, no architecture, and that the rugosities of its dirty lanes affect the feet like knife-blades. It was not then, on the other hand, that I saw the arena best. The second day of my stay at Arles I devoted to a pilgrimage to the strange old hill town of Les Baux, the mediæval Pompeii, of which I shall give myself the pleasure of speaking. The evening of that day, however (my friend and I returned in time for a late dinner), I wandered among the Roman remains of the place by the light of a magnificent moon, and gathered an impression which has lost little of its silvery glow. The moon of the evening before had been aqueous and erratic; but if on the present occasion it was guilty of any irregularity, the worst it did was only to linger beyond its time in the heavens in order to let us look at things comfortably. The effect was admirable; it brought back the impression of the way, in Rome itself, on evenings like that, the moonshine rests upon broken shafts and slabs of antique pavement. As we sat in the theatre looking at the two lone columns that survive—part of the decoration of the back of the stage—and at the fragments of ruin around them, we might have been in the Roman Forum. The arena at Arles, with its great magnitude, is less complete than that of Nîmes; it has suffered even more the assaults of time and the children of time, and it has been less repaired. The seats are almost wholly wanting; but the external walls, minus the topmost tier of arches, are massively, ruggedly complete; and the vaulted corridors seem as solid as the day they were built. The whole thing is superbly vast, and as monumental, for place of light amusement—what is called in America a "variety show"—as it entered only into the Roman mind to make such establishments. The *podium* is much higher than at Nîmes, and many of the great white slabs that faced it have been recovered and put into their places. The proconsular box has been more or less reconstructed, and the great converging passages of approach to it are still majestically distinct; so that, as I sat there in the moon-charmed stillness, leaning my elbows on the battered parapet of the ring, it was not impossible to listen to the murmurs and shudders, the thick voice of the circus, that died away fifteen hundred years ago.

The theatre has a voice as well, but it lingers on the ear of time with a different music. The Roman theatre at Arles seemed to me one of the most charming and touching ruins I had ever beheld; I took a particular fancy to it. It is less than a skeleton—the arena may be called a skeleton; for it consists only of half a dozen bones. The traces of the row of columns which formed the scene—the permanent back-scene—remain; two marble pillars—I just mentioned them—are upright, with a fragment of their entablature. Before them is the vacant space which was filled by the stage, with the line of the proscenium distinct, marked by a deep groove impressed upon slabs of stone, which looks as if the bottom of a high screen had been intended to fit into it. The semicircle formed by the seats—half a cup—rises opposite; some of the rows are distinctly marked. The floor, from the bottom of the stage, in the shape of an arc of which the chord is formed by the line of the orchestra, is covered by slabs of colored marble—red, yellow, and green—which, though terribly battered and cracked to-day, give one an idea of the elegance of the interior. Everything shows that it was on a great scale: the large sweep of its inclosing walls, the massive corridors that passed behind the auditorium, and of which we can still perfectly take the measure. The way in which every seat commanded the stage is a lesson to the architects of our epochs, as also the immense size of the place is a proof of extraordinary power of voice on the part of the Roman actors. It was after we had spent half an hour in the moonshine at the arena that we came on to this more ghostly and more exquisite ruin. The principal entrance was locked, but we effected an easy *escalade,* scaled a low parapet, and descended into the place behind the scenes. It was as light as day, and the solitude was complete. The two slim columns, as we sat on the broken benches, stood there like a pair of silent actors. What I called touching just now was the thought that here the human voice, the utterance of a great language, had been supreme. The air was full of intonations and cadences; not of the echo of smashing blows, of riven armor, of howling victims, and roaring beasts. The spot is, in short, one of the sweetest legacies of the ancient world; and there seems no profanation in the fact that by day it is open to the good people of Arles, who use it to pass, by no means in great numbers, from one part of the town to the other; treading the old marble floor and brushing, if need be, the empty benches. This familiarity does not kill the place again; it makes it, on the contrary, live a little—makes the present and the past touch each other.

II

Arles: The Museum

The third lion of Arles has nothing to do with the ancient world, but only with the old one. The church of Saint Trophimus, whose wonderful romanesque porch is the principal ornament of the principal *place*—a *place* otherwise distinguished by the presence of a slim and tapering obelisk in the middle, as well as by that of the hôtel de ville and the museum—the interesting church of Saint Trophimus swears a little, as the French say, with the peculiar character of Arles. It is very remarkable, but I would rather it were in another place. Arles is delightfully pagan, and Saint Trophimus, with its apostolic sculptures, is rather a false note. These sculptures are equally remarkable for their primitive vigor and for the perfect preservation in which they have come down to us. The deep recess of a round-arched porch of the twelfth century is covered with quaint figures which have not lost a nose or a finger. An angular, Byzantine-looking Christ sits in a diamond-shaped frame at the summit of the arch, surrounded by little angels, by great apostles, by winged beasts, by a hundred sacred symbols and grotesque ornaments. It is a dense embroidery of sculpture, black with time, but as uninjured as if it had been kept under glass. One good mark for the French Revolution! Of the interior of the church, which has a nave of the twelfth century and a choir three hundred years more recent, I chiefly remember the odd feature that the romanesque aisles are so narrow that you literally—or almost—squeeze through them. You do so with some eagerness, for your natural purpose is to pass out to the cloister. This cloister, as distinguished and as perfect as the porch, has a great deal of charm. Its four sides, which are not of the same period (the earliest and best are of the twelfth century), have an elaborate arcade, supported on delicate pairs of columns, the capitals of which show an extraordinary variety of device and ornament. At the corners of the quadrangle these columns take the form of curious human figures. The whole thing is a gem of lightness and preservation and is often cited for its beauty; but—if it doesn't sound too profane—I prefer, especially at Arles, the ruins of the Roman theatre. The antique element is too precious to be mingled with anything less rare. This truth was very present to my mind during a ramble of a couple of hours that I took just before leaving the place; and the glowing beauty of the morning gave the last touch to the impression. I spent half an hour at the Museum; then I took another look at the Roman theatre; after which I walked a little out of the town to the Aliscamps, the old Elysian Fields, the meagre remnant of the old pagan place of sepulture, which was afterwards used by the Christians, but has been for ages deserted, and now consists only of a melancholy avenue of cypresses lined with a succession of ancient sarcophagi, empty, mossy, and mutilated. An iron foundry, or some horrible establishment which is conditioned upon tall chimneys and a noise of hammering and banging, has been established near at hand; but the cypresses shut it out well enough, and this small patch of Elysium is a very romantic corner.

The door of the Museum stands ajar, and a vigilant custodian, with the usual batch of photographs on his mind, peeps out at you disapprovingly while you linger opposite, before the charming portal of Saint Trophimus, which you may look at for nothing. When you succumb to the silent influence of his eye and go over to visit his collection, you find yourself in a desecrated church, in which a variety of ancient objects disinterred in Arlesian soil have been arranged without any pomp. The best of these, I believe, were found in the ruins of the theatre. Some of the most curious of them are early Christian sarcophagi, exactly on the pagan model, but covered with rude yet vigorously wrought images of the apostles and with illustrations of scriptural history. Beauty of the highest kind, either of conception or of execution, is absent from most of the Roman fragments, which belong to the taste of a late period and a provincial civilization. But a gulf divides them from the bristling little imagery of the Christian sarcophagi, in which, at the same time, one detects a vague emulation of the rich examples by which their authors were surrounded. There is a certain element of style in all the pagan things; there is not a hint of it in the early Christian relics, among which, according to M. Joanne, of the Guide, are to be found more fine sarcophagi than in any collection but that of Saint John Lateran. In two or three of the Roman fragments there is a noticeable distinction; principally in a charming bust of a boy, quite perfect, with those salient eyes that one sees in antique portraits, and to which the absence of vision in the marble mask gives a look, often very touching, as of a baffled effort to see; also in the head of a woman, found in the ruins of the theatre, who, alas! has lost her nose, and whose noble, simple contour, barring this deficiency, recalls the great manner of the Venus of Milo. There are various rich architectural fragments which indicate that that edifice was a very splendid affair. This little Museum at Arles, in short, is the most Roman thing I know out of Rome.

Nîmes

1882

After this I was free to look about me at Nîmes, and I did so with such attention as the place appeared to require. At the risk of seeming too easily and too frequently disappointed, I will say that it required rather less than I had been prepared to give. It is a town of three or four fine features rather than a town with, as I may say, a general figure. In general, Nîmes is poor; its only treasures are its Roman remains, which are of the first order. The new French fashions prevail in many of its streets; the old houses are paltry, and the good houses are new; while beside my hotel rose a big spick-and-span church, which had the oddest air of having been intended for Brooklyn or Cleveland. It is true that this church looked out on a square completely French—a square of a fine modern disposition, flanked on one side by a classical *palais de justice* embellished with trees and parapets and occupied in the centre with a group of allegorical statues such as one encounters only in the cities of France, the chief of these being a colossal figure by Pradier representing Nîmes. An English, an American town, which should have such a monument, such a square, as this, would be a place of great pretensions;

but, like so many little *villes de province* in the country of which I write, Nîmes is easily ornamental. What nobler element can there be than the Roman baths at the foot of Mont Cavalier and the delightful old garden that surrounds them? All that quarter of Nîmes has every reason to be proud of itself; it has been revealed to the world at large by copious photography. A clear, abundant stream gushes from the foot of a high hill (covered with trees and laid out in paths), and is distributed into basins which sufficiently refer themselves to the period that gave them birth —the period that has left its stamp on that pompous Peyrou which we admired at Montpellier. Here are the same terraces and steps and balustrades, and a system of waterworks less impressive perhaps, but very ingenious and charming. The whole place is a mixture of old Rome and of the French eighteenth century; for the remains of the antique baths are in a measure incorporated in the modern fountains. In a corner of this umbrageous precinct stands a small Roman ruin, which is known as a temple of Diana, but was more apparently a *nymphæum,* and appears to have had a graceful connection with the adjacent baths. I learn from Murray that this little temple, of the period of Augustus, "was reduced to its present state of ruin in 1577;" the moment at which the townspeople, threatened with a siege by the troops of the Crown, partly demolished it lest it should serve as a cover to the enemy. The remains are very fragmentary, but they serve to show that the place was lovely. I spent half an hour in it on a perfect Sunday morning (it is inclosed by a high *grille,* carefully tended, and has a warden of its own), and with the help of my imagination tried to reconstruct a little the aspect of things in the Gallo-Roman days. I do wrong perhaps to say that I *tried;* from a flight so deliberate I should have shrunk. But there was a certain contagion of antiquity in the air; and among the ruins of baths and temples, in the very spot where the aqueduct that crosses the Gardon in the wondrous manner I had seen discharged itself, the picture of a splendid paganism seemed vaguely to glow. Roman baths —Roman baths; those words alone were a scene. Everything was changed: I was strolling in a *jardin français;* the bosky slope of the Mont Cavalier (a very modest mountain), hanging over the place, is crowned with a shapeless tower, which is as likely to be of mediæval as of antique origin; and yet, as I leaned on the parapet of one of the fountains, where a flight of curved steps (a hemicycle, as the French say) descended into a basin full of dark, cool recesses, where the slabs of the Roman foundations gleam through the clear green water—as in this attitude I surrendered myself to contemplation and reverie, it seemed to me that I touched for a moment the ancient world. Such moments are illuminating, and the light of this one mingles, in my memory, with the dusky greenness of the Jardin de la Fontaine.

The fountain proper—the source of all these distributed waters—is the prettiest thing in the world, a reduced copy of Vaucluse. It gushes up at the foot of the Mont Cavalier, at a point where that eminence rises with a certain cliff-like effect, and, like other springs in the same circumstances, appears to issue from the rock with a sort of quivering stillness. I trudged up the Mont Cavalier—it is a matter of five minutes—and having committed this cockneyism enhanced it presently by another. I ascended the stupid Tour Magne, the mysterious structure I mentioned a moment ago. The only feature of this dateless tube, except the inevitable collection of photographs to which you are introduced by the doorkeeper, is the view you enjoy from its summit. This view is of course remarkably fine, but I am ashamed to say I have not the smallest recollection of it; for while I looked into the brilliant spaces of the air I seemed still to see only what I saw in the depths of the Roman baths—the image, disastrously confused and vague, of a vanished world. This world, however, has left at Nîmes a far more considerable memento than a few old stones covered with water-moss. The Roman arena is the rival of those of Verona and of Arles; at a respectful distance it emulates the Colosseum. It is a small Colosseum, if I may be allowed the expression, and is in much better preservation than the great circus at Rome. This is especially true of the external walls, with their arches, pillars, cornices. I must add that one should not speak of preservation, in regard to the arena at Nîmes, without speaking also of repair. After the great ruin ceased to be despoiled it began to be protected, and most of its wounds have been dressed with new material. These matters concern the archæologist; and I felt here, as I felt afterwards at Arles, that one of the profane, in the presence of such a monument, can only admire and hold his tongue. The great impression, on the whole, is an impression of wonder that so much should have survived. What remains at Nîmes, after all dilapidation is estimated, is astounding. I spent an hour in the Arènes on that same sweet Sunday morning, as I came back from the Roman baths, and saw that the corridors, the vaults, the staircases, the external casing, are still virtually there. Many of these parts are wanting in the Colosseum, whose sublimity of size, however, can afford to dispense with detail. The seats at Nîmes, like those at Verona, have been largely renewed; not that this mattered much, as I lounged on the cool surface of one of them and admired the mighty concavity of the place and the elliptical sky-line, broken by uneven blocks and forming the rim of the monstrous cup—a cup that had been filled with horrors. And yet I made my reflections; I said to myself that though a Roman arena is one of the most impressive of the works of man, it has a touch of that same stupidity which I ventured to discover in the Pont du Gard. It is brutal; it is monotonous; it is not at all exquisite. The

Arènes at Nîmes were arranged for a bull-fight—a form of recreation that, as I was informed, is much *dans les habitudes Nîmoises,* and very common throughout Provence, where (still according to my information) it is the usual pastime of a Sunday afternoon. At Arles and Nîmes it has a characteristic setting, but in the villages the patrons of the game make a circle of carts and barrels, on which the spectators perch themselves. I was surprised at the prevalence in mild Provence of the Iberian vice, and hardly know whether it makes the custom more respectable that at Nîmes and Arles the thing is shabbily and imperfectly done. The bulls are rarely killed, and indeed often are bulls only in the Irish sense of the term—being domestic and motherly cows. Such an entertainment of course does not supply to the arena that element of the exquisite which I spoke of as wanting. The exquisite at Nîmes is mainly represented by the famous Maison Carrée. The first impression you receive from this delicate little building, as you stand before it, is that you have already seen it many times. Photographs, engravings, models, medals, have placed it definitely in your eye, so that from the sentiment with which you regard it curiosity and surprise are almost completely, and perhaps deplorably, absent. Admiration remains, however—admiration of a familiar and even slightly patronizing kind. The Maison Carrée does not overwhelm you; you can conceive it. It is not one of the great sensations of antique art; but it is perfectly felicitous, and, in spite of having been put to all sorts of incongruous uses, marvelously preserved. Its slender columns, its delicate proportions, its charming compactness, seem to bring one nearer to the century that built it than the great superpositions of arenas and bridges, and give it the interest that vibrates from one age to another when the note of taste is struck. If anything were needed to make this little toy-temple a happy production the service would be rendered by the second-rate boulevard that conducts to it, adorned with inferior cafés and tobacco-shops. Here, in a respectable recess, surrounded by vulgar habitations and with the theatre, of a classic pretension, opposite, stands the small "square house," so called because it is much longer than it is broad. I saw it first in the evening, in the vague moonlight, which made it look as if it were cast in bronze. Stendhal says, justly, that it has the shape of a playing-card, and he expresses his admiration for it by the singular wish that an "exact copy" of it should be erected in Paris. He even goes so far as to say that in the year 1880 this tribute will have been rendered to its charms; nothing would be more simple, to his mind, than to "have" in that city "le Panthéon de Rome, quelques temples de Grèce." Stendhal found it amusing to write in the character of a *commis-voyageur*, and sometimes it occurs to his reader that he really was one.

Part IV

The Lover of Italy

Travels in Italy

1873—1900

Editor's Note

Of all the countries of Europe, Italy excited in James the strongest romantic feeling, the most intense sensuous emotion, and perhaps the richest evocations to be found in his essays and tales. The country had not figured in the youthful travels of the James family; it remained for James to discover it in the autumn of 1869, and his letters home resound with the "wonderment," the "enthrallment and the passion," of his first encounter with "the Italian feeling," "the melodious Italian voice," the "vital principle of grace," and "the Spirit of the South." Those emotions mounted as he descended from France and Switzerland over the old Saint-Gothard road and the Simplon toward Maggiore and Como and Milan, then onward through Brescia, Verona, Mantua, Padua, and Vicenza to Venice, shrine of his lifelong devotion, and thus downward to Florence and Rome, where his excitement burst out in an ecstatic panegyric written to his brother William on October 30: "At last—for the first time—I live! It beats everything: it leaves the Rome of your fancy—your education—nowhere. . . . I went reeling and moaning thro' the streets, in a fever of enjoyment. . . . The effect is something indescribable."

This attachment was never to exhaust itself in James. He returned to Italy many times—in 1872 with his sister Alice and his Aunt Catherine Walsh, in 1873, in 1874 with his brother William, in 1877 and 1879, and often thereafter. He wrote tales and novels in Venice, in Florence, at Bellosguardo, and in Rome. From early stories like "Traveling Companions," "At Isella," "The Last of the Valerii," and "The Madonna of the Future," through Roderick Hudson, Daisy Miller, The Portrait of a Lady, The Aspern Papers, and The Wings of the Dove, the charms and splendors of Italy serve as backgrounds to the dramas he laid there. His memoir of William Wetmore Story and His Friends in 1903 evokes his richest memories of Rome, the Campagna, Florence, and Vallombrosa; and while it has not been possible to include portions of that work here, it counts as one of James's most eloquent tributes to "the old Italy" he never ceased to love.

Transatlantic Sketches (1875) included twelve of James's early essays on Italian scenes and cities, dating from 1873–74. Portraits of Places (1883) included the long essays on "Venice" and "Italy Revisited." In 1909 James assembled all his Italian essays in revised versions in his book Italian Hours, from which all the present texts are taken. They describe his early approaches to the South out of France and Switzerland ("From Chambéry to Milan" and "The Old Saint-Gothard"); five are devoted to Venice; his Roman sojourns and holidays are recounted in six; Florence and other Tuscan cities are described in four; Siena, Ravenna, and "A Chain of Cities" (Narni, Spoleto, Assisi, Perugia, Cortona, Arezzo) in three others; Naples and its Bay, Sorrento, and Capri in a last tribute called "The Saint's Afternoon and Others." The six pictures from Italy included here describe various scenes from James's Italian pilgrimages ranging from 1873 to 1900 (four of them being excerpts from longer papers). The reader will wish to add to "Venice" the essay on "The Grand Canal"; to "A Roman Holiday" the essays on "Roman Rides," "Roman

Neighbourhoods," "The After-Season in Rome," "From a Roman Notebook," and "A Few Other Roman Neighbourhoods"; to "Florence," "The Autumn in Florence," "Florentine Notes," "Tuscan Cities," and "Other Tuscan Cities"; and to the whole group the essays on "Italy Revisited," "Ravenna," and many scenes from the Story memoir, not least the beautiful account of Story's death at Vallombrosa, in which James's love of the South speaks in its deepest and most memorable accents.

A Roman Holiday

1873

It is certainly sweet to be merry at the right moment; but the right moment hardly seems to me the ten days of the Roman Carnival. It was my rather cynical suspicion perhaps that they wouldn't keep to my imagination the brilliant promise of legend; but I have been justified by the event and have been decidedly less conscious of the festal influences of the season than of the inalienable gravity of the place. There was a time when the Carnival was a serious matter—that is a heartily joyous one; but, thanks to the seven-league boots the kingdom of Italy has lately donned for the march of progress in quite other directions, the fashion of public revelry has fallen woefully out of step. The state of mind and manners under which the Carnival was kept in generous good faith I doubt if an American can exactly conceive: he can only say to himself that for a month in the year there must have been things—things considerably of humiliation—it was comfortable to forget. But now that Italy is made the Carnival is unmade; and we are not especially tempted to envy the attitude of a population who have lost their relish for play and not yet acquired to any striking extent an enthusiasm for work. The spectacle on the Corso has seemed to me, on the whole, an illustration of that great breach with the past of which Catholic Christendom felt the somewhat muffled shock in September, 1870. A traveller acquainted with the fully papal Rome, coming back any time during the past winter, must have immediately noticed that something momentous had happened—something hostile to the elements of picture and colour and "style." My first warning was that ten minutes after my arrival I found myself face to face with a newspaper stand. The impossibility in the other days of having anything in the journalistic line but the *Osservatore Romano* and the *Voce della Verità* used to seem to me much connected with the extraordinary leisure of thought and stillness of mind to which the place admitted you. But now the slender piping of the Voice of Truth is stifled by the raucous note of eventide vendors of the *Capitale*, the *Libertà* and the *Fanfulla;* and Rome reading unexpurgated news is another Rome indeed. For every subscriber to the *Libertà* there may well be an antique masker and reveller less. As striking a sign of the new régime is the extraordinary increase of population. The Corso was always a well-filled street, but now it's a perpetual crush. I never cease to wonder where the new-comers are lodged, and how such spotless flowers of fashion as the gentlemen who stare at the carriages can bloom in the atmosphere of those *camere mobiliate* of which I have had glimpses. This, however, is their own question, and bravely enough they meet it. They proclaimed somehow, to the first freshness of my wonder, as I say, that by force of numbers Rome had been secularised. An Italian dandy is a figure visually to reckon with, but these goodly throngs of them scarce offered compensation for the absent monsignori, treading the streets in their purple stockings and followed by the solemn servants who returned on their behalf the bows of the meaner sort; for the mourning gear of the cardinals' coaches that formerly glittered with scarlet and swung with the weight of the footmen clinging behind; for the certainty that you'll not, by the best of traveller's luck, meet the Pope sitting deep in the shadow of his great chariot with uplifted fingers like some inaccessible idol in his shrine. You may meet the King indeed, who is as ugly, as imposingly ugly, as some idols, though not so inaccessible. The other day as I passed the Quirinal he drove up in a low carriage with a single attendant; and a group of men and women who had been waiting near the gate rushed at him with a number of folded papers. The carriage slackened pace and he pocketed their offerings with a business-like air—that of a good-natured man accepting handbills at a street-corner. Here was a monarch at his palace gate receiving petitions from his subjects—being adjured to right their wrongs. The scene ought to have thrilled me, but somehow it had no more intensity than a woodcut in an illustrated newspaper. Homely I should call it at most; admirably so, certainly, for there were lately few sovereigns standing, I believe, with whom their people enjoyed these filial hand-to-hand relations. The King this year, however, has had as little to do with the Carnival as the Pope, and the innkeepers and Americans have marked it for their own.

It was advertised to begin at half-past two o'clock of a certain Saturday, and punctually at the stroke of the hour, from my room across a wide court, I heard a sudden multiplication of sounds and confusion of tongues in the Corso. I was writing to a friend for whom I cared more than for any mere romp; but as the minutes elapsed and the hubbub deepened curiosity got the better of affection, and I remembered that I was really within eye-shot of an affair the fame of which had ministered to the daydreams of my infancy. I used to have a scrap-book with a coloured print of the starting of the bedizened wild horses, and the use of a library rich in keepsakes and annuals with a frontispiece commonly of a masked lady in a balcony, the heroine of a delightful tale further on. Agitated by these tender memories I descended into the street; but I confess I looked in vain for a masked lady who might serve as a frontispiece, in vain for any object whatever that might adorn a tale. Masked and muffled ladies there were in abundance; but their masks were of ugly wire, perfectly resembling the little covers placed upon strong cheese in German hotels, and their drapery was a shabby water-proof with the hood pulled over their chignons. They were armed with great tin scoops or funnels, with which they solemnly shovelled lime and flour out of bushel-baskets and down on the heads of the people in the street. They were packed into balconies all the way along the straight vista of the Corso, in which their calcareous shower maintained a dense, gritty, unpalatable fog. The crowd was compact in the street, and the Americans in it were tossing back confetti out of great satchels hung round their necks. It was quite the "you're another" sort of repartee, and less seasoned than I had hoped with the airy mockery tradition hangs about this festival. The scene was striking, in a word; but somehow not as I had dreamed of its being. I stood regardful, I suppose, but with a peculiarly tempting blankness of visage, for in a moment I received half a bushel of flour on my too-philosophic head. Decidedly it was an ignoble form of humour. I shook my ears like an emergent diver, and had a sudden vision of how still and sunny and solemn, how peculiarly and undisturbedly themselves, how secure from any intrusion less sympathetic than one's own, certain outlying parts of Rome must just then be. The Carnival had received its death-blow in my imagination; and it has been ever since but a thin and dusky ghost of pleasure that has flitted at intervals in and out of my consciousness.

I turned my back accordingly on the Corso and wandered away to the grass-grown quarters delightfully free even from the possibility of a fellow-countryman. And so having set myself an example I have been keeping Carnival by strolling perversely along the silent circumference of Rome. I have doubtless lost a great deal. The Princess Margaret has occupied a balcony opposite the open space which leads into Via Condotti and, I believe, like the discreet princess she is, has dealt in no missiles but bonbons, bouquets and white doves. I would have waited half an hour any day to see the Princess Margaret hold a dove on her forefinger; but I never chanced to notice any preparation for that effect. And yet do what you will you can't really elude the Carnival. As the days elapse it filters down into the manners of the common people, and before the week is over the very beggars at the church-doors seem to have gone to the expense of a domino. When you meet these specimens of dingy drollery capering about in dusky back-streets at all hours of the day and night, meet them flitting out of black doorways between the greasy groups that cluster about Roman thresholds, you feel that a love of "pranks," the more vivid the better, must from far back have been implanted in the Roman temperament with a strong hand. An unsophisticated American is wonderstruck at the number of persons, of every age and various conditions, whom it costs nothing in the nature of an ingenuous blush to walk up and down the streets in the costume of a theatrical supernumerary. Fathers of families do it at the head of an admiring progeniture; aunts and uncles and grandmothers do it; all the family does it, with varying splendour but with the same good conscience. "A pack of babies!" the doubtless too self-conscious alien pronounces it for its pains, and tries to imagine himself strutting along Broadway in a battered tin helmet and a pair of yellow tights. Our vices are certainly different; it takes those of the innocent sort to be so ridiculous. A self-consciousness lapsing so easily, in fine, strikes me as so near a relation to amenity, urbanity and general gracefulness that, for myself, I should be sorry to lay a tax on it, lest these other commodities should also cease to come to market.

I was rewarded, when I had turned away with my ears full of flour, by a glimpse of an intenser life than the dingy foolery of the Corso. I walked down by the back streets to the steps mounting to the Capitol—that long inclined plane, rather, broken at every two paces, which is the unfailing disappointment, I believe, of tourists primed for retrospective raptures. Certainly the Capitol seen from this side isn't commanding. The hill is so low, the ascent so narrow, Michael Angelo's architecture in the quadrangle at the top so meagre, the whole place somehow so much more of a mole-hill than a mountain, that for the first ten minutes of your standing there Roman history seems suddenly to have sunk through a trap-door. It emerges however on the other side, in the Forum; and here meanwhile, if you get no sense of the sublime, you get gradually a sense of exquisite composition. Nowhere in Rome is more colour, more charm, more sport for the eye. The mild incline, during the winter months, is always covered with lounging sun-seekers, and especially with those more constantly obvious members of the Roman population—beggars, soldiers, monks and tourists. The beggars and peasants lie kicking their heels along that grandest of loafing-places the great steps of the Ara Cœli. The dwarfish look of the Capitol is intensified, I think, by the neighbourhood of this huge blank staircase, mouldering away in disuse, the weeds thick in its crevices, and climbing to the rudely solemn façade of the church. The sunshine glares on this great unfinished wall only to light up its featureless despair, its expression of conscious, irremediable incompleteness. Sometimes, massing its rusty screen against the deep blue sky, with the little cross and the sculptured porch casting a clear-cut shadow on the bricks, it seems to have even more than a Roman desolation, it confusedly suggests Spain and Africa—lands with no latent *risorgimenti,* with absolutely nothing but a fatal past. The legendary wolf of Rome has lately been accommodated with a little artificial grotto, among the cacti and the palms, in the fantastic triangular garden squeezed between the steps of the church and the ascent to the Capitol, where she holds a perpetual levee and "draws" apparently as powerfully as the Pope himself. Above, in the piazzetta before the stuccoed palace which rises so jauntily on a basement of thrice its magnitude, are more loungers and knitters in the sun, seated round the massively inscribed base of the statue of Marcus Aurelius. Hawthorne has perfectly expressed the attitude of this admirable figure in saying that it extends its arm with "a command which is in itself a benediction." I doubt if any statue of king or captain in the public places of the world has more to commend it to the general heart. Irrecoverable simplicity—residing so in irrecoverable Style—has no sturdier representative. Here is an impression that the sculptors of the last three hundred years have been laboriously trying to reproduce; but contrasted with this mild old monarch their prancing horsemen suggest a succession of riding-masters taking out young ladies' schools. The admirably human character of the figure survives the rusty decomposition of the bronze and the slight "debasement" of the art; and one may call it singular that in the capital of Christendom the portrait most suggestive of a Christian conscience is that of a pagan emperor.

You recover in some degree your stifled hopes of sublimity as you pass beyond the palace and take your choice of either curving slope to descend into the Forum. Then you see that the little stuccoed edifice is but a modern excrescence on the mighty cliff of a primitive construction, whose great squares of porous tufa, as they underlie each other, seem to resolve themselves back into the colossal cohesion of unhewn rock. There are prodigious strangenesses in the union of this airy and comparatively fresh-faced superstructure and these deep-plunging, hoary foundations; and few things in Rome are more entertaining to the eye than to measure the long plumb-line which drops from the inhabited windows of the palace, with their little overpeeping balconies, their muslin curtains and their birdcages, down to the rugged constructional work of the Republic. In the Forum proper the sublime is eclipsed again, though the late extension of the excavations gives a chance for it.

Nothing in Rome helps your fancy to a more vigorous backward flight than to lounge on a sunny day over the railing which guards the great central researches. It "says" more things to you than you can repeat to see the past, the ancient world, as you stand there, bodily turned up with the spade and transformed from an immaterial, inaccessible fact of time into a matter of soils and surfaces. The pleasure is the same—in kind—as what you enjoy of Pompeii, and the pain the same. It wasn't here, however, that I found my compensation for forfeiting the spectacle on the Corso, but in a little church at the end of the narrow byway which diverges up the Palatine from just beside the Arch of Titus. This byway leads you between high walls, then takes a bend and introduces you to a long row of rusty, dusty little pictures of the stations of the cross. Beyond these stands a small church with a front so modest that you hardly recognise it till you see the leather curtain. I never see a leather curtain without lifting it; it is sure to cover a constituted *scene* of some sort—good, bad or indifferent. The scene this time was meagre—whitewash and tarnished candlesticks and mouldy muslin flowers being its principal features. I shouldn't have remained if I hadn't been struck with the attitude of the single worshipper—a young priest kneeling before one of the side-altars, who, as I entered, lifted his head and gave me a sidelong look so charged with the langour of devotion that he immediately became an object of interest. He was visiting each of the altars in turn and kissing the balustrade beneath them. He was alone in the church, and indeed in the whole region. There were no beggars even at the door; they were plying their trade on the skirts of the Carnival. In the entirely deserted place he alone knelt for religion, and as I sat respectfully by it seemed to me I could hear in the perfect silence the faraway uproar of the maskers. It was my late impression of these frivolous people, I suppose, joined with the extraordinary gravity of the young priest's face—his pious fatigue, his droning prayer and his isolation—that gave me just then and there a supreme vision of the religious passion, its privations and resignations and exhaustions and its terribly small share of amusement. He was young and strong and evidently of not too refined a fibre to enjoy the Carnival; but, planted there with his face pale with fasting and his knees stiff with praying, he seemed so stern a satire on it and on the crazy thousands who were preferring it to *his* way, that I half expected to see some heavenly portent out of a monastic legend come down and confirm his choice. Yet I confess that though I wasn't enamoured of the Carnival myself, his seemed a grim preference and this forswearing of the world a terrible game—a gaining one only if your zeal never falters; a hard fight when it does. In such an hour, to a stout young fellow like the hero of my anecdote, the smell of incense must seem horribly stale and the muslin flowers and gilt candlesticks to figure no great bribe. And it wouldn't have helped him much to think that not so very far away, just beyond the Forum, in the Corso, there was sport for the million, and for nothing. I doubt on the other hand whether my young priest had thought of this. He had made himself a temple out of the very elements of his innocence, and his prayers followed each other too fast for the tempter to slip in a whisper. And so, as I say, I found a solider fact of human nature than the love of *coriandoli*.

One of course never passes the Colosseum without paying it one's respects—without going in under one of the hundred portals and crossing the long oval and sitting down a while, generally at the foot of the cross in the centre. I always feel, as I do so, as if I were seated in the depths of some Alpine valley. The upper portions of the side toward the Esquiline look as remote and lonely as an Alpine ridge, and you raise your eyes to their rugged sky-line, drinking in the sun and silvered by the blue air, with much the same feeling with which you would take in a grey cliff on which an eagle might lodge. This roughly mountainous quality of the great ruin is its chief interest; beauty of detail has pretty well vanished, especially since the high-growing wild-flowers have been plucked away by the new government, whose functionaries, surely, at certain points of their task, must have felt as if they shared the dreadful trade of those who gather samphire. Even if you are on your way to the Lateran you won't grudge the twenty minutes it will take you, on leaving the Colosseum, to turn away under the Arch of Constantine, whose noble battered bas-reliefs, with the chain of tragic statues—fettered, drooping barbarians—round its summit, I assume you to have profoundly admired, toward the piazzetta of the church of San Giovanni e Paolo, on the slope of Cælian. No spot in Rome can show a cluster of more charming accidents. The ancient brick apse of the church peeps down into the trees of the little wooded walk before the neighbouring church of San Gregorio, intensely venerable beneath its excessive modernisation; and a series of heavy brick buttresses, flying across to an opposite wall, overarches the short, steep, paved passage which leads into the small square. This is flanked on one side by the long mediæval portico of the church of the two saints, sustained by eight time-blackened columns of granite and marble. On another rise the great scarce-windowed walls of a Passionist convent, and on the third the portals of a grand villa, whose tall porter, with his cockade and silver-topped staff, standing sublime behind his grating, seems a kind of mundane St. Peter, I suppose, to the beggars who sit at the church door or lie in the sun along the farther slope which leads to the gate of the convent. The place always seems to me the perfection of an out-of-the-way corner—a place you would think twice before telling people about, lest you should find them there the next time you were to go. It is such a group of objects, singly and in their happy combination, as one must come to Rome to find at one's house door; but what makes it peculiarly a picture is the beautiful dark red campanile of the church, which stands embedded in the mass of the convent. It begins, as so many things in Rome begin, with a stout foundation of antique travertine, and rises high, in delicately quaint mediæval brickwork—little tiers and apertures sustained on miniature columns and adorned with small cracked slabs of green and yellow marble, inserted almost at random. When there are three or four brown-breasted contadini sleeping in the sun before the convent doors, and a departing monk leading his shadow down over them, I think you will not find anything in Rome more *sketchable*.

If you stop, however, to observe everything worthy of your water-colours you will never reach St. John Lateran. My business was much less with the interior of that vast and empty, that cold clean temple, which I have never found peculiarly interesting, than with certain charming features of its surrounding precinct—the crooked old court beside it, which admits you to the Baptistery and to a delightful rear-view of the queer architectural odds and ends that may in Rome compose a florid ecclesiastical façade. There are more of these, a stranger jumble of chance detail, of lurking recesses and wanton projections and inexplicable windows, than I have memory or phrase for; but the gem of the collection is the oddly perched peaked turret, with its yellow travertine welded upon the rusty brickwork, which was not meant to be suspected, and the brickwork retreating beneath and leaving it in the odd position of a tower *under* which you may see the sky. As to the great front of the church overlooking the Porta San Giovanni, you are not admitted behind the scenes; the term is quite in keeping, for the architecture has a vastly theatrical air. It is extremely imposing—that of St. Peter's alone is more so; and when from far off on the Campagna you see the colossal images of the mitred saints along the top standing distinct against the sky, you forget their coarse construction and their inflated draperies. The view from the great space which stretches from the church steps to the city wall is the very prince of views. Just beside you, beyond the great alcove of mosaic, is the Scala Santa, the marble staircase which (says the legend) Christ descended under the weight of Pilate's judgment, and which all Christians must for ever ascend on their knees; before you is the city gate which opens upon the Via Appia Nuova, the long gaunt file of arches of the Claudian aqueduct, their jagged ridge stretching away like the vertebral column of some monstrous mouldering skeleton, and upon the blooming brown and purple flats and dells of the Campagna and the glowing blue of the Alban Mountains, spotted with their white, high-nestling towns; while to your left is the great grassy space, lined with dwarfish mulberry-trees, which stretches across to the damp little sister-basilica of Santa Croce in Gerusalemme. During a former visit to Rome I lost my heart to this idle tract,[1] and wasted much time in sitting on the steps of the church and watching certain white-cowled friars who were sure to be passing there for

[1] Utterly overbuilt and gone—1909.

the delight of my eyes. There are fewer friars now, and there are a great many of the king's recruits, who inhabit the ex-conventual barracks adjoining Santa Croce and are led forward to practise their goose-step on the sunny turf. Here too the poor old cardinals who are no longer to be seen on the Pincio descend from their mourning-coaches and relax their venerable knees. These members alone still testify to the traditional splendour of the princes of the Church; for as they advance the lifted black petticoat reveals a flash of scarlet stockings and makes you groan at the victory of civilisation over colour.

If St. John Lateran disappoints you internally, you have an easy compensation in pacing the long lane which connects it with Santa Maria Maggiore and entering the singularly perfect nave of that most delightful of churches. The first day of my stay in Rome under the old dispensation I spent in wandering at random through the city, with accident for my *valet-de-place*. It served me to perfection and introduced me to the best things; among others to an immediate happy relation with Santa Maria Maggiore. First impressions, memorable impressions, are generally irrecoverable; they often leave one the wiser, but they rarely return in the same form. I remember, of my coming uninformed and unprepared into the place of worship and of curiosity that I have named, only that I sat for half an hour on the edge of the base of one of the marble columns of the beautiful nave and enjoyed a perfect revel of—what shall I call it?—taste, intelligence, fancy, perceptive emotion? The place proved so endlessly suggestive that perception became a throbbing confusion of images, and I departed with a sense of knowing a good deal that is not set down in Murray. I have seated myself more than once again at the base of the same column; but you live your life only once, the parts as well as the whole. The obvious charm of the church is the elegant grandeur of the nave—

its perfect shapeliness and its rich simplicity, its long double row of white marble columns and its high flat roof, embossed with intricate gildings and mouldings. It opens into a choir of an extraordinary splendour of effect, which I recommend you to look out for of a fine afternoon. At such a time the glowing western light, entering the high windows of the tribune, kindles the scattered masses of colour into sombre brightness, scintillates on the great solemn mosaic of the vault, touches the porphyry columns of the superb baldachino with ruby lights, and buries its shining shafts in the deep-toned shadows that hang about frescoes and sculptures and mouldings. The deeper charm even than in such things, however, is the social or historic note or tone or atmosphere of the church—I fumble, you see, for my right expression; the sense it gives you, in common with most of the Roman churches, and more than any of them, of having been prayed in for several centuries by an endlessly curious and complex society. It takes no great attention to let it come to you that the authority of Italian Catholicism has lapsed not a little in these days; not less also perhaps than to feel that, as they stand, these deserted temples were the fruit of a society leavened through and through by ecclesiastical manners, and that they formed for ages the constant background of the human drama. They are, as one may say, the *churchiest* churches in Europe—the fullest of gathered memories, of the experience of their office. There's not a figure one has read of in old-world annals that isn't to be imagined on proper occasion kneeling before the lamp-decked Confession beneath the altar of Santa Maria Maggiore. One sees after all, however, even among the most palpable realities, very much what the play of one's imagination projects there; and I present my remarks simply as a reminder that one's constant excursions into these places are not the least interesting episodes of one's walks in Rome.

I had meant to give a simple illustration of the church-habit, so to speak, but I have given it at such a length as leaves scant space to touch on the innumerable topics brushed by the pen that begins to take Roman notes. It is by the aimless *flânerie* which leaves you free to follow capriciously every hint of entertainment that you get to know Rome. The greater part of the life about you goes on in the streets; and for an observer fresh from a country in which town scenery is at the least monotonous incident and character and picture seem to abound. I become conscious with compunction, let me hasten to add, that I have launched myself thus on the subject of Roman churches and Roman walks without so much as a preliminary allusion to St. Peter's. One is apt to proceed thither on rainy days with intentions of exercise—to put the case only at that—and to carry these out body and mind. Taken as a walk not less than as a church, St. Peter's of course reigns alone. Even for the profane "constitutional" it serves where the Boulevards, where Piccadilly and Broadway, fall short, and if it didn't offer to our use the grandest area in the world it would still offer the most diverting. Few great works of art last longer to the curiosity, to the perpetually transcended attention. You think you have taken the whole thing in, but it expands, it rises sublime again, and leaves your measure itself poor. You never let the ponderous leather curtain bang down behind you—your weak lift of a scant edge of whose padded vastness resembles the liberty taken in folding back the parchment corner of some mighty folio page—without feeling all former visits to have been but missed attempts at apprehension and the actual to achieve your first real possession. The conventional question is ever as to whether one hasn't been "disappointed in the size," but a few honest folk here and there, I hope, will never cease to say no. The place struck me from the first as the hugest thing conceivable—a real exaltation of one's idea of space; so that one's entrance, even from the great empty square which either glares beneath the deep blue sky or makes of the cool far-cast shadow of the immense front something that resembles a big slate-coloured country on a map, seems not so much a going in somewhere as a going out. The mere man of pleasure in quest of new sensations might well not know where to better his encounter there of the sublime shock that brings him, within the threshold, to an immediate gasping pause. There are days when the vast nave looks mysteriously vaster than on others and the gorgeous baldachino a longer journey beyond the far-spreading tessellated plain of the pavement, and when the light has yet a quality which lets things loom their largest, while the scattered figures—I mean the human, for there are plenty of others—mark happily the scale of items and parts. Then you have only to stroll and stroll and gaze and gaze; to watch the glorious altar-canopy lift its bronze architecture, its colossal embroidered contortions, like a temple within a temple, and feel yourself, at the bottom of the abysmal shaft of the dome, dwindle to a crawling dot.

Much of the constituted beauty resides in the fact that it is all general beauty, that you are appealed to by no specific details, or that these at least, practically never importunate, are as taken for granted as the lieutenants and captains are taken for granted in a great standing army—among whom indeed individual aspects may figure here the rather shifting range of decorative dignity in which details, when observed, often prove poor (though never not massive and substantially precious) and sometimes prove ridiculous. The sculptures, with the sole exception of Michael Angelo's ineffable "Pietà," which lurks obscurely in a side-chapel—this indeed to my sense the rarest artistic *combination* of the greatest things the hand of man has produced —are either bad or indifferent; and the universal incrustation of marble, though sumptuous enough, has a less brilliant effect than much later work of the same sort, that for instance of St. Paul's without the Walls. The supreme beauty is the splendidly sustained simplicity of the whole. The thing represents a prodigious imagination extraordinarily strained, yet strained, at its happiest pitch, without breaking. Its happiest pitch I say, because this is the only creation of its strenuous author in presence of which you are in presence of serenity. You may invoke the idea of ease at St. Peter's without a sense of sacrilege—which you can hardly do, if you are at all spiritually nervous, in Westminster Abbey or Notre Dame. The vast enclosed clearness has much to do with the idea. There are no shadows to speak of, no marked effects of shade; only effects of light innumerable—points at which this element seems to mass itself in airy density and scatter itself in enchanting gradations and cadences. It performs the office of gloom or of mystery in Gothic churches; hangs like a rolling mist along the gilded vault of the nave, melts into bright interfusion the mosaic scintillations of the dome, clings and clusters and lingers, animates the whole huge and otherwise empty shell. A good Catholic, I suppose, is the same Catholic anywhere, before the grandest as well as the humblest altars; but to a visitor not formally enrolled St. Peter's speaks less of aspiration than of full and convenient assurance. The soul infinitely expands there, if one will, but all on its quite human level. It marvels at the reach of our dream and the immensity of our resources. To be so impressed and put in our place, we say, is to be sufficiently "saved"; we can't be more than that in heaven itself; and what specifically celestial beauty such a show or such a substitute may lack it makes up for in certainty and tangibility. And yet if one's hours on the scene are not actually spent in praying, the spirit seeks it again as for the finer comfort, for the blessing, exactly, of its example, its protection and its exclusion. When you are weary of the swarming democracy of your fellow-tourists, of the unremunerative aspects of human nature on Corso and Pincio, of the oppressively frequent combination of coronets on carriage panels and stupid faces in carriages, of addled brains and lacquered boots, of ruin and dirt and decay, of priests and beggars and takers of advantage, of the myriad tokens of a halting civilisation, the image of the great temple depresses the balance of your doubts, seems to rise above even the highest tide of vulgarity and make you still believe in the heroic will and the heroic act. It's a relief, in other words, to feel that there's nothing but a cab-fare between your pessimism and one of the greatest of human achievements.

This might serve as a Lenten peroration to these remarks of mine which have strayed so woefully from their jovial text, save that I ought fairly to confess that my last impression of the Carnival was altogether Carnivalesque. The merry-making of Shrove Tuesday had life and felicity; the dead letter of tradition broke out into nature and grace. I pocketed my scepticism and spent a long afternoon on the Corso. Almost every one was a masker, but you had no need to conform; the pelting rain of confetti effectually disguised you. I can't say I found it all very exhilarating; but here and there I noticed a brighter episode—a capering clown inflamed with contagious jollity, some finer humourist forming a circle every thirty yards to crow at his indefatigable sallies. One clever performer so especially pleased me that I should have been glad to catch a glimpse of the natural man. You imagined for him that he was taking a prodigious intellectual holiday and that his gaiety was in inverse ratio to his daily mood. Dressed as a needy scholar, in an ancient evening-coat and with a rusty black hat and gloves fantastically patched, he carried a little volume carefully under his arm. His humours were in excellent taste, his whole manner the perfection of genteel comedy. The crowd seemed to relish him vastly, and he at once commanded a gleefully attentive audience. Many of his sallies I lost; those I caught were excellent. His trick was often to begin by taking some one urbanely and caressingly by the chin and complimenting him on the *intelligenza della sua fisionomia.* I kept near him as long as I could; for he struck me as a real ironic artist, cherishing a disinterested, and yet at the same time a motived and a moral, passion for the grotesque. I should have liked, however—if indeed I shouldn't have feared—to see him the next morning, or when he unmasked that night over his hard-earned supper in a smoky *trattoría.* As the evening went on the crowd thickened and became a motley press of shouting, pushing, scrambling, everything but squabbling, revellers. The rain of missiles ceased at dusk, but the universal deposit of chalk and flour was trampled into a cloud made lurid by flaring pyramids of the gas-lamps that replaced for the occasion the stingy Roman luminaries. Early in the evening came off the classic exhibition of the *moccoletti,* which I but half saw, like a languid reporter resigned beforehand to be cashiered for want of enterprise. From the mouth of a side-street, over a thousand heads, I caught a huge slow-moving illuminated car, from which blue-lights and rockets and Roman candles were in course of discharge, meeting all in a dim fuliginous glare far above the house-tops. It was like a glimpse of some public orgy in ancient Babylon. In the small hours of the morning, walking homeward from a private entertainment, I found Ash Wednesday still kept at bay. The Corso, flaring with light, smelt like a circus. Every one was taking friendly liberties with every one else and using up the dregs of his festive energy in convulsive hootings and gymnastics. Here and there certain indefatigable spirits, clad all in red after the manner of devils and leaping furiously about with torches, were supposed to affright you. But they shared the universal geniality and bequeathed me no midnight fears as a pretext for keeping

Lent, the *carnevale dei preti*, as I read in that profanely radical sheet the *Capitale*. Of this too I have been having glimpses. Going lately into Santa Francesca Romana, the picturesque church near the Temple of Peace, I found a feast for the eyes—a dim crimson-toned light through curtained windows, a great festoon of tapers round the altar, a bulging girdle of lamps before the sunken shrine beneath, and a dozen white-robed Dominicans scattered in the happiest composition on the pavement. It was better than the *moccoletti*.

A Chain of Cities

1873

One day in midwinter, some years since, during a journey from Rome to Florence perforce too rapid to allow much wayside sacrifice to curiosity, I waited for the train at Narni. There was time to stroll far enough from the station to have a look at the famous old bridge of Augustus, broken short off in mid-Tiber. While I stood admiring the measure of impression was made to overflow by the gratuitous grace of a white-cowled monk who came trudging up the road that wound to the gate of the town. Narni stood, in its own presented felicity, on a hill a good space away, boxed in behind its perfect grey wall, and the monk, to oblige me, crept slowly along and disappeared within the aperture. Everything was distinct in the clear air, and the view exactly as like the bit of background by an Umbrian master as it ideally should have been. The winter is bare and brown enough in southern Italy and the earth reduced to more of a mere anatomy than among ourselves, for whom the very *crânerie* of its exposed state, naked and unashamed, gives it much of the robust serenity, not of a fleshless skeleton, but of a fine nude statue. In these regions at any rate, the tone of the air, for the eye, during the brief desolation, has often an extraordinary charm: nature still smiles as with the deputed and provisional charity of colour and light, the duty of not ceasing to cheer man's heart. Her whole behaviour, at the time, cast such a spell on the broken bridge, the little walled town and the trudging friar, that I turned away with the impatient vow and the fond vision of how I would take the journey again and pause to my heart's content at Narni, at Spoleto, at Assisi, at Perugia, at Cortona, at Arezzo. But we have generally to clip our vows a little when we come to fulfil them; and so it befell that when my blest springtime arrived I had to begin as resignedly as possible, yet with comparative meagreness, at Assisi.

I suppose enjoyment would have a simple zest which it often lacks if we always did things at the moment we want to, for it's mostly when we can't that we're thoroughly sure we *would*, and we can answer too little for moods in the future conditional. Winter at least seemed to me to have put something into these seats of antiquity that the May sun had more or less melted away—a desirable strength of tone, a depth upon depth of queerness and quaintness. Assisi had been in the January twilight, after my mere snatch at Narni, a vignette out of some brown old missal. But you'll have to be a fearless explorer now to find of a fine spring day any such cluster of curious objects as doesn't seem made to match before anything else Mr. Baedeker's polyglot estimate of its chief recommendations. This great man was at Assisi in force, and a brand-new inn for his accommodation has just been opened cheek by jowl with the church of St. Francis. I don't know that even the dire discomfort of this harbourage makes it seem less impertinent; but I confess I sought its protection, and the great view seemed hardly less beautiful from my window than from the gallery of the convent. This view embraces the whole wide reach of Umbria, which becomes as twilight deepens a purple counterfeit of the misty sea. The visitor's first errand is with the church; and it's fair furthermore to admit that when he has crossed that threshold the position and quality of his hotel cease for the time to be matters of moment. This twofold temple of St. Francis is one of the very sacred places of Italy, and it would be hard to breathe anywhere an air more heavy with holiness. Such seems especially the case if you happen thus to have come from Rome, where everything ecclesiastical is, in aspect, so very much of this world—so florid, so elegant, so full of accommodations and excrescences. The mere site here makes for authority, and they were brave builders who laid the foundation-stones. The thing rises straight from a steep mountain-side and plunges forward on its great substructure of arches even as a crowned headland may frown over the main. Before it stretches a long, grassy piazza, at the end of which you look up a small grey street, to see it first climb a little way the rest of the hill and then pause and leave a broad green slope, crested, high in the air, with a ruined castle. When I say before it I mean before the upper church; for by way of doing something supremely handsome and impressive the sturdy architects of the thirteenth century piled temple upon temple and bequeathed a double version of their idea. One may imagine them to have intended perhaps an architectural image of the relation between heart and head. Entering the lower church at the bottom of the great flight of steps which leads from the upper door, you seem to push at least into the very heart of Catholicism.

For the first minutes after leaving the clearer gloom you catch nothing but a vista of low black columns closed by the great fantastic cage surrounding the altar, which is thus placed, by your impression, in a sort of gorgeous cavern. Gradually you distinguish details, become accustomed to the penetrating chill, and even manage to make out a few frescoes; but the general effect remains splendidly sombre and subterranean. The vaulted roof is very low and the pillars dwarfish, though immense in girth, as befits pillars supporting substantially a cathedral. The tone of the place is a triumph of mystery, the richest harmony of lurking shadows and dusky corners, all relieved by scattered images and scintillations. There was little light but what came through the windows of the choir over which the red curtains had been dropped and were beginning to glow with the downward sun. The choir was guarded by a screen behind which a dozen venerable voices droned vespers; but over the top of the screen came the heavy radiance and played among the ornaments of the high fence round the shrine, casting the shadow of the whole elaborate mass forward into the obscured nave. The darkness of vaults and side-chapels is overwrought with vague frescoes, most of them by Giotto and his school, out of which confused richness the terribly distinct little faces characteristic of these artists stare at you with a solemn formalism. Some are faded and injured, and many so ill-lighted and ill-placed that you can only glance at them with decent conjecture; the great group, however—four paintings by Giotto on the ceiling above the altar—may be examined with some success. Like everything of that grim and beautiful master they deserve examination; but with the effect ever of carrying one's appreciation in and in, as it were, rather than of carrying it out and out, off and off, as happens for us with those artists who have been helped by the process of "evolution" to grow wings. This one, "going in" for emphasis at any price, stamps hard, as who should say, on the very spot of his idea—thanks to which fact he has a concentration that has never been surpassed. He was in other words, in proportion to his means, a genius supremely expressive; he makes the very shade of an intended meaning or a represented attitude so unmistakable that his figures affect us at moments as creatures all too suddenly, too alarmingly, too menacingly met. Meagre, primitive, undeveloped, he yet is immeasurably strong; he even suggests that if he had lived the due span of years later Michael Angelo might have found a rival. Not that he is given, however, to complicated postures or superhuman flights. The something strange that troubles and haunts us in his work springs rather from a kind of fierce familiarity.

It is part of the wealth of the lower church that it contains an admirable primitive fresco by an artist of genius rarely encountered, Pietro Cavallini, pupil of Giotto. This represents the Crucifixion; the three crosses rising into a sky spotted with the winged heads of angels while a dense crowd presses below. You will nowhere see anything more direfully lugubrious, or more approaching for direct force, though not of course for amplitude of style, Tintoretto's great renderings of the scene in Venice. The abject anguish of the crucified and the straddling authority and brutality of the mounted guards in the foreground are contrasted in a fashion worthy of a great dramatist. But the most poignant touch is the tragic grimaces of the little angelic heads that fall like hailstones through the dark air. It is genuine realistic weeping, the act of irrepressible "crying," that the painter has depicted, and the effect is pitiful at the same time as grotesque. There are many more frescoes besides; all the chapels on one side are lined with them, but these are chiefly interesting in their general impressiveness—as they people the dim recesses with startling presences, with apparitions out of scale. Before leaving the place I lingered long near the door, for I was sure I shouldn't soon again enjoy such a feast of scenic composition. The opposite end glowed with subdued colour; the middle portion was vague and thick and brown, with two or three scattered worshippers looming through the obscurity; while, all the way down, the polished pavement, its uneven slabs glittering dimly in the obstructed light, was of the very essence of expensive picture. It is certainly desirable, if one takes the lower church of St. Francis to represent the human heart, that one should find a few bright places there. But if the general effect is of brightness terrorised and smothered, is the symbol less valid? For the contracted, prejudiced, passionate heart let it stand.

One thing at all events we can say, that we should rejoice to boast as capacious, symmetrical and well-ordered a head as the upper sanctuary. Thanks to these merits, in spite of a brave array of Giottesque work which has the advantage of being easily seen, it lacks the great character of its counterpart. The frescoes, which are admirable, represent certain leading events in the life of St. Francis, and suddenly remind you, by one of those anomalies that are half the secret of the consummate *mise-en-scène* of Catholicism, that the apostle of beggary, the saint whose only tenement in life was the ragged robe which barely covered him, is the hero of this massive structure. Church upon church, nothing less will adequately shroud his consecrated clay. The great reality of Giotto's designs adds to the helpless wonderment with which we feel the passionate pluck of the Hero, the sense of being separated from it by an impassable gulf, the reflection on all that has come and gone to make morality at that vertiginous pitch impossible. There are no such high places of humility left to climb to. An observant friend who has lived long in Italy lately declared to me, however, that she detested the name of this moralist, deeming him chief propagator of the Italian vice most trying to the would-be lover of the people, the want of personal self-respect. There is a solidarity in the use of soap, and every cringing beggar, idler, liar and pilferer flourished for her under the shadow of the great Francisan indifference to it. She was possibly right; at Rome, at Naples, I might have admitted she was right; but at Assisi, face to face with

Giotto's vivid chronicle, we admire too much in its main subject the exquisite play of that subject's genius—we don't remit to him, and this for very envy, a single throb of his consciousness. It took in, that human, that divine embrace, everything *but* soap.

I should find it hard to give an orderly account of my next adventures or impressions at Assisi, which couldn't well be anything more than mere romantic *flânerie*. One may easily plead as the final result of a meditation at the shrine of St. Francis a great and even an amused charity. This state of mind led me slowly up and down for a couple of hours through the steep little streets, and at last stretched itself on the grass with me in the shadow of the great ruined castle that decorates so grandly the eminence above the town. I remember edging along the sunless side of the small mouldy houses and pausing very often to look at nothing in particular. It was all very hot, very hushed, very resignedly but very persistently old. A wheeled vehicle in such a place is an event, and the *forestiero's* interrogative tread in the blank sonorous lanes has the privilege of bringing the inhabitants to their doorways. Some of the better houses, however, achieve a sombre stillness that protests against the least curiosity as to what may happen in any such century as this. You wonder, as you pass, what lingering old-world social types vegetate there, but you won't find out; albeit that in one very silent little street I had a glimpse of an open door which I have not forgotten. A long-haired peddler who must have been a Jew, and who yet carried without prejudice a burden of mass-books and rosaries, was offering his wares to a stout old priest. The priest had opened the door rather stingily and appeared half-heartedly to dismiss him. But the peddler held up something I couldn't see; the priest wavered with a timorous concession to profane curiosity and then furtively pulled the agent of sophistication, or whatever it might be, into the house. I should have liked to enter with that worthy.

I saw later some gentlemen of Assisi who also seemed bored enough to have found entertainment in his tray. They were at the door of the café on the Piazza, and were so thankful to me for asking them the way to the cathedral that, answering all in chorus, they lighted up with smiles as sympathetic as if I had done them a favour. Of that type were my mild, my delicate adventures. The Piazza has a fine old portico of an ancient Temple of Minerva—six fluted columns and a pediment, of beautiful proportions, but sadly battered and decayed. Goethe, I believe, found it much more interesting than the mighty mediæval church, and Goethe, as a cicerone, doubtless could have persuaded one that it was so; but in the humble society of Murray we shall most of us find a richer sense in the later monument. I found quaint old meanings enough in the dark yellow façade of the small cathedral as I sat on a stone bench by the oblong green stretched before it. This is a pleasing piece of Italian Gothic and, like several of its companions at Assisi, has an elegant wheel window and a number of grotesque little carvings of creatures human and bestial. If with Goethe I were to balance anything against the attractions of the double church I should choose the ruined castle on the hill above the town. I had been having glimpses of it all the afternoon at the end of steep street-vistas, and promising myself half-an-hour beside its grey walls at sunset. The sun was very late setting, and my half-hour became a long lounge in the lee of an abutment which arrested the gentle uproar of the wind. The castle is a splendid piece of ruin, perched on the summit of the mountain to whose slope Assisi clings and dropping a pair of stony arms to enclose the little town in its embrace. The city wall, in other words, straggles up the steep green hill and meets the crumbling skeleton of the fortress. On the side off from the town the mountain plunges into a deep ravine, the opposite face of which is formed by the powerful undraped shoulder of Monte Subasio, a fierce reflector of the sun. Gorge and mountain are wild enough, but their frown expires in the teeming softness of the great vale of Umbria. To lie aloft there on the grass, with silver-grey ramparts at one's back and the warm rushing wind in one's ears, and watch the beautiful plain mellow into the tones of twilight, was as exquisite a form of repose as ever fell to a tired tourist's lot.

Perugia too has an ancient stronghold, which one must speak of in earnest as that unconscious humorist the classic American traveller is supposed invariably to speak of the Colosseum: it will be a very handsome building when it's finished. Even Perugia is going the way of all Italy—straightening out her streets, preparing her ruins, laying her venerable ghosts. The castle is being completely *remis à neuf*—a Massachusetts schoolhouse couldn't cultivate a "smarter" ideal. There are shops in the basement and fresh putty on all the windows; so that the only thing proper to a castle it has kept is its magnificent position and range, which you may enjoy from the broad platform where the Perugini assemble at eventide. Perugia is chiefly known to fame as the city of Raphael's master; but it has a still higher claim to renown and ought to figure in the gazetteer of fond memory as the little City of the infinite View. The small dusky, crooked place tries by a hundred prompt pretensions, immediate contortions, rich mantling flushes and other ingenuities, to waylay your attention and keep it at home; but your consciousness, alert and uneasy from the first moment, is all abroad even when your back is turned to the vast alternative or when fifty house-walls conceal it, and you are for ever rushing up by-streets and peeping round corners in the hope of another glimpse or reach of it. As it stretches away before you in that eminent indifference to limits which is at the same time at every step an eminent homage to style, it is altogether too free and fair for compasses and terms. You can only say, and rest upon it, that you prefer it to any other visible fruit of position or claimed empire of the eye that you are anywhere likely to enjoy.

For it is such a wondrous mixture of blooming plain and gleaming river and wavily-multitudinous mountain vaguely dotted with pale grey cities, that, placed as you are, roughly speaking, in the centre of Italy, you all but span the divine peninsula from sea to sea. Up the long vista of the Tiber you look—almost to Rome; past Assisi, Spello, Foligno, Spoleto, all perched on their respective heights and shining through the violet haze. To the north, to the east, to the west, you see a hundred variations of the prospect, of which I have kept no record. Two notes only I have made: one—though who hasn't made it over and over again?—on the exquisite elegance of mountain forms in this endless play of the excrescence, it being exactly as if there were variation of sex in the upheaved mass, with the effect here mainly of contour and curve and complexion determined in the feminine sense. It further came home to me that the command of such an outlook on the world goes far, surely, to give authority and centrality and experience, those of the great seats of dominion, even to so scant a cluster of attesting objects as here. It must deepen the civic consciousness and take off the edge of ennui. It performs this kindly office, at any rate, for the traveller who may overstay his curiosity as to Perugino and the Etruscan relics. It continually solicits his wonder and praise—it reinforces the historic page. I spent a week in the place, and when it was gone I had had enough of Perugino, but hadn't had enough of the View.

I should perhaps do the reader a service by telling him just how a week at Perugia may be spent. His first care must be to ignore the very dream of haste, walking everywhere very slowly and very much at random, and to impute an esoteric sense to almost anything his eye may happen to encounter. Almost everything in fact lends itself to the historic, the romantic, the æsthetic fallacy—almost everything has an antique queerness and richness that ekes out the reduced state; that of a grim and battered old adventuress, the heroine of many shames and scandals, surviving to an extraordinary age and a considerable penury, but with ancient gifts of princes and other forms of the wages of sin to show, and the most beautiful garden of all the world to sit and doze and count her beads in and remember. He must hang a great deal about the huge Palazzo Pubblico, which indeed is very well worth any acquaintance you may scrape with it. It masses itself gloomily above the narrow street to an immense elevation, and leads up the eye along a cliff-like surface of rugged wall, mottled with old scars and new repairs, to the loggia dizzily perched on its cornice. He must repeat his visit to the Etruscan Gate, by whose immemorial composition he must indeed linger long to resolve it back into the elements originally attending it. He must uncap to the irrecoverable, the inimitable style of the statue of Pope Julius III before the cathedral, remembering that Hawthorne fabled his Miriam, in an air of romance from which we are well-nigh as far to-day as from the building of Etruscan gates, to have given rendezvous to Kenyon at its base. Its material is a vivid green bronze, and the mantle and tiara are covered with a delicate embroidery worthy of a silversmith.

Then our leisurely friend must bestow on Perugino's frescoes in the Exchange, and on his pictures in the University, all the placid contemplation they deserve. He must go to the theatre every evening, in an orchestra-chair at twenty-two soldi, and enjoy the curious didacticism of *Amore senza Stima, Severità e Debolezza, La Società Equivoca,* and other popular specimens of contemporaneous

Italian comedy—unless indeed the last-named be not the edifying title applied, for peninsular use, to *Le Demi-Monde* of the younger Dumas. I shall be very much surprised if, at the end of a week of this varied entertainment, he hasn't learnt how to live, not exactly in, but with, Perugia. His strolls will abound in small accidents and mercies of vision, but of which a dozen pencil-strokes would be a better memento than this poor word-sketching. From the hill on which the town is planted radiate a dozen ravines, down whose sides the houses slide and scramble with an alarming indifference to the cohesion of their little rugged blocks of flinty red stone. You ramble really nowhither without emerging on some small court or terrace that throws your view across a gulf of tangled gardens or vineyards and over to a cluster of serried black dwellings which have to hollow in their backs to keep their balance on the opposite ledge. On archways and street-staircases and dark alleys that bore through a density of massive basements, and curve and climb and plunge as they go, all to the truest mediæval tune, you may feast your fill. These are the local, the architectural, the compositional commonplaces. Some of the little streets in out-of-the-way corners are so rugged and brown and silent that you may imagine them passages long since hewn by the pick-axe in a deserted stone-quarry. The battered black houses, of the colour of buried things—things buried, that is, in accumulations of time, closer packed, even as such are, than spadefuls of earth—resemble exposed sections of natural rock; none the less so when, beyond some narrow gap, you catch the blue and silver of the sublime circle of landscape.

But I oughtn't to talk of mouldy alleys, or yet of azure distances, as if they formed the main appeal to taste in this accomplished little city. In the Sala del Cambio, where in ancient days the money-changers rattled their embossed coin and figured up their profits, you may enjoy one of the serenest æsthetic pleasures that the golden age of art anywhere offers us. Bank parlours, I believe, are always handsomely appointed, but are even those of Messrs. Rothschild such models of mural bravery as this little counting-house of a bygone fashion? The bravery is Perugino's own; for, invited clearly to do his best, he left it as a lesson to the ages, covering the four low walls and the vault with scriptural and mythological figures of extraordinary beauty. They are ranged in artless attitudes round the upper half of the room—the sibyls, the prophets, the philosophers, the Greek and Roman heroes—looking down with broad serene faces, with small mild eyes and sweet mouths that commit them to nothing in particular unless to being comfortably and charmingly alive, at the incongruous proceedings of a Board of Brokers. Had finance a very high tone in those days, or were genius and faith then simply as frequent as capital and enterprise are among ourselves? The great distinction of the Sala del Cambio is that it has a friendly Yes for both these questions. There was a rigid transactional probity, it seems to say; there was also a high tide of inspiration. About the artist himself many things come up for us—more than I can attempt in their order; for he was not, I think, to an attentive observer, the mere smooth and entire and devout spirit we at first are inclined to take him for. He has that about him which leads us to wonder if he may not, after all, play a proper part enough here as the patron of the money-changers. He is the delight of a million of young ladies; but who knows whether we shouldn't find in his works, might we "go into" them a little, a trifle more of manner than of conviction, and of system than of deep sincerity?

This, I allow, would put no great affront on them, and one speculates thus partly but because it's a pleasure to hang about him on any pretext, and partly because his immediate effect is to make us quite inordinately embrace the pretext of his lovely soul. His portrait, painted on the wall of the Sala (you may see it also in Rome and Florence) might at any rate serve for the likeness of Mr. Worldly-Wiseman in Bunyan's allegory. He was fond of his glass, I believe, and he made his art lucrative. This tradition is not refuted by his preserved face, and after some experience—or rather after a good deal, since you can't have a *little* of Perugino, who abounds wherever old masters congregate, so that one has constantly the sense of being "in" for all there is—you may find an echo of it in the uniform type of his creatures, their monotonous grace, their prodigious invariability. He may very well have wanted to produce figures of a substantial, yet at the same time of an impeccable innocence; but we feel that he had taught himself *how* even beyond his own belief in them, and had arrived at a process that acted at last mechanically. I confess at the same time that, so interpreted, the painter affects me as hardly less interesting, and one can't but become conscious of one's style when one's style has become, as it were, so conscious of one's, or at least of its own, fortune. If he was the inventor of a remarkably calculable *facture*, a calculation that never fails is in its way a grace of the first order, and there are things in this special appearance of perfection of practice that make him the forerunner of a mighty and more modern race. More than any of the early painters who strongly charm, you may take all his measure from a single specimen. The other samples infallibly match, reproduce unerringly the one type he had mastered, but which had the good fortune to be adorably fair, to seem to have dawned on a vision unsullied by the shadows of earth. Which truth, moreover, leaves Perugino all delightful as composer and draughtsman; he has in each of these characters a sort of spacious neatness which suggests that the whole conception has been washed clean by some spiritual chemistry the last thing before reaching the canvas;

after which it has been applied to that surface with a rare economy of time and means. Giotto and Fra Angelico, beside him, are full of interesting waste and irrelevant passion. In the sacristy of the charming church of San Pietro —a museum of pictures and carvings—is a row of small heads of saints formerly covering the frame of the artist's Ascension, carried off by the French. It is almost miniature work, and here at least Perugino triumphs in sincerity, in apparent candour, as well as in touch. Two of the holy men are reading their breviaries, but with an air of infantine innocence quite consistent with their holding the book upside down.

Between Perugia and Cortona lies the large weedy water of Lake Thrasymene, turned into a witching word for ever by Hannibal's recorded victory over Rome. Dim as such records have become to us and remote such realities, he is yet a passionless pilgrim who doesn't, as he passes, of a heavy summer's day, feel the air and the light and the very faintness of the breeze all charged and haunted with them, all interfused as with the wasted ache of experience and with the vague historic gaze. Processions of indistinguishable ghosts bore me company to Cortona itself, most sturdily ancient of Italian towns. It must have been a seat of ancient knowledge even when Hannibal and Flaminius came to the shock of battle, and have looked down afar from its grey ramparts on the contending swarm with something of the philosophic composure suitable to a survivor of Pelasgic and Etruscan revolutions. These grey ramparts are in great part still visible, and form the chief attraction of Cortona. It is perched on the very pinnacle of a mountain, and I wound and doubled interminably over the face of the great hill, while the jumbled roofs and towers of the arrogant little city still seemed nearer to the sky than to the railway-station. "Rather rough," Murray pronounces the local inn; and rough indeed it was; there was scarce a square foot of it that you would have cared to stroke with your hand. The landlord himself, however, was all smoothness and the best fellow in the world; he took me up into a rickety old loggia on the tip-top of his establishment and played showman as to half the kingdoms of the earth. I was free to decide at the same time whether my loss or my gain was the greater for my seeing Cortona through the medium of a festa. On the one hand the museum was closed (and in a certain sense the smaller and obscurer the town the more I like the museum); the churches—an interesting note of manners and morals—were impenetrably crowded, though, for that matter, so was the café, where I found neither an empty stool nor the edge of a table. I missed a sight of the famous painted Muse, the art-treasure of Cortona and supposedly the most precious, as it falls little short of being the only, sample of the Greek painted picture that has come down to us. On the other hand, I saw—but this is what I saw.

A part of the mountain-top is occupied by the church of St. Margaret, and this was St. Margaret's day. The houses pause roundabout it and leave a grassy slope, planted here and there with lean black cypresses. The contadini from near and far had congregated in force and were crowding into the church or winding up the slope. When I arrived they were all kneeling or uncovered; a bedizened procession, with banners and censers, bearing abroad, I believe, the relics of the saint, was re-entering the church. The scene made one of those pictures that Italy still brushes in for you with an incomparable hand and from an inexhaustible palette when you find her in the mood. The day was superb—the sky blazed overhead like a vault of deepest sapphire. The grave brown peasantry, with no great accent of costume, but with sundry small ones—decked, that is, in cheap fineries of scarlet and yellow —made a mass of motley colour in the high wind-stirred light. The procession halted in the pious hush, and the lovely land around and beneath us melted away, almost to either sea, in tones of azure scarcely less intense than the sky. Behind the church was an empty crumbling citadel, with half-a-dozen old women keeping the gate for coppers. Here were views and breezes and sun and shade and grassy corners to the heart's content, together with one couldn't say what huge seated mystic melancholy presence, the after-taste of everything the still open maw of time had consumed. I chose a spot that fairly combined all these advantages, a spot from which I seemed to look, as who should say, straight down the throat of the monster, no dark passage now, but with all the glorious day playing into it, and spent a good part of my stay at Cortona lying there at my length and observing the situation over the top of a volume that I must have brought in my pocket just for that especial wanton luxury of the resource provided and slighted. In the afternoon I came down and hustled a while through the crowded little streets, and then strolled forth under the scorching sun and made the outer circuit of the wall. There I found tremendous uncemented blocks; they glared and twinkled in the powerful light, and I had to put on a blue eye-glass in order to throw into its proper perspective the vague Etruscan past, obtruded and magnified in such masses quite as with the effect of inadequately-withdrawn hands and feet in photographs.

I spent the next day at Arezzo, but I confess in very much the same uninvestigating fashion—taking in the "general impression," I dare say, at every pore, but rather systematically leaving the dust of the ages unfingered on the stored records: I should doubtless, in the poor time at my command, have fingered it to so little purpose. The seeker for the story of things has moreover, if he be worth his salt, a hundred insidious arts; and in that case indeed—by which I mean when his sensibility has come duly to adjust itself

—the story assaults him but from too many sides. He even feels at moments that he must sneak along on tiptoe in order not to have too much of it. Besides which the case all depends on the kind of use, the range of application, his tangled consciousness, or his intelligible genius, say, may come to recognize for it. At Arezzo, however this might be, one was far from Rome, one was well within genial Tuscany, and the historic, the romantic decoction seemed to reach one's lips in less stiff doses. There at once was the "general impression"—the exquisite sense of the scarce expressible Tuscan quality, which makes immediately, for the whole pitch of one's perception, a grateful, a not at all strenuous difference, attaches to almost any coherent group of objects, to any happy aspect of the scene, for a main note, some mild recall, through pleasant friendly colour, through settled ample form, through something homely and economic too at the very heart of "style," of an identity of temperament and habit with those of the divine little Florence that one originally knew. Adorable Italy in which, for the constant renewal of interest, of attention, of affection, these refinements of variety, these so harmoniously-grouped and individually-seasoned fruits of the great garden of history, keep presenting themselves! It seemed to fall in with the cheerful Tuscan mildness for instance—sticking as I do to that ineffectual expression of the Tuscan charm, of the yellow-brown Tuscan dignity at large—that the ruined castle on the hill (with which agreeable feature Arezzo is no less furnished than Assisi and Cortona) had been converted into a great blooming, and I hope all profitable, podere or market-garden. I lounged away the half-hours there under a spell as potent as the "wildest" forecast of propriety—propriety to all the particular conditions—could have figured it. I had seen Santa Maria della Pieve and its campanile of quaint colonnades, the stately, dusky cathedral—grass-plotted and residenced about almost after the fashion of an English "close"—and John of Pisa's elaborate marble shrine; I had seen the museum and its Etruscan vases and majolica platters. These were very well, but the old pacified citadel somehow, through a day of soft saturation, placed me most in relation. Beautiful hills surrounded it, cypresses cast straight shadows at its corners, while in the middle grew a wondrous Italian tangle of wheat and corn, vines and figs, peaches and cabbages, memories and images, anything and everything.

Siena

1873

Florence being oppressively hot and delivered over to the mosquitoes, the occasion seemed to favour that visit to Siena which I had more than once planned and missed. I arrived late in the evening, by the light of a magnificent moon, and while a couple of benignantly-mumbling old crones were making up my bed at the inn strolled forth in quest of a first impression. Five minutes brought me to where I might gather it unhindered as it bloomed in the white moonshine. The great Piazza of Siena is famous, and though in this day of multiplied photographs and blunted surprises and profaned revelations none of the world's wonders can pretend, like Wordsworth's phantom of delight, really to "startle and waylay," yet as I stepped upon the waiting scene from under a dark archway I was conscious of no loss of the edge of a precious presented sensibility. The waiting scene, as I have called it, was in the shape of a shallow horse-shoe—as the untravelled reader who has turned over his travelled friends' portfolios will respectfully remember; or, better, of a bow in which the high wide face of the Palazzo Pubblico forms the cord and everything else the arc. It was void of any human presence that could figure to me the current year; so that, the moonshine assisting, I had half-an-hour's infinite vision of mediæval Italy. The Piazza being built on the side of a hill—or rather, as I believe science affirms, in the cup of a volcanic crater—the vast pavement converges downwards in slanting radiations of stone, the spokes of a great wheel, to a point directly before the Palazzo, which may mark the hub, though it is nothing more ornamental than the mouth of a drain. The great monument stands on the lower side and might seem, in spite of its goodly mass and its embattled cornice, to be rather defiantly out-countenanced by vast private constructions occupying the opposite eminence. This *might* be, without the extraordinary dignity of the architectural gesture with which the huge high-shouldered pile asserts itself.

On the firm edge of the palace, from bracketed base to grey-capped summit against the sky, where grows a tall slim tower which soars and soars till it has given notice of the city's greatness over the blue mountains that mark the horizon. It rises as slender and straight as a pennoned lance planted on the steel-shod toe of a mounted knight, and keeps all to itself in the blue air, far above the changing fashions of the market, the proud consciousness or rare arrogance once built into it. This beautiful tower, the finest thing in Siena and, in its rigid fashion, as permanently fine thus as a really handsome nose on a face of no matter what accumulated age, figures there still as a Declaration of Independence beside which such an affair as ours, thrown off at Philadelphia, appears to have scarce done more than helplessly give way to time. Our Independence has become a dependence on a thousand such dreadful things as the incorrupt declaration of Siena strikes us as looking for ever straight over the level of. As it stood silvered by the moonlight, while my greeting lasted, it seemed to speak, all as from soul to soul, very much indeed as some ancient worthy of a lower order, buttonholing one on the coveted chance and at the quiet hour, might have done, of a state of things long and vulgarly superseded, but to the pride and power, the once prodigious vitality, of which who could expect any one effect to testify more incomparably, more indestructibly, quite, as it were, more immortally? The gigantic houses enclosing the rest of the Piazza took up the tale and mingled with it their burden. "We are very old and a trifle weary, but we were built strong and piled high, and we shall last for many an age. The present is cold and heedless, but we keep ourselves in heart by brooding over our store of memories and traditions. We are haunted houses in every creaking timber and aching stone." Such were the gossiping connections I established with Siena before I went to bed.

Since that night I have had a week's daylight knowledge of the surface of the subject at least, and don't know how I can better present it than simply as another and a vivider page of the lesson that the ever-hungry artist has only to *trust* old Italy for her to feed him at every single step from her hand—and if not with one sort of sweetly-stale grain from that wondrous mill of history which during so many ages ground finer than any other on earth, why then always with something else. Siena has at any rate "preserved appearances"—kept the greatest number of them, that is, unaltered for the eye—about as consistently as one can imagine the thing done. Other places perhaps may treat you to as drowsy an odour of antiquity, but few exhale it from so large an area. Lying massed within her walls on a dozen clustered hill-tops, she shows you at every turn in how much greater a way she once lived; and if so much of the grand manner is extinct, the receptacle of the ashes still solidly rounds itself. This heavy general stress of all her emphasis on the past is what she constantly keeps in your eyes and your ears, and if you be but a casual observer and admirer the generalised response is mainly what you give her. The casual observer, however beguiled, is mostly not very learned, not over-equipped in advance with data; he hasn't specialised, his notions are necessarily vague, the chords of his imagination, for all his good-will, are inevitably muffled and weak. But such as it is, his received, his welcome impression serves his turn so far as the life of sensibility goes, and reminds him from time to time that even the lore of German doctors is but the shadow of satisfied curiosity. I have been living at the inn, walking about the streets, sitting in the Piazza; these are the simple terms of my experience. But streets and inns in Italy are the vehicles of half one's knowledge; if one has no fancy for their lessons one may burn one's note-book. In Siena everything is Sienese. The inn has an English sign over the door—a little battered plate with a rusty representation of the lion and the unicorn; but advance hopefully into the mouldy stone alley which serves as vestibule and you will find local colour enough. The landlord, I was told, had been servant in an English family, and I was curious to see how he met the probable argument of the casual Anglo-Saxon after the latter's first twelve hours in his establishment. As he failed to appear I asked the waiter if he weren't at home. "Oh," said the latter, "he's a *piccolo grasso vecchiotto* who doesn't like to move." I'm afraid this little fat old man has simply a bad conscience. It's no small burden for one who likes the Italians—as who doesn't, under this restriction?—to have so much indifference even to rudimentary purifying processes to dispose of. What is the real philosophy of dirty habits, and are foul surfaces merely superficial? If unclean manners have in truth the moral meaning which I suspect in them we must love Italy better than consistency. This a number of us are prepared to do, but while we are making the sacrifice it is as well we should be aware.

We may plead moreover for these impecunious heirs of

the past that even if it were easy to be clean in the midst of their mouldering heritage it would be difficult to appear so. At the risk of seeming to flaunt the silly superstition of restless renovation for the sake of renovation, which is but the challenge of the infinitely precious principle of duration, one is still moved to say that the prime result of one's contemplative strolls in the dusky alleys of such a place is an ineffable sense of disrepair. Everything is cracking, peeling, fading, crumbling, rotting. No young Sienese eyes rest upon anything youthful; they open into a world battered and befouled with long use. Everything has passed its meridian except the brilliant façade of the cathedral, which is being diligently retouched and restored, and a few private palaces whose broad fronts seem to have been lately furbished and polished. Siena was long ago mellowed to the pictorial tone; the operation of time is now to deposit shabbiness upon shabbiness. But it's for the most part a patient, sturdy, sympathetic shabbiness, which soothes rather than irritates the nerves, and has in many cases doubtless as long a career to run as most of our pert and shallow freshnesses. It projects at all events a deeper shadow into the constant twilight of the narrow streets—that vague historic dusk, as I may call it, in which one walks and wonders. These streets are hardly more than sinuous flagged alleys, into which the huge black houses, between their almost meeting cornices, suffer a meagre light to filter down over rough-hewn stone, past windows often of graceful Gothic form, and great pendent iron rings and twisted sockets for torches. Scattered over their many-headed hill, they suffer the roadway often to incline to the perpendicular, becoming so impracticable for vehicles that the sound of wheels is only a trifle less anomalous than it would be in Venice. But all day long there comes up to my window an incessant shuffling of feet and clangour of voices. The weather is very warm for the season, all the world is out of doors, and the

Tuscan tongue (which in Siena is reputed to have a classic purity) wags in every imaginable key. It doesn't rest even at night, and I am often an uninvited guest at concerts and *conversazioni* at two o'clock in the morning. The concerts are sometimes charming. I not only don't curse my wakefulness, but go to my window to listen. Three men come carolling by, trolling and quavering with voices of delightful sweetness, or a lonely troubadour in his shirt-sleeves draws such artful love-notes from his clear, fresh tenor, that I seem for the moment to be behind the scenes at the opera, watching some Rubini or Mario go "on" and waiting for the round of applause. In the intervals a couple of friends or enemies stop—Italians always make their points in conversation by pulling up, letting you walk on a few paces, to turn and find them standing with finger on nose and engaging your interrogative eye—they pause, by a happy instinct, directly under my window, and dispute their point or tell their story or make their confidence. One scarce is sure which it may be; everything has such an explosive promptness, such a redundancy of inflection and action. But everything for that matter takes on such dramatic life as *our* lame colloquies never know—so that almost any uttered communications here become an acted play, improvised, mimicked, proportioned and rounded, carried bravely to its *dénoûment*. The speaker seems actually to establish his stage and face his foot-lights, to create by a gesture a little scenic circumscription about him; he rushes to and fro and shouts and stamps and postures, he ranges through every phase of his inspiration. I noted the other evening a striking instance of the spontaneity of the Italian gesture, in the person of a small Sienese of I hardly know what exact age—the age of inarticulate sounds and the experimental use of a spoon. It was a Sunday evening, and this little man had accompanied his parents to the café. The Caffè Greco at Siena is a most delightful institution; you get a capital *demi-tasse* for three sous, and an excellent ice for eight, and while you consume these easy luxuries you may buy from a little hunchback the local weekly periodical, the *Vita Nuova,* for three centimes (the two centimes left from your sou, if you are under the spell of this magical frugality, will do to give the waiter). My young friend was sitting on his father's knee and helping himself to the half of a strawberry-ice with which his mamma had presented him. He had so many misadventures with his spoon that this lady at length confiscated it, there being nothing left of the ice but a little crimson liquid which he might dispose of by the common instinct of childhood. But he was no friend, it appeared, to such freedoms; he was a perfect little gentleman and he resented it being expected of him that he should drink down his remnant. He protested therefore, and it was the manner of his protest that struck me. He didn't cry audibly, though he made a very wry face. It was no stupid squall, and yet he was too young to speak. It was a penetrating concord of inarticulately pleading, accusing sounds, accompanied by gestures of the most exquisite propriety. These were perfectly mature; he did everything that a man of forty would have done if he had been pouring out a flood of sonorous eloquence. He shrugged his shoulders and wrinkled his eyebrows, tossed out his hands and folded his arms, obtruded his chin and bobbed about his head—and at last, I am happy to say, recovered his spoon. If I had had a solid little silver one I would have presented it to him as a testimonial to a perfect, though as yet unconscious, artist.

My actual tribute to him, however, has diverted me from what I had in mind—a much weightier matter—the great private palaces which are the massive majestic syllables, sentences, periods, of the strange message the place addresses to us. They are extraordinarily spacious and numerous, and one wonders what part they can play in the meagre economy of the actual city. The Siena of to-day is a mere shrunken semblance of the rabid little republic which in the thirteenth century waged triumphant war with Florence, cultivated the arts with splendour, planned a cathedral (though it had ultimately to curtail the design) of proportions almost unequalled, and contained a population of two hundred thousand souls. Many of these dusky piles still bear the names of the old mediæval magnates the vague mild occupancy of whose descendants has the effect of armour of proof worn over "pot" hats and tweed jackets and trousers. Half-a-dozen of them are as high as the Strozzi and Riccardi palaces in Florence; they couldn't well be higher. The very essence of the romantic and the scenic is in the way these colossal dwellings are packed together in their steep streets, in the depths of their little enclosed, agglomerated city. When we, in our day and country, raise a structure of half the mass and dignity, we leave a great space about it in the manner of a pause after a showy speech. But when a Sienese countess, as things are here, is doing her hair near the window, she is a wonderfully near neighbour to the cavalier opposite, who is being shaved by his valet. Possibly the countess doesn't object to a certain chosen publicity at her toilet; what does an Italian gentleman assure me but that the aristocracy make very free with each other? Some of the palaces are shown, but only when the occupants are at home, and now they are in *villeggiatura.* Their villeggiatura lasts eight months of the year, the waiter at the inn informs me, and they spend little more than the carnival in the city. The gossip of an inn-waiter ought perhaps to be beneath the dignity of even such thin history as this; but I confess that when, as a story-seeker always and ever, I have come in from my strolls with an irritated sense of the dumbness of stones and mortar, it has been to listen with avidity, over my dinner, to the proffered confidences of the worthy man who stands by with a napkin. His talk is really very fine, and he prides himself greatly on his cultivated tone, to which he calls my attention. He has very little good to say about the Sienese nobility. They are "proprio d' origine egoista"—whatever that may be—and there are many who can't write their names. This may be calumny; but I doubt whether the most blameless of them all could have spoken more delicately of a lady of peculiar personal appearance who had been dining near me. "She's too fat," I grossly said on her leaving the room. The waiter shook his head with a little sniff: "È troppo materiale." This lady and her companion were the party whom, thinking I might relish a little company—I had been dining alone for a week—he gleefully announced to me as newly arrived Americans. They were Americans, I found, who wore, pinned to their heads in permanence, the black lace veil or mantilla, conveyed their beans to their mouth with a knife, and spoke a strange raucous Spanish. They were in fine compatriots from Montevideo. The genius of old Siena, however, would make little of any stress of such distinctions; one representative of a far-off social platitude being about as much in order as another as he stands before the great loggia of the Casino di Nobili, the club of the best society. The nobility, which is very numerous and very rich, is still, says the apparently competent native I began by quoting, perfectly feudal and uplifted and separate. Morally and intellectually, behind the walls of its palaces, the fourteenth century, it's thrilling to think, hasn't ceased to hang on. There is no bourgeoisie to speak of; immediately after the aristocracy come the poor people, who are very poor indeed. My friend's account of these matters made me wish more than ever, as a lover of the preserved social specimen, of type at almost any price, that one weren't, a helpless victim of the historic sense, reduced simply to staring at black stones and peeping up stately staircases; and that when one had examined the street-face of the palace, Murray in hand, one might walk up to the great drawing-room, make one's bow to the master and mistress, the old abbé and the young count, and invite them to favour one with a sketch of their social philosophy or a few first-hand family anecdotes.

The dusky labyrinth of the streets, we must in default of such initiations content ourselves with noting, is interrupted by two great candid spaces: the fan-shaped piazza, of which I just now said a word, and the smaller square in which the cathedral erects its walls of many-coloured marble. Of course since paying the great piazza my compliments by moonlight I have strolled through it often at sunnier and shadier hours. The market is held there, and wherever Italians buy and sell, wherever they count and chaffer—as indeed you hear them do right and left, at almost any moment, as you take your way among them—the pulse of life beats fast. It has been doing so on the spot just named, I suppose, for the last five hundred years, and during that time the cost of eggs and earthen pots has been gradually but inexorably increasing. The buyers nevertheless wrestle over their purchases as lustily as so many fourteenth-century burghers suddenly waking up in horror to current prices. You have but to walk aside, however, into the Palazzo Pubblico really to feel yourself a thrifty old mediævalist. The state affairs of the Republic were formerly transacted here, but it now gives shelter to modern law-courts and other prosy business. I was marched through a number of vaulted halls and chambers, which, in the intervals of the administrative sessions held in them, are peopled only by the great mouldering archaic frescoes—anything but inanimate these even in their present ruin—that cover the walls and ceiling. The chief painters of the Sienese school lent a hand in producing the works I name, and you may complete there the connoisseurship in which, possibly, you will have embarked at the Academy. I say "possibly" to be very judicial, my own observation having led me no great length. I have rather than otherwise cherished the thought that the Sienese school suffers one's eagerness peacefully to slumber—benignantly abstains in fact from whipping up a languid curiosity and a tepid faith. "A formidable rival to the Florentine," says some book—I forget which—into which I recently glanced. Not a bit of it thereupon boldly say I; the Florentines may rest on their laurels and the lounger on his lounge. The early painters of the two groups have indeed much in common; but the Florentines had the good fortune to see their efforts gathered up and applied by a few pre-eminent spirits, such as never came to the rescue of the groping Sienese. Fra Angelico and Ghirlandaio said all their feebler *confrères* dreamt of and a great deal more beside, but the inspiration of Simone Memmi and Ambrogio Lorenzetti and Sano di Pietro has a painful air of never efflorescing into a maximum. Sodoma and Beccafumi are to my taste a rather abortive maximum. But one should speak of them all gently—and I do, from my soul; for their labour, by their lights, has wrought a precious heritage of still-living colour and rich figure-peopled shadow for the echoing chambers of their old civic fortress. The faded frescoes cover the walls like quaintly-storied tapestries; in one way or another they cast their spell. If one owes a large debt of pleasure to pictorial art one comes to think tenderly and easily of its whole evolution, as of the conscious experience of a single mysterious, striving spirit, and one shrinks from saying rude things about any particular phase of it, just as one would from referring without precautions to some error or lapse in the life of a person one esteemed. You don't care to remind a grizzled veteran of his defeats, and why should we linger in Siena to talk about Beccafumi? I by no means go so far as to say, with an amateur with whom I have just been discussing the matter, that "Sodoma is a precious poor painter and Beccafumi no painter at all"; but, opportunity being limited, I am willing to let the remark about Beccafumi pass for true. With regard to Sodoma, I remember seeing four years ago in the choir of the Cathedral of Pisa a certain small dusky specimen of the painter—an Abraham and Isaac, if I am not mistaken—which was charged with a gloomy grace. One rarely meets him in general collections, and I had never done so till the other day. He was not prolific, apparently; he had however his own elegance, and his rarity is a part of it.

Here in Siena are a couple of dozen scattered frescoes and three or four canvases; his masterpiece, among others, an harmonious Descent from the Cross. I wouldn't give a fig for the equilibrium of the figures or the ladders; but while it lasts the scene is all intensely solemn and graceful and sweet—too sweet for so bitter a subject. Sodoma's women are strangely sweet; an imaginative sense of morbid appealing attitude—as notably in the sentimental, the pathetic, but the none the less pleasant, "Swooning of St. Catherine," the great Sienese heroine, at San Domenico—seems to me the author's finest accomplishment. His frescoes have all the same almost appealing evasion of difficulty, and a kind of mild melancholy which I am inclined to think the sincerest part of them, for it strikes me as practically the artist's depressed suspicion of his own want of force. Once he determined, however, that if he couldn't be strong he would make capital of his weakness, and painted the Christ bound to the Column, of the Academy. Here he got much nearer and I have no doubt mixed his colours with his tears; but the result can't be better described than by saying that it is, pictorially, the first of the modern Christs. Unfortunately it hasn't been the last.

The main strength of Sienese art went possibly into the erection of the Cathedral, and yet even here the strength is not of the greatest strain. If, however, there are more interesting temples in Italy, there are few more richly and variously scenic and splendid, the comparative meagreness of the architectural idea being overlaid by a marvellous wealth of ingenious detail. Opposite the church—with the dull old archbishop's palace on one side and a dismantled residence of the late Grand Duke of Tuscany on the other —is an ancient hospital with a big stone bench running all along its front. Here I have sat a while every morning for a week, like a philosophic convalescent, watching the florid façade of the cathedral glitter against the deep blue sky. It has been lavishly restored of late years, and the fresh white marble of the densely clustered pinnacles and statues and beasts and flowers flashes in the sunshine like a mosaic of jewels. There is more of this goldsmith's work in stone than I can remember or describe; it is piled up over three great doors with immense margins of exquisite decorative sculpture—still in the ancient cream-coloured marble—and beneath three sharp pediments embossed with images relieved against red marble and tipped with golden mosaics. It is in the highest degree fantastic and luxuriant—it is on the whole very lovely. As a triumph of the many-hued it prepares you for the interior, where the same parti-coloured splendour is endlessly at play—a confident complication of harmonies and contrasts and of the minor structural refinements and braveries. The internal surface is mainly wrought in alternate courses of black and white marble; but as the latter has been dimmed by the centuries to a fine mild brown the place is all a concert of relieved and dispersed glooms. Save for Pinturicchio's brilliant frescoes in the Sacristy there are no pictures to speak of; but the pavement is covered with many elaborate designs in black and white mosaic after cartoons by Beccafumi. The patient skill of these compositions makes them a rare piece of decoration; yet even here the friend whom I lately quoted rejects this over-ripe fruit of the Sienese school. The designs are nonsensical, he declares, and all his admiration is for the cunning artisans who have imitated the hatchings and shadings and hair-strokes of the pencil by the finest curves of inserted black stone. But the true romance of handiwork at Siena is to be seen in the wondrous stalls of the choir, under the coloured light of the great wheel-window. Wood-carving has ever been a cherished craft of the place, and the best masters of the art during the fifteenth century lavished themselves on this prodigious task. It is the frost-work on one's window-panes interpreted in polished oak. It would be hard to find, doubtless, a more moving illustration of the peculiar patience, the sacred candour, of the great time. Into such artistry as this the author seems to put more of his personal substance than into any other; he has to wrestle not only with his subject, but with his material. He is richly fortunate when his subject is charming—when his devices, inventions and fantasies spring lightly to his hand; for in the material itself, after age and use have ripened and polished and darkened it to the richness of ebony and to a greater warmth, there is something surpassingly delectable and venerable. Wander behind the altar at Siena when the chanting is over and the incense has faded, and look well at the stalls of the Barili.

From "Siena Early and Late" (1874–1909)

Florence

1877

I

I had never known Florence more herself, or in other words more attaching, than I found her for a week in that brilliant October.[1] She sat in the sunshine beside her yellow river like the little treasure-city she has always seemed, without commerce, without other industry than the manufacture of mosaic paperweights and alabaster Cupids, without actuality or energy or earnestness or any of those rugged virtues which in most cases are deemed indispensable for civic cohesion; with nothing but the little unaugmented stock of her mediæval memories, her tender-coloured mountains, her churches and palaces, pictures and statues. There were very few strangers; one's detested fellow-pilgrim was infrequent; the native population itself seemed scanty; the sound of wheels in the streets was but occasional; by eight o'clock at night, apparently, every one had gone to bed, and the musing wanderer, still wandering and still musing, had the

[1] James had left Paris in October 1877 and entered Italy by way of the Jura and the Mont Cenis Tunnel, so approaching Florence by way of Turin, Genoa, and Spezia. He describes the journey in the essay "Italy Revisited," of 1878, from which this account of his visit to Florence is taken. [Editor's note.]

place to himself—had the thick shadow-masses of the great palaces, and the shafts of moonlight striking the polygonal paving-stones, and the empty bridges, and the silvered yellow of the Arno, and the stillness broken only by a homeward step, a step accompanied by a snatch of song from a warm Italian voice. My room at the inn looked out on the river and was flooded all day with sunshine. There was an absurd orange-coloured paper on the walls; the Arno, of a hue not altogether different, flowed beneath; and on the other side of it rose a line of sallow houses, of extreme antiquity, crumbling and mouldering, bulging and protruding over the stream. (I seem to speak of their fronts; but what I saw was their shabby backs, which were exposed to the cheerful flicker of the river, while the fronts stood for ever in the deep damp shadow of a narrow mediæval street.) All this brightness and yellowness was a perpetual delight; it was a part of that indefinably charming colour which Florence always seems to wear as you look up and down at it from the river, and from the bridges and quays. This is a kind of grave radiance—a harmony of high tints—which I scarce know how to describe. There are yellow walls and green blinds and red roofs, there are intervals of brilliant brown and natural-looking blue; but the picture is not spotty nor gaudy, thanks to the distribution of the colours in large and comfortable masses, and to the washing-over of the scene by some happy softness of sunshine. The river-front of Florence is in short a delightful composition. Part of its charm comes of course from the generous aspect of those high-based Tuscan palaces which a renewal of acquaintance with them has again commended to me as the most dignified dwellings in the world. Nothing can be finer than that look of giving up the whole immense ground-floor to simple purposes of vestibule and staircase, of court and high-arched entrance; as if this were all but a massive pedestal for the real habitation and people weren't properly housed unless, to begin with, they should be lifted fifty feet above the pavement. The great blocks of the basement; the great intervals, horizontally and vertically, from window to window (telling of the height and breadth of the rooms within); the armorial shield hung forward at one of the angles; the wide-brimmed roof, overshadowing the narrow street; the rich old browns and yellows of the walls: these definite elements put themselves together with admirable art.

Take a Tuscan pile of this type out of its oblique situation in the town; call it no longer a palace, but a villa; set it down by a terrace on one of the hills that encircle Florence, place a row of high-waisted cypresses beside it, give it a grassy courtyard and a view of the Florentine towers and the valley of the Arno, and you will think it perhaps even more worthy of your esteem. It was a Sunday noon, and brilliantly warm, when I again arrived; and after I had looked from my windows a while at that quietly-basking river-front I have spoken of I took my way across one of the bridges and then out of one of the gates—that immensely tall Roman Gate in which the space from the top of the arch to the cornice (except that there is scarcely a cornice, it is all a plain massive piece of wall) is as great, or seems to be, as that from the ground to the former point. Then I climbed a steep and winding way—much of it a little dull if one likes, being bounded by mottled, mossy garden-walls—to a villa on a hill-top, where I found various things that touched me with almost too fine a point. Seeing them again, often, for a week, both by sunlight and moonshine, I never quite learned not to covet them; not to feel that not being a part of them was somehow to miss an exquisite chance. What a tranquil, contented life it seemed, with romantic beauty as a part of its daily texture!—the sunny terrace, with its tangled *podere* beneath it; the bright grey olives against the bright blue sky; the long, serene, horizontal lines of other villas, flanked by their upward cypresses, disposed upon the neighbouring hills; the richest little city in the world in a softly-scooped hollow at one's feet, and beyond it the most appealing of views, the most majestic, yet the most familiar. Within the villa was a great love of art and a painting-room full of felicitous work, so that if human life there confessed to quietness, the quietness was mostly but that of the intent act. A beautiful occupation in that beautiful position, what could possibly be better? That is what I spoke just now of envying—a way of life that doesn't wince at such refinements of peace and ease. When labour self-charmed presents itself in a dull or an ugly place we esteem it, we admire it, but we scarce feel it to be the ideal of good fortune. When, however, its votaries move as figures in an ancient, noble landscape, and their walks and contemplations are like a turning of the leaves of history, we seem to have before us an admirable case of virtue made easy; meaning here by virtue contentment and concentration, a real appreciation of the rare, the exquisite though composite, medium of life. You needn't want a rush or a crush when the scene itself, the mere scene, shares with you such a wealth of consciousness.

It is true indeed that I might after a certain time grow weary of a regular afternoon stroll among the Florentine lanes; of sitting on low parapets, in intervals of flower-topped wall, and looking across at Fiesole or down the rich-hued valley of the Arno; of pausing at the open gates of villas and wondering at the height of cypresses and the depth of loggias; of walking home in the fading light and noting on a dozen westward-looking surfaces the glow of the opposite sunset. But for a week or so all this was delightful. The villas are innumerable, and if you're an aching alien half the talk is about villas. This one has a story; that one has another; they all look as if they had stories—none in truth predominantly gay. Most of them are offered to rent (many of them for sale) at prices unnaturally low; you may have a tower and a garden, a chapel and an expanse of thirty windows, for five hundred dollars a year. In imagination you hire three or four; you take possession and settle and stay. Your sense of the fineness of the finest is of something very grave and stately; your sense of the bravery of two or three of the best something quite tragic and sinister. From what does this latter impression come? You gather it as you stand there in the early dusk, with your eyes on the long, pale-brown façade, the enormous windows, the iron cages fastened to the lower ones. Part of the brooding expression of these great houses comes, even when they have not fallen into decay, from their look of having outlived their original use. Their extraordinary largeness and massiveness are a satire on their present fate. They weren't built with such a thickness of wall and depth of embrasure, such a solidity of staircase and superfluity of stone, simply to afford an economical winter residence to English and American families. I don't know whether it was the appearance of these stony old villas, which seemed so dumbly conscious of a change of manners, that threw a tinge of melancholy over the general prospect; certain it is that, having always found this note as of a myriad old sadnesses in solution in the view of Florence, it seemed to me now particularly strong. "Lovely, lovely, but it makes me 'blue,'" the sensitive stranger couldn't but murmur to himself as, in the late afternoon, he looked at the landscape from over one of the low parapets, and then, with his hands in his pockets, turned away indoors to candles and dinner.

II

Below, in the city, through all frequentation of streets and churches and museums, it was impossible not to have a good deal of the same feeling; but here the impression was more easy to analyse. It came from a sense of the perfect separateness of all the great productions of the Renaissance from the present and the future of the place, from the actual life and manners, the native ideal. I have already spoken of the way in which the vast aggregation of beautiful works of art in the Italian cities strikes the visitor nowadays—so far as present Italy is concerned—as the mere stock-in-trade of an impecunious but thrifty people. It is this spiritual solitude, this conscious disconnection of the great works of architecture and sculpture that deposits a certain weight upon the heart; when we see a great tradition broken we feel something of the pain with which we hear a stifled cry. But regret is one thing and resentment is another. Seeing one morning, in a shop-window, the series of *Mornings in Florence* published a few years since by Mr. Ruskin, I made haste to enter and purchase these amusing little books, some passages of which I remembered formerly to have read. I couldn't turn over many pages without observing that the "separateness" of the new and old which I just mentioned had produced in their author the liveliest irritation. With the more acute phases of this condition it was difficult to sympathise, for the simple reason, it seems to me, that it savours of arrogance to demand of any people, as a right of one's own, that they shall be artistic. "Be artistic yourselves!" is the very natural reply that young Italy has at hand for English critics and censors. When a people produces beautiful statues and pictures it gives us something more than is set down in the bond, and we must thank it for its generosity; and when it stops producing them or caring for them we may cease thanking, but we hardly have a right to begin and rail. The wreck of Florence, says Mr. Ruskin, "is now too ghastly and heart-breaking to any human soul that remembers the days of old"; and these desperate words are an allusion to the fact that the little square in front of the cathedral, at the foot of Giotto's Tower, with the grand Baptistery on the other side, is now the resort of a number of hackney-coaches and omnibuses. This fact is doubtless lamentable, and it would be a hundred times more agreeable to see among people who have been made the heirs of so priceless a work of art as the sublime campanile some such feeling about it as would keep it free even from the danger of defilement. A cab-stand is a very ugly and dirty thing, and Giotto's Tower should have nothing in common with such conveniences. But there is more than one way of taking such things, and the sensitive stranger who has been walking about for a week with his mind full of the sweetness and suggestiveness of a hundred Florentine places may feel at last in looking into Mr. Ruskin's little tracts that, discord for discord, there isn't much to choose between the importunity of the author's personal ill-humour and the incongruity of horse-pails and bundles of hay. And one may say this without being at all a partisan of the doctrine of the inevitableness of new desecrations. For my own part, I believe there are few things in this line that the new Italian spirit isn't capable of, and not many indeed that we aren't destined to see. Pictures and buildings won't be completely destroyed, because in that case the *forestieri,* scatterers of cash, would cease to arrive and the turn-stiles at the doors of the old palaces and convents, with the little patented slit for absorbing your half-franc, would grow quite rusty, would stiffen with disuse. But it's safe to say that the new Italy growing into an old Italy again will continue to take her elbow-room wherever she may find it.

I am almost ashamed to say what I did with Mr. Ruskin's little books. I put them into my pocket and betook myself to Santa Maria Novella. There I sat down and, after I had looked about for a while at the beautiful church, drew them forth one by one and read the greater part of them.

Occupying one's self with light literature in a great religious edifice is perhaps as bad a piece of profanation as any of those rude dealings which Mr. Ruskin justly deplores; but a traveller has to make the most of odd moments, and I was waiting for a friend in whose company I was to go and look at Giotto's beautiful frescoes in the cloister of the church. My friend was a long time coming, so that I had an hour with Mr. Ruskin, whom I called just now a light *littérateur* because in these little *Mornings in Florence* he is for ever making his readers laugh. I remembered of course where I was, and in spite of my latent hilarity felt I had rarely got such a snubbing. I had really been enjoying the good old city of Florence, but I now learned from Mr. Ruskin that this was a scandalous waste of charity. I should have gone about with an imprecation on my lips, I should have worn a face three yards long. I had taken great pleasure in certain frescoes by Ghirlandaio in the choir of that very church; but it appeared from one of the little books that these frescoes were as naught. I had much admired Santa Croce and had thought the Duomo a very noble affair; but I had now the most positive assurance I knew nothing about them. After a while, if it was only ill-humour that was needed for doing honour to the city of the Medici, I felt that I had risen to a proper level; only now it was Mr. Ruskin himself I had lost patience with, not the stupid Brunelleschi, not the vulgar Ghirlandaio. Indeed I lost patience altogether, and asked myself by what right this informal votary of form pretended to run riot through a poor charmed *flâneur's* quiet contemplations, his attachment to the noblest of pleasures, his enjoyment of the loveliest of cities. The little books seemed invidious and insane, and it was only when I remembered that I had been under no obligation to buy them that I checked myself in repenting of having done so.

Then at last my friend arrived and we passed together

out of the church, and, through the first cloister beside it, into a smaller enclosure where we stood a while to look at the tomb of the Marchesa Strozzi-Ridolfi, upon which the great Giotto has painted four superb little pictures. It was easy to see the pictures were superb; but I drew forth one of my little books again, for I had observed that Mr. Ruskin spoke of them. Hereupon I recovered my tolerance; for what could be better in this case, I asked myself, than Mr. Ruskin's remarks? They are in fact excellent and charming—full of appreciation of the deep and simple beauty of the great painter's work. I read them aloud to my companion; but my companion was rather, as the phrase is, "put off" by them. One of the frescoes—it is a picture of the birth of the Virgin—contains a figure coming through a door. "Of ornament," I quote, "there is only the entirely simple outline of the vase which the servant carries; of colour two or three masses of sober red and pure white, with brown and grey. That is all," Mr. Ruskin continues. "And if you are pleased with this you can see Florence. But if not, by all means amuse yourself there, if you find it amusing, as long as you like; you can never see it." *You can never see it.* This seemed to my friend insufferable, and I had to shuffle away the book again, so that we might look at the fresco with the unruffled geniality it deserves. We agreed afterwards, when in a more convenient place I read aloud a good many more passages from the precious tracts, that there are a great many ways of seeing Florence, as there are of seeing most beautiful and interesting things, and that it is very dry and pedantic to say that the happy vision depends upon our squaring our toes with a certain particular chalk-mark. We see Florence wherever and whenever we enjoy it, and for enjoying it we find a great many more pretexts than Mr. Ruskin seems inclined to allow. My friend and I convinced ourselves also, however, that the little books were an excellent purchase, on account of the great charm and felicity of much of their incidental criticism; to say nothing, as I hinted just now, of their being extremely amusing. Nothing in fact is more comical than the familiar asperity of the author's style and the pedagogic fashion in which he pushes and pulls his unhappy pupils about, jerking their heads toward this, rapping their knuckles for that, sending them to stand in corners and giving them Scripture texts to copy. But it is neither the felicities nor the aberrations of detail, in Mr. Ruskin's writings, that are the main affair for most readers; it is the general tone that, as I have said, puts them off or draws them on. For many persons he will never bear the test of being read in this rich old Italy, where art, so long as it really lived at all, was spontaneous, joyous, irresponsible. If the reader is in daily contact with those beautiful Florentine works which do still, in a way, force themselves into notice through the vulgarity and cruelty of modern profanation, it will seem to him that this commentator's comment is pitched in the strangest falsetto key. "One may read a hundred pages of this sort of thing," said my friend, "without ever dreaming that he is talking about *art*. You can say nothing worse about him than that." Which is perfectly true. Art is the one corner of human life in which we may take our ease. To justify our presence there the only thing demanded of us is that we shall have felt the representational impulse. In other connections our impulses are conditioned and embarrassed; we are allowed to have only so many as are consistent with those of our neighbours; with their convenience and well-being, with their convictions and prejudices, their rules and regulations. Art means an escape from all this. Wherever her shining standard floats the need for apology and compromise is over; there it is enough simply that we please or are pleased. There the tree is judged only by its fruits. If these are sweet the tree is justified—and not less so the consumer.

One may read a great many pages of Mr. Ruskin without getting a hint of this delightful truth; a hint of the not unimportant fact that art after all is made for us and not we for art. This idea that the value of a work is in the amount of illusion it yields is conspicuous by its absence. And as for Mr. Ruskin's world's being a place—his world of art—where we may take life easily, woe to the luckless mortal who enters it with any such disposition. Instead of a garden of delight, he finds a sort of assize court in perpetual session. Instead of a place in which human responsibilities are lightened and suspended, he finds a region governed by a kind of Draconic legislation. His responsibilities indeed are tenfold increased; the gulf between truth and error is for ever yawning at his feet; the pains and penalties of this same error are advertised, in apocalyptic terminology, upon a thousand sign-posts; and the rash intruder soon begins to look back with infinite longing to the lost paradise of the artless. There can be no greater want of tact in dealing with those things with which men attempt to ornament life than to be perpetually talking about "error." A truce to all rigidities is the law of the place; the only thing absolute there is that some force and some charm have worked. The grim old bearer of the scales excuses herself; she feels this not to be her province. Differences here are not iniquity and righteousness; they are simply variations of temperament, kinds of curiosity. We are not under theological government.

III

It was very charming, in the bright, warm days, to wander from one corner of Florence to another, paying one's respects again to remembered masterpieces. It was pleasant also to find that memory had played no tricks and that the rarest things of an earlier year were as rare as ever. To enumerate these felicities would take a great deal of space; for I never had been more struck with the mere quantity of brilliant Florentine work. Even giving up the Duomo and Santa Croce to Mr. Ruskin as very ill-arranged edifices, the list of the Florentine treasures is almost inexhaustible. Those long outer galleries of the Uffizi had never beguiled me more; sometimes there were not more than two or three figures standing there, Baedeker in hand, to break the charming perspective. One side of this upstairs portico, it will be remembered, is entirely composed of glass; a continuity of old-fashioned windows, draped with white curtains of rather primitive fashion, which hang there till they acquire a perceptible tone. The light, passing through them, is softly filtered and diffused; it rests mildly upon the old marbles—chiefly antique Roman busts—which stand in the narrow intervals of the casements. It is projected upon the numerous pictures that cover the opposite wall and that are not by any means, as a general thing, the gems of the great collection; it imparts a faded brightness to the old ornamental arabesques upon the painted wooden ceiling, and it makes a great soft shining upon the marble floor, in which, as you look up and down, you see the strolling tourists and the motionless copyists almost reflected. I don't know why I should find all this very pleasant, but in fact, I have seldom gone into the Uffizi without walking the length of this third-story cloister, between the (for the most part) third-rate canvases and panels and the faded cotton curtains. Why is it that in Italy we see a charm in things in regard to which in other countries we always take vulgarity for granted? If in the city of New York a great museum of the arts were to be provided, by way of decoration, with a species of verandah enclosed on one side by a series of small-paned windows draped in dirty linen, and furnished on the other with an array of pictorial feebleness, the place being surmounted by a thinly-painted wooden roof, strongly suggestive of summer heat, of winter cold, of frequent leakage, those amateurs who had had the advantage of foreign travel would be at small pains to conceal their contempt.

Contemptible or respectable, to the judicial mind, this quaint old loggia of the Uffizi admitted me into twenty chambers where I found as great a number of ancient favourites. I don't know that I had a warmer greeting for any old friend than for Andrea del Sarto, that most touching of painters who is not one of the first. But it was on the other side of the Arno that I found him in force, in those dusky drawing-rooms of the Pitti Palace to which you take your way along the tortuous tunnel that wanders through the houses of Florence and is supported by the little goldsmiths' booths on the Ponte Vecchio. In the rich insufficient light of these beautiful rooms, where, to look at the pictures, you sit in damask chairs and rest your elbows on tables of malachite, the elegant Andrea becomes deeply effective. Before long he has drawn you close. But the great pleasure, after all, was to revisit the earlier masters, in those specimens of them chiefly that bloom so unfadingly on the big plain walls of the Academy. Fra Angelico and Filippo Lippi, Botticelli and Lorenzo di Credi are the clearest, the sweetest and best of all painters; as I sat for an hour in their company, in the cold great hall of the institution I have mentioned—there are shabby rafters above and an immense expanse of brick tiles below, and many bad pictures as well as good—it seemed to me more than ever that if one really had to choose one couldn't do better than choose here. You may rest at your ease at the Academy, in this big first room—at the upper end especially, on the left—because more than many other places it savours of old Florence. More for instance, in reality, than the Bargello, though the Bargello makes great pretensions. Beautiful and masterful though the Bargello is, it smells too strongly of restoration, and, much of old Italy as still lurks in its furbished and renovated chambers, it speaks even more distinctly of the ill-mannered young kingdom that has—as "unavoidably" as you please—lifted down a hundred delicate works of sculpture from the convent-walls where their pious authors placed them. If the early Tuscan painters are exquisite I can think of no praise pure enough for the sculptors of the same period, Donatello and Luca della Robbia, Matteo Civitale and Mina da Fiesole, who, as I refreshed my memory of them, seemed to me to leave absolutely nothing to be desired in the way of straightness of inspiration and grace of invention. The Bargello is full of early Tuscan sculpture, most of the pieces of which have come from suppressed religious houses; and even if the visitor be an ardent liberal he is uncomfortably conscious of the rather brutal process by which it has been collected. One can hardly envy young Italy the number of odious things she has had to do.

From "Italy Revisited" (1878)

Venice

1882

It is a great pleasure to write the word; but I am not sure there is not a certain impudence in pretending to add anything to it. Venice has been painted and described many thousands of times, and of all the cities of the world is the easiest to visit without going there. Open the first book and you will find a rhapsody about it; step into the first picture-dealer's and you will find three or four high-coloured "views" of it. There is notoriously nothing more to be said on the subject. Every one has been there, and every one has brought back a collection of photographs. There is as little mystery about the Grand Canal as about our local thoroughfare, and the name of St. Mark is as familiar as the postman's ring. It is not forbidden, however, to speak of familiar things, and I hold that for the true Venice-lover Venice is always in order. There is nothing new to be said about her certainly, but the old is better than any novelty. It would be a sad day indeed when there should be something new to say. I write these lines with the full consciousness of having no information whatever to offer. I do not pretend to enlighten the reader; I pretend only to give a fillip to his memory; and I hold any writer sufficiently justified who is himself in love with his theme.

I

Mr. Ruskin has given it up, that is very true; but only after extracting half a lifetime of pleasure and an immeasurable quantity of fame from it. We all may do the same, after it has served our turn, which it probably will not cease to do for many a year to come. Meantime it is Mr. Ruskin who beyond any one helps us to enjoy. He has indeed lately produced several aids to depression in the shape of certain little humorous—ill-humorous—pamphlets (the series of *St. Mark's Rest*) which embody his latest reflections on the subject of our city and describe the latest atrocities perpetrated there. These latter are numerous and deeply to be deplored; but to admit that they have spoiled Venice would be to admit that Venice may be spoiled—an admission pregnant, as it seems to us, with disloyalty. Fortunately one reacts against the Ruskinian contagion, and one hour of the lagoon is worth a hundred pages of demoralised prose. This queer late-coming prose of Mr. Ruskin (including the revised and condensed issue of the *Stones of Venice,* only one little volume of which has been published, or perhaps ever will be) is all to be read, though much of it appears addressed to children of tender age. It is pitched in the nursery-key, and might be supposed to emanate from an angry governess. It is, however, all suggestive, and much of it is delightfully just. There is an inconceivable want of form in it, though the author has spent his life in laying down the principles of form and scolding people for departing from them; but it throbs and flashes with the love of his subject—a love disconcerted and abjured, but which has still much of the force of inspiration. Among the many strange things that have befallen

Venice, she has had the good fortune to become the object of a passion to a man of splendid genius, who has made her his own and in doing so has made her the world's. There is no better reading at Venice therefore, as I say, than Ruskin, for every true Venice-lover can separate the wheat from the chaff. The narrow theological spirit, the moralism *à tout propos,* the queer provincialities and pruderies, are mere wild weeds in a mountain of flowers. One may doubtless be very happy in Venice without reading at all—without criticising or analysing or thinking a strenuous thought. It is a city in which, I suspect, there is very little strenuous thinking, and yet it is a city in which there must be almost as much happiness as misery. The misery of Venice stands there for all the world to see; it is part of the spectacle—a thoroughgoing devotee of local colour might consistently say it is part of the pleasure. The Venetian people have little to call their own—little more than the bare privilege of leading their lives in the most beautiful of towns. Their habitations are decayed; their taxes heavy; their pockets light; their opportunities few. One receives an impression, however, that life presents itself to them with attractions not accounted for in this meagre train of advantages, and that they are on better terms with it than many people who have made a better bargain. They lie in the sunshine; they dabble in the sea; they wear bright rags; they fall into attitudes and harmonies; they assist at an eternal *conversazione.* It is not easy to say that one would have them other than they are, and it certainly would make an immense difference should they be better fed. The number of persons in Venice who evidently never have enough to eat is painfully large; but it would be more painful if we did not equally perceive that the rich Venetian temperament may bloom upon a dog's allowance. Nature has been kind to it, and sunshine and leisure and conversation and beautiful views form the greater part of its sustenance. It takes a great deal to make a successful American, but to make a happy Venetian takes only a handful of quick sensibility. The Italian people have at once the good and the evil fortune to be conscious of few wants; so that if the civilisation of a society is measured by the number of its needs, as seems to be the common opinion to-day, it is to be feared that the children of the lagoon would make but a poor figure in a set of comparative tables. Not their misery, doubtless, but the way they elude their misery, is what pleases the sentimental tourist, who is gratified by the sight of a beautiful race that lives by the aid of its imagination. The way to enjoy Venice is to follow the example of these people and make the most of simple pleasures. Almost all the pleasures of the place are simple; this may be maintained even under the imputation of ingenious paradox. There is no simpler pleasure than looking at a fine Titian, unless it be looking at a fine Tintoret or strolling into St. Mark's,—abominable the way one falls into the habit,—and resting one's light-wearied eyes upon the windowless gloom; or than floating in a gondola or than hanging over a balcony or than taking one's coffee at Florian's. It is of such superficial pastimes that a Venetian day is composed, and the pleasure of the matter is in the emotions to which they minister. These are fortunately of the finest—otherwise Venice would be insufferably dull. Reading Ruskin is good; reading the old records is perhaps better; but the best thing of all is simply staying on. The only way to care for Venice as she deserves it is to give her a chance to touch you often—to linger and remain and return.

II

The danger is that you will not linger enough—a danger of which the author of these lines had known something. It is possible to dislike Venice, and to entertain the sentiment in a responsible and intelligent manner. There are travellers who think the place odious, and those who are not of this opinion often find themselves wishing that the others were only more numerous. The sentimental tourist's sole quarrel with his Venice is that he has too many competitors there. He likes to be alone; to be original; to have (to himself, at least) the air of making discoveries. The Venice of to-day is a vast museum where the little wicket that admits you is perpetually turning and creaking, and you march through the institution with a herd of fellow-gazers. There is nothing left to discover or describe, and originality of attitude is completely impossible. This is often very annoying; you can only turn your back on your impertinent playfellow and curse his want of delicacy. But this is not the fault of Venice; it is the fault of the rest of the world. The fault of Venice is that, though she is easy to admire, she is not so easy to live with as you count living in other places. After you have stayed a week and the bloom of novelty has rubbed off you wonder if you can accommodate yourself to the peculiar conditions. Your old habits become impracticable and you find yourself obliged to form new ones of an undesirable and unprofitable character. You are tired of your gondola (or you think you are) and you have seen all the principal pictures and heard the names of the palaces announced a dozen times by your gondolier, who brings them out almost as impressively as if he were an English butler bawling titles into a drawing-room. You have walked several hundred times round the Piazza and bought several bushels of photographs. You have visited the antiquity mongers whose horrible sign-boards dishonour some of the grandest vistas in the Grand Canal; you have tried the opera and found it very bad; you have bathed at the Lido and found the water flat. You have begun to have a shipboard-feeling—to regard the Piazza as an enormous saloon and the Riva degli Schiavoni as a promenade-deck. You are obstructed and encaged; your desire for space is unsatisfied; you miss your usual exercise. You try to take a walk and you fail, and meantime, as I say, you have come to regard your gondola as a sort of magnified baby's cradle. You have no desire to be rocked to sleep, though you are sufficiently kept awake by the irritation produced, as you gaze across the shallow lagoon, by the attitude of the perpetual gondolier, with his turned-out toes, his protruded chin, his absurdly unscientific stroke. The canals have a horrible smell, and the everlasting Piazza, where you have looked repeatedly at every article in every shop-window and found them all rubbish, where the young Venetians who sell bead bracelets and "panoramas" are perpetually thrusting their wares at you, where the same tightly-buttoned officers are for ever sucking the same black weeds, at the same empty tables, in front of the same cafés—the Piazza, as I say, has resolved itself into a magnificent tread-mill. This is the state of mind of those shallow inquirers who find Venice all very well for a week; and if in such a state of mind you take your departure you act with fatal rashness. The loss is your own, moreover; it is not—with all deference to your personal attractions—that of your companions who remain behind; for though there are some disagreeable things in Venice there is nothing so disagreeable as the visitors. The conditions are peculiar, but your intolerance of them evaporates before it has had time to become a prejudice. When you have called for the bill to go, pay it and remain, and you will find on the morrow that you are deeply attached to Venice. It is by living there from day to day that you feel the fulness of her charm; that you invite her exquisite influence to sink into your spirit. The creature varies like a nervous woman, whom you know only when you know all the aspects of her beauty. She has high spirits or low, she is pale or red, grey or pink, cold or warm, fresh or wan, according to the weather or the hour. She is always interesting and almost always sad; but she has a thousand occasional graces and is always liable to happy accidents. You become extraordinarily fond of these things; you count upon them; they make part of your life. Tenderly fond you become; there is something indefinable in those depths of personal acquaintance that gradually establish themselves. The place seems to personify itself, to become human and sentient and conscious of your affection. You desire to embrace it, to caress it, to possess it; and finally a soft sense of possession grows up and your visit becomes a perpetual love-affair. It is very true that if you go, as the author of these lines on a certain occasion went, about the middle of March, a certain amount of disappointment is possible. He had paid no visit for several years, and in the interval the beautiful and helpless city had suffered an increase of injury. The barbarians are in full possession and you tremble for what they may do. You are reminded from the moment of your arrival that Venice scarcely exists any more as a city at all; that she exists only as a battered peep-show and bazaar. There was a horde of savage Germans encamped in the Piazza, and they filled the Ducal Palace and the Academy with their uproar. The English and Americans came a little later. They came in good time, with a great many French, who were discreet enough to make very long repasts at the Caffè Quadri, during which they were out of the way. The months of April and May of the year 1881 were not, as a general thing, a favourable season for visiting the Ducal Palace and the Academy. The *valet-de-place* had marked them for his own and held triumphant possession of them. He celebrates his triumphs in a terrible brassy voice, which resounds all over the place, and has, whatever language he be speaking, the accent of some other idiom. During all the spring months in Venice these gentry abound in the great resorts, and they lead their helpless captives through churches and galleries in dense irresponsible groups. They infest the Piazza; they pursue you along the Riva; they hang about the bridges and the doors of the cafés. In saying just now that I was disappointed at first, I had chiefly in mind the impression that assails me to-day in the whole precinct of St. Mark's. The condition of this ancient sanctuary is surely a great scandal. The pedlars and commissioners ply their trade—often a very unclean one—at the very door of the temple; they follow you across the threshold, into the sacred dusk, and pull your sleeve, and hiss into your ear, scuffling with each other for customers. There is a great deal of dishonour about St. Mark's altogether, and if Venice, as I say, has become a great bazaar, this exquisite edifice is now the biggest booth.

III

It is treated as a booth in all ways, and if it had not somehow a great spirit of solemnity within it the traveller would soon have little warrant for regarding it as a religious affair. The restoration of the outer walls, which has lately been so much attacked and defended, is certainly a great shock. Of the necessity of the work only an expert is, I suppose, in a position to judge; but there is no doubt that, if a necessity it be, it is one that is deeply to be regretted. To no more distressing necessity have people of taste lately had to resign themselves. Wherever the hand of the restorer has been laid all semblance of beauty has vanished; which is a sad fact, considering that the external loveliness of St. Mark's has been for ages less impressive only than that of the still comparatively uninjured interior. I know not what is the measure of necessity in such a case, and it appears indeed to be a very delicate question. To-day, at any rate, that admirable harmony of faded mosaic and marble which, to the eye of the traveller emerging from the narrow streets that lead to the Piazza, filled all the further end of it with a sort of dazzling silver presence—to-day this lovely vision is in a way to be completely reformed and indeed well-nigh abolished. The old softness and mellowness of colour—the work of the quiet centuries and of the breath of the salt sea—is giving way to large crude patches of new material which have the effect of a monstrous malady rather than of a restoration to health. They look like blotches of red and white paint and dishonourable smears of chalk on the cheeks of a noble matron. The face toward the Piazzetta is in especial the newest-looking thing conceivable—as new as a new pair of boots or as the morning's paper. We do not profess, however, to undertake a scientific quarrel with these changes; we admit that our complaint is a purely sentimental one. The march of industry in united Italy must doubtless be looked at as a whole, and one must endeavour to believe that it is through innumerable lapses of taste that this deeply interesting country is groping her way to her place among the nations. For the present, it is not to be denied, certain odd phases of the process are more visible than the result, to arrive at which it seems necessary that, as she was of old a passionate votary of the beautiful, she should to-day burn everything that she has adored. It is doubtless too soon to judge her, and there are moments when one is willing to forgive her even the restoration of St. Mark's. Inside as well there has been a considerable attempt to make the place more tidy; but the general effect, as yet, has not seriously suffered. What I chiefly remember is the straightening out of that dark and rugged old pavement—those deep undulations of primitive mosaic in which the fond spectator was thought to perceive an intended resemblance to the waves of the ocean. Whether intended or not the analogy was an image the more in a treasure-house of images; but from a considerable portion of the church it has now disappeared. Throughout the greater part indeed the pavement remains as recent generations have known it—dark, rich, cracked, uneven, spotted with porphyry and time-blackened malachite, polished by the knees of innumerable worshippers; but in other large stretches the idea imitated by the restorers is that of the ocean in a dead calm, and the model they have taken the floor of a London club-house or of a New York hotel. I think no Venetian and scarcely any Italian cares much for such differences; and when, a year ago, people in England were writing to the *Times* about the whole business and holding meetings to protest against it the dear children of the lagoon—so far as they heard or heeded the rumour—thought them partly busy-bodies and partly asses. Busy-bodies they doubtless were, but they took a good deal of disinterested trouble. It never occurs to the Venetian mind of to-day that such trouble may be worth taking; the Venetian mind vainly endeavours to conceive a state of existence in which personal questions are so insipid that people have to look for grievances in the wrongs of brick and marble. I must not, however, speak of St. Mark's as if I had the pretension of giving a description of it or as if the reader desired one. The reader has been too well served already. It is surely the best-described building in the world. Open the *Stones of Venice,* open Théophile Gautier's *Italia,* and you will see. These writers take it very seriously, and it is only because there is another way of taking it that I venture to speak of it; the way that offers itself after you have been in Venice a couple of months, and the light is hot in the great Square, and you pass in under the pictured porticoes with a feeling of habit and friendliness and a desire for something cool and dark. There are moments, after all, when the church is comparatively quiet and empty, and when you may sit there with an easy consciousness of its beauty. From the moment, of course, that you go into any Italian church for any purpose but to say your prayers or look at the ladies, you rank yourself among the trooping barbarians I just spoke of; you treat the place as an orifice in the peep-show. Still, it is almost a spiritual function—or, at the worst, an amorous one—to feed one's eyes on the molten colour that drops from the hollow vaults and thickens the air with its richness. It is all so quiet and sad and faded and yet all so brilliant and living. The strange figures in the mosaic pictures, bending with the curve of niche and vault, stare down through the glowing dimness; the burnished gold that stands behind them catches the light on its little uneven cubes. St. Mark's owes nothing of its character to the beauty of proportion or perspective; there is nothing grandly balanced or far-arching; there are no long lines nor triumphs of the perpendicular. The church arches indeed, but arches like a dusky cavern. Beauty of surface, of tone, of detail, of things near enough to touch and kneel upon and lean against—it is from this the effect proceeds. In this sort of beauty the place is incredibly rich, and you may go there every day and find afresh some lurking pictorial nook. It is a treasury of bits, as the painters say; and there are usually three or four of the fraternity with their easels set up in uncertain equilibrium on the undulating floor. It is not easy to catch the real complexion of St. Mark's, and these laudable attempts at portraiture are apt to look either lurid or livid. But if you cannot paint the old loose-looking marble slabs, the great panels of basalt and jasper, the crucifixes of which the lonely anguish looks deeper in the vertical light, the tabernacles whose open doors disclose a dark Byzantine image spotted with dull, crooked gems—if you cannot paint these things you can at least grow fond of them. You grow fond even of the old benches of red marble, partly worn away by the breeches of many generations and attached to the base of those wide pilasters of which the precious plating, delightful in its faded brownness, with a faint grey bloom upon it, bulges and yawns a little with honourable age.

IV

Even at first, when the vexatious sense of the city of the Doges reduced to earning its living as a curiosity-shop was in its keenness, there was a great deal of entertainment to be got from lodging on Riva Schiavoni and looking out at the far-shimmering lagoon. There was entertainment indeed in simply getting into the place and observing the queer incidents of a Venetian installation. A great many persons contribute indirectly to this undertaking, and it is surprising how they spring out at you during your novitiate to remind you that they are bound up in some mysterious manner with the constitution of your little establishment. It was an interesting problem for instance to trace the subtle connection existing between the niece of the landlady and the occupancy of the fourth floor. Superficially it was none too visible, as the young lady in question was a dancer at the Fenice theatre—or when that was closed at the Rossini—and might have been supposed absorbed by her professional duties. It proved necessary, however, that she should hover about the premises in a velvet jacket and a pair of black kid gloves with one little white button; as also, that she should apply a thick coating of powder to her face, which had a charming oval and a sweet weak expression, like that of most of the Venetian maidens, who, as a general thing—it was not a peculiarity of the landlady's niece—are fond of besmearing themselves with flour. You soon recognise that it is not only the many-twinkling lagoon you behold from a habitation on the Riva; you see a little of everything Venetian. Straight across, before my windows, rose the great pink mass of San Giorgio Maggiore, which has for an ugly Palladian church a success beyond all reason. It is a success of position, of colour, of the immense detached Campanile, tipped with a tall gold angel. I know not whether it is because San Giorgio is so grandly conspicuous, with a great deal of worn, faded-looking brickwork; but for many persons the whole place has a kind of suffusion of rosiness. Asked what may be the leading colour in the Venetian concert, we should inveterately say Pink, and yet without remembering after all that this elegant hue occurs very often. It is a faint, shimmering, airy, watery pink; the bright sea-light seems to flush with it and the pale whiteish-green of lagoon and canal to drink it in. There is indeed a great deal of very evident brickwork, which is never fresh or loud in colour, but always burnt out, as it were, always exquisitely mild.

Certain little mental pictures rise before the collector of memories at the simple mention, written or spoken, of the places he has loved. When I hear, when I see, the magical name I have written above these pages, it is not of the great Square that I think, with its strange basilica and its high arcades, nor of the wide mouth of the Grand Canal, with the stately steps and the well-poised dome of the Salute; it is not of the low lagoon, nor the sweet Piazzetta, nor the dark chambers of St. Mark's. I simply see a narrow canal in the heart of the city—a patch of green water and a surface of pink wall. The gondola moves slowly; it gives a great smooth swerve, passes under a bridge, and the gondolier's cry, carried over the quiet water, makes a kind of splash in the stillness. A girl crosses the little bridge, which has an arch like a camel's back, with an old shawl on her head, which makes her characteristic and charming; you see her against the sky as you float beneath. The pink of the old wall seems to fill the whole place; it sinks even into the opaque water. Behind the wall is a garden, out of which the long arm of a white June rose—the roses of Venice are splendid—has flung itself by way of spontaneous ornament.

On the other side of this small water-way is a great shabby façade of Gothic windows and balconies—balconies on which dirty clothes are hung and under which a cavernous-looking doorway opens from a low flight of slimy water-steps. It is very hot and still, the canal has a queer smell, and the whole place is enchanting.

It is poor work, however, talking about the colour of things in Venice. The fond spectator is perpetually looking at it from his window, when he is not floating about with that delightful sense of being for the moment a part of it, which any gentleman in a gondola is free to entertain. Venetian windows and balconies are a dreadful lure, and while you rest your elbows on these cushioned ledges the precious hours fly away. But in truth Venice isn't in fair weather a place for concentration of mind. The effort required for sitting down to a writing-table is heroic, and the brightest page of MS. looks dull beside the brilliancy of your *milieu.* All nature beckons you forth and murmurs to you sophistically that such hours should be devoted to collecting impressions. Afterwards, in ugly places, at unprivileged times, you can convert your impressions into prose. Fortunately for the present proser the weather wasn't always fine; the first month was wet and windy, and it was better to judge of the matter from an open casement than to respond to the advances of persuasive gondoliers. Even then however there was a constant entertainment in the view. It was all cold colour, and the steel-grey floor of the lagoon was stroked the wrong way by the wind. Then there were charming cool intervals, when the churches, the houses, the anchored fishing-boats, the whole gently-curving line of the Riva, seemed to be washed with a pearly white. Later it all turned warm—warm to the eye as well as to other senses. After the middle of May the whole place was in a glow. The sea took on a thousand shades, but they were only infinite variations of blue, and those rosy walls

I just spoke of began to flush in the thick sunshine. Every patch of colour, every yard of weather-stained stucco, every glimpse of nestling garden or daub of sky above a *calle*, began to shine and sparkle—began, as the painters say, to "compose." The lagoon was streaked with odd currents, which played across it like huge smooth finger-marks. The gondolas multiplied and spotted it all over; every gondola and gondolier looking, at a distance, precisely like every other.

There is something strange and fascinating in this mysterious impersonality of the gondola. It has an identity when you are in it, but, thanks to their all being of the same size, shape and colour, and of the same deportment and gait, it has none, or as little as possible, as you see it pass before you. From my windows on the Riva there was always the same silhouette—the long, black, slender skiff, lifting its head and throwing it back a little, moving yet seeming not to move, with the grotesquely-graceful figure on the poop. This figure inclines, as may be, more to the graceful or to the grotesque—standing in the "second position" of the dancing-master, but indulging from the waist upward in a freedom of movement which that functionary would deprecate. One may say as a general thing that there is something rather awkward in the movement even of the most graceful gondolier, and something graceful in the movement of the most awkward. In the graceful men of course the grace predominates, and nothing can be finer than the large, firm way in which, from their point of vantage, they throw themselves over their tremendous oar. It has the boldness of a plunging bird and the regularity of a pendulum. Sometimes, as you see this movement in profile, in a gondola that passes you—see, as you recline on your own low cushions, the arching body of the gondolier lifted up against the sky—it has a kind of nobleness which suggests an image on a Greek frieze. The gondolier at Venice is your very good friend—if you choose him happily—and on the quality of the personage depends a good deal that of your impressions. He is a part of your daily life, your double, your shadow, your complement. Most people, I think, either like their gondolier or hate him; and if they like him, like him very much. In this case they take an interest in him after his departure; wish him to be sure of employment, speak of him as the gem of gondoliers and tell their friends to be certain to "secure" him. There is usually no difficulty in securing him; there is nothing elusive or reluctant about a gondolier. Nothing would induce me not be believe them for the most part excellent fellows, and the sentimental tourist must always have a kindness for them. More than the rest of the population, of course, they are the children of Venice; they are associated with its idiosyncrasy, with its essence, with its silence, with its melancholy.

When I say they are associated with its silence I should immediately add that they are associated also with its sound. Among themselves they are an extraordinarily talkative company. They chatter at the *traghetti,* where they always have some sharp point under discussion; they bawl across the canals; they bespeak your commands as you approach; they defy each other from afar. If you happen to have a *traghetto* under your window, you are well aware that they are a vocal race. I should go even further than I went just now, and say that the voice of the gondolier is in fact for audibility the dominant or rather the only note of Venice. There is scarcely another heard sound, and that indeed is part of the interest of the place. There is no noise there save distinctly human noise; no rumbling, no vague uproar, nor rattle of wheels and hoofs. It is all articulate and vocal and personal. One may say indeed that Venice is emphatically the city of conversation; people talk all over the place because there is nothing to interfere with its being caught by the ear. Among the populace it is a general family party. The still water carries the voice, and good Venetians exchange confidences at a distance of half a mile. It saves a world of trouble, and they don't like trouble. Their delightful garrulous language helps them to make Venetian life a long *conversazione*. This language, with its soft elisions, its odd transpositions, its kindly contempt for consonants and other disagreeables, has in it something peculiarly human and accommodating. If your gondolier had no other merit he would have the merit that he speaks Venetian. This may rank as a merit even—some people perhaps would say especially—when you don't understand what he says. But he adds to it other graces which make him an agreeable feature in your life. The price he sets on his services is touchingly small, and he has a happy art of being obsequious without being, or at least without seeming, abject. For occasional liberalities he evinces an almost lyrical gratitude. In short he has delightfully good manners, a merit which he shares for the most part with the Venetians at large. One grows very fond of these people, and the reason of one's fondness is the frankness and sweetness of their address. That of the Italian family at large has much to recommend it; but in the Venetian manner there is something peculiarly ingratiating. One feels that the race is old, that it has a long and rich civilisation in its blood, and that if it hasn't been blessed by fortune it has at least been polished by time. It hasn't a genius for stiff morality, and indeed makes few pretensions in that direction. It scruples but scantly to represent the false as the true, and has been accused of cultivating the occasion to grasp and to overreach, and of steering a crooked course—not to your and my advantage—amid the sanctities of property. It has been accused further of loving if not too well at least too often, of being in fine as little austere as possible. I am not sure it is very brave, nor struck with its being very industrious. But it has an unfailing sense of the amenities of life; the poorest Venetian is a natural man of the world. He is better company than persons of his class are apt to be among the nations of industry and virtue—where people are also sometimes perceived to lie and steal and otherwise misconduct themselves. He has a great desire to please and to be pleased.

V

In that matter at least the cold-blooded stranger begins at last to imitate him; begins to lead a life that shall be before all things easy; unless indeed he allow himself, like Mr. Ruskin, to be put out of humour by Titian and Tiepolo. The hours he spends among the pictures are his best hours in Venice, and I am ashamed to have written so much of common things when I might have been making festoons of the names of the masters. Only, when we have covered our page with such festoons what more is left to say? When one has said Carpaccio and Bellini, the Tintoret and the Veronese, one has struck a note that must be left to resound at will. Everything has been said about the mighty painters, and it is of little importance that a pilgrim the more has found them to his taste. "Went this morning to the Academy; was very much pleased with Titian's 'Assumption.'" That honest phrase has doubtless been written in many a traveller's diary, and was not indiscreet on the part of its author. But it appeals little to the general reader, and we must moreover notoriously not expose our deepest feelings. Since I have mentioned Titian's "Assumption" I must say that there are some people who have been less pleased with it than the observer we have just imagined. It is one of the possible disappointments of Venice, and you may if you like take advantage of your privilege of not caring for it. It imparts a look of great richness to the side of the beautiful room of the Academy on which it hangs; but the same room contains two or three works less known to fame which are equally capable of inspiring a passion. "The 'Annunciation' struck me as coarse and superficial": that note was once made in a simple-minded tourist's book. At Venice, strange to say, Titian is altogether a disappointment; the city of his adoption is far from containing the best of him. Madrid, Paris, London, Florence, Dresden, Munich—these are the homes of his greatness.

There are other painters who have but a single home, and the greatest of these is the Tintoret. Close beside him sit Carpaccio and Bellini, who make with him the dazzling Venetian trio. The Veronese may be seen and measured in other places; he is most splendid in Venice, but he shines in Paris and in Dresden. You may walk out of the noon-day dusk of Trafalgar Square in November, and in one of the chambers of the National Gallery see the family of Darius rustling and pleading and weeping at the feet of Alexander. Alexander is a beautiful young Venetian in crimson pantaloons, and the picture sends a glow into the cold London twilight. You may sit before it for an hour and dream you are floating to the water-gate of the Ducal Palace, where a certain old beggar who has one of the handsomest heads in the world—he has sat to a hundred painters for Doges and for personages more sacred—has a prescriptive right to pretend to pull your gondola to the steps and to hold out a greasy immemorial cap. But you must go to Venice in very fact to see the other masters, who form part of your life while you are there, who illuminate your view of the universe. It is difficult to express one's relation to them; the whole Venetian art-world is so near, so familiar, so much an extension and adjunct of the spreading actual, that it seems almost invidious to say one owes more to one of them than to the other. Nowhere, not even in Holland, where the correspondence between the real aspects and the little polished canvases is so constant and so exquisite, do art and life seem so interfused and, as it were, so consanguineous. All the splendour of light and colour, all the Venetian air and the Venetian history are on the walls and ceilings of the palaces; and all the genius of the masters, all the images and visions they have left upon canvas, seem to tremble in the sunbeams and dance upon the waves. That is the perpetual interest of the place—that you live in a certain sort of knowledge as in a rosy cloud. You don't go into the churches and galleries by way of a change from the streets; you go into them because they offer you an exquisite reproduction of the things that surround you. All Venice was both model and painter, and life was so pictorial that art couldn't help becoming so. With all diminutions life is pictorial still, and this fact gives an extraordinary freshness to one's perception of the great Venetian works. You judge of them not as a connoisseur, but as a man of the world, and you enjoy them because they are so social and so true. Perhaps of all works of art that are equally great they demand least reflection on the part of the spectator—they make least of a mystery of being enjoyed. Reflection only confirms your admiration, yet is almost ashamed to show its head. These things speak so frankly and benignantly to the sense that even when they arrive at the highest style—as in the Tintoret's "Presentation of the little Virgin at the Temple"—they are still more familiar.

But it is hard, as I say, to express all this, and it is painful as well to attempt it—painful because in the memory of vanished hours so filled with beauty the consciousness of present loss oppresses. Exquisite hours, enveloped in light and silence, to have known them once is to have always a terrible standard of enjoyment. Certain lovely mornings of May and June come back with an ineffaceable fairness. Venice isn't smothered in flowers at this season, in the manner of Florence and Rome; but the sea and sky themselves seem to blossom and rustle. The gondola waits at the wave-washed steps, and if you are wise you will take your place beside a discriminating companion. Such a companion in Venice should of course be of the sex that discriminates most finely. An intelligent woman who knows her Venice seems doubly intelligent, and it makes no woman's perceptions less keen to be aware that she can't help looking graceful as she is borne over the waves. The handsome Pasquale, with uplifted oar, awaits your command, knowing, in a general way, from observation of your habits, that your intention is to go to see a picture or two. It perhaps doesn't immensely matter what picture you choose: the whole affair is so charming. It is charming to wander through the light and shade of intricate canals, with perpetual architecture above you and perpetual fluidity beneath. It is charming to disembark at the polished steps of a little empty *campo*—a sunny shabby square with an old well in the middle, an old church on one side and tall Venetian windows looking down. Sometimes the windows are tenantless; sometimes a lady in a faded dressing-gown leans vaguely on the sill. There is always an old man holding out his hat for coppers; there are always three or four small boys dodging possible umbrella-pokes while they precede you, in the manner of custodians, to the door of the church.

VI

The churches of Venice are rich in pictures, and many a masterpiece lurks in the unaccommodating gloom of side-chapels and sacristies. Many a noble work is perched behind the dusty candles and muslin roses of a scantily-visited altar; some of them indeed, hidden behind the altar, suffer in a darkness that can never be explored. The facilities offered you for approaching the picture in such cases are a mockery of your irritated wish. You stand at tip-toe on a three-legged stool, you climb a rickety ladder, you almost mount upon the shoulders of the *custode*. You do everything but see the picture. You see just enough to be sure it's beautiful. You catch a glimpse of a divine head, of a fig-tree against a mellow sky, but the rest is impenetrable mystery. You renounce all hope, for instance, of approaching the magnificent Cima da Conegliano in San Giovanni in Bragora; and bethinking yourself of the immaculate purity that shines in the spirit of this master, you renounce it with chagrin and pain. Behind the high altar in that church hangs a Baptism of Christ by Cima which I believe has been more or less repainted. You make the thing out in spots, you see it has a fulness of perfection. But you turn away from it with a stiff neck and promise yourself consolation in the Academy and at the Madonna dell' Orto, where two noble works by the same hand—pictures as clear as a summer twilight—present themselves in better circumstances. It may be said as a general thing that you never see the Tintoret. You admire him, you adore him, you think him the greatest of painters, but in the great majority of cases your eyes fail to deal with him. This is partly his own fault; so many of his works have turned to blackness and are positively rotting in their frames. At the Scuola di San Rocco, where there are acres of him, there is scarcely anything at all adequately visible save the immense "Crucifixion" in the upper story. It is true that in looking at this huge composition you look at many pictures; it has not only a multitude of figures but a wealth of episodes; and you pass from one of these to the other as if you were "doing" a gallery. Surely no single picture in the world contains more of human life; there is everything in it, including the most exquisite beauty. It is one of the greatest things of art; it is always interesting. There are works of the artist which contain touches more exquisite, revelations of beauty more radiant, but there is no other vision of so intense a reality, an execution so splendid. The interest, the impressiveness, of that whole corner of Venice, however melancholy the effect of its gorgeous and ill-lighted chambers, gives a strange importance to a visit to the Scuola. Nothing that all travellers go to see appears to suffer less from the incursions of travellers. It is one of the loneliest booths of the bazaar, and the author of these lines has always had the good fortune, which he wishes to every other traveller, of having it to himself. I think most visitors find the place rather alarming and wicked-looking. They walk about a while among the fitful figures that gleam here and there out of the great tapestry (as it were) with which the painter has hung all the walls, and then, depressed and bewildered by the portentous solemnity of these objects, by strange glimpses of unnatural scenes, by the echo of their lonely footsteps on the vast stone floors, they take a hasty departure, finding themselves again, with a sense of release from danger, a sense that the *genius loci* was a sort of mad white-washer who worked with a bad mixture, in the bright light of the *campo,* among the beggars, the orange-vendors and the passing gondolas. Solemn indeed is the place, solemn and strangely suggestive, for the simple reason that we shall scarcely find four walls elsewhere that inclose within a like area an equal quantity of genius. The air is thick with it and dense and difficult to breathe; for it was genius that was not happy, inasmuch as it lacked the art to fix itself for ever. It is not immortality that we breathe at the Scuola di San Rocco, but conscious, reluctant mortality.

Fortunately, however, we can turn to the Ducal Palace, where everything is so brilliant and splendid that the poor dusky Tintoret is lifted in spite of himself into the concert. This deeply original building is of course the loveliest thing in Venice, and a morning's stroll there is a wonderful illumination. Cunningly select your hour—half the enjoyment of Venice is a question of dodging—and enter at about one o'clock, when the tourists have flocked off to lunch and the echoes of the charming chambers have gone to sleep among the sunbeams. There is no brighter place in Venice—by which I mean that on the whole there is none half so bright. The reflected sunshine plays up through the great windows from the glittering lagoon and shimmers and twinkles over gilded walls and ceilings. All the history of Venice, all its splendid stately past, glows around you in a strong sea-light. Every one here is magnificent, but the great Veronese is the most magnificent of all. He swims before you in a silver cloud; he thrones in an eternal morning. The deep blue sky burns behind him, streaked across with milky bars; the white colonnades sustain the richest canopies, under which the first gentlemen and ladies in the world both render homage and receive it. Their glorious garments rustle in the air of the sea and their sun-lighted faces are the very complexion of Venice. The mixture of pride and piety, of politics and religion, of art and patriotism, gives a splendid dignity to every scene. Never was a painter more nobly joyous, never did an artist take a greater delight in life, seeing it all as a kind of breezy festival and feeling it through the medium of perpetual success. He revels in the gold-framed ovals of the ceilings, multiplies himself there with the fluttering movement of an embroidered banner that tosses itself into the blue. He was the happiest of painters and produced the happiest picture in the world. "The Rape of Europa" surely deserves this title; it is impossible to look at it without aching with envy. Nowhere else in art is such a temperament revealed; never did inclination and opportunity combine to express such enjoyment. The mixture of flowers and gems and brocade, of blooming flesh and shining sea and waving groves, of youth, health, movement, desire—all this is the brightest vision that ever descended upon the soul of a painter. Happy the artist who could entertain such a vision; happy the artist who could paint it as the masterpiece I here recall is painted.

The Tintoret's visions were not so bright as that; but he had several that were radiant enough. In the room that contains the work just cited are several smaller canvases by the greatly more complex genius of the Scuola di San Rocco, which are almost simple in their loveliness, almost happy in their simplicity. They have kept their brightness through the centuries, and they shine with their neighbours in those golden rooms. There is a piece of painting in one of them which is one of the sweetest things in Venice and which reminds one afresh of those wild flowers of execution that bloom so profusely and so unheeded in the dark corners of all of the Tintoret's work. "Pallas chasing away Mars" is, I believe, the name that is given to the picture; and it represents in fact a young woman of noble appearance administering a gentle push to a fine young man in armour, as if to tell him to keep his distance. It is of the gentleness of this push that I speak, the charming way in which she puts out her arm, with a single bracelet on it, and rests her young hand, its rosy fingers parted, on his dark breastplate. She bends her enchanting head with the effort —a head which has all the strange fairness that the Tintoret always sees in women—and the soft, living, flesh-like glow of all these members, over which the brush has scarcely paused in its course, is as pretty an example of genius as all Venice can show. But why speak of the Tintoret when I can say nothing of the great "Paradise," which unfolds its somewhat smoky splendour and the wonder of its multitudinous circles in one of the other chambers? If it were not one of the first pictures in the world it would be about the biggest, and we must confess that the spectator gets from it at first chiefly an impression of quantity. Then he sees that this quantity is really wealth; that the dim confusion of faces is a magnificent composition, and that some of the details of this composition are extremely beautiful. It is impossible however in a retrospect of Venice to specify one's happiest hours, though as one looks backward certain ineffaceable moments start here and there into vividness. How is it possible to forget one's visits to the sacristy of the Frari, however frequent they may have been, and the great work of John Bellini which forms the treasure of that apartment?

VII

Nothing in Venice is more perfect than this, and we know of no work of art more complete. The picture is in three compartments; the Virgin sits in the central division with her child; two venerable saints, standing close together, occupy each of the others. It is impossible to imagine anything more finished or more ripe. It is one of those things that sum up the genius of a painter, the experience of a life, the teaching of a school. It seems painted with molten gems, which have only been clarified by time, and it is as solemn as it is gorgeous and as simple as it is deep. Giovanni Bellini is more or less everywhere in Venice, and, wherever he is, almost certain to be first—first, I mean, in his own line: he paints little else than the Madonna and the saints; he has not Carpaccio's care for human life at large, nor the Tintoret's nor that of the Veronese. Some of his greater pictures, however, where several figures are clustered together, have a richness of sanctity that is almost profane. There is one of them on the dark side of the room at the Academy that contains Titian's "Assumption," which if we could only see it—its position is an inconceivable scandal—would evidently be one of the mightiest of so-called sacred pictures. So too is the Madonna of San Zaccaria, hung in a cold, dim, dreary place, ever so much too high, but so mild and serene, and so grandly disposed and accompanied, that the proper attitude for even the most critical amateur, as he looks at it, strikes one as the bended knee. There is another noble John Bellini, one of the very few in which there is no Virgin, at San Giovanni Crisostomo—a St. Jerome, in a red dress, sitting aloft upon the rocks and with a landscape of extraordinary purity behind him. The absence of the peculiarly erect Madonna makes it an interesting surprise among the works of the painter and gives it a somewhat less strenuous air. But it has brilliant beauty and the St. Jerome is a delightful old personage.

The same church contains another great picture for which the haunter of these places must find a shrine apart in his memory; one of the most interesting things he will have seen, if not the most brilliant. Nothing appeals more to him than three figures of Venetian ladies which occupy the foreground of a smallish canvas of Sebastian del Piombo, placed above the high altar of San Giovanni Crisostomo. Sebastian was a Venetian by birth, but few of his productions are to be seen in his native place; few indeed are to be seen anywhere. The picture represents the patron-saint of the church, accompanied by other saints and by the worldly votaries I have mentioned. These ladies stand together on the left, holding in their hands little white caskets; two of them are in profile, but the foremost turns her face to the spectator. This face and figure are almost unique among the beautiful things of Venice, and they leave the susceptible observer with the impression of having made, or rather having missed, a strange, a dangerous, but a most valuable, acquaintance. The lady, who is superbly handsome, is the typical Venetian of the sixteenth century, and she remains for the mind the perfect flower of that society. Never was there a greater air of breeding, a deeper expression of tranquil superiority. She walks a goddess—as if she trod without sinking the waves of the Adriatic. It is impossible to conceive a more perfect expression of the aristocratic spirit either in its pride or in its benignity. This magnificent creature is so strong and secure that she is gentle, and so quiet that in comparison all minor assumptions of calmness suggest only a vulgar alarm. But for all this there are depths of possible disorder in her light-coloured eye.

I had meant however to say nothing about her, for it's not right to speak of Sebastian when one hasn't found room for Carpaccio. These visions come to one, and one can neither hold them nor brush them aside. Memories of Carpaccio, the magnificent, the delightful—it's not for want of such visitations, but only for want of space, that I haven't said of him what I would. There is little enough need of it for Carpaccio's sake, his fame being brighter to-day—thanks to the generous lamp Mr. Ruskin has held up to it—than it has ever been. Yet there is something ridiculous in talking of Venice without making him almost the refrain. He and the Tintoret are the two great realists, and it is hard to say which is the more human, the more various. The Tintoret had the mightier temperament, but Carpaccio, who had the advantage of more newness and more responsibility, sailed nearer to perfection. Here and there he quite touches it, as in the enchanting picture, at the Academy, of St. Ursula asleep in her little white bed, in her high clean room, where the angel visits her at dawn; or in the noble St. Jerome in his study at S. Giorgio Schiavoni. This latter work is a pearl of sentiment, and I may add without being fantastic a ruby of colour. It unites the most masterly finish with a kind of universal largeness of feeling, and he who has it well in his memory will never hear the name of Carpaccio without a throb of almost personal affection. Such indeed is the feeling that descends upon you in that wonderful little chapel of St. George of the Slaves, where this most personal and sociable of artists has expressed all the sweetness of his imagination. The place is small and incommodious, the pictures are out of sight and ill-lighted, the custodian is rapacious, the visitors are mutually intolerable, but the shabby little chapel is a palace of art. Mr. Ruskin has written a pamphlet about it which is a real aid to enjoyment, though I can't but think the generous artist, with his keen senses and his just feeling, would have suffered to hear his eulogist declare that one of his other productions —in the Museo Civico of Palazzo Correr, a delightful portrait of two Venetian ladies with pet animals—is the "finest picture in the world." It has no need of that to be thought admirable; and what more can a painter desire?

VIII

May in Venice is better than April, but June is best of all. Then the days are hot, but not too hot, and the nights are more beautiful than the days. Then Venice is rosier than ever in the morning and more golden than ever as the day descends. She seems to expand and evaporate, to multiply all her reflections and iridescences. Then the life of her people and the strangeness of her constitution become a perpetual comedy, or at least a perpetual drama. Then the gondola is your sole habitation, and you spend days between sea and sky. You go to the Lido, though the Lido has been spoiled. When I first saw it, in 1869, it was a very natural place, and there was but a rough lane across the little island from the landing-place to the beach. There was a bathing-place in those days, and a restaurant, which was very bad, but where in the warm evenings your dinner didn't much matter as you sat letting it cool on the wooden terrace that stretched out into the sea. To-day the Lido is a part of united Italy and has been made the victim of villainous improvements. A little cockney village has sprung up on its rural bosom and a third-rate boulevard leads from

Santa Elisabetta to the Adriatic. There are bitumen walks and gas-lamps, lodging-houses, shops and a *teatro diurno*. The bathing-establishment is bigger than before, and the restaurant as well; but it is a compensation perhaps that the cuisine is no better. Such as it is, however, you won't scorn occasionally to partake of it on the breezy platform under which bathers dart and splash, and which looks out to where the fishing-boats, with sails of orange and crimson, wander along the darkening horizon. The beach at the Lido is still lonely and beautiful, and you can easily walk away from the cockney village. The return to Venice in the sunset is classical and indispensable, and those who at that glowing hour have floated toward the towers that rise out of the lagoon will not easily part with the impression. But you indulge in larger excursions—you go to Burano and Torcello, to Malamocco and Chioggia. Torcello, like the Lido, has been improved; the deeply interesting little cathedral of the eighth century, which stood there on the edge of the sea, as touching in its ruin, with its grassy threshold and its primitive mosaics, as the bleached bones of a human skeleton washed ashore by the tide, has now been restored and made cheerful, and the charm of the place, its strange and suggestive desolation, has well-nigh departed.

It will still serve you as a pretext, however, for a day on the lagoon, especially as you will disembark at Burano and admire the wonderful fisher-folk, whose good looks—and bad manners, I am sorry to say—can scarcely be exaggerated. Burano is celebrated for the beauty of its women and the rapacity of its children, and it is a fact that though some of the ladies are rather bold about it every one of them shows you a handsome face. The children assail you for coppers, and in their desire to be satisfied pursue your gondola into the sea. Chioggia is a larger Burano, and you carry away from either place a half-sad, half-cynical, but altogether pictorial impression; the impression of bright-coloured hovels, of bathing in stagnant canals, of young girls with faces of a delicate shape and a susceptible expression, with splendid heads of hair and complexions smeared with powder, faded yellow shawls that hang like old Greek draperies, and little wooden shoes that click as they go up and down the steps of the convex bridges; of brown-cheeked matrons with lustrous tresses and high tempers, massive throats encased with gold beads, and eyes that meet your own with a certain traditional defiance. The men throughout the islands of Venice are almost as handsome as the women; I have never seen so many good-looking rascals. At Burano and Chioggia they sit mending their nets, or lounge at the street corners, where conversation is always high-pitched, or clamour to you to take a boat; and everywhere they decorate the scene with their splendid colour—cheeks and throats as richly brown as the sails of their fishing-smacks—their sea-faded tatters which are always a "costume," their soft Venetian jargon, and the gallantry with which they wear their hats, an article that nowhere sits so well as on a mass of dense Venetian curls. If you are happy you will find yourself, after a June day in Venice (about ten o'clock), on a balcony that overhangs the Grand Canal, with your elbows on the broad ledge, a cigarette in your teeth and a little good company beside you. The gondolas pass beneath, the watery surface gleams here and there from their lamps, some of which are coloured lanterns that move mysteriously in the darkness. There are some evenings in June when there are too many gondolas, too many lanterns, too many serenades in front of the hotels. The serenading in particular is overdone; but on such a balcony as I speak of you needn't suffer from it, for in the apartment behind you—an accessible refuge—there is more good company, there are more cigarettes. If you are wise you will step back there presently.

Capri and the Bay of Naples

1900

Before and above all was the sense that, with the narrow limits of past adventure, I had never yet had such an impression of what the summer could be in the south or the south in the summer; but I promptly found it, for the occasion, a good fortune that my terms of comparison were restricted. It was really something, at a time when the stride of the traveller had become as long as it was easy, when the seven-league boots positively hung, for frequent use, in the closet of the most sedentary, to have kept one's self so innocent of strange horizons that the Bay of Naples in June might still seem quite final. That picture struck me—a particular corner of it at least, and for many reasons—as the last word; and it is this last word that comes back to me, after a short interval, in a green, grey northern nook, and offers me again its warm, bright golden meaning before it also inevitably catches the chill. Too precious, surely, for us not to suffer it to help us as it may is the faculty of putting together again in an order the sharp minutes and hours that the wave of time has been as ready to pass over as the salt sea to wipe out the letters and words your stick has traced in the sand. Let me, at any rate, recover a sufficient number of such signs to make a sort of sense.

I

Far aloft on the great rock was pitched, as the first note, and indeed the highest, of the wondrous concert, the amazing creation of the friend who had offered me hospitality, and whom, more almost than I had ever envied any one anything, I envied the privilege of being able to reward a heated, artless pilgrim with a revelation of effects so incalculable. There was none but the loosest prefigurement as the creaking and puffing little boat, which had conveyed me only from Sorrento, drew closer beneath the prodigious island—beautiful, horrible and haunted—that does most, of all the happy elements and accidents, towards making the Bay of Naples, for the study of composition, a lesson in the grand style. There was only, above and below, through the blue of the air and sea, a great confused shining of hot cliffs and crags and buttresses, a loss, from nearness, of the splendid couchant outline and the more comprehensive mass, and an opportunity—oh, not lost, I assure you—to sit and meditate, even moralise, on the empty deck, while a happy brotherhood of American and German tourists, including, of course, many sisters, scrambled down into little waiting, rocking tubs and, after a few strokes, popped systematically into the small orifice of the Blue Grotto. There was an appreciable moment when they were all lost to view in that receptacle, the daily "psychological" moment during which it must so often befall the recalcitrant observer on the deserted deck to find himself aware of how delightful it might be if none of them should come out again. The charm, the fascination of the idea is not a little—though also not wholly—in the fact that, as the wave rises over the aperture, there is the most encouraging appearance that they perfectly may not. There it is. There is no more of them. It is a case to which nature has, by the neatest stroke and with the best taste in the world, just quietly attended.

Beautiful, horrible, haunted: that is the essence of what, about itself, Capri says to you—dip again into your Tacitus and see why; and yet, while you roast a little under the awning and in the vaster shadow, it is not because the trail of Tiberius is ineffaceable that you are most uneasy. The trail of Germanicus in Italy to-day ramifies further and bites perhaps even deeper; a proof of which is, precisely, that his eclipse in the Blue Grotto is inexorably brief, that here he is popping out again, bobbing enthusiastically back and scrambling triumphantly back. The spirit, in truth, of his effective appropriation of Capri has a broad-faced candour against which there is no standing up, supremely expressive as it is of the well-known "love that kills," of Germanicus's fatal susceptibility. If I were to let myself, however, incline to *that* aspect of the serious case of Capri I should embark on strange depths. The straightness and simplicity, the classic, synthetic directness of the German passion for Italy, make this passion probably the sentiment in the world that is in the act of supplying enjoyment in the largest, sweetest mouthfuls; and there is something unsurpassably marked in the way that on this irresistible shore it has seated itself to ruminate and digest. It keeps the record in its own loud accents; it breaks out in the folds of the hills and on the crests of the crags into every manner of symptom and warning. Huge advertisements and portents stare across the bay; the acclivities bristle with breweries and "restorations" and with great ugly Gothic names. I hasten, of course, to add that some such general consciousness as this may well oppress, under any sky, at the century's end, the brooding tourist who makes himself a prey by staying anywhere, when the gong sounds, "behind." It is behind, in the track and the reaction, that he least makes out the end of it all, perceives that to visit any one's country for any one's sake is more and more to find some one quite other in possession. No one, least of all the brooder himself, is in his own.

II

I certainly, at any rate, felt the force of this truth when, on scaling the general rock with the eye of apprehension, I made out at a point much nearer its summit than its base the gleam of a dizzily-perched white sea-gazing front which I knew for my particular landmark and which promised so much that it would have been welcome to keep even no more than half. Let me instantly say that it kept still more than it promised, and by no means least in the way of leaving far below it the worst of the outbreak of restorations and breweries. There is a road at present to the upper village, with which till recently communication was all by rude steps cut in the rock and diminutive donkeys scrambling on the flints; one of those fine flights of construction which the great road-making "Latin races" take, wherever they prevail, without advertisement or bombast; and even while I followed along the face of the cliff its climbing consolidated ledge, I asked myself how I could think so well of it without consistently thinking better still of the temples of beer so obviously destined to enrich its terminus. The perfect answer to that was of course that the brooding tourist is never bound to be consistent. What happier law for him than this very one, precisely, when on at last alighting, high up in the blue air, to stare and gasp and almost disbelieve, he embraced little by little the beautiful truth particularly, on this occasion, reserved for himself, and took in the stupendous picture? For here above all had the thought and the hand come from far away—even from *ultima Thule*, and yet were in possession triumphant and acclaimed. Well, all one could say was that the way they had felt their opportunity, the divine conditions of the place, spoke of the advantage of some such intellectual perspective as a remote original standpoint alone perhaps can give. If what had finally, with infinite patience, passion, labour, taste, got itself done there, was like some supreme reward of an old dream of Italy, something perfect after long delays, was it not verily in *ultima Thule* that the vow would have been piously enough made and the germ tenderly enough nursed? For a certain art of asking of Italy all she can give, you must doubtless either be a rare *raffiné* or a rare genius, a sophisticated Norseman or just a Gabriele d' Annunzio.

All she can give appeared to me, assuredly, for that day and the following, gathered up and enrolled there: in the wondrous cluster and dispersal of chambers, corners, courts, galleries, arbours, arcades, long white ambulatories and vertiginous points of view. The greatest charm of all perhaps was that, thanks to the particular conditions, she seemed to abound, to overflow, in directions in which I had never yet enjoyed the chance to find her so free. The indispensable thing was therefore, in observation, in reflection, to press the opportunity hard, to recognise that as the abundance was splendid, so, by the same stroke, it was immensely suggestive. It dropped into one's lap, naturally, at the end of an hour or two, the little white flower of its formula: the brooding tourist, in other words, could only continue to brood till he had made out in a measure, as I may say, what was so wonderfully the matter with him. He was simply then in the presence, more than ever yet, of the possible poetry of the personal and social life of the south, and the fun would depend much—as occasions are fleeting—on his arriving in time, in the interest of that imagination which is his only field of sport, at adequate new notations of it. The sense of all this, his obscure and special fun in the general bravery, mixed, on the morrow, with the long, human hum of the bright, hot day and filled up the golden cup with questions and answers. The feast of St. Antony, the patron of the upper town, was the one thing in the air, and of the private beauty of the place, there on the narrow shelf, in the shining, shaded loggias and above the blue gulfs, all comers were to be made free.

III

The church-feast of its saint is of course for Anacapri, as for any self-respecting Italian town, the great day of the year, and the smaller the small "country," in native parlance, as well as the simpler, accordingly, the life, the less the chance for leakage, on other pretexts, of the stored wine of loyalty. This pure fluid, it was easy to feel overnight, had not sensibly lowered its level; so that nothing indeed, when the hour came, could well exceed the outpouring. All up and down the Sorrentine promontory the early summer happens to be the time of the saints, and I had just been witness there of a week on every day of which one might have travelled, through kicked-up clouds and other demonstrations, to a different hot holiday. There had been no bland evening that, somewhere or other, in the hills or by the sea, the white dust and the red glow didn't rise to the dim stars. Dust, perspiration, illumination, conversation—these were the regular elements. "They're very civilised," a friend who knows them as well as they can be known had said to me of the people in general; "plenty of fireworks and plenty of talk—that's all they ever want." That they were "civilised"—on the side on which they were most to show—was therefore to be the word of the whole business, and nothing could have, in fact, had more interest than the meaning that for the thirty-six hours I read into it.

Seen from below and diminished by distance, Anacapri makes scarce a sign, and the road that leads to it is not traceable over the rock; but it sits at its ease on its high, wide table, of which it covers—and with picturesque southern culture as well—as much as it finds convenient. As much of it as possible was squeezed all the morning, for St. Antony, into the piazzetta before the church, and as much more into that edifice as the robust odour mainly prevailing there allowed room for. It was the odour that was in prime occupation, and one could only wonder how so many men, women and children could cram themselves into so much smell. It was surely the smell, thick and resisting, that was least successfully to be elbowed. Meanwhile the good saint, before he could move into the air, had, among the tapers and the tinsel, the opera-music and the pulpit poundings, bravely to snuff it up. The shade outside was hot, and the sun was hot; but we waited as densely for him to come out, or rather to come "on," as the pit at the opera waits for the great tenor. There were people from below and people from the mainland and people from Pomerania and a brass band from Naples. There were other figures at the end of longer strings—strings that, some of them indeed, had pretty well given way and were now but little snippets trailing in the dust. Oh, the queer sense of the good old Capri of artistic legend, of which the name itself was, in the more benighted years—years of the contadina and the pifferaro—a bright evocation! Oh, the echo, on the spot, of each romantic tale! Oh, the loafing painters, so bad and so happy, the conscious models, the vague personalities! The "beautiful Capri girl" was of course not missed, though not perhaps so beautiful as in her ancient glamour, which none the less didn't at all exclude the probable presence—with *his* legendary light quite undimmed—of the English lord in disguise who will at no distant date marry her. The whole thing was there; one held it in one's hand.

The saint comes out at last, borne aloft in long procession and under a high canopy: a rejoicing, staring, smiling saint, openly delighted with the one happy hour in the year on which he may take his own walk. Frocked and tonsured, but not at all macerated, he holds in his hand a small wax puppet of an infant Jesus and shows him to all their friends, to whom he nods and bows: to whom, in the dazzle of the sun he literally seems to grin and wink, while his litter sways and his banners flap and every one gaily greets him. The ribbons and draperies flutter, and the white veils of the marching maidens, the music blares and the guns go off and the chants resound, and it is all as holy and merry and noisy as possible. The procession—down to the delightful little tinselled and bare-bodied babies, miniature St. Antonys irrespective of sex, led or carried by proud papas or brown grandsires—includes so much of the population that you marvel there is such a muster to look on—like the charades given in a family in which every one wants to act. But it is all indeed in a manner one house, the little high-niched island community, and nobody therefore, even in the presence of the head of it, puts on an air of solemnity. Singular and suggestive before everything else is the absence of any approach to our notion of the posture of respect, and this among people whose manners in general struck one as so good and, in particular, as so cultivated. The office of the saint—of which the festa is but the annual reaffirmation—involves not the faintest attribute of remoteness or mystery.

While, with my friend, I waited for him, we went for coolness into the second church of the place, a considerable and bedizened structure, with the rare curiosity of a wondrous pictured pavement of majolica, the garden of Eden done in large coloured tiles or squares, with every beast, bird and river, and a brave *diminuendo*, in especial, from portal to altar, of perspective, so that the animals and objects of the foreground are big and those of the successive distances differ with much propriety. Here in the sacred shade the old women were knitting, gossipping, yawning, shuffling about; here the children were romping and "larking"; here, in a manner, were the open parlour, the nursery, the kindergarten and the *conversazione* of the poor. This is everywhere the case by the southern sea. I remember near Sorrento a wayside chapel that seemed the scene of every function of domestic life, including cookery and others. The odd thing is that it all appears to interfere so little with that special civilised note—the note of manners—which is so constantly touched. It is barbarous to expectorate in the temple of your faith, but that doubtless is an extreme case. Is civilisation really measured by the number of things people do respect? There would seem to be much evidence against it. The oldest societies, the societies with most traditions, are naturally not the least ironic, the least *blasées*, and the African tribes who take so many things into account that they fear to quit their huts at night are not the fine flower.

IV

Where, on the other hand, it was impossible not to feel to the full all the charming *riguardi*—to use their own good word—in which our friends *could* abound, was, that afternoon, in the extraordinary temple of art and hospitality that had been benignantly opened to me. Hither, from three o'clock to seven, all the world, from the small in particular to the smaller and the smallest, might freely flock, and here, from the first hour to the last, the huge straw-bellied flasks of purple wine were tilted for all the thirsty. They were many, the thirsty, they were three hundred, they were unending; but the draughts they drank were neither countable nor counted. This boon was dispensed in a long, pillared portico, where everything was white and light save the blue of the great bay as it played up from far below or as you took it in, between shining columns, with your elbows on the parapet. Sorrento and Vesuvius were over against you; Naples furthest off, melted, in the middle of the picture, into shimmering vagueness and innocence; and the long arm of Posilippo and the presence of the other islands, Procida, the stricken Ischia, made themselves felt to the left. The grand air of it all was in one's very nostrils and seemed to come from sources too numerous and too complex to name. It was antiquity in solution, with every brown, mild figure, every note of the old speech, every tilt of the great flask, every shadow cast by every classic fragment, adding its touch to the impression. What was the secret of the surprising amenity?—to the essence of which one got no nearer than simply by feeling afresh the old story of the deep interfusion of the present with the past. You had felt that often before, and all that could, at the most, help you now was that, more than ever yet, the present appeared to become again really classic, to sigh with strange elusive sounds of Virgil and Theocritus. Heaven only knows how little they would in truth have had to say to it, but we yield to these visions as we must, and when the imagination fairly turns in its pain almost any soft name is good enough to soothe it.

It threw such difficulties but a step back to say that the secret of the amenity was "style"; for what in the world was the secret of style, which you might have followed up and down the abysmal old Italy for so many a year only to be still vainly calling for it? Everything, at any rate, that happy afternoon, in that place of poetry, was bathed and blessed with it. The castle of Barbarossa had been on the height behind; the villa of black Tiberius had overhung the immensity from the right; the white arcades and the cool chambers offered to every step some sweet old "piece" of the past, some rounded porphyry pillar supporting a bust, some shaft of pale alabaster upholding a trellis, some mutilated marble image, some bronze that had roughly resisted. Our host, if we came to that, had the secret; but he could only express it in grand practical ways. One of them was precisely this wonderful "afternoon tea," in which tea only—*that*, good as it is, has never the note of style—was not to be found. The beauty and the poetry, at all events, were clear enough, and the extraordinary uplifted distinction; but where, in all this, it may be asked, was the element of "horror" that I have spoken of as sensible?—what obsession that was not charming could find a place in that splendid light, out of which the long summer squeezes every secret and shadow? I'm afraid I'm driven to plead that these evils were exactly in one's imagination, a predestined victim always of the cruel, the fatal historic sense. To make so much distinction, how much history had been needed! —so that the whole air still throbbed and ached with it, as with an accumulation of ghosts to whom the very climate was pitiless, condemning them to blanch for ever in the general glare and grandeur, offering them no dusky northern nook, no place at the friendly fireside, no shelter of legend or song.

From "The Saint's Afternoon and Others" (1900–1909)

Part V

The Return of the Native

The American Scene

1904—1905

Editor's Note

James's return to America in the autumn of 1904, after an absence of twenty-one years, was one of the most challenging and momentous events of his life. It brought him back to his native land not only as a famous man but as a rediscoverer of all that had happened to his country in rapid growth and change, in acquisitions of wealth and power, and in the enhanced prestige of material success and assertive nationhood, during the decades he had spent abroad. As he had made his earlier explorations of Europe from the vantage-point of his American origins, so he now approached America from a long commitment to foreign residence and associations. He felt himself approaching a "dire confrontation"; he knew his long-pondered "international subject" now faced its most acute test; he told his nephew he was prepared to alight on the New York docks "in abject and craven terror." Yet once he had arrived, though he confessed himself to friends back in England as "transcendently homesick" and at times "almost crushed by the sense of accumulated and congested matter" around him in a land that was "such a living and breathing and feeling and moving great monster as this one is," he also found how "very interesting and quite unexpectedly and almost uncannily delightful and sympathetic" it was to be "seeing, feeling, how agreeable it is, in the maturity of age, to revisit the long neglected and long unseen land of one's birth," and how he could "quite thrill with the romance of elderly and belated discovery."

His journey took him first from New York into New England, to spend the autumn weeks with his brother William and his family at Chocorua, New Hampshire; then to old scenes in Boston, Cambridge, Concord, Salem, and Newport; then for Christmas to New York with its memories of his Washington Square childhood and its impact of startling changes; then down to Philadelphia and Washington; and so south into regions never previously explored—Virginia, Richmond, Charleston, Florida. In March, 1905, he crossed the country for the first time to Indianapolis, Chicago, St. Louis, and so westward to California. He lectured along the way on "The Lesson of Balzac" and "The Question of Our Speech." He returned finally to New York and Cambridge, and by August he was back in Lamb House, prepared to turn his journey to account.

Two projects resulted from the American journey. In New York he arranged with Scribners for the publication of the twenty-four-volume New York Edition of his novels and tales. He also carried out a commission for Chapman and Hall of London, and for Harpers of New York, for the writing of a book on his American impressions. By the time this appeared in 1907 as The American Scene, *it had become the most complex and searching study of travel, sociology, American criticism, and personal assessment James had yet succeeded in writing, and one of the travel classics of modern literature.*

All or parts of seven of its fourteen chapters are reproduced here, all of them dealing with scenes or cities that touched James's native roots and sympathies most closely—New England, New York, Boston, Newport, Concord and Salem, and Washington. Two other chapters were devoted to New York, and the remaining essays to Philadelphia, Baltimore, Richmond, Charleston, and Florida. James never wrote the supplementary volume he hoped to devote to the Middle and Far West, but he did write two essays on "The Speech of American Women" and "The Manners of American Women" for Harper's Bazar *in 1906–7. What James saw, felt, observed, and discovered in America the present selections partly indicate; but the entire book, combining as it does travel with social criticism and personal self-examination, must be grouped with the prefaces and revisions of the New York Edition and his three memoirs of 1913–17–*A Small Boy and Others, Notes of a Son and Brother, *and* The Middle Years*–as forming the huge project in reassessment of his life, origins, art, and nationality which was James's major undertaking in the last decade of his life.*

The titles used for the earlier sections of this book–"The Sentimental Tourist," "The Passionate Pilgrim," "The Cosmopolite," "The Lover of Italy"–are Jamesian phrases suggested by his texts. The title given to the present part–which might have been appropriately called "The Restless Analyst"–suggests another modern novelist, yet it was a title that James himself had in mind for his book on America. When, after arriving in the United States in the autumn of 1904, he wrote in October to George Harvey, then editor of The North American Review, *in which seven of the American essays were to be serialized, and president of Harper and Brothers, who were to publish* The American Scene, *he said that "his impulse toward them was gathering force and volume in his mind, every day and every hour; 'so that, verily,' he continued in his most characteristic vein, 'I am moved inwardly to believe that I shall be able not only to write the best book (of social and pictorial and, as it were, human observations) ever devoted to this country, but one of the best–or why drag in* "one of," *why not say frankly* the *best?—ever devoted to any country at all.' He regretted deeply that Thomas Hardy had made it impossible for him to give the work the caption, 'The Return of the Native,' as he would have liked to do; and he suggested instead calling it 'The Return of the Novelist,' 'if that would not seem too light and airy or free and easy.' He did not adopt that title, however, but three years later produced* The American Scene." (George Harvey: "A Passionate Patriot," *by Willis Fletcher Johnson* [1929], *p.* 91. *I am indebted to Mr. Leon Edel for this reference.*)

Indications are given at the end of each of the following selections as to which chapters or parts of chapters of The American Scene *they represent. This book, more unified than any of James's other travel volumes, must properly be read in its entirety; less than half of its 465 pages are reproduced here because of limitations of space. Though now out of print in America, it was most recently reissued by Charles Scribner's Sons in 1946 with an introduction by W. H. Auden.*

New England: An Autumn Impression

1904

I

Conscious that the impressions of the very first hours have always the value of their intensity, I shrink from wasting those that attended my arrival, my return after long years, even though they be out of order with the others that were promptly to follow and that I here gather in, as best I may, under a single head. They referred partly, these instant vibrations, to a past recalled from very far back; fell into a train of association that receded, for its beginning, to the dimness of extreme youth. One's extremest youth had been full of New York, and one was absurdly finding it again, meeting it at every turn, in sights, sounds, smells, even in the chaos of confusion and change; a process under which, verily, recognition became more interesting and more amusing in proportion as it became more difficult, like the spelling-out of foreign sentences of which one knows but half the words. It was not, indeed, at Hoboken, on emerging from the comparatively assured order of the great berth of the ship, that recognition *was* difficult: there, only too confoundingly familiar and too serenely exempt from change, the waterside squalor of the great city put forth again its most inimitable notes, showed so true to the barbarisms it had not outlived that one could only fall to wondering what obscure inward virtue had preserved it. There was virtue evident enough in the crossing of the water, that brave sense of the big, bright, breezy bay; of light and space and multitudinous movement; of the serried, bristling city, held in the easy embrace of its great good-natured rivers very much as a battered and accommodating beauty may sometimes be "distinguished" by a gallant less fastidious, with his open arms, than his type would seem to imply. But what was it that was still holding together, for observation, on the hither shore, the same old sordid facts, all the ugly items that had seemed destined so long ago to fall apart from their very cynicism?—the rude cavities, the loose cobbles, the dislodged supports, the unreclaimed pools, of the roadway; the unregulated traffic, as of innumerable desperate drays charging upon each other with tragic long-necked, sharp-ribbed horses (a length and a sharpness all emphasized by the anguish of effort); the corpulent constables, with helmets askew, swinging their legs, in high detachment, from coigns of contemplation; the huddled houses of the other time, red-faced, off their balance, almost prone, as from too conscious an affinity with "saloon" civilization.

It was, doubtless, open to the repentant absentee to feel these things sweetened by some shy principle of picturesqueness; and I admit that I asked myself, while I considered and bumped, why what was "sauce for the goose" should *not* be in this case sauce for the gander; and why antique shabbiness shouldn't plead on this particular waterside the cause it more or less successfully pleads on so many others. The light of the September day was lovely, and the sun of New York rests mostly, with a laziness all its own, on that dull glaze of crimson paint, as thick as on the cheek of the cruder coquetry, which is, in general, beneath its range, the sign of the old-fashioned. Yes; I could remind myself, as I went, that Naples, that Tangiers or Constantinople has probably nothing braver to flaunt, and mingle with excited recognition the still finer throb of seeing in advance, seeing even to alarm, many of the responsibilities lying in wait for the habit of headlong critical or fanciful reaction, many of the inconsistencies in which it would probably have, at the best, more or less defiantly to drape itself. Such meditations, at all events, bridged over alike the weak places of criticism and some of the rougher ones of my material passage. Nothing was left, for the rest of the episode, but a kind of fluidity of appreciation—a mild, warm wave that broke over the succession of aspects and objects according to some odd inward rhythm, and often, no doubt, with a violence that there was little in the phenomena themselves flagrantly to justify. It floated me, my wave, all that day and the next; so that I still think tenderly—for the short backward view is already a distance with "tone"—of the service it rendered me and of the various perceptive penetrations, charming coves of still blue water, that carried me up into the subject, so to speak, and enabled me to step ashore. The subject was everywhere—that was the beauty, that the advantage: it was thrilling, really, to find one's self in presence of a theme to which everything directly contributed, leaving no touch of experience irrelevant. That, at any rate, so far as feeling it went; treating it, evidently, was going to be a matter of prodigious difficulty and selection—in consequence of which, indeed, there might even be a certain recklessness in the largest surrender to impressions. Clearly, however, these were not for the present—and such as they were—to be kept at bay; the hour of reckoning, obviously, would come, with more of them heaped up than would prove usable, a greater quantity of vision, possibly, than might fit into decent form: whereby, assuredly, the part of wisdom was to put in as much as possible of one's recklessness while it was fresh.

It was fairly droll, for instance, the quantity of vision that began to press during a wayside rest in a house of genial but discriminating hospitality that opened its doors just where the fiddle-string of association could most intensely vibrate, just where the sense of "old New York," of the earlier stages of the picture now so violently overpainted, found most of its occasions—found them, to extravagance, within and without. The good easy Square, known in childhood, and as if the light were yellower there from that small accident, bristled with reminders as vague as they were sweet; within, especially, the place was a cool backwater, for time as well as for space; out of the slightly dim depths of which, at the turn of staircases and from the walls of communicating rooms, portraits and relics and records, faintly, quaintly æsthetic, in intention at least, and discreetly—yet bravely, too, and all so archaically and pathetically—Bohemian, laid traps, of a pleasantly primitive order, for memory, for sentiment, for relenting irony; gross little devices, on the part of the circumscribed past, which appealed with scarce more emphasis than so many tail-pieces of closed chapters. The whole impression had fairly a rococo tone; and it was in this perceptibly golden air, the air of old empty New York afternoons of the waning summer-time, when the long, the perpendicular rattle, as of buckets, forever thirsty, in the bottomless well of fortune, almost dies out in the merciful cross-streets, that the ample rearward loggia of the Club seemed serenely to hang; the glazed, disglazed, gallery dedicated to the array of small spread tables for which blank "backs," right and left and opposite, made a privacy; backs blank with the bold crimson of the New York house-painter, and playing upon the chord of remembrance, all so absurdly, with the scarcely less simplified green of their great cascades of Virginia creeper, as yet unturned: an admonition, this, for piety, as well as a reminder—since one had somehow failed to treasure it up—that the rather pettifogging plan of the city, the fruit, on the spot, of an artless age, happened to leave even so much margin as that for consoling chances. There were plenty of these—which I perhaps seem unduly to patronize in speaking of them as only "consoling"—for many hours to come and while the easy wave that I have mentioned continued to float me: so abysmal are the resources of the foredoomed student of manners, or so helpless, at least, his case when once adrift in that tide.

If in Gramercy Park already, three hours after his arrival, he had felt himself, this victim, up to his neck in what I have called his "subject," the matter was quite beyond calculation by the time he had tumbled, in such a glorified "four-wheeler," and with such an odd consciousness of roughness superimposed upon smoothness, far down-town again, and, on the deck of a shining steamer bound for the Jersey shore, was taking all the breeze of the Bay. The note of manners, the note that begins to sound, everywhere, for the spirit newly disembarked, with the first word exchanged, seemed, on the great clean deck, fairly to vociferate in the breeze—and not at all, so far, as was pleasant to remark, to the harshening of that element. Nothing could have been more to the spectator's purpose, moreover, than the fact he was ready to hail as the most characteristic in the world, the fact that what surrounded him was a rare collection of young men of business returning, as the phrase is, and in the pride of their youth and their might, to their "homes," and that, if treasures of "type" were not here to be disengaged, the fault would be all his own. It was perhaps this simple sense of treasure to be gathered in, it was doubtless this very confidence in the objective reality of impressions, so that they could deliciously be left to ripen, like golden apples, on the tree—it was all this that gave a charm to one's sitting in the orchard, gave a strange and inordinate charm both to the prospect of the Jersey shore and to every inch of the entertainment, so divinely inexpensive, by the way. The immense liberality of the Bay, the noble amplitude of the boat, the great unlocked and tumbled-out city on one hand, and the low, accessible mystery of the opposite State on the other, watching any approach, to all appearance, with so gentle and patient an eye; the gaiety of the light, the gladness of the air, and, above all (for it most came back to that), the unconscious affluence, the variety in identity, of the young men of business: these things somehow left speculation, left curiosity exciting, yet kept it beguilingly safe. And what shall I say more of all that presently followed than that it sharpened to the last pleasantness—quite draining it of fears of fatuity—that consciousness of strolling in the orchard that was all one's own to pluck, and counting, overhead, the apples of gold? I figure, I repeat, under this name those thick-growing items of the characteristic that were surely going to drop into one's hand, for vivid illustration, as soon as one could begin to hold it out.

Heavy with fruit, in particular, was the whole spreading bough that rustled above me during an afternoon, a very wonderful afternoon, that I spent in being ever so wisely driven, driven further and further, into the large lucidity of—well, of what else shall I call it but a New Jersey condition? That, no doubt, is a loose label for the picture; but impressions had to range themselves, for the hour, as they could. I had come forth for a view of such parts of the condition as might peep out at the hour and on the spot, and it was clearly not going to be the restless analyst's own fault if conditions in general, everywhere, should strike him as peculiarly, as almost affectingly, at the mercy of observation. They came out to meet us, in their actuality, in the soft afternoon; they stood, artless, unconscious, unshamed, at the very gates of Appearance; they might, verily, have been there, in their plenitude, at the call of some procession of drums and banners—the principal facts of the case being collected along our passage, to my fancy, quite as if they had been principal citizens. And then there was the further fact of the case, one's own ridiculous property and sign—the romantic, if not the pathetic, circumstance of one's having had to wait till now to read even such meagre meanings as this into a page at which one's geography might so easily have opened. It might have threatened, for twenty minutes, to be almost complicating, but the truth was recorded: it was an adventure, unmistakably, to have a revelation made so convenient—to be learning at last, in the maturity of one's powers, what New Jersey might "connote." This was nearer than I had ever come to any such experience; and it was now as if, all my life, my curiosity had been greater than I knew. Such, for an excited sensibility, are the refinements of personal contact. These influences then were present, as a source of glamour, at every turn of our drive, and especially present, I imagined, during that longest perspective when the road took no turn, but showed us, with a large, calm consistency, the straight blue band of summer sea, between the sandy shore and the reclaimed margin of which the chain of big villas was stretched tight, or at least kept straight, almost as for the close stringing of more or less monstrous pearls. The association of the monstrous thrusts itself somehow into my retrospect, for all the decent humility of the low, quiet coast, where the shadows of the waning afternoon could lengthen at their will and the chariots of Israel, on the wide and admirable road, could advance, in the glittering eye of each array of extraordinarily exposed windows, as through an harmonious golden haze.

There was gold-dust in the air, no doubt—which would have been again an element of glamour if it had not rather lighted the scene with too crude a confidence. It was one of the phases, full of its own marks and signs, of New York, the immense, in *villeggiatura*—and, presently, with little room left for doubt of what particular phase it might be. The huge new houses, up and down, looked over their smart, short lawns as with a certain familiar prominence in their profiles, which was borne out by the accent, loud, assertive, yet benevolent withal, with which they confessed to their extreme expensiveness. "Oh, yes; we were awfully dear, for what we are and for what we do"—it was proud, but it was rather rueful; with the odd appearance everywhere as of florid creations waiting, a little bewilderingly, for their justification, waiting for the next clause in the sequence, waiting in short for life, for time, for interest, for character, for identity itself to come to them, quite as large spread tables or superfluous shops may wait for guests and customers. The scene overflowed with curious suggestion; it comes back to me with the afternoon air and the amiable flatness, the note of the sea in a drowsy mood; and I thus somehow think of the great white boxes as standing there with the silvered ghostliness (for all the silver involved) of a series of candid new moons. It could only be the occupants, moreover, who were driving on the vast, featureless highway, to and fro in front of their ingenuous palaces and as if pretending not to recognize them when they passed; German Jewry—wasn't it conceivable?—tending to the stout, the simple, the kind, quite visibly to the patriarchal, and with the old superseded shabbiness of Long Branch partly for the goal of their course; the big brown wooden barracks of the hotels, the bold rotunda of the gaming-room—monuments already these, in truth, of a more artless age, and yet with too little history about them for dignity of ruin. Dignity, if not of ruin at least of reverence, was what, at other points, doubtless, we failed considerably less to read into the cottage where Grant lived and the cottage where Garfield died; though they had, for all the world, those modest structures, exactly the effect of objects diminished by recession into space—as if to symbolize the rapidity of their recession into time. They have been left so far behind by the expensive, as the expensive is now practised; in spite of having apparently been originally a sufficient expression of it.

This could pass, it seemed, for the greatest vividness of the picture—that the expensive, for New York in *villeggiatura,* even on such subordinate showing, is like a train covering ground at maximum speed and pushing on, at present, into regions unmeasurable. It included, however, other lights, some of which glimmered, to my eyes, as with the promise of great future intensity—hanging themselves as directly over the question of manners as if they had been a row of lustres reflected in the polished floor of a ball-room. Here was the expensive as a power by itself, a power unguided, undirected, practically unapplied, really exerting itself in a void that could make it no response, that had nothing—poor gentle, patient, rueful, but altogether helpless, void!—to offer in return. The game was that of its doing, each party to the whole combination, what it could, but with the result of the common effort's falling so short. Nothing could be of a livelier interest—with the question of manners always in view—than to note that the most as yet accomplished at such a cost was the air of unmitigated publicity, publicity as a condition, as a doom, from which there could be no appeal; just as in all the topsy-turvy order, the defeated scheme, the misplaced confidence, or whatever one may call it, there was no achieved protection, no constituted mystery of retreat, no saving complexity, not so much as might be represented by a foot of garden wall or a preliminary sketch of interposing shade. The homely principle under which the picture held at all together was that of the famous freedom of the cat to look at the king; that seemed, so clearly, throughout, the only motto that would work. The ample villas, in their full dress, planted each on its little square of brightly-green carpet, and as with their stiff skirts pulled well down, eyed each other, at short range, from head to foot; while the open road, the chariots, the buggies, the motors, the pedestrians—which last number, indeed, was remarkably small—regarded at their ease both this reciprocity and the parties to it. It was in fact all *one* participation, with an effect deterrent to those ingenuities, or perhaps indeed rather to those commonplaces, of conjecture produced in general by the outward show of the fortunate life. That, precisely, appeared the answer to the question of manners: the fact that in such conditions there couldn't *be* any manners to speak of; that the basis of privacy was somehow wanting for them; and that nothing, accordingly, no image, no presumption of constituted relations, possibilities, amenities, in the social, the domestic order, was inwardly projected. It was as if the projection had been so completely outward that one could but find one's self almost uneasy about the mere perspective required for the common acts of the personal life, that minimum of vagueness as to what takes place in it for which the complete "home" aspires to provide.

What had it been their idea to *do,* the good people—do, exactly, *for* their manners, their habits, their intercourse, their relations, their pleasures, their general advantage and justification? Do, that is, in affirming their wealth with such innocent emphasis and yet not at the same time affirming anything else. It would have rested on the cold-blooded critic, doubtless, to explain why the crudity of wealth did strike him with so direct a force; accompanied after all with no paraphernalia, no visible redundancies of possession, not so much as a lodge at any gate, nothing but the scale of many of the houses and their candid look of having cost as much as they knew how. Unmistakably they all proclaimed it—they would have cost still more had the way but been shown them; and, meanwhile, they added as with one voice, they would take a fresh start as soon as ever it should be. "We are only instalments, symbols, stopgaps," they practically admitted, and with no shade of embarrassment; "expensive as we are, we have nothing to do with continuity, responsibility, transmission, and don't in the least care what becomes of us after we have served our present purpose." On the detail of this impression, however, I needn't insist; the essence of it, which was all that was worth catching, was one's recognition of the odd treachery that may practically lie in wait for isolated opulence. The highest luxury of all, the supremely expensive thing, is constituted privacy—and yet it was the supremely expensive thing that the good people had supposed themselves to be getting: all of which, I repeat, enriched the case, for the restless analyst, with an illustrative importance. For what did it offer but the sharp interest of the match everywhere and everlastingly played between the short-cut and the long road?—an interest never so sharp as since the short-cut has been able to find itself so endlessly backed by money. Money in fact *is* the short-cut—or the short-cut money; and the long road having, in the instance before me, so little operated, operated for the effect, as we may say, of the cumulative, the game remained all in the hands of its adversary.

The example went straight to the point, and thus was the drama presented: what turn, on the larger, the general stage, was the game going to take? The whole spectacle, with the question, opened out, diffusing positively a multitudinous murmur that was in my ears, for some of the more subtly-romantic parts of the drive, as who should say (the sweet American vaguenesses, hailed again, the dear old nameless, promiscuous lengths of woodside and waterside), like the collective afternoon hum of invisible insects. Yes; it was all actually going to be drama, and *that* drama; than which nothing could be more to the occult purpose of the confirmed, the systematic story-seeker, or to that even of the mere ancient contemplative person curious of character. The very *donnée* of the piece could be given, the subject formulated: the great adventure of a society reaching out into the apparent void for the amenities, the consummations, after having earnestly gathered in so many of the preparations and necessities. "Into the apparent void"—I had to insist on that, since without it there would be neither comedy nor tragedy; besides which so little was wanting, in the way of vacancy, to the completeness of the appearance. What would lurk beneath this—or indeed what wouldn't, what mightn't—to thicken the plot from stage to stage and to intensify the action? The story-seeker would be present, quite intimately present, at the general effort—showing, doubtless, as quite heroic in many a case—to gouge an interest *out* of the vacancy, gouge it with tools of price, even as copper and gold and diamonds are extracted, by elaborate processes, from earth-sections of small superficial expression. What was such an effort, on its associated side, for the attentive mind, but a more or less adventurous fight, carried on from scene to scene, with fluctuations and variations, the shifting quantity of success and failure? Never would be such a chance to see how the short-cut works, and if there be really any substitute for roundabout experience, for troublesome history, for the long, the immitigable process of time. It was a promise, clearly, of the highest entertainment.

II

It was presently to come back to me, however, that there were other sorts, too—so many sorts, in fact, for the ancient contemplative person, that selection and omission, in face of them, become almost a pain, and the sacrifice of even the least of these immediate sequences of impression in its freshness a lively regret. But without much foreshortening is no representation, and I was promptly to become conscious, at all events, of quite a different part of the picture, and of personal perceptions, to match it, of a different order. I woke up, by a quick transition, in the New Hampshire mountains, in the deep valleys and the wide woodlands, on the forest-fringed slopes, the far-seeing crests of the high places, and by the side of the liberal streams and the lonely lakes; things full, at first, of the sweetness of belated recognition, that of the sense of some bedimmed summer of the distant prime flushing back into life and asking to give again as much as possible of what it had given before—all in spite, too, of much unacquaintedness, of the newness, to my eyes, through the mild September glow, of the particular rich region. I call it rich without compunction, despite its several poverties, caring little that half the charm, or half the response to it, may have been shamelessly "subjective"; since that but slightly shifts the ground of the beauty of the impression. When you wander about in Arcadia you ask as few questions as possible. That *is* Arcadia in fact, and questions drop, or at least get themselves deferred and shiftlessly shirked; in conformity with which truth the New England hills and woods—since they were not all, for the weeks to come, of mere New Hampshire—the mild September glow and even the clear October blaze were things to play on the chords of memory and association, to say nothing of those of surprise, with an admirable art of their own. The tune may have dropped at last, but it succeeded for a month in being strangely sweet, and in producing, quite with intensity, the fine illusion. Here, moreover, was "interest" of the sort that could come easily, and therefore not of the sort—quite the contrary—that involved a consideration of the millions spent; a fact none the fainter, into the bargain, for having its curious, unexpected, inscrutable side.

Why was the whole connotation so *delicately* Arcadian, like that of the Arcadia of an old tapestry, an old legend, an old love-story in fifteen volumes, one of those of Mademoiselle de Scudéri? Why, in default of other elements of the higher finish, did all the woodwalks and nestled nooks and shallow, carpeted dells, why did most of the larger views themselves, the outlooks to purple crag and blue horizon, insist on referring themselves to the idyllic *type* in its purity?—as if the higher finish, even at the hand of nature, were in some sort a perversion, and hillsides and rocky eminences and wild orchards, in short any common sequestered spot, could strike one as the more exquisitely and ideally Sicilian, Theocritan, poetic, romantic, academic, from their not bearing the burden of too much history. The history was there in its degree, and one came upon it, on sunny afternoons, in the form of the classic abandoned farm of the rude forefather who had lost patience with his fate. These scenes of old, hard New England effort, defeated by the soil and the climate and reclaimed by nature and time—the crumbled, lonely chimney-stack, the overgrown threshold, the dried-up well, the cart-track vague and lost—these seemed the only notes to interfere, in their meagreness, with the queer *other,* the larger, eloquence that one kept reading into the picture. Even the wild legend, immediately local, of the Indian who, having, a hundred years ago, murdered a husbandman, was pursued, by roused avengers, to the topmost peak of Chocorua Mountain, and thence, to escape, took his leap into the abyss—even so sharp an echo of a definite far-off past, enriching the effect of an admirable silvered summit (for Chocorua Mountain carries its grey head quite with the grandest air), spent itself in the mere idleness of the undiscriminated, tangled actual. There was one thinkable reason, of course, for everything, which hung there as a possible answer to any question, should any question insist. Did one by chance exaggerate, did one rhapsodize amiss, and was the apparent superior charm of the whole thing mainly but an accident of one's own situation, the state of having happened to be deprived to excess—that is for too long—of naturalism in *quantity*? Here it was in such quantity as one hadn't for years had to deal with; and that might by itself be a luxury corrupting the judgment.

It was absurd, perhaps, to have one's head so easily turned; but there was perfect convenience, at least, in the way the parts of the impression fell together and took a particular light. This light, from whatever source proceeding, cast an irresistible spell, bathed the picture in the confessed resignation of early autumn, the charming sadness that resigned itself with a silent smile. I say "silent" because the voice of the air had dropped as forever, dropped to a stillness exquisite, day by day, for a pilgrim from a land of stertorous breathing, one of the windiest corners of the world; the leaves of the forest turned, one by one, to crimson and to gold, but never broke off: all to the enhancement of this strange conscious hush of the landscape, which kept one in presence as of a world created, a stage set, a sort of ample capacity constituted, for—well, for things that wouldn't, after all, happen: more the pity for them, and for me and for you. This view of so many of the high places of the hills and deep places of the woods, the lost trails and wasted bowers, the vague, empty, rock-roughened pastures, the lonely intervals where the afternoon lingered and the hidden ponds over which the season itself seemed to bend as a young bedizened, a slightly melodramatic mother, before taking some guilty flight, hangs over the crib of her sleeping child—these things put you, so far as you were preoccupied with the human history of places, into a mood in which appreciation became a positive wantonness and the sense of quality, plucking up unexpectedly a spirit, fairly threatened to take the game into its hands. You discovered, when once it was stirred, an elegance in the commonest objects, and a mystery even in accidents that really represented, perhaps, mere plainness unashamed. Why otherwise, for instance, the inveterate charm of the silver-grey rock cropping through thinly-grassed acres with a placed and "composed" felicity that suggested the furniture of a drawing-room? The great boulders in the woods, the pulpit-stones, the couchant and rampant beasts, the isolated cliffs and lichened cathedrals, had all, seen, as one passed, through their drizzle of forest light, a special New Hampshire beauty; but I never tired of finding myself of a sudden in some lonely confined place, that was yet at the same time both wide and bright, where I could recognize, after the fashion of the old New Hampshire sociability, every facility for spending the day. There was the oddity—the place was furnished by its own good taste; its bosky ring shut it in, the two or three gaps of the old forgotten enclosure made symmetrical doors, the sweet old stones had the surface of grey velvet, and the scattered wild apples were like figures in the carpet.

It might be an ado about trifles—and half the poetry, roundabout, the poetry in solution in the air, was doubtless but the alertness of the touch of autumn, the imprisoned painter, the Bohemian with a rusty jacket, who had already broken out with palette and brush; yet the way the colour begins in those days to be dabbed, the way, here and there, for a start, a solitary maple on a woodside flames in single scarlet, recalls nothing so much as the daughter of a noble house dressed for a fancy-ball, with the whole family gathered round to admire her before she goes. One speaks, at the same time, of the orchards; but there are properly no orchards where half the countryside shows, all September, the easiest, most familiar sacrifice to Pomona. The apple-tree, in New England, plays the part of the olive in Italy, charges itself with the effect of detail, for the most part otherwise too scantly produced, and, engaged in this charming care, becomes infinitely decorative and delicate. What it must do for the too under-dressed land in May and June is easily supposable; but its office in the early autumn is to scatter coral and gold. The apples are everywhere and every interval, every old clearing, an orchard; they have "run down" from neglect and shrunken from cheapness—you pick them up from under your feet but to bite into them, for fellowship, and throw them away; but as you catch their young brightness in the blue air, where they suggest strings of strange-coloured pearls tangled in the knotted boughs, as you note their manner of swarming for a brief and wasted gaiety, they seem to ask to be praised only by the cheerful shepherd and the oaten pipe. The question of the encircled waters too, larger and smaller—that again was perhaps an ado about trifles; but you can't, in such conditions, and especially at first, resist the appeal of their extraordinarily mild faces and wooded brims, with the various choice spots where the great straight pines, interspaced beside them, and yielding to small strands as finely curved as the eyebrows of beauty, make the sacred grove and the American classic temple, the temple for the worship of the evening sky, the cult of the Indian canoe, of Fenimore Cooper, of W. C. Bryant, of the immortalizable water-fowl. They look too much alike, the lakes and the ponds, and this is, indeed, all over the world, too much a reproach to lakes and ponds—to all save the pick of the family, say, like George and Champlain; the American idea, moreover, is too inveterately that woods shall grow thick to the water. Yet there is no feature of grace the landscape could so ill spare—let alone one's not knowing what other, what baser, promiscuity mightn't oppress the banks if that of the free overgrowth didn't. Each surface of this sort is a breathing-space in the large monotony; the rich recurrence of water gives a polish to the manner itself, so to speak, of nature; thanks to which, in any case, the memory of a characteristic perfection attaches, I find, to certain hours of declining day spent, in a shallow cove, on a fallen log, by the scarce-heard plash of the largest liquid expanse under Chocorua; a situation interfused with every properest item of sunset and evening star, of darkening circle of forest, of boat that, across the water, put noiselessly out—of analogy, in short, with every typical triumph of the American landscape "school," now as rococo as so many squares of ingenious wool-work, but the remembered delight of our childhood. On *terra firma,* in New England, too often dusty or scrubby, the guarantee is small that some object at variance, cruelly at variance, with the glamour of the landscape school may not "put out." But that boat across the water is safe, is sustaining as far as it goes; it puts out from the cove of romance, from the inlet of poetry, and glides straight over, with muffled oar, to the —well, to the right place.

The consciousness of quantity, rather, as opposed to quality, to which I just alluded, quantity inordinate, quantity duly impressive and duly, if need be, overwhelming, had been the form of vigilance posting itself at the window —whence, incontestably, after a little, yielding to the so marked agitation of its sister-sense, it stepped back into the shadow of the room. If memory, at any rate, with its message so far to carry, had played one a trick, imagination, or some finer faculty still, could play another to match it. If it had settled to a convenience of the mind that "New England scenery" was hard and dry and thin, scrubby and meagre and "plain," here was that comfort routed by every plea of fancy—though of a fancy indeed perhaps open to the charge of the morbid—and by every refinement of appeal. The oddest thing in the world would delightfully have happened—and happened just there—in case one had really found the right word for the anomaly of one's surprise. What would the right word be but that nature, in these lights, was no single one of the horrid things I have named, but was, instead of them all, that quite other happy and charming thing, *feminine?*—feminine from head to foot, in expression, tone and touch, mistress throughout of the feminine attitude and effect. That had by no means the figure recalled from far back, but when once it had fully glimmered out it fitted to perfection, it became the case like a crown of flowers and provided completely for one's relation to the subject.

"Oh Italy, thou woman-land!" breaks out Browning, more than once, straight at *that* mark, and with a force of example that, for this other collocation, served much more as an incitement than as a warning. Reminded vividly of the identities of latitude and living so much in the same relation to the sun, you never really in New Hampshire—nor in Massachusetts, I was soon able to observe—look out at certain hours for the violet spur of an Apennine or venture to speak, in your admiration, of Tuscan or Umbrian forms, without feeling that the ground has quite gratefully borne you. The matter, however, the matter of the insidious grace, is not at all only a question of amusing coincidence; something intrinsically lovable everywhere lurks—which most comes out indeed, no doubt, under the consummate art of autumn. How shall one lightly enough express it, how describe it or to what compare it?—since, unmistakably, after all, the numbered items, the few flagrant facts, fail perfectly to account for it. It is like some diffused, some slightly confounding, sweetness of voice, charm of tone and accent, on the part of some enormous family of rugged, of almost ragged, rustics—a tribe of sons and daughters too numerous to be counted and homogeneous perhaps to monotony. There was a voice in the air, from week to week, a spiritual voice: "Oh, the *land's* all right!"—it took on fairly a fondness of emphasis, it rebounded from other aspects, at times, with such a tenderness. Thus it sounded, the blessed note, under many promptings, but always in the same form and to the effect that the poor dear land itself—if that was all that was the matter—would beautifully "do." It seemed to plead, the pathetic presence, to be liked, to be loved, to be stayed with, lived with, handled with some kindness, shown even some courtesy of admiration. What was that but the feminine attitude?—not the actual, current, impeachable, but the old ideal and classic; the air of meeting you everywhere, standing in wait everywhere, yet always without conscious defiance, only in mild submission to your doing what you would with it. The mildness was of the very essence, the essence of all the forms and lines, all the postures and surfaces, all the slimness and thinness and elegance, all the consent, on the part of trees and rocks and streams, even of vague happy valleys and fine undistinguished hills, to be viewed, to their humiliation, in the mass, instead of being viewed in the piece.

It is perhaps absurd to have to hasten to add that doing what you would with it, in these irresponsible senses, simply left out of account, for the country in general, the proved, the notorious fact that nothing useful, nothing profitable, nothing directly economic, *could* be done at all. Written over the great New Hampshire region at least, and stamped, in particular, in the shadow of the admirable high-perched cone of Chocorua, which rears itself, all granite, over a huge interposing shoulder, quite with the *allure* of a minor Matterhorn—everywhere legible was the hard little historic record of agricultural failure and defeat. It had to pass for the historic background, that traceable truth that a stout human experiment had been tried, had broken down. One was in presence, everywhere, of the refusal to consent to history, and of the consciousness, on the part of every site, that this precious compound is in no small degree being insolently made, on the other side of the continent, at the expense of such sites. The touching appeal of nature, as I have called it therefore, the "Do something kind for me," is not so much a "Live upon me and thrive by me" as a "Live *with* me, somehow, and let us make out together what we may do for each other—something that is not merely estimable in more or less greasy greenbacks. See how 'sympathetic' I am," the still voice seemed everywhere to proceed, "and how I am therefore better than my fate; see how I lend myself to poetry and sociability—positively to æsthetic use: give me that consolation." The appeal was thus not only from the rude absence of the company that had gone, and the still ruder presence of the company left, the scattered families, of poor spirit and loose habits, who had feared the risk of change; it was to a listening ear, directly—that of the "summer people," to whom, in general, one soon began to figure so much of the country, in New England, as looking for its future; with the consequence in fact that, from place to place, the summer people themselves almost promised to glow with a reflected light. It was a clue, at any rate, in the maze of contemplation, for this vision of the relation so established, the disinherited, the impracticable land throwing itself, as for a finer argument, on the non-rural, the intensely urban class, and the class in question throwing itself upon the land for reasons of its own. What would come of such an *entente*, on the great scale, for both parties?—that special wonderment was to strike me everywhere as in order. How populations with money to spare may extract a vulgar joy from "show" sections of the earth, like Switzerland and Scotland, we have seen abundantly proved, so that this particular lesson has little more to teach us; in America, however, evidently, the difference in the conditions, and above all in the scale of demonstration, is apt to make lessons new and larger.

Once the whole question had ranged itself under that head—what would the "summer people," as a highly comprehensive term, do with the aspects (perhaps as a highly comprehensive term also), and what would the aspects do with the summer people?—it became conveniently portable and recurrently interesting. Perhaps one of the best reasons I can give for this last side of it was that it kept again and again presenting the idea of that responsibility for *appearances* which, in such an association as loomed thus large, was certain to have to fix itself somewhere. What was one to say of appearances as they actually prevailed—from the moment, I mean, they were not of the charming order that nature herself could care for? The appearances of man, the appearances of woman, and of their conjoined life, the general latent spectacle of their arrangements, appurtenances, manners, devices, opened up a different chapter, the leaves of which one could but musingly turn. A better expression of the effect of most of this imagery on the mind should really be sought, I think, in its seeming, through its sad consistency, a mere complete negation of appearances—using the term in the sense of any familiar and customary "care for looks." Even the recognition that, the scattered summer people apart, the thin population was poor and bare had its bewilderment, on which I shall presently touch; but the poverty and the bareness were, as we seemed to measure them, a straight admonition of all we had, from far back, so easily and comfortably taken for granted, in the rural picture, on the other side of the world. There was a particular thing that, more than any other, had been pulled out of the view and that left the whole show, humanly and socially, a collapse. This particular thing was exactly the fact of the *importance*, the significance, imputable, in a degree, to appearances. In the region in which these observations first languished into life that importance simply didn't exist at all, and its absence was everywhere forlornly, almost tragically, attested. There was the little white wooden village, of course, with its houses in queer alignment and its rudely-emphasized meeting-house, in particular, very nearly as unconsecrated as the store or the town pump; but this represented, throughout, the highest tribute to the amenities. A sordid ugliness and shabbiness hung, inveterately, about the wayside "farms," and all their appurtenances and incidents—above all, about their inmates; when the idea of appearance was anywhere expressed (and its highest flights were but in the matter of fresh paint or a swept dooryard), a summer person was usually the author of the boon. The teams, the carts, the conveyances in their kinds, the sallow, saturnine natives in charge of them, the enclosures, the fences, the gates, the wayside "bits," of whatever sort, so far as these were referable to human attention or human neglect, kept telling the tale of the difference made, in a land of long winters, by the suppression of the two great factors of the familiar English landscape, the squire and the parson.

What the squire and the parson do, between them, for appearances (which is what I am talking of) in scenes, predominantly Anglo-Saxon, subject to their sway, is brought home, as in an ineffable glow, when the elements are reduced to "composing," in the still larger Anglo-Saxon light, without them. Here was no church, to begin with; and the shrill effect of the New England meeting-house, in general, so merely continuous and congruous, as to type and tone, with the common objects about it, the single straight breath with which it seems to blow the ground clear of the seated solidity of religion, is an impression that responds to the renewed sight of one of these structures as promptly as the sharp ring to the pressure of the electric button. One lives among English ancientries, for instance, as in a world toward the furnishing of which religion has done a large part. And here, immediately, was a room vast and vacant, with a vacancy especially reducible, for most of the senses, to the fact of that elimination. Perpetually, inevitably, moreover, as the restless analyst wandered, the eliminated thing *par excellence* was the thing most absent to sight—and for which, oh! a thousand times, the small substitutes, the mere multiplication of the signs of theological enterprise, in the tradition and on the scale of commercial and industrial enterprise, had no attenuation worth mentioning. The case, in the New Hampshire hills at least, was quite the same for the pervasive Patron, whose absence made such a hole. We went on counting up all the blessings we had, too unthankfully, elsewhere owed to him; we lost ourselves in the intensity of the truth that to compare a simplified social order with a social order in which feudalism had once struck deep was the right way to measure the penetration of feudalism. If there was no point here at which they had perceptibly begun, there was on the other side of the world no point at which they had perceptibly ceased. One's philosophy, one's logic might perhaps be muddled, but one clung to them for the convenience of their explanation of so much of the ugliness. The ugliness—one pounced, indeed, on this as on a talisman for the future—was the so complete abolition of *forms;* if, with so little reference to their past, present or future possibility, they could be said to have been even so much honoured as to be abolished.

The pounce at any rate was, for a guiding light, effectual; the guiding light worked to the degree of seeming at times positively to save the restless analyst from madness. He could make the absence of forms responsible, and he could thus react without bitterness—react absolutely with pity; he could judge without cruelty and condemn without despair; he could think of the case as perfectly definite and say to himself that, could forms only *be,* as a recognized accessory to manners, introduced and developed, the ugliness might begin scarcely to know itself. He could play with the fancy that the people might at last grow fairly to like them—far better, at any rate, than the class in question may in its actual ignorance suppose: the necessity would be to give it, on an adequate scale and in some lucid way, a taste of the revelation. What "form," meanwhile, *could* there be in the almost sophisticated dinginess of the present destitution? One thoughtfully asked that, though at the cost of being occasionally pulled up by odd glimpses of the underlying existence of a standard. There was the wage-standard, to begin with; the well-nigh awestruck view of the high rate of remuneration open to the most abysmally formless of "hired" men, indeed to field or house labour, expert or inexpert, on the part of either sex, in any connection: the ascertainment of which was one of the "bewilderments" I just now spoke of, one of the failures of consistency in the grey revelation. After this there was the standard, ah! the very high standard, of sensibility and propriety, so far as tribute on this ground was not owed by the parties themselves, but owed *to* them, not to be rendered, but to be received, and with a stiff, a warningly stiff, account kept of it. Didn't it appear at moments a theme for endless study, this queer range of the finer irritability in the breasts of those whose fastidiousness was compatible with the violation of almost every grace in life *but* that one? "Are you the woman of the house?" a rustic cynically squalid, and who makes it a condition of *any* intercourse that he be received at the front door of the house, not at the back, asks of a *maîtresse de maison,* a summer person trained to resignation, as preliminary to a message brought, as he then mentions, from the "washerlady." These are the phenomena, of course, that prompt the woman of the house, and perhaps still more the man, to throw herself, as I say, on the land, for what it may give her of balm and beauty—a character to which, as I also say, the land may affect these unfortunates as so consciously and tenderly playing up. The lesson had perhaps to be taught; if the Patron is at every point so out of the picture, the end is none the less not yet of the demonstration, on the part of the figures peopling it, that they are not to be patronized. Once to see this, however, was again to focus the possible evolution of manners, the latent drama to come: the æsthetic enrichment of the summer people, so far as they should be capable or worthy of it, by contact with the consoling background, so full of charming secrets, and the forces thus conjoined for the production and the imposition of forms. Thrown back again almost altogether, as by the Jersey shore, on the excitement of the speculative, one could extend unlimitedly—by which I mean one could apply to a thousand phases of the waiting spectacle—the idea of the possible drama. So everything worked round, afresh, to the promise of the large interest.

From Chapter I of The American Scene (1907)

New York Revisited

1904–5

I

The single impression or particular vision most answering to the greatness of the subject would have been, I think, a certain hour of large circumnavigation that I found prescribed, in the fulness of the spring, as the almost immediate crown of a return from the Far West. I had arrived at one of the transpontine stations of the Pennsylvania Railroad; the question was of proceeding to Boston, for the occasion, without pushing through the terrible town—why "terrible," to my sense, in many ways, I shall presently explain—and the easy and agreeable attainment of this great advantage was to embark on one of the mightiest (as appeared to me) of train-bearing barges and, descending the western waters, pass round the bottom of the city and remount the other current to Harlem; all without "losing touch" of the Pullman that had brought me from Washington. This absence of the need of losing touch, this breadth of effect, as to the whole process, involved in the prompt floating of the huge concatenated cars not only without arrest or confusion, but as for positive prodigal beguilement of the artless traveller, had doubtless much to say to the ensuing state of mind, the happily-excited and amused view of the great face of New York. The extent, the ease, the energy, the quantity and number, all notes scattered about as if, in the whole business and in the splendid light, nature and science were joyously romping together, might have been taking on again, for their symbol, some collective presence of great circling and plunging, hovering and perching sea-birds, white-winged images of the spirit, of the restless freedom of the Bay. The Bay had always, on other opportunities, seemed to blow its immense character straight into one's face—coming "at" you, so to speak, bearing down on you, with the full force of a thousand prows of steamers seen exactly on the line of their longitudinal axis; but I had never before been so conscious of its boundless cool assurance or seemed to see its genius so grandly at play. This was presumably indeed because I had never before enjoyed the remarkable adventure of taking in so much of the vast bristling promontory from the water, of ascending the East River, in especial, to its upper diminishing expanses.

Something of the air of the occasion and of the mood of the moment caused the whole picture to speak with its largest suggestion; which suggestion is irresistible when once it is sounded clear. It is all, absolutely, an expression of things lately and currently *done,* done on a large impersonal stage and on the basis of inordinate gain—it is not an expression of any other matters whatever; and yet the sense of the scene (which had at several previous junctures, as well, put forth to my imagination its power) was commanding and thrilling, was in certain lights almost charming. So it befell, exactly, that an element of mystery and wonder entered into the impression—the interest of trying to make out, in the absence of features of the sort usually supposed indispensable, the reason of the beauty and the joy. It is indubitably a "great" bay, a great harbour, but no one item of the romantic, or even of the picturesque, as commonly understood, contributes to its effect. The shores are low and for the most part depressingly furnished and prosaically peopled; the islands, though numerous, have not a grace to exhibit, and one thinks of the other, the real flowers of geography in this order, of Naples, of Capetown, of Sydney, of Seattle, of San Francisco, of Rio, asking how if *they* justify a reputation, New York should seem to justify one. Then, after all, we remember that there are reputations and reputations; we remember above all that the imaginative response to the conditions here presented may just happen to proceed from the intellectual extravagance of the given observer. When this personage is open to corruption by almost any large view of an intensity of life, his vibrations tend to become a matter difficult even for *him* to explain. He may have to confess that the group of evident facts fails to account by itself for the complacency of his appreciation. Therefore it is that I find myself rather backward with a perceived sanction, of an at all proportionate kind, for the fine exhilaration with which, in this free wayfaring relation to them, the wide waters of New York inspire me. There is the beauty of light and air, the great scale of space, and, seen far away to the west, the open gates of the Hudson, majestic in their degree, even at a distance, and announcing still nobler things. But the real appeal, unmistakably, is in that note of vehemence in the local life of which I have spoken, for it is the appeal of a particular type of dauntless power.

The aspect the power wears then is indescribable; it is the power of the most extravagant of cities, rejoicing, as with the voice of the morning, in its might, its fortune, its unsurpassable conditions, and imparting to every object and element, to the motion and expression of every floating, hurrying, panting thing, to the throb of ferries and tugs, to the plash of waves and the play of winds and the glint of lights and the shrill of whistles and the quality and authority of breeze-borne cries—all, practically, a diffused, wasted clamour of *detonations*—something of its sharp free accent and, above all, of its sovereign sense of being "backed" and able to back. The universal *applied* passion struck me as shining unprecedentedly out of the composition; in the bigness and bravery and insolence, especially, of everything that rushed and shrieked; in the air as of a great intricate frenzied dance, half merry, half desperate, or at least half defiant, performed on the huge watery floor. This appearance of the bold lacing-together, across the waters, of the scattered members of the monstrous organism—lacing as by the ceaseless play of an enormous system of steam-shuttles or electric bobbins (I scarce know what to call them), commensurate in form with their infinite work—does perhaps more than anything else to give the pitch of the vision of energy. One has the sense that the monster grows and grows, flinging abroad its loose limbs even as some unmannered young giant at his "larks," and that the binding stitches must for ever fly further and faster and draw harder; the future complexity of the web, all under the sky and over the sea, becoming thus that of some colossal set of clockworks, some steel-souled machine-room of brandished arms and hammering fists and opening and closing jaws. The immeasurable bridges are but as the horizontal sheaths of pistons working at high pressure, day and night, and subject, one apprehends with perhaps inconsistent gloom, to certain, to fantastic, to merciless multiplication. In the light of this apprehension indeed the breezy brightness of the Bay puts on the semblance of the vast white page that awaits beyond any other perhaps the black over-scoring of science.

Let me hasten to add that its present whiteness is precisely its charming note, the frankest of the signs you recognize and remember it by. That is the distinction I was just feeling my way to name as the main ground of its doing so well, for effect, without technical scenery. There are great imposing ports—Glasgow and Liverpool and London—that have already their page blackened almost beyond redemption from any such light of the picturesque as can hope to irradiate fog and grime, and there are others, Marseilles and Constantinople say, or, for all I know to the contrary, New Orleans, that contrive to abound before everything else in colour, and so to make a rich and instant and obvious show. But memory and the actual impression keep investing New York with the tone, predominantly, of summer dawns and winter frosts, of sea-foam, of bleached sails and stretched awnings, of blanched hulls, of scoured decks, of new ropes, of polished brasses, of streamers clear in the blue air; and it is by this harmony, doubtless, that the projection of the individual character of the place, of the candour of its avidity and the freshness of its audacity, is most conveyed. The "tall buildings," which have so promptly usurped a glory that affects you as rather surprised, as yet, at itself, the multitudinous sky-scrapers standing up to the view, from the water, like extravagant pins in a cushion already overplanted, and stuck in as in the dark, anywhere and anyhow, have at least the felicity of carrying out the fairness of tone, of taking the sun and the shade in the manner of towers of marble. They are not all of marble, I believe, by any means, even if some may be, but they are impudently new and still more impudently "novel"—this in common with so many other terrible things in America—and they are triumphant payers of dividends; all of which uncontested and unabashed pride, with flash of innumerable windows and flicker of subordinate gilt attributions, is like the flare, up and down their long, narrow faces, of the lamps of some general permanent "celebration."

You see the pin-cushion in profile, so to speak, on passing between Jersey City and Twenty-third Street, but you get it broadside on, this loose nosegay of architectural flowers, if you skirt the Battery, well out, and embrace the whole plantation. Then the "American beauty," the rose of interminable stem, becomes the token of the cluster at large—to that degree that, positively, this is all that is wanted for emphasis of your final impression. Such growths, you feel, have confessedly arisen but to be "picked," in time, with a shears; nipped short off, by waiting fate, as soon as "science," applied to gain, has put upon the table, from far up its sleeve, some more winning card. Crowned not only with no history, but with no credible possibility of time for history, and consecrated by no uses save the commercial at any cost, they are simply the most piercing notes in that concert of the expensively provisional into which your supreme sense of New York resolves itself. They never begin to speak to you, in the manner of the builded majesties of the world as we have heretofore known such—towers or temples or fortresses or palaces—with the authority of things of permanence or even of things of long duration. One story is good only till another is told, and sky-scrapers are the last word of economic ingenuity only till another word be written. This shall be possibly a word of still uglier meaning, but the vocabulary of thrift at any price shows boundless resources, and the consciousness of that truth, the consciousness of the finite, the menaced, the essentially *invented* state, twinkles ever, to my perception, in the thousand glassy eyes of these giants of the mere market. Such a structure as the comparatively windowless bell-tower of Giotto, in Florence, looks supremely serene in its beauty. You don't feel it to have risen by the breath of an interested passion that, restless beyond all passions, is for ever seeking more pliable forms. Beauty has been the object of its creator's idea, and, having found beauty, it has found the form in which it splendidly rests.

Beauty indeed was the aim of the creator of the spire of Trinity Church, so cruelly overtopped and so barely distinguishable, from your train-bearing barge, as you stand off, in its abject helpless humility; and it may of course be asked how much of this superstition finds voice in the actual shrunken presence of that laudable effort. Where, for the eye, is the felicity of simplified Gothic, of noble pre-eminence, that once made of this highly-pleasing edifice the pride of the town and the feature of Broadway? The answer is, as obviously, that these charming elements are still there, just where they ever were, but that they have been mercilessly deprived of their visibility. It aches and throbs, this smothered visibility, we easily feel, in its caged and dishonoured condition, supported only by the consciousness that the dishonour is no fault of its own. We commune with it, in tenderness and pity, through the encumbered air; our eyes, made, however unwillingly, at home in strange vertiginous upper atmospheres, look down on it as on a poor ineffectual thing, an architectural object addressed, even in its prime aspiration, to the patient pedestrian sense and permitting thereby a relation of intimacy. It was to speak to me audibly enough on two or three other occasions—even through the thick of that frenzy of Broadway just where Broadway receives from Wall Street the fiercest application of the maddening lash; it was to put its tragic case there with irresistible lucidity. "Yes, the wretched figure I am making is as little as you see my fault —it is the fault of the buildings whose very first care is to deprive churches of their visibility. There are but two or three—two or three outward and visible churches—left in New York 'anyway,' as you must have noticed, and even they are hideously threatened: a fact at which no one, indeed, appears to be shocked, from which no one draws the least of the inferences that stick straight out of it, which every one seems in short to take for granted either with remarkable stupidity or with remarkable cynicism." So, at any rate, they may still effectively communicate, ruddy-brown (where not browny-black) old Trinity and any pausing, any attending survivor of the clearer age—and there is yet more of the bitterness of history to be tasted in such a tacit passage, as I shall presently show.

Was it not the bitterness of history, meanwhile, that on that day of circumnavigation, that day of highest intensity of impression, of which I began by speaking, the ancient rotunda of Castle Garden, viewed from just opposite, should have lurked there as a vague nonentity? One had known it from far, far back and with the indelibility of the childish vision—from the time when it was the commodious concert-hall of New York, the firmament of long-extinguished stars; in spite of which extinction there outlives for me the image of the infant phenomenon Adelina Patti, whom (another large-eyed infant) I had been benevolently taken to hear: Adelina Patti, in a fan-like little white frock and "pantalettes" and a hussar-like red jacket, mounted on an armchair, its back supporting her, wheeled to the front of the stage and warbling like a tiny thrush even in the nest. Shabby, shrunken, barely discernible today, the ancient rotunda, adjusted to other uses, had afterwards, for many decades, carried on a conspicuous life—and it was the present remoteness, the repudiated barbarism of all this, foreshortened by one's own experience, that dropped the acid into the cup. The sky-scrapers and the league-long bridges, present and to come, marked the point where the age—the age for which Castle Garden could have been, in its day, a "value"—had come out. That in itself was nothing—ages do come out, as a matter of course, so far from where they have gone in. But it had done so, the latter half of the nineteenth century, in one's own more or less immediate presence; the difference, from pole to pole, was so vivid and concrete that no single shade of any one of its aspects was lost. This impact of the whole condensed past at once produced a horrible, hateful sense of personal antiquity.

Yet was it after all that those monsters of the mere market, as I have called them, had more to say, on the question of "effect," than I had at first allowed?—since they are the element that looms largest for me through a particular impression, with remembered parts and pieces melting together rather richly now, of "downtown" seen and felt from the inside. "Felt"—I use that word, I dare say, all presumptuously, for a relation to matters of magnitude and mystery that I could begin neither to measure nor to penetrate, hovering about them only in magnanimous wonder, staring at them as at a world of immovably-closed doors behind which immense "material" lurked, material for the artist, the painter of life, as we say, who shouldn't have begun so early and so fatally to fall away from possible initiations. This sense of a baffled curiosity, an intellectual adventure forever renounced, was surely enough a state of feeling, and indeed in presence of the different half-hours, as memory presents them, at which I gave myself up both to the thrill of Wall Street (by which I mean that of the whole wide edge of the whirlpool), and the too accepted, too irredeemable ignorance, I am at a loss to see what intensity of response was wanting. The imagination might have responded more if there had been a slightly less settled inability to understand what every one, what any one, was really doing; but the picture, as it comes back to me, is, for all this foolish subjective poverty, so crowded with its features that I rejoice, I confess, in not having more of them to handle. No open apprehension, even if it be as open as a public vehicle plying for hire, can carry more than a certain amount of life, of a kind; and there was nothing at play in the outer air, at least, of the scene, during these glimpses, that didn't scramble for admission into mine very much as I had seen the mob seeking entrance to an up-town or a down-town electric car fight for life at one of the apertures. If it had been the final function of the Bay to make one feel one's age, so, assuredly, the mouth of Wall Street proclaimed it, for one's private ear, distinctly enough; the breath of existence being taken, wherever one turned, as that of youth on the run and with the prize of the race in sight, and the new landmarks crushing the old quite as violent children stamp on snails and caterpillars.

The hour I first recall was a morning of winter drizzle and mist, of dense fog in the Bay, one of the strangest sights of which I was on my way to enjoy; and I had stopped in the heart of the business quarter to pick up a friend who was to be my companion. The weather, such as it was, worked wonders for the upper reaches of the buildings, round which it drifted and hung very much as about the flanks and summits of emergent mountain-masses —for, to be just all round, there *was* some evidence of their having a message for the eyes. Let me parenthesize, once for all, that there are other glimpses of this message, up and down the city, frequently to be caught; lights and shades of winter and summer air, of the literally "finishing" afternoon in particular, when refinement of modelling descends from the skies and lends the white towers, all new and crude and commercial and over-windowed as they are, a fleeting distinction. The morning I speak of offered me my first chance of seeing one of them from the inside —which was an opportunity I sought again, repeatedly, in respect to others; and I became conscious of the force with which this vision of their prodigious working, and of the multitudinous life, as if each were a swarming city in itself, that they are capable of housing, may beget, on the part of the free observer, in other words of the restless analyst, the impulse to describe and present the facts and express the sense of them. Each of these huge constructed and compressed communities, throbbing, through its myriad arteries and pores, with a single passion, even as a complicated watch throbs with the one purpose of telling you the hour and the minute, testified overwhelmingly to the *character* of New York—and the passion of the restless analyst, on his side, is for the extraction of character. But there would be too much to say, just here, were this incurable eccentric to let himself go; the impression in question, fed by however brief an experience, kept overflowing the cup and spreading in a wide waste of speculation. I must dip into these depths, if it prove possible, later on; let me content myself for the moment with remembering how from the first, on all such ground, my thought went straight to poor great wonder-working Émile Zola and *his* love of the human aggregation, the artificial microcosm, which had to spend itself on great shops, great businesses, great "apartment-houses," of inferior, of mere Parisian scale. His image, it seemed to me, really asked for compassion—in the presence of this material that his energy of evocation, his alone, would have been of a stature to meddle with. What if *Le Ventre de Paris,* what if *Au Bonheur des Dames,* what if *Pot-Bouille* and *L'Argent,* could but have come into being under the New York inspiration?

The answer to that, however, for the hour, was that, in all probability, New York was not going (as it turns such remarks) to produce both the maximum of "business" spectacle and the maximum of ironic reflection of it. Zola's huge reflector got itself formed, after all, in a far other air; it had hung there, in essence, awaiting the scene that was to play over it, long before the scene really approached it in scale. The reflecting surfaces, of the ironic, of the epic order, suspended in the New York atmosphere, have yet to show symptoms of shining out, and the monstrous phenomena themselves, meanwhile, strike me as having, with their immense momentum, got the start, got ahead of, in proper parlance, any possibility of poetic, of dramatic capture. That conviction came to me most perhaps while I gazed across at the special sky-scraper that overhangs poor old Trinity to the north—a south face as high and wide as the mountain-wall that drops the Alpine avalanche, from time to time, upon the village, and the village spire, at its foot; the interest of this case being above all, as I learned, to my stupefaction, in the fact that the very creators of the extinguisher are the churchwardens themselves, or at least the trustees of the church property. What was the case but magnificent for pitiless ferocity?—that inexorable law of the growing invisibility of churches, their everywhere reduced or abolished *presence*, which is nine-tenths of their virtue, receiving thus, at such hands, its supreme consecration. This consecration was positively the greater that just then, as I have said, the vast money-making structure quite horribly, quite romantically justified itself, looming through the weather with an insolent cliff-like sublimity. The weather, for all that experience, mixes intimately with the fulness of my impression; speaking not least, for instance, of the way "the state of the streets" and the assault of the turbid air seemed all one with the look, the tramp, the whole quality and *allure*, the consummate monotonous commonness, of the pushing male crowd, moving in its dense mass—with the confusion carried to chaos for any intelligence, any perception; a welter of objects and sounds in which relief, detachment, dignity, meaning, perished utterly and lost all rights. It appeared, the muddy medium, all one with every other element and note as well, all the signs of the heaped industrial battle-field, all the sounds and silences, grim, pushing, trudging silences too, of the universal will to move—to move, move, move, as an end in itself, an appetite at any price.

In the Bay, the rest of the morning, the dense raw fog that delayed the big boat, allowing sight but of the immediate ice-masses through which it thumped its way, was not less of the essence. Anything blander, as a medium, would have seemed a mockery of the facts of the terrible little Ellis Island, the first harbour of refuge and stage of patience for the million or so of immigrants annually knocking at our official door. Before this door, which opens to them there only with a hundred forms and ceremonies, grindings and grumblings of the key, they stand appealing and waiting, marshalled, herded, divided, subdivided, sorted, sifted, searched, fumigated, for longer or shorter periods—the effect of all which prodigious process, an intendedly "scientific" feeding of the mill, is again to give the earnest observer a thousand more things to think of than he can pretend to retail. The impression of Ellis Island, in fine, would be—as I was to find throughout that so many of my impressions would be—a chapter by itself; and with a particular page for recognition of the degree in which the liberal hospitality of the eminent Commissioner of this wonderful service, to whom I had been introduced, helped to make the interest of the whole watched drama poignant and unforgettable. It is a drama that goes on, without a pause, day by day and year by year, this visible act of ingurgitation on the part of our body politic and social, and constituting really an appeal to amazement beyond that of any sword-swallowing or fire-swallowing of the circus. The wonder that one couldn't keep down was the thought that these two or three hours of one's own chance vision of the business were but as a tick or two of the mighty clock, the clock that never, never stops—least of all when it strikes, for a sign of so much winding-up, some louder hour of our national fate than usual. I think indeed that the simplest account of the action of Ellis Island on the spirit of any sensitive citizen who may have happened to "look in" is that he comes back from his visit not at all the same person that he went. He has eaten of the tree of knowledge, and the taste will be for ever in his mouth. He had thought he knew before, thought he had the sense of the degree in which it is his American fate to share the sanctity of his American consciousness, the intimacy of his American patriotism, with the inconceivable alien; but the truth had never come home to him with any such force. In the lurid light projected upon it by those courts of dismay it shakes him—or I like at least to imagine it shakes him—to the depths of his being; I like to think of him, I positively *have* to think of him, as going about ever afterwards with a new look, for those who can see it, in his face, the outward sign of the new chill in his heart. So is stamped, for detection, the questionably privileged person who has had an apparition, seen a ghost in his supposedly safe old house. Let not the unwary, therefore, visit Ellis Island.

The after-sense of that acute experience, however, I myself found, was by no means to be brushed away; I felt it grow and grow, on the contrary, wherever I turned: other impressions might come and go, but this affirmed claim of the alien, however immeasurably alien, to share in one's supreme relation was everywhere the fixed element, the reminder not to be dodged. One's supreme relation, as one had always put it, was one's relation to one's country—a conception made up so largely of one's countrymen and one's countrywomen. Thus it was as if, all the while, with such a fond tradition of what these products predominantly were, the idea of the country itself underwent something of that profane overhauling through which it appears to suffer the indignity of change. Is not our instinct in this matter, in general, essentially the safe one—that of keeping the idea simple and strong and continuous, so that it shall be perfectly sound? To touch it overmuch, to pull it about, is to put it in peril of weakening; yet on this free assault upon it, this readjustment of it in *their* monstrous, presumptuous interest, the aliens, in New York, seemed perpetually to insist. The combination there of their quantity and their quality—that loud primary stage of alienism which New York most offers to sight—operates, for the native, as their note of settled possession, something they have nobody to thank for; so that *un*settled possession is what we, on our side, seem reduced to—the implication of which, in its turn, is that, to recover confidence and regain lost ground, we, not they, must make the surrender and accept the orientation. We must go, in other words, *more* than half-way to meet them; which is all the difference, for us, between possession and dispossession. This sense of dispossession, to be brief about it, haunted me so, I was to feel, in the New York streets and in the packed trajectiles to which one clingingly appeals from the streets, just as one tumbles back into the streets in appalled reaction from *them,* that the art of beguiling or duping it became an art to be cultivated—though the fond alternative vision was never long to be obscured, the imagination, exasperated to envy, of the ideal, in the order in question; of the luxury of some such close and sweet and *whole* national consciousness as that of the Switzer and the Scot.

II

My recovery of impressions, after a short interval, yet with their flush a little faded, may have been judged to involve itself with excursions of memory—memory directed to the antecedent time—reckless almost to extravagance. But I recall them to-day, none the less, for that value in them which ministered, at happy moments, to an artful evasion of the actual. There was no escape from the ubiquitous alien into the future, or even into the present; there was an escape but into the past. I count as quite a triumph in this interest an unbroken ease of frequentation of that ancient end of Fifth Avenue to the whole neighbourhood of which one's earlier vibrations, a very far-away matter now, were attuned. The precious stretch of space between Washington Square and Fourteenth Street had a value, had even a charm, for the revisiting spirit—a mild and melancholy glamour which I am conscious of the difficulty of "rendering" for new and heedless generations. Here again the assault of suggestion is too great; too large, I mean, the number of hares started, before the pursuing imagination, the quickened memory, by this fact of the felt moral and social value of this comparatively unimpaired morsel of the Fifth Avenue heritage. Its reference to a pleasanter, easier, hazier past is absolutely comparative, just as the past in question itself enjoys as such the merest courtesy-title. It is all recent history enough, by the measure of the whole, and there are flaws and defacements enough, surely, even in its appearance of decency of duration. The tall building, grossly tall and grossly ugly, has failed of an admirable chance of distinguished consideration for it, and the dignity of many of its peaceful fronts has succumbed to the presence of those industries whose foremost need is to make "a good thing" of them. The good thing is doubtless being made, and yet this lower end of the once agreeable street still just escapes being a wholly bad thing. What held the fancy in thrall, however, as I say, was the admonition, proceeding from all the facts, that values of this romantic order are at best, anywhere, strangely relative. It was an extraordinary statement on the subject of New York that the space between Fourteenth Street and Washington Square *should* count for "tone," figure as the old ivory of an overscored tablet.

True wisdom, I found, was to let it, to make it, so count and figure as much as it would, and charming assistance came for this, I also found, from the young good-nature of May and June. There had been neither assistance nor good-nature during the grim weeks of mid-winter; there had been but the meagre fact of a discomfort and an ugliness less formidable here than elsewhere. When, toward the top of the town, circulation, alimentation, recreation, every art of existence, gave way before the full onset of winter, when the upper avenues had become as so many congested bottle-necks, through which the wine of life simply refused to be decanted, getting back to these latitudes resembled really a return from the North Pole to the Temperate Zone: it was as if the wine of life had been poured for you, in advance, into some pleasant old punch-bowl that would support you through the temporary stress. Your condition was not reduced to the endless vista of a clogged tube, of a thoroughfare occupied as to the narrow central ridge with trolley-cars stuffed to suffocation, and as to the mere margin, on either side, with snow-banks resulting from the cleared rails and offering themselves as a field for all remaining action. Free existence and good manners, in New York, are too much brought down to a bare rigour of marginal relation to the endless electric coil, the monstrous chain that winds round the general neck and body, the general middle and legs, very much as the boa-constrictor winds round the group of the Laocoön. It struck me that when these folds are tightened in the terrible stricture of the snow-smothered months of the year, the New York predicament leaves far behind the anguish represented in the Vatican figures. To come and go where East Eleventh Street, where West Tenth, opened their kind short arms was at least to keep clear of the awful hug of the serpent. And this was a grace that grew large, as I have hinted, with the approach of summer, and that made in the afternoons of May and of the first half of June, above all, an insidious appeal. There, I repeat, was the delicacy, there the mystery, there the wonder, in especial, of the unquenchable intensity of the impressions received in childhood. They are made then once for all, be their intrinsic beauty, interest, importance, small or great; the stamp is indelible and never wholly fades. This in fact gives it an importance when a lifetime has intervened. I found myself intimately recognizing every house my officious tenth year had, in the way of imagined adventure, introduced to me—incomparable master of ceremonies after all; the privilege had been offered since to millions of other objects that had made nothing of it, that had gone as they came; so that here were Fifth Avenue corners with which one's connection was fairly exquisite. The lowered light of the days' ends of early summer became them, moreover, exceedingly, and they fell, for the quiet northward perspective, into a dozen delicacies of composition and tone.

One could talk of "quietness" now, for the shrinkage of life so marked, in the higher latitudes of the town, after Easter, the visible early flight of that "society" which, by the old custom, used never to budge before June or July, had almost the effect of clearing some of the streets, and indeed of suggesting that a truly clear New York might have an unsuspected charm or two to put forth. An approach to peace and harmony might have been, in a manner, promised, and the sense of other days took advantage of it to steal abroad with a ghostly tread. It kept meeting, half the time, to its discomfiture, the lamentable little Arch of Triumph which bestrides these beginnings of Washington Square—lamentable because of its poor and lonely and unsupported and unaffiliated state. With this melancholy monument it could make no terms at all, but turned its back to the strange sight as often as possible, helping itself thereby, moreover, to do a little of the pretending required, no doubt, by the fond theory that nothing hereabouts was changed. Nothing *was*, it could occasionally appear to me—there was no new note in the picture, not one, for instance, when I paused before a low house in a small row on the south side of Waverley Place and lived again into the queer mediæval costume (preserved by the daguerreotypist's art) of the very little boy for whom the scene had once embodied the pangs and pleasures of a dame's small school. The dame must have been Irish, by her name, and the Irish tradition, only intensified and coarsened, seemed still to possess the place, the fact of the survival, the sturdy sameness, of which arrested me, again and again, to fascination. The shabby red house, with its mere two storeys, its lowly "stoop," its dislocated ironwork of the forties, the early fifties, the record, in its face, of blistering summers and of the long stages of the loss of self-respect, made it as consummate a morsel of the old liquor-scented, heated-looking city, the city of no pavements, but of such a plenty of politics, as I could have desired. And neighbouring Sixth Avenue, overstraddled though it might be with feats of engineering unknown to the primitive age that otherwise so persisted, wanted only, to carry off the illusion, the warm smell of the bakery on the corner of Eighth Street, a blessed repository of doughnuts, cookies, cream-cakes and pies, the slow passing by which, on returns from school, must have had much in common with the experience of the shipmen of old who came, in long voyages, while they tacked and hung back, upon those belts of ocean that are haunted with the balm and spice of tropic islands.

These were the felicities of the backward reach, which, however, had also its melancholy checks and snubs; nowhere quite so sharp as in presence, so to speak, of the rudely, the ruthlessly suppressed birth-house on the other side of the Square. That was where the pretence that nearly nothing was changed had most to come in; for a high, square, impersonal structure, proclaiming its lack of interest with a crudity all its own, so blocks, at the right moment for its own success, the view of the past, that the effect for me, in Washington Place, was of having been amputated of half my history. The grey and more or less "hallowed" University building—wasn't it somehow, with a desperate bravery, both castellated and gabled?—has vanished from the earth, and vanished with it the two or three adjacent houses, of which the birthplace was one. This was the snub, for the complacency of retrospect, that, whereas the inner sense had positively erected there for its private contemplation a commemorative mural tablet, the very wall that should have borne this inscription had been smashed as for demonstration that tablets, in New York, are unthinkable. And I have had indeed to permit myself this free fantasy of the hypothetic rescued identity of a given house —taking the vanished number in Washington Place as most pertinent—in order to invite the reader to gasp properly with me before the fact that we not only fail to remember, in the whole length of the city, one of these frontal records of birth, sojourn, or death, under a celebrated name, but that we have only to reflect an instant to see any such form of civic piety inevitably and for ever absent. The form is cultivated, to the greatly quickened interest of street-scenery, in many of the cities of Europe; and is it not verily bitter, for those who feel a poetry in the noted passage, longer or shorter, here and there, of great lost spirits, that the institution, the profit, the glory of any such association is denied in advance to communities tending, as the phrase is, to "run" preponderantly to the sky-scraper? Where, in fact, is the point of inserting a mural tablet, at any legible height, in a building certain to be destroyed to make room for a sky-scraper? And from where, on the other hand, in a façade of fifty floors, does one "see" the pious plate recording the honour attached to one of the apartments look down on a responsive people? We have but to ask the question to recognize our necessary failure to answer it as a supremely characteristic local note—a note in the light of which the great city is projected into its future as, practically, a huge, continuous fifty-floored conspiracy against the very idea of the ancient graces, those that strike us as having flourished just in proportion as the parts of life and the signs of character have *not* been lumped together, not been indistinguishably sunk in the common fund of mere economic convenience. So interesting, as object-lessons, may the developments of the American gregarious ideal become; so traceable, at every turn, to the restless analyst at least, are the heavy footprints, in the finer texture of life, of a great commercial democracy seeking to abound supremely in its own sense and having none to gainsay it.

Let me not, however, forget, amid such contemplations, what may serve here as a much more relevant instance of the operation of values, the price of the as yet undiminished dignity of the two most southward of the Fifth Avenue churches. Half the charm of the prospect, at that extremity, is in their still being there, and being as they are; this charm, this serenity of escape and survival positively works as a blind on the side of the question of their architectural importance. The last shade of pedantry or priggishness drops from your view of that element; they illustrate again supremely your grasped truth of the *comparative* character, in such conditions, of beauty and of interest. The special standard they may or may not square with signifies, you feel, not a jot: all you know, and want to know, is that they are probably menaced—some horrible voice of the air has murmured it—and that with them will go, if fate overtakes them, the last cases worth mentioning (with a single exception), of the modest felicity that sometimes used to be. Remarkable certainly the state of things in which mere exemption from the "squashed" condition can shed such a glamour; but we may accept the state of things if only we can keep the glamour undispelled. It reached its maximum for me, I hasten to add, on my penetrating into the Ascension, at chosen noon, and standing for the first time in presence of that noble work of John La Farge, the representation, on the west wall, in the grand manner, of the theological event from which the church takes its title. Wonderful enough, in New York, to find one's self, in a charming and considerably dim "old" church, hushed to admiration before a great religious picture; the sensation, for the moment, upset so all the facts. The hot light, outside, might have been that of an Italian *piazzetta;* the cool shade, within, with the important work of art shining through it, seemed part of some other-world pilgrimage—all the more that the important work of art itself, a thing of the highest distinction, spoke, as soon as one had taken it in, with that authority which makes the difference, ever afterwards, between the remembered and the forgotten quest. A rich note of interference came, I admit, through the splendid window-glass, the finest of which, unsurpassably fine, to my sense, is the work of the same artist; so that the church, as it stands, is very nearly as commemorative a monument as a great reputation need wish. The deeply pictorial windows, in which clearness of picture and fulness of expression consort so successfully with a tone as of magnified gems, did not strike one as looking into a yellow little square of the south—they put forth a different implication; but the flaw in the harmony was, more than anything else, that sinister voice of the air of which I have spoken, the fact that one *could* stand there, vibrating to such impressions, only to remember the suspended danger, the possibility of the doom. Here was the loveliest cluster of images, begotten on the spot, that the preoccupied city had ever taken thought to offer itself; and here, to match them, like some black shadow they had been condemned to cast, was this particular prepared honour of "removal" that appeared to hover about them.

One's fear, I repeat, was perhaps misplaced—but what an air to live in, the shuddering pilgrim mused, the air in which such fears are not misplaced only when we are conscious of very special reassurances! The vision of the doom that does descend, that had descended all round, was at all events, for the half-hour, all that was wanted to charge with the last tenderness one's memory of the transfigured interior. Afterwards, outside, again and again, the powers of removal struck me as looming, awfully, in the newest mass of multiplied floors and windows visible at this point. *They*, ranged in this terrible recent erection, were going to bring in money—and was not money the only thing a self-respecting structure could be thought of as bringing in? Hadn't one heard, just before, in Boston, that the security, that the sweet serenity of the Park Street Church, charmingest, there, of aboriginal notes, the very light, with its perfect position and its dear old delightful Wren-like spire, of the starved city's eyes, had been artfully practised against, and that the question of saving it might become, in the near future, acute? Nothing, fortunately, I think, is so much the "making" of New York, at its central point, for the visual, almost for the romantic, sense, as the Park Street Church is the making, by its happy coming-in, of Boston; and, therefore, if it were thinkable that the peculiar rectitude of Boston might be laid in the dust, what mightn't easily come about for the reputedly less austere conscience of New York? Once such questions had obtained lodgment, to take one's walks was verily to look at almost everything in their light; and to commune with the sky-scraper under this influence was really to feel worsted, more and more, in any magnanimous attempt to adopt the æsthetic view of it. I may appear to make too much of these invidious presences, but it must be remembered that they represent, for our time, the only claim to any consideration other than merely statistical established by the resounding growth of New York. The attempt to take the æsthetic view is invariably blighted sooner or later by their most salient characteristic, *the* feature that speaks loudest for the economic idea. Window upon window, at any cost, is a condition never to be reconciled with any grace of building, and the logic of the matter here happens to put on a particularly fatal front. If quiet interspaces, always half the architectural battle, exist no more in such a structural scheme than quiet tones, blest breathing-spaces, occur, for the most part, in New York conversation, so the reason is, demonstrably, that the building can't afford them. (It is by very much the same law, one supposes, that New York conversation cannot afford stops.) The building can only afford lights, each light having a superlative value as an aid to the transaction of business and the conclusion of sharp bargains. Doesn't it take in fact acres of window-glass to help even an expert New Yorker to get the better of another expert one, or to see that the other expert one doesn't get the better of *him?* It is easy to conceive that, after all, with this origin and nature stamped upon their foreheads, the last word of the mercenary monsters should not be their address to our sense of formal beauty.

Still, as I have already hinted, there was always the case of the one other rescued identity and preserved felicity, the happy accident of the elder day still ungrudged and finally legitimated. When I say ungrudged, indeed, I seem to remember how I had heard that the divine little City Hall had *been* grudged, at a critical moment, to within an inch of its life; had but just escaped, in the event, the extremity of grudging. It lives on securely, by the mercy of fate—lives on in the delicacy of its beauty, speaking volumes again (more volumes, distinctly, than are anywhere else spoken) for the exquisite truth of the *conferred* value of interesting objects, the value derived from the social, the civilizing function for which they have happened to find their opportunity. It is the opportunity that gives them their price, and the luck of there being, round about them, nothing greater than themselves to steal it away from them. They strike thus, virtually, the supreme note, and—such is the mysterious play of our finer sensibility!—one takes this note, one is glad to work it, as the phrase goes, for all it is worth. I so work the note of the City Hall, no doubt, in speaking of the spectacle there constituted as "divine"; but I do it precisely by reason of the spectacle taken *with* the delightful small facts of the building: largely by reason, in other words, of the elegant, the gallant little structure's situation and history, the way it has played, artistically, ornamentally, its part, has held out for the good cause, through the long years, alone and unprotected. The fact is it has been the very centre of that assault of vulgarity of which the innumerable mementos rise within view of it and tower, at a certain distance, over it; and yet it has never parted with a square inch of its character, it has forced them, in a manner, to stand off. I hasten to add that in expressing thus its uncompromised state I speak of its outward, its æsthetic character only. So, at all events, it has discharged the civilizing function I just named as inherent in such cases—that of representing, to the community possessed of it, all the Style the community is likely to get, and of making itself responsible for the same.

The consistency of this effort, under difficulties, has been the story that brings tears to the eyes of the hovering kindly critic, and it is through his tears, no doubt, that such a personage reads the best passages of the tale and makes out the proportions of the object. Mine, I recognize, didn't prevent my seeing that the pale yellow marble (or whatever it may be) of the City Hall has lost, by some late excoriation, the remembered charm of its old surface, the pleasant promiscuous patina of time; but the perfect taste and finish, the reduced yet ample scale, the harmony of parts, the just proportions, the modest classic grace, the living look of the type aimed at, these things, with gaiety of detail undiminished and "quaintness" of effect augmented, are all there; and I see them, as I write, in that glow of appreciation which made it necessary, of a fine June morning, that I should somehow pay the whole place my respects. The simplest, in fact the only way, was, obviously, to pass under the charming portico and brave the consequences: this impunity of such audacities being, in America, one of the last of the lessons the repatriated absentee finds himself learning. The crushed spirit he brings back from European discipline never quite rises to the height of the native argument, the brave sense that the public, the civic building is his very own, for any honest use, so that he may tread even its most expensive pavements and staircases (and very expensive, for the American citizen, these have lately become), without a question asked. This further and further unchallenged penetration begets in the perverted person I speak of a really romantic thrill: it is like some assault of the dim seraglio, with the guards bribed, the eunuchs drugged and one's life carried in one's hand. The only drawback to such freedom is that penetralia it is so easy to penetrate fail a little of a due impressiveness, and that if stationed sentinels are bad for the temper of the freeman they are good for the "prestige" of the building.

Never, in any case, it seemed to me, had any freeman made so free with the majesty of things as I was to make on this occasion with the mysteries of the City Hall—even to the point of coming out into the presence of the Representative of the highest office with which City Halls are associated, and whose thoroughly gracious condonation of my act set the seal of success upon the whole adventure. Its dizziest intensity in fact sprang precisely from the unexpected view opened into the old official, the old so thick-peopled local, municipal world: upper chambers of council and state, delightfully of their nineteenth-century time, as to design and ornament, in spite of rank restoration; but replete, above all, with portraits of past worthies, past celebrities and city fathers, Mayors, Bosses, Presidents, Governors, Statesmen at large, Generals and Commodores at large, florid ghosts, looking so unsophisticated now, of years not remarkable, municipally, for the absence of sophistication. Here were types, running mainly to ugliness and all bristling with the taste of their day and the quite touching provincialism of their conditions, as to many of which nothing would be more interesting than a study of New York annals in the light of their personal look, their very noses and mouths and complexions and heads of hair—to say nothing of their waistcoats and neckties; with such colour, such sound and movement would the thick stream of local history then be interfused. Wouldn't its thickness fairly become transparent? since to walk through the collection was not only to see and feel so much that had happened, but to understand, with the truth again and again inimitably pointed, why nothing could have happened otherwise; the whole array thus presenting itself as an unsurpassed demonstration of the real reasons of things. The florid ghosts look out from their exceedingly gilded frames—all that *that* can do is bravely done for them—with the frankest responsibility for everything; their collective presence becomes a kind of copious tell-tale document signed with a hundred names. There are few of these that at this hour, I think, we particularly desire to repeat; but the place where they may be read is, all the way from river to river and from the Battery to Harlem, the place in which there is most of the terrible town.

. . . .

IV

The huge jagged city, it must be nevertheless said, has always at the worst, for propitiation, the resource of its easy reference to its almost incomparable river. New York may indeed be jagged, in her long leanness, where she lies looking at the sky in the manner of some colossal hair-comb turned upward and so deprived of half its teeth that the others, at their uneven intervals, count doubly as sharp spikes; but, unmistakably, you can bear with some of her aspects and her airs better when you have really taken in that reference—which I speak of as easy because she has in this latter time begun to make it with an appearance of some intention. She has come at last, far up on the West side, into possession of her birthright, into the roused consciousness that some possibility of a river-front may still remain to her; though, obviously, a justified pride in this property has yet to await the birth of a more responsible sense of style in her dealings with it, the dawn of some adequate plan or controlling idea. Splendid the elements of position, on the part of the new Riverside Drive (over the small suburbanizing name of which, as at the effect of a second-rate shop-worn article, we sigh as we pass); yet not less irresistible the pang of our seeing it settle itself on meagre, bourgeois, happy-go-lucky lines. The pity of this is sharp in proportion as the "chance" has been magnificent, and the soreness of perception of what merely might have been is as constant as the flippancy of the little vulgar "private houses" or the big vulgar "apartment hotels" that are having their own way, so unchallenged, with the whole question of composition and picture. The fatal "tall" pecuniary enterprise rises where it will, in the candid glee of new worlds to conquer; the intervals between take whatever foolish little form they like; the sky-line, eternal victim of the artless jumble, submits again to the type of the broken hair-comb turned up; the streets that abut from the East condescend at their corners to any crudity or poverty that may suit their convenience. And all this in presence of an occasion for noble congruity such as one scarce knows where to seek in the case of another great city.

A sense of the waste of criticism, however, a sense that

is almost in itself consoling, descends upon the fond critic after his vision has fixed the scene awhile in this light of its lost accessibility to some informed and benevolent despot, some power working in one great way and so that the interest of beauty should have been better saved. Is not criticism wasted, in other words, just by the reason of the constant remembrance, on New York soil, that one is almost impudently cheated by any part of the show that pretends to prolong its actuality or to rest on its present basis? Since every part, however blazingly new, fails to affect us as doing more than hold the ground for something else, some conceit of the bigger dividend, that is still to come, so we may bind up the æsthetic wound, I think, quite as promptly as we feel it open. The particular ugliness, or combination of uglinesses, is no more final than the particular felicity (since there are several even of these up and down the town to be noted), and whatever crudely-extemporized look the Riverside heights may wear to-day, the spectator of fifty years hence will find his sorrow, if not his joy, in a different extemporization. The whole thing is the vividest of lectures on the subject of individualism, and on the strange truth, no doubt, that this principle may in the field of art—at least if the art be architecture—often conjure away just that mystery of distinction which it sometimes so markedly promotes in the field of life. It is also quite as suggestive perhaps on the ever-interesting question, for the artist, of the entirely relative nature and value of "treatment." A manner so right in one relation may be so wrong in another, and a house-front so "amusing" for its personal note, or its perversity, in a short perspective, may amid larger elements merely dishonour the harmony. And yet why *should* the charm ever fall out of the "personal," which is so often the very condition of the exquisite? Why should conformity and subordination, that acceptance of control and assent to collectivism in the name of which our age has seen such dreary things done, become on a given occasion the one *not* vulgar way of meeting a problem?

Inquiries these, evidently, that are answerable only in presence of the particular cases provoking them; when indeed they may hold us as under a spell. Endless for instance the æsthetic nobleness of such a question as that of the authority with which the spreading Hudson, at the opening of its gates, would have imposed on the constructive powers, if listened to, some proportionate order—would, in other words, have admirably given us collectivism at its highest. One has only to stand there and *see*—of such value are lessons in "authority." But the great vista of the stream alone speaks of it—save in so far at least as the voice is shared, and to so different, to so dreadful a tune, by the grossly-defacing railway that clings to the bank. The authority of railways, in the United States, sits enthroned as none other, and has always, of course, in any vision of aspects, to be taken into account. Here, at any rate, it is the rule that has prevailed; the other, the high interest of the possible picture, is one that lapses; so that the cliffs overhang the water, and at various points descend to it in green slopes and hollows (where the landscape-gardener does what he can), only to find a wealth of visible baseness installed there before them. That so familiar circumstance, in America, of the completion of the good thing ironically and, as would often seem for the time, insuperably baffled, meets here one of its liveliest illustrations. It at all events helps to give meanwhile the mingled pitch of the whole concert that Columbia College (to sound the old and easier name) should have "moved up"—moved up twice, if I am not mistaken—to adorn with an ampler presence this very neighbourhood. It has taken New York to invent, for the thickening of classic shades, the "moving" University; and does not that quite mark the tune of the dance, of the local unwritten law that forbids almost *any* planted object to gather in a history where it stands, forbids in fact any accumulation that may not be recorded in the mere bank-book? This last became long ago *the* historic page.

It is, however, just because the beauty of the Hudson seems to speak of other matters, and because the sordid city has the honour, after all, of sitting there at the Beautiful Gate, that I alluded above to her profiting in a manner, even from the point of view of "taste," by this close and fortunate connection. The place puts on thus, not a little, the likeness of a large loose family which has had queer adventures and fallen into vulgar ways, but for which a glorious cousinship never quite repudiated by the indifferent princely cousin—*bon prince* in this as in other matters —may still be pleaded. At the rate New York is growing, in fine, she will more and more "command," in familiar intercourse, the great perspective of the River; so that here, a certain point reached, her whole case must change and her general opportunity, swallowing up the mainland, become a new question altogether. Let me hasten to add that in the light of this opportunity even the most restless analyst can but take the hopeful view of her. I fear I am finding too many personal comparisons for her—than which indeed there can be no greater sign of a confessed pre-occupation; but she figures, once again, as an heir whose expectations are so vast and so certain that no temporary sowing of wild oats need be felt to endanger them. As soon as the place begins to spread at ease real responsibility of all sorts will begin, and the good-natured feeling must surely be that the civic conscience in her, at such a stage, will fall into step. Of the spreading woods and waters amid which the future in question appears still half to lurk, that mainland region of the Bronx, vast above all in possibilities of Park, out of which it already appears half to emerge, I unluckily failed of occasion to take the adequate measure. But my confused impression was of a kind of waiting abundance, an extraordinary quantity of "nature," for the reformed rake, that is the sobered heir, to play with. It is the fashion in the East to speak of New York as poor of environment, unpossessed of the agreeable, accessible countryside that crowns the convenience not only of London and of Paris, but even, with more humiliating promptitude, that of Boston, of Philadelphia, of Baltimore. In spite, however, of the memory, from far back, of a hundred marginal Manhattanese miseries, an immediate belt of the most sordid character, I cannot but think of this invidious legend as attempting to prove too much.

The countryside is there, on the most liberal of scales—it is the townside, only, that, having the great waters and the greater distances generally to deal with, has worn so rude and demoralized a face as to frighten the country away. And if the townside is now making after the countryside fast, as I say, and with a little less of the mere roughness of the satyr pursuing the nymph, what finer warrant could be desired than such felicities of position as those enjoyed, on the Riverside heights, by the monument erected to the soldiers and sailors of the Civil War and, even in a greater degree, by the tomb of General Grant? These are verily monumental sites of the first order, and I confess that, though introduced to them on a bleak winter morning, with no ingratiation in any element, I felt the critical question, as to the structures themselves, as to taste or intention, as to the amount of involved or achieved consecration or profanation, carried off in the general greatness of the effect. I shall in fact always remember that icy hour, with the temple-crowned headlands, the wide Hudson vista white with the cold, all nature armour-plated and grim, as an extraordinarily strong and simple composition; made stern and kept simple as for some visit of the God of Battles to his chosen. He might have been riding there, on the north wind, to look down at them, and one caught for the moment, the true hard light in which military greatness should be seen. It shone over the miles of ice with its lustre of steel, and if what, thus attested, it makes one think of was its incomparable, indestructible "prestige," so that association affected me both then and on a later occasion as with a strange indefinable consequence—an influence in which the æsthetic consideration, the artistic value of either memorial, melted away and became irrelevant. For here, if ever, was a great democratic demonstration caught in the fact, the nakedest possible effort to strike the note of the august. The tomb of the single hero in particular presents itself in a manner so opposed to our common ideas of the impressive, to any past vision of sepulchral state, that we can only wonder if a new kind and degree of solemnity may not have been arrived at in this complete rupture with old consecrating forms.

The tabernacle of Grant's ashes stands there by the pleasure-drive, unguarded and unenclosed, the feature of the prospect and the property of the people, as open as an hotel or a railway-station to any coming and going, and as dedicated to the public use as builded things in America (when not mere closed churches) only can be. Unmistakable its air of having had, all consciously, from the first, to raise its head and play its part without pomp and circumstance to "back" it, without mystery or ceremony to protect it, without Church or State to intervene on its behalf, with only its immediacy, its familiarity of interest to circle it about, and only its proud outlook to preserve, so far as possible, its character. The tomb of Napoleon at the Invalides is a great national property, and the play of democratic manners sufficiently surrounds it; but as compared to the small pavilion on the Riverside bluff it is a holy of holies, a great temple jealously guarded and formally approached. And yet one doesn't conclude, strange to say, that the Riverside pavilion fails of its expression a whit more than the

Paris dome; one perhaps even feels it triumph by its use of its want of reserve as a very last word. The admonition of all of which possibly is—I confess I but grope for it—that when there has been in such cases a certain other happy combination, an original sincerity of intention, an original propriety of site, and above all an original high value of name and fame, something in this line really supreme, publicity, familiarity, immediacy, as I have called them, *carried far enough,* may stalk in and out of the shrine with their hands in their pockets and their hats on their heads, and yet not dispel the Presence. The question at any rate puts itself—as new questions in America are always putting themselves: Do certain impressions there represent the absolute extinction of old sensibilities, or do they represent only new forms of them? The inquiry would be doubtless easier to answer if so many of these feelings were not mainly known to us just *by* their attendant forms. At this rate, or on such a showing, in the United States, attendant forms being, in every quarter, remarkably scarce, it would indeed seem that the sentiments implied *are* extinct; for it would be an abuse of ingenuity, I fear, to try to read mere freshness of form into some of the more rank failures of observance. There are failures of observance that stand, at the best, for failures of sense—whereby, however, the question grows too great. One must leave the tomb of Grant to its conditions and its future with the simple note for it that if it be not in fact one of the most effective of commemorations it is one of the most missed. On the whole I distinctly "liked" it.

V

It is still vivid to me that, returning in the spring-time from a few weeks in the Far West, I re-entered New York State with the absurdest sense of meeting again a ripe old civilization and travelling through a country that showed the mark of established manners. It will seem, I fear, one's perpetual refrain, but the moral was yet once more that values of a certain order are, in such conditions, all relative, and that, as some wants of the spirit *must* somehow be met, one knocks together any substitute that will fairly stay the appetite. We had passed great smoky Buffalo in the raw charm, whatever it might be, too needfully sacrificed, op- vernal dawn—with a vision, for me, of curiosity, character, portunity perhaps forever missed, yet at the same time a vision in which the lost object failed to mock at me with the last concentration of shape; and history, as we moved Eastward, appeared to meet us, in the look of the land, in its more overwrought surface and thicker detail, quite as if she had ever consciously declined to cross the border and were aware, precisely, of the queer feast we should find in her. The recognition, I profess, was a preposterous ecstasy: one couldn't have felt more if one had passed into the presence of some seated, placid, rich-voiced gentlewoman after leaving that of an honest but boisterous hoyden. It was doubtless a matter only of degrees and shades, but never was such a pointing of the lesson that a sign of any sort may count double if it be but artfully placed. I spent that day, literally, in the company of the rich-voiced gentlewoman, making my profit of it even in spite of a second privation, the doom I was under of having only, all wistfully, all ruefully, to avert my lips from the quaint silver bowl, as I here quite definitely figured it, in which she offered me the entertainment of antique Albany. At antique Albany, to a certainty, the mature matron involved in my metaphor would have put on a particular grace, and as our train crossed the river for further progress I almost seemed to see her stand at some gable-window of Dutch association, one of the two or three impressed there on my infantile imagination, to ask me why then I had come so far at all.

I could have replied but in troubled tones, and I looked at the rest of the scene for some time, no doubt, as through the glaze of all-but filial tears. Thus it was, possibly, that I saw the River shine, from that moment on, as a great romantic stream, such as could throw not a little of its glamour, for the mood of that particular hour, over the city at its mouth. I had not even known, in my untravelled state, that we were to "strike" it on our way from Chicago, so that it represented, all that afternoon, so much beauty thrown in, so much benefit beyond the bargain—the so hard bargain, for the traveller, of the American railway-journey at its best. That ordeal was in any case at its best here, and the perpetually interesting river kept its course, by my right elbow, with such splendid consistency that, as I recall the impression, I repent a little of having just now reflected with acrimony on the cost of the obtrusion of track and stations to the Riverside view. One must of course choose between dispensing with the ugly presence and enjoying the scenery by the aid of the same—which but means, really, that to use the train at all had been to put one's self, for any proper justice to the scenery, in a false position. That, however, takes us too far back, and one can only save one's dignity by laying all such blames on our detestable age. A decent respect for the Hudson would confine us to the use of the boat—all the more that American river-steamers have had, from the earliest time, for the true *raffiné*, their peculiar note of romance. A possible commerce, on the other hand, with one's time—which is always also the time of so many other busy people—has long since made mincemeat of the rights of contemplation; rights as reduced, in the United States, to-day, and by quite the same argument, as those of the noble savage whom we have banished to his narrowing reservation. Letting that pass, at all events, I still remember that I was able to put, from the car-window, as many questions to the scene as it could have answered in the time even had its face been clearer to read.

Its face was veiled, for the most part, in a mist of premature spring heat, an atmosphere draping it indeed in luminous mystery, hanging it about with sun-shot silver and minimizing any happy detail, any element of the definite, from which the romantic effect might here and there have gained an accent. There was not an accent in the picture from the beginning of the run to Albany to the end—for which thank goodness! one is tempted to say on remembering how often, over the land in general, the accents are wrong. Yet if the romantic effect as we know it elsewhere mostly depends on them, why *should* that glamour have so shimmered before me in their absence?—how should the picture have managed to be a constant combination of felicities? Was it just *because* the felicities were all váguenesses, and the "beauties," even the most celebrated, all blurs?—was it perchance on that very account that I could meet my wonder so promptly with the inference that what I had in my eyes on so magnificent a scale was simply, was famously, "style"? I was landed by that conclusion in the odd further proposition that style could then exist without accents—a quandary soon after to be quenched, however, in the mere blinding radiance of a visit to West Point. I was to make that memorable pilgrimage a fortnight later—and I was to find my question, when it in fact took place, shivered by it to mere silver atoms. The very powers of the air seemed to have taken the case in hand and positively to have been interested in making it transcend all argument. Our Sunday of mid-May, wet and windy, let loose, over the vast stage, the whole procession of storm-effects; the raw green of wooded heights and hollows was only everywhere rain-brightened, the weather playing over it all day as with some great grey water-colour brush. The essential character of West Point and its native nobleness of position can have been but intensified, I think, by this artful process; yet what was mainly unmistakable was the fact again of the suppression of detail as in the positive interest of the grand style. One had therefore only to take detail as another name for accent, the accent that might prove compromising, in order to see it made good that style *could* do without them, and that the grand style in fact almost always must. How on this occasion the trick was played is more than I shall attempt to say; it is enough to have been conscious of our being, from hour to hour, literally bathed in that high element, with the very face of nature washed, so to speak, the more clearly to express and utter it.

Such accordingly is the strong silver light, all simplifying and ennobling, in which I see West Point; see it as a cluster of high promontories, of the last classic elegance, overhanging vast receding reaches of river, mountain-guarded and dim, which took their place in the geography of the ideal, in the long perspective of the poetry of association, rather than in those of the State of New York. It was as if the genius of the scene had said: "No, you *shan't* have accent, because accent is, at the best, local and special, and might here by some perversity—how do I know after all?—interfere. I want you to have something unforgettable, and therefore you shall have *type*—yes, absolutely have type, and even tone, without accent; an impossibility, you may hitherto have supposed, but which you have only to look about you now really to see expressed. And type and tone of the very finest and rarest; type and tone good enough for Claude or Turner, if they could have walked by these rivers instead of by their thin rivers of France and Italy; type and tone, in short, that gather in shy detail under wings as wide as those with which a motherly hen covers her endangered brood. So there you are—deprived of all 'accent' as a peg for criticism, and reduced thereby, you see, to asking me no more questions." I was able so to take home, I may add, this formula of the matter, that even the interesting facts of the School of the Soldier which have carried the name of the place about the world almost put on the shyness, the air of conscious evasion and escape, noted in the above allocution: they struck me as forsaking the foreground of the picture. It was part of the play again, no doubt, of the grey water-colour brush: there was to be no consent of the elements, that day, to anything but a generalized elegance—in which effect certainly the clustered, the scattered Academy played, on its high green stage, its part. But, of all things in the world, it massed, to my vision, more mildly than I had somehow expected; and I take that for a feature, precisely, of the pure poetry of the impression. It lurked there with grace, it insisted without swagger—and I could have hailed it just for this reason indeed as a presence of the last distinction. It is doubtless too much to say, in fine, that the Institution, at West Point, "suffers" comparatively, for vulgar individual emphasis, from the overwhelming liberality of its setting—and I perhaps chanced to see it in the very conditions that most invest it with poetry. The fact remains that, both as to essence and as to quantity, its prose seemed washed away, and I shall recall it in the future much less as the sternest, the world over, of all the seats of Discipline, than as some great Corot-composition of young, vague, wandering figures in splendidly-classic shades.

From Chapters II and III of The American Scene (1907)

The Sense of Newport

1904–5

I

Newport, on my finding myself back there, threatened me sharply, quite at first, with that predicament at which I have glanced in another connection or two—the felt condition of having known it too well and loved it too much for description or definition. What was one to say about it except that one *had* been so affected, so distraught, and that discriminations and reasons were buried under the dust of use? There was a chance indeed that the breath of the long years (of the interval of absence, I mean) would have blown away this dust—and that, precisely, was what one was eager to see. To go out, to look about, to recover the sense, was accordingly to put the question, without delay, to the proof—and with the happy consequence, I think, of an escape from a grave discomfiture. The charm was there again, unmistakably, the little old strange, very simple charm—to be expressed, as a fine proposition, or to be given up; but the answer came in the fact that to have walked about for half-an-hour was to have felt the question clear away. It cleared away so conveniently, so blissfully, in the light of the benign little truth that nothing had been less possible, even in the early, ingenuous, infatuated days than to describe or define Newport. It had clearly had nothing about it *to* describe or define, so that one's fondness had fairly rested on this sweet oddity in it. One had only to look back to recognize that it had never condescended to give a scrap of reasoned account of itself (as a favourite of fortune and the haunt of the *raffiné*); it had simply lain there like a little bare, white, open hand, with slightly-parted fingers, for the observer with a presumed sense for hands to take or to leave. The observer with a real sense never failed to pay this image the tribute of quite tenderly grasping the hand, and even of raising it, delicately, to his lips; having no less, at the same time, the instinct of not shaking it too hard, and that above all of never putting it to any rough work.

Such had been from the first, under a chastened light and in a purple sea, the dainty isle of Aquidneck; which might have avoided the weak mistake of giving up its pretty native name and of becoming thereby as good as nameless—with an existence as Rhode Island practically monopolized by the State and a Newport identity borrowed at the best and applicable but to a corner. Does not this vagueness of condition, however, fitly symbolize the small virtual promontory, of which, superficially, nothing could be predicated but its sky and its sea and its sunsets? One views it as placed there, by some refinement in the scheme of nature, just as a touchstone of taste—with a beautiful little sense to be read into it by a few persons, and nothing at all to be made of it, as to its essence, by most others. I come back, for its essence, to that figure of the little white hand, with the gracefully-spread fingers and the fine grain of skin, even the dimples at the joints and the shell-like delicacy of the pink nails—all the charms in short that a little white hand may have. I see all the applications of the image—I see a special truth in each. It is the back of the hand, rising to the swell of the wrist, that is exposed—which is the way, I think, the true lover takes and admires it. He makes out in it, bending over it—or he used to in the old days—innumerable shy and subtle beauties, almost requiring, for justice, a magnifying-glass; and he winces at the sight of certain other obtruded ways of dealing with it. The touchstone of taste was indeed to operate, for the critical, the tender spirit, from the moment the pink palm was turned up on the chance of what might be "in" it. For nine persons out of ten, among its visitors, its purchasers of sites and builders of (in the old parlance) cottages, there had never been anything in it at all—except of course an opportunity: an opportunity for escaping the summer heat of other places, for bathing, for boating, for riding and driving, and for many sorts of more or less expensive riot. The pink palm being empty, in other words, to their vision, they had begun, from far back, to put things into it, things of their own, and of all sorts, and of many ugly, and of more and more expensive, sorts; to fill it substantially, that is, with gold, the gold that they have ended by heaping up there to an amount so oddly out of proportion to the scale of nature and of space.

This process, one was immediately to perceive with that renewal of impression, this process of injection and elaboration, of creating the palpable pile, had been going on for years to such a tune that the face of nature was now as much obliterated as possible, and the original shy sweetness as much as possible bedizened and bedevilled: all of which, moreover, might also at present be taken as having led, in turn, to the most unexpected climax, a matter of which I shall presently speak. The original shy sweetness, however, that range of effect which I have referred to as practically too latent and too modest for notation, had meanwhile had its votaries, the fond pedestrian minority, for whom the little white hand (to return for an instant to my figure, with which, as you see, I am charmed) had always been so full of treasures of its own as to discredit, from the point of view of taste, any attempt, from without, to stuff it fuller. Such attempts had, in the nature of the case, and from far back, been condemned to show for violations; violations of taste and discretion, to begin with—violations, more intimately, as the whole business became brisker, of a thousand delicate secret places, dear to the disinterested rambler, small, mild "points" and promontories, far away little lonely, sandy coves, rock-set, lily-sheeted ponds, almost hidden, and shallow Arcadian summer-haunted valleys, with the sea just over some stony shoulder: a whole world that called out to the long afternoons of youth, a world with its scale so measured and intended and happy, its detail so finished and pencilled and stippled (certainly for American detail!) that there comes back to me, across the many years, no better analogy for it than that of some fine foreground in an old "line" engraving. There remained always a sense, of course, in which the superimpositions, the multiplied excrescences, were a tribute to the value of the place; where no such liberty was ever taken save exactly *because* (as even the most blundering builder would have claimed) it was all so beautiful, so solitary and so "sympathetic." And that indeed has been, thanks to the "pilers-on" of gold, the fortune, the history of its beauty: that it now bristles with the villas and palaces into which the cottages have all turned, and that these monuments of pecuniary power rise thick and close, precisely, in order that their occupants may constantly remark to each other, from the windows to the "grounds," and from house to house, that it *is* beautiful, it *is* solitary and sympathetic. The thing has been done, it is impossible not to perceive, with the best faith in the world—though not altogether with the best light, which is always so different a matter; and it is with the general consequence only, at the end of the story, that I find myself to-day concerned.

So much concerned I found myself, I profess, after I had taken in this fact of a very distinct general consequence, that the whole interest of the vision was quickened by it; and that when, in particular, on one of the last days of June, among the densely-arrayed villas, I had followed the beautiful "ocean drive" to its uttermost reach and back without meeting either another vehicle or a single rider, let alone a single pedestrian, I recognized matter for the intellectual thrill that attests a social revolution foreseen and completed. The term I use may appear extravagant, but it was a fact, none the less, that I seemed to take full in my face, on this occasion, the cold stir of air produced when the whirligig of time has made one of its liveliest turns. It is always going, the whirligig, but its effect is so to blow up the dust that we must wait for it to stop a moment, as it now and then does with a pant of triumph, in order to see what it has been at. I saw, beyond all doubt, on the spot—and *there* came in, exactly, the thrill; I could remember far back enough to have seen it begin to blow all the artless buyers and builders and blunderers into their places, leaving them there for half a century or so of fond security, and then to see it, of a sudden, blow them quite out again, as with the happy consciousness of some new amusing use for them, some other game still to play with them. This acquaintance, as it practically had been, with the whole rounding of the circle (even though much of it from a distance), was tantamount to the sense of having sat out the drama, the social, the local, that of a real American period, from the rise to the fall of the curtain—always assuming that truth of the reached catastrophe or *dénouement. How* this climax or solution had been arrived at—that, clearly, for the spectator, would have been worth taking note of; but what he made of it I shall not glance at till I have shown him as first of all, on the spot, quite modestly giving in to mere primary beguilement. It had been certain in advance that he would find the whole picture over-painted, and the question could only be, at the best, of how much of the ancient surface would here and there glimmer through. The ancient surface had been the concern, as I have hinted, of the small fond minority, the comparatively few people for whom the lurking shy charm, all there, but all to be felt rather than published, did in fact constitute a surface. The question, as soon as one arrived, was of whether some ghost of that were recoverable.

II

There was always, to begin with, the Old Town—we used, before we had become Old ourselves, to speak of it that way, in the manner of an allusion to Nuremberg or to Carcassonne, since it had been leading its little historic life for centuries (as we implied) before "cottages" and house-agents were dreamed of. It was not that we had great illusions about it or great pretensions for it; we only thought it, without interference, very "good of its kind," and we had as to its *being* of that kind no doubt whatever. Would it still be of that kind, and what had the kind itself been?—these questions made one's heart beat faster as one went forth in search of it. Distinctly, if it had been of a kind it *would* still be of it; for the kind wouldn't at the worst or at the best (one scarce knew how to put it) have been worth changing: so that the question for the restored absentee, who so palpitated with the sense of it, all hung, absolutely, on the validity of the past. One might well hold one's breath if the past, with the dear little blue distances in it, were in danger now of being given away. One might well pause before the possible indication that a cherished impression of youth had been but a figment of the mind. Fortunately, however, at Newport, and especially where the antiquities cluster, distances are short, and the note of reassurance awaited me almost round the first corner. One had been a hundred times right—for how *was* one to think of it all, as one went on, if one didn't think of it as Old? There played before one's eyes again, in fine, in that unmistakable silvery shimmer, a particular property of the local air, the exquisite law of the relative—the application of which, on the spot, is required to make even such places as Viterbo and Bagdad not seem new. One may sometimes be tired of the word, but anything that has succeeded in living long enough to become conscious of its *note,* is capable on occasion of making that note effectively sound. It *will* sound, we gather, if we listen for it, and the small silver whistle of the past, with its charming quaver of weak gaiety, quite played the tune I asked of it up and down the tiny, sunny, empty Newport vistas, perspectives coming to a stop like the very short walks of very old ladies. What indeed but little very old ladies did they resemble, the little very old streets? with the same suggestion of present timidity and frugality of life, the same implication in their few folds of drab, of mourning, of muslin still mysteriously starched, the implication of no adventure at any time, however far back, that mightn't have been suitable to a lady.

The whole low promontory, in its wider and remoter measurements, is a region of jutting tide-troubled "points," but we had admired the Old Town too for the emphasis of its peculiar point, *the* Point; a quarter distinguished, we considered, by a really refined interest. Here would have been my misadventure, if I was to have any—that of missing, on the grey page of to-day, the suggestive passages I remembered; but I was to find, to my satisfaction, that there was still no more mistaking their pleasant sense than there had ever been: a quiet, mild waterside sense, not that of the bold, bluff outer sea, but one in which shores and strands and small coast things played the greater part; with overhanging back verandahs, with little private wooden piers, with painted boat-houses and boats laid up, with still-water bathing (the very words, with their old slightly prim discrimination, as of ladies and children jumping up and down, reach me across the years), with a wide-curving Bay and dim landward distances that melted into a mysterious, rich, superior, but quite disconnected and not at all permittedly patronizing Providence. There were stories, anciently, for the Point—so prescribed a feature of it that one made them up, freely and handsomely, when they were not otherwise to be come by; though one was never quite sure if they ought most to apply to the rather blankly and grimly Colonial houses, fadedly drab at their richest and mainly, as the legend ran, appurtenant to that Quaker race whom Massachusetts and Connecticut had prehistorically cast forth and the great Roger Williams had handsomely welcomed, or to the other habitations, the felicitous cottages, with their galleries on the Bay and toward the sunset, their pleasure-boats at their little wharves, and the supposition, that clung to them, of their harbouring the less fashionable of the outer Great, but also the more cultivated and the more artistic. Everything was there still, as I say, and quite as much as anything the prolonged echo of that ingenuous old-time distinction. It was a marvel, no doubt, that the handful of light elements I have named should add up to any total deserving the name of *picture,* and if I must produce an explanation I seek it with a certain confidence in the sense of the secret enjoyed by that air for bathing or, as one figures, for dipping, the objects it deals with. It takes them uninteresting, but feels immediately what submersion can do for them; tips them in, keeps them down, holds them under, just for the proper length of time: after which they come up, as I say, irradiating vague silver—the reflection of which I have perhaps here been trying to catch even to extravagance.

I did nothing, at any rate, all an autumn morning, but

discover again how "good" everything had been—positively better than one had ventured to suppose in one's care to make the allowance for one's young simplicity. Some things indeed, clearly, had been better than one knew, and now seemed to surpass any fair probability: else why, for instance, should I have been quite awestruck by the ancient State House that overlooks the ancient Parade?—an edifice ample, majestic, archaic, of the finest proportions and full of a certain public Dutch dignity, having brave, broad, high windows, in especial, the distinctness of whose innumerable square white-framed panes is the recall of some street view of Haarlem or Leyden. Here was the charming impression of a treasure of antiquity to the vague image of which, through the years, one hadn't done justice—any more than one had done it, positively, to three or four of the other old-time ornaments of the Parade (which, with its wide, cobbly, sleepy space, of those years, in the shadow of the State House, must have been much more of a Van der Heyden, or somebody of that sort, than one could have dreamed). There was a treasure of modernity to reckon with, in the form of one of the Commodores Perry (they are somehow much multiplied at Newport, and quite monumentally ubiquitous) engaged in his great naval act; but this was swept away in the general flood of justice to be done. I continued to do it all over the place, and I remember doing it next at a certain ample old-time house which used to unite with the still prettier and archaic Vernon, near it, to form an honourable pair. In this mild town-corner, where it was so indicated that the grass should be growing between the primitive paving-stones, and where indeed I honestly think it mainly is, amid whatever remains of them, ancient peace had appeared formerly to reign—though attended by the ghost of ancient war, inasmuch as these had indubitably been the haunts of our auxiliary French officers during the Revolution, and no self-respecting legend could fail to report that it was in the Vernon house Washington would have visited Rochambeau. There had hung about this structure, which is, architecturally speaking, all "rusticated" and indefinable decency, the implication of an inward charm that refined even on its outward, and this was the tantalizing message its clean, serious windows, never yet debased, struck me as still giving. But it was still (something told me) a question of not putting, anywhere, too many presumptions to the touch; so that my hand quitted the knocker when I was on the point of a tentative tap, and I fell back on the neighbour and mate, as to which there was unforgotten acquaintance to teach me certainty. Here, alas, cold change was installed; the place had become a public office—none of the "artistic" supercivilized, no *raffiné* of them all, among the passing fanciers or collectors, having, strangely enough, marked it for his own. This mental appropriation it is, or it was a few months ago, really impossible not to make, at sight of its delightful hall and almost "grand" staircase, its charming recessed, cupboarded, window-seated parlours, its general panelled amplitude and dignity: the due taster of such things putting himself straight into possession on the spot, and, though wondering at the indifference and neglect, breathing thanks for the absence of positive ravage. For me there were special ghosts on the staircase, known voices in the brown old rooms—presences that one would have liked, however, to call a little to account. "People don't do those things"; people didn't let so clear a case—clear for sound curiosity—go like that; they didn't, somehow, even if they were only ghosts. But I thought too, as I turned away, of all the others of the foolish, or at least of the responsible, those who for so long have swarmed in the modern quarter and who make profession of the finer sense.

This impression had been disturbing, but it had served its purpose in reconstituting, with a touch, a link—in laying down again every inch of the train of association with the human, the social, personal Newport of what I may call the middle years. To go further afield, to measure the length of the little old Avenue and tread again the little old cliff-walk, to hang over, from above, the little old white crescent of the principal bathing-sands, with the big pond, behind them, set in its stone-walled featureless fields; to do these things and many others, every one of them thus accompanied by the admission that all that *had* been had been little, was to feel dead and buried generations push off even the transparence of their shroud and get into motion for the peopling of a scene that a present posterity has outgrown. The company of the middle years, the so considerably prolonged formative, tentative, imaginative Newport time, hadn't outgrown it—this catastrophe was still to come, as it constitutes, precisely, the striking dramatic *dénouement* I have already referred to. American society—so far as that free mixture was to have arrived at cohesion—had for half a century taken its whole relation with the place seriously (which was by intention very gaily); it long remained, for its happiness, quite at one with this most favoured resort of its comparative innocence. In the attesting presence of all the constant elements, of natural conditions that have, after all, persisted more than changed, a hundred far-away passages of the extinct life and joy, and of the comparative innocence, came back to me with an inevitable grace. A glamour as of the flushed ends of beautiful old summers, making a quite rich medium, a red sunset haze, as it were, for a processional throng of charioteers and riders, fortunate folk, fortunate above all in their untouched good faith, adjourning from the pleasures of the day to those of the evening—this benignity in particular overspread the picture, hanging it there as the Newport aspect that most lived again. Those good people all could make discoveries within the frame itself—beginning of course to push it out, in all directions, so as sufficiently to enlarge it, as they fondly fancied, even for the experience of a sophisticated world. They danced and they drove and they rode, they dined and wined and dressed and flirted and yachted and polo'd and Casino'd, responding to the subtlest inventions of their age; on the old lawns and verandahs I saw them gather, on the old shining sands I saw them gallop, past the low headlands I saw their white sails verily flash, and through the dusky old shrubberies came the light and sound of their feasts.

It had all been in truth a history—for the imagination that could take it so; and when once that kindly stage was offered them it was a wonder how many figures and faces, how many names and voices, images and embodiments of youth mainly, and often of Beauty, and of felicity and fortune almost always, or of what then passed for such, pushed, under my eyes, in blurred gaiety, to the front. Hadn't it been above all, in its good faith, the Age of Beauties—the blessed age when it was so easy to *be*, "on the Avenue," a Beauty, and when it was so easy, not less, not to doubt of the unsurpassability of such as appeared there? It was through the fact that the whole scheme and opportunity satisfied them, the fact that the place was, as I say, good enough for them—it was through this that, with ingenuities and audacities and refinements of their own (some of the more primitive of which are still touching to think of) they extended the boundaries of civilization, and fairly taught themselves to believe they were doing it in the interest of nature. Beautiful the time when the Ocean Drive had been hailed at once as a triumph of civilization and as a proof of the possible appeal of Scenery even to the dissipated. It was spoken of as of almost boundless extent—as one of the wonders of the world; as indeed it does turn often, in the gloaming, to purple and gold, and as the small sea-coves then gleam on its edge like barbaric gems on a mantle. Yet if it was a question of waving the wand and of breathing again, till it stirred, on the quaintness of the old manners—I refer to those of the fifties, sixties, seventies, and don't exclude those of the eighties—it was most touching of all to go back to dimmest days, days, such as now appear antediluvian, when ocean-drives, engineered by landscape artists and literally macadamized all the way, were still in the lap of time; when there was only an afternoon for the Fort, and another for the Beach, and another for the "Boat-house"—inconceivable innocence!—and even the shortness of the Avenue seemed very long, and even its narrowness very wide, and even its shabbiness very promising for the future, and when, in fine, chariots and cavaliers took their course, across country, to Bateman's, by inelegant precarious tracts and returned, through the darkling void, with a sense of adventure and fatigue. That, I can't but think, was the *pure* Newport time, the most perfectly guarded by a sense of margin and of mystery.

It was the time of settled possession, and yet furthest removed from these blank days in which margin has been consumed and the palaces, on the sites but the other day beyond price, stare silently seaward, monuments to the *blasé* state of their absent proprietors. Purer still, however, I remind myself, was that stretch of years which I have reasons for thinking sacred, when the custom of seeking hibernation on the spot partly prevailed, when the local winter inherited something of the best social grace (as it liked at least to think) of the splendid summer, and when the strange sight might be seen of a considerable company of Americans, not gathered at a mere rest-cure, who confessed brazenly to not being in business. Do I grossly exaggerate in saying that this company, candidly, quite excitedly self-conscious, as all companies not commercial, in America, may be pleasantly noted as being, formed, for the time of its persistence, an almost unprecedented small body

—unprecedented in American conditions; a collection of the detached, the slightly disenchanted and casually disqualified, and yet of the resigned and contented, of the socially orthodox: a handful of mild, oh delightfully mild, cosmopolites, united by three common circumstances, that of their having for the most part more or less lived in Europe, that of their sacrificing openly to the ivory idol whose name is leisure, and that, not least, of a formed critical habit. These things had been felt as making them excrescences on the American surface, where nobody ever criticized, especially after the grand tour, and where the great black ebony god of business was the only one recognized. So I see them, at all events, in fond memory, lasting as long as they could and finding no successors; and they are most embalmed for me, I confess, in that scented, somewhat tattered, but faintly spiced, wrapper of their various "European" antecedents. I see them move about in the light of these, and I understand how it was this that made them ask what would have become of them, and where in the world, the hard American world, they *could* have hibernated, how they could even, in the Season, have bowed their economic heads and lurked, if it hadn't been for Newport. I think of that question as, in their reduced establishments, over their winter whist, under their private theatricals, and pending, constantly, their loan and their return of the *Revue des Deux Mondes,* their main conversational note. I find myself in fact tenderly evoking them as special instances of the great—or perhaps I have a right only to say of the small —American complication; the state of one's having been so pierced, betimes, by the sharp outland dart as to be able ever afterwards but to move about, vaguely and helplessly, with the shaft still in one's side.

Their nostalgia, however exquisite, was, I none the less gather, sterile, for they appear to have left no seed. They must have died, some of them, in order to "go back"—to go back, that is, to Paris. If I make, at all events, too much of them, it is for their propriety as a delicate subjective value matching with the intrinsic Newport delicacy. They must have felt that they, obviously, notably, notoriously, did match—the proof of which was in the fact that to them alone, of the customary thousands, was the beauty of the good walk, over the lovely little land, revealed. The customary thousands here, as throughout the United States, never set foot to earth—yet this had happened so, of old, to be the particular corner of *their* earth that made that adventure most possible. At Newport, as the phrase was, in autumnal, in vernal hibernation, you *could* walk—failing which, in fact, you failed of impressions the most consolatory; and it is mainly to the far ends of the low, densely shrubbed and perfectly finished little headlands that I see our friends ramble as if to stretch fond arms across the sea. There used to be distant places beyond Bateman's, or better still on the opposite isle of Conanicut, now blighted with ugly uses, where nursing a nostalgia on the sun-warmed rocks was almost as good as having none at all. So it was not only not our friends who had overloaded and overcrowded, but it was they at last, I infer, who gave way before that grossness. How should they have wished to leave seed only to be trampled by the white elephants?

The white elephants, as one may best call them, all cry and no wool, all house and no garden, make now, for three or four miles, a barely interrupted chain, and I dare say I think of them best, and of the distressful, inevitable waste they represent, as I recall the impression of a divine little drive, roundabout them and pretty well everywhere, taken, for renewal of acquaintance, while November was still mild. I sought another renewal, as I have intimated, in the vacant splendour of June, but the interesting evidence then only refined on that already gathered. The place itself, as man —and often, no doubt, alas, as woman, with her love of the immediate and contiguous—had taken it over, was more than ever, to the fancy, like some dim, simplified ghost of a small Greek island, where the clear walls of some pillared portico or pavilion, perched afar, looked like those of temples of the gods, and where Nature, deprived of that ease in merely massing herself on which "American scenery," as we lump it together, is too apt to depend for its effect, might have shown a piping shepherd on any hillside or attached a mythic image to any point of rocks. What an idea, originally, to have seen this miniature spot of earth, where the sea-nymphs on the curved sands, at the worst, might have chanted back to the shepherds, as a mere breeding-ground for white elephants! They look queer and conscious and lumpish—some of them, as with an air of the brandished proboscis, really grotesque—while their averted owners, roused from a witless dream, wonder what in the world is to be done with them. The answer to which, I think, can only be that there is absolutely nothing to be done; nothing but to let them stand there always, vast and blank, for reminder to those concerned of the prohibited degrees of witlessness, and of the peculiarly awkward vengeances of affronted proportion and discretion.

Chapter VI of The American Scene (1907)

Boston

1904–5

It sometimes uncomfortably happens for a writer, consulting his remembrance, that he remembers too much and finds himself knowing his subject too well; which is but the case of the bottle too full for the wine to start. There has to be room for the air to circulate between one's impressions, between the parts of one's knowledge, since it is the air, or call it the intervals on the sea of one's ignorance, of one's indifference, that sets these floating fragments into motion. This is more or less what I feel in presence of the invitation—even the invitation written on the very face of the place itself, of its actual aspects and appearances—to register my "impression" of Boston. Can one *have*, in the conditions, an impression of Boston, any that has not been for long years as inappreciable as a "sunk" picture?—that dead state of surface which requires a fresh application of varnish. The situation I speak of is the consciousness of "old" knowledge, knowledge so compacted by the years as to be unable, like the bottled wine, to flow. The answer to such questions as these, no doubt, however, is the practical one of trying a shake of the bottle or a brushful of the varnish. My "sunk" sense of Boston found itself vigorously varnished by mere renewal of vision at the end of long years; though I confess that under this favouring influence I ask myself why I should have had, after all, the notion of overlaid deposits of experience. The experience had anciently been small—so far as smallness may be imputed to any of our prime initiations; yet it had left consequences out of proportion to its limited seeming self. Early contacts had been brief and few, and the slight bridge had long ago collapsed; wherefore the impressed condition that acquired again, on the spot, an intensity, struck me as but half explained by the inordinate power of assimilation of the imaginative young. I should have had none the less to content myself with this evidence of the magic of past sensibilities had not the question suddenly been lighted for me as by a sudden flicker of the torch—and for my special benefit—carried in the hand of history. This light, waving for an instant over the scene, gave me the measure of my relation to it, both as to immense little extent and to quite subjective character.

I

It was in strictness only a matter of noting the harshness of change—since I scarce know what else to call it—on the part of the approaches to a particular spot I had wished to revisit. I made out, after a little, the entrance to Ashburton Place; but I missed on that spacious summit of Beacon Hill more than I can say the pleasant little complexity of the other time, marked with its share of the famous old-world "crookedness" of Boston, that element of the mildly tortuous which did duty, for the story-seeker, as an ancient and romantic note, and was half envied, half derided by the merely rectangular criticism. Didn't one remember the day when New Yorkers, when Philadelphians, when pilgrims from the West, sated with their eternal equi-distances, with the quadrilateral scheme of life, "raved" about Cornhill and appeared to find in the rear of the State House a recall of one of the topographical, the architectural jumbles of Europe or Asia? And did not indeed the small happy accidents of the disappearing Boston exhale in a comparatively sensible manner the warm breath of history, the history of something as against the history of nothing? —so that, being gone, or generally going, they enabled one at last to feel and almost to talk about them as one had found one's self feeling and talking about the sacrificed relics of old Paris and old London. In this immediate neighbourhood of the enlarged State House, where a great raw clearance has been made, memory met that pang of loss, knew itself sufficiently bereft to see the vanished objects, a scant but adequate cluster of "nooks," of such odds and ends as parochial schemes of improvement sweep away, positively overgrown, within one's own spirit, by a wealth of legend. There was at least the gain, at any rate, that one was now going to be free to picture them, to embroider them, at one's ease—to tangle them up in retrospect and make the real romantic claim for them. This accordingly is what I am doing, but I am doing it in particular for the sacrificed end of Ashburton Place, the Ashburton Place that I anciently knew. This eminently respectable by-way, on my return to question it, opened its short vista for me honestly enough, though looking rather exposed and undermined, since the mouth of the passage to the west, formerly measured and narrow, had begun to yawn into space, a space peopled in fact, for the eye of appreciation, with the horrific glazed perpendiculars of the future. But the pair of ancient houses I was in quest of kept their tryst; a pleasant individual pair, mated with nothing else in the street, yet looking at that hour as if their old still faces had lengthened, their shuttered, lidded eyes had closed, their brick complexions had paled, above the good granite basements, to a fainter red—all as with the cold consciousness of a possible doom.

That possibility, on the spot, was not present to me, occupied as I was with reading into one of them a short page of history that I had my own reasons for finding of supreme interest, the history of two years of far-away youth spent there at a period—the closing-time of the War—full both of public and of intimate vibrations. The two years had been those of a young man's, a very young man's earliest fond confidence in a "literary career," and the effort of actual attention was to recover on the spot some echo of ghostly footsteps—the sound as of taps on the window-pane heard in the dim dawn. The place itself was meanwhile, at all events, a conscious memento, with old secrets to keep and old stories to witness for, a saturation of life as closed together and preserved in it as the scent lingering in a folded pocket-handkerchief. But when, a month later, I returned again (a justly-rebuked mistake) to see if another whiff of the fragrance were not to be caught, I found but a gaping void, the brutal effacement, at a stroke, of every related object, of the whole precious past. Both the houses had been levelled and the space to the corner cleared; hammer and pickaxe had evidently begun to swing on the very morrow of my previous visit—which had moreover been precisely the imminent doom announced, without my understanding it, in the poor scared faces. I had been present, by the oddest hazard, at the very last moments of the victim in whom I was most interested; the act of obliteration had been breathlessly swift, and if I had often seen how fast history could be made I had doubtless never so felt that it could be unmade still faster. It was as if the bottom had fallen out of one's own biography, and one plunged backward into space without meeting anything. That, however, seemed just to give me, as I have hinted, the whole figure of my connection with everything about, a connection that had been sharp, in spite of brevity, and then had broken short off. Thus it was the sense of the rupture, more than of anything else, that I was, and for a still much briefer time, to carry with me. It seemed to leave me with my early impression of the place on my hands, inapt, as might be, for use; so that I could only try, rather vainly, to fit it to present conditions, among which it tended to shrink and stray.

It was on two or three such loitering occasions, wondering and invoking pauses that had, a little vaguely and helplessly perhaps, the changed crest of Beacon Hill for their field—it was at certain of these moments of charged, yet rather chilled, contemplation that I felt my small cluster of early associations shrivel to a scarce discernible point. I recall a Sunday afternoon in particular when I hung about on the now vaster platform of the State House for a near view of the military monuments erected there, the statues of Generals Hooker and Devens, and for the charm at once and the pang of feeling the whole backward vista, with all its features, fall from that eminence into grey perspective. The top of Beacon Hill quite rakes, with a but slightly shifting range, the old more definite Boston; for there seemed no item, nor any number, of that remarkable sum that it would not anciently have helped one to distinguish or divine. There all these things essentially were at the moment I speak of, but only again as something ghostly and dim, something overlaid and smothered by the mere modern thickness. I lingered half-an-hour, much of the new disposition of the elements here involved being duly impressive, and the old uplifted front of the State House, surely, in its spare and austere, its ruled and pencilled kind, a thing of beauty, more delightful and harmonious even than I had remembered it; one of the inestimable values again, in the eye of the town, for taste and temperance, as the perfectly felicitous "Park Street" Church hard by, was another. The irresistible spell, however, I think, was something sharper yet—the coercion, positively, of feeling one's case, the case of one's deeper discomfiture, completely made out. The day itself, toward the winter's end, was all benignant, like the immense majority of the days of the American year, and there went forward across the top of the hill a continuous passage of men and women, in couples and talkative companies, who struck me as labouring wage-earners, of the simpler sort, arrayed, very comfortably, in their Sunday best and decently enjoying their leisure. They came up as from over the Common, they passed or they paused, exchanging remarks on the beauty of the scene, but rapidly presenting themselves to me as of more interest, for the moment, than anything it contained.

For no sound of English, in a single instance, escaped their lips; the greater number spoke a rude form of Italian, the others some outland dialect unknown to me—though I waited and waited to catch an echo of antique refrains. No note of any shade of American speech struck my ear, save in so far as the sounds in question represent to-day so much of the substance of that idiom. The types and faces bore them out; the people before me were gross aliens to a man, and they were in serene and triumphant possession. Nothing, as I say, could have been more effective for figuring the hitherward bars of a grating through which I might make out, far-off in space, "my" small homogeneous Boston of the more interesting time. It was not of course that our gross little aliens were immediate "social" figures in the narrower sense of the term, or that any personal commerce of which there might be question could colour itself, to its detriment, from their presence; but simply that they expressed, as everywhere and always, the great cost at which every place on my list had become braver and louder, and that they gave the measure of the distance by which the general movement was *away*—away, always and everywhere, from the old presumptions and conceivabilities. Boston, the bigger, braver, louder Boston, was "away," and it was quite, at that hour, as if each figure in my procession were there on purpose to leave me no doubt of it. Therefore had I the vision, as filling the sky, no longer of the great Puritan "whip," the whip for the conscience and the nerves, of the local legend, but that of a huge applied sponge, a sponge saturated with the foreign mixture and passed over almost everything I remembered and might still have recovered. The detail of this obliteration would take me too far, but I had even then (on a previous day as well as only half-an-hour before) caught at something that might stand for a vivid symbol of the general effect of it. To come up from School Street into Beacon was to approach the Athenæum—exquisite institution, to fond memory, joy of the aspiring prime; yet to approach the Athenæum only to find all disposition to enter it drop as dead as if from quick poison, what did *that* denote but the dreadful chill of change, and of the change in especial that was most completely dreadful? For had not this honoured haunt of all the most civilized—library, gallery, temple of culture, the place that was to Boston at large as Boston at large was to the rest of New England—had it not with peculiar intensity had a "value," the most charming of its kind, no doubt, in all the huge country, and had not this value now, evidently, been brought so low that one shrank, in delicacy, from putting it to the test?

It was a case of the detestable "tall building" again, and of its instant destruction of quality in everything it overtowers. Put completely out of countenance by the mere masses of brute ugliness beside it, the temple of culture looked only rueful and snubbed, hopelessly down in the world; so that, far from being moved to hover or to penetrate, one's instinct was to pass by on the other side, averting one's head from an humiliation one could do nothing to make less. And this indeed though one would have liked to do something; the brute masses, above the comparatively small refined façade (one saw how happy one had always thought it) having for the inner ear the voice of a pair of school-bullies who hustle and pummel some studious little boy. "'Exquisite' was what they called you, eh? We'll teach you, then, little sneak, to be exquisite! We allow none of that rot round here." It was heart-breaking, this presentation of a Boston practically void of an Athenæum; though perhaps not without interest as showing how much one's own sense of the small city of the earlier time had been dependent on that institution. I found it of no use, at any rate, to think, for a compensatory sign of the new order, of the present Public Library; the present Public Library, however remarkable in its pomp and circumstance, and of which I had at that hour received my severe impression, being neither exquisite nor on the way to become so—a difficult, an impassable way, no doubt, for Public Libraries. Nor did I cast about, in fact, very earnestly, for consolation—so much more was I held by the vision of the closed order which shaped itself, continually, in the light of the differing present; an order gaining an interest for this backward view precisely as one felt that all the parts and tokens of it, while it lasted, had hung intimately together. Missing those parts and tokens, or as many of them as one could, became thus a constant slightly painful joy: it made them fall so into their place as items of the old character, or proofs, positively, as one might say, of the old distinction. It was impossible not to see Park Street itself, for instance —while I kept looking at the matter from my more "swagger" hilltop as violently vulgarized; and it was incontestable that, whatever might be said, there had anciently not been, on the whole continent, taking everything together, an equal animated space more exempt from vulgarity. There had probably been comparable spaces—impressions, in

New York, in Philadelphia, in Baltimore, almost as good; but only almost, by reason of their lacking (which was just the point) the indefinable perfection of Park Street.

It seems odd to have to borrow from the French the right word in this association—or would seem so, rather, had it been less often indicated that that people have better names than ours even for the qualities we are apt to suppose ourselves more in possession of than they. Park Street, in any case, had been magnificently *honnête*—the very type and model, for a pleasant street-view, of the character. The aspects that might elsewhere have competed were *honnêtes* and weak, whereas Park Street was *honnête* and strong—strong as founded on *all* the moral, material, social solidities, instead of on some of them only; which made again all the difference. Personal names, as notes of that large emanation, need scarcely be invoked—they might even have a weakening effect; the force of the statement was in its collective, cumulative look, as if each member of the row, from the church at the Tremont Street angle to the amplest, squarest, most purple presence at the Beacon Street corner (where it always had a little the air of a sturdy proprietor with back to the fire, legs apart and thumbs in the armholes of an expanse of high-coloured plush waistcoat), was but a syllable in the word Respectable several times repeated. One had somehow never heard it uttered with so convincing an emphasis. But the shops, up and down, are making all this as if it had never been, pleasant "premises" as they have themselves acquired; and it was to strike me from city to city, I fear, that the American shop in general pleads but meagrely—whether on its outer face or by any more intimate art—for indulgence to its tendency to swarm, to bristle, to vociferate. The shop-front, observed at random, produced on me from the first, and almost everywhere alike, a singular, a sinister impression, which left me uneasy till I had found a name for it: the sense of an economic law of which one had not for years known the unholy rigour, the vision of "protected" production and of commodities requiring certainly, in many cases, every advantage Protection could give them. They looked to me always, these exhibitions, consciously and defiantly protected —insolently safe, able to be with impunity anything they would; and when once that lurid light had settled on them I could see them, I confess, in none other; so that the objects composing them fell, throughout, into a vicious and villainous category—quite as if audibly saying: "Oh come; don't look among us for what you won't, for what you shan't find, the best quality attainable; but only for that quite other matter, the best value we allow you. You must take us or go without, and if you feel your nose thus held to the grindstone by the hard fiscal hand, it's no more than you deserve for harbouring treasonable thoughts."

So it was, therefore, that while the imagination and the memory strayed—strayed away to other fiscal climates, where the fruits of competition so engagingly ripen and flush—the streets affected one at moments as a prolonged show-case for every arrayed vessel of humiliation. The fact that several classes of the protected products appeared to consist of articles that one might really anywhere have preferred did little, oddly enough, to diminish the sense of severe discipline awaiting the restored absentee on contact with these occasions of traffic. The discipline indeed is general, proceeding as it does from so many sources, but it earns its name, in particular, from the predicament of the ingenuous inquirer who asks himself if he can "really bear" the combination of such general manners and such general prices, of such general prices and such general manners. He has a helpless bewildered moment during which he wonders if he mightn't bear the prices a little better if he were a little better addressed, or bear the usual form of address a little better if the prices were in themselves, given the commodity offered, a little less humiliating to the purchaser. Neither of these elements of his dilemma strikes him as likely to abate—the general cost of the things to drop, or the general grimness of the person he deals with over the counter to soften; so that he reaches out again for balm to where he has had to seek it under other wounds, falls back on the cultivation of patience and regret, on large international comparison. He is confronted too often, to his sense, with the question of what may be "borne"; but what does he see about him if not a vast social order in which the parties to certain relations are all the while marvellously, inscrutably, desperately "bearing" each other? He may wonder, at his hours, how, under the strain, social cohesion does not altogether give way; but that is another question, which belongs to a different plane of speculation. For he asks himself quite as much as anything else how the shopman or the shoplady can bear to be barked at in the manner he constantly hears used to them by customers—he recognizes that no agreeable form of intercourse *could* survive a day in such air: so that what is the only relation finding ground there but a necessary vicious circle of gross mutual endurance?

These reflections connect themselves moreover with that most general of his restless hauntings in the United States —not only with the lapse of all wonderment at the immense number of absentees unrestored and making their lives as they may in other countries, but with the preliminary American postulate or basis for any successful accommodation of life. This basis is that of active pecuniary gain and of active pecuniary gain only—that of one's making the conditions so triumphantly pay that the prices, the manners, the other inconveniences, take their place as a friction it is comparatively easy to salve, wounds directly treatable with the wash of gold. What prevails, what sets the tune, is the American scale of gain, more magnificent than any other, and the fact that the whole assumption, the whole theory of life, is that of the individual's participation in it, that of his being more or less punctually and more or less effectually "squared." To make so much money that you won't, that you don't "mind," don't mind anything—that is absolutely, I think, the main American formula. Thus your making no money—or so little that it passes there for none—and being thereby distinctly reduced to minding, amounts to your being reduced to the knowledge that America is no place for you. To mind as one minds, for instance, in Europe, under provocation or occasion offered, and yet to have to live under the effect of American pressure, is speedily to perceive that the knot can be untied but by a definite pull of one or the other string. The immense majority of people pull, luckily for the existing order, the string that consecrates their connection with it; the minority (small, however, only in comparison) pull the string that loosens that connection. The existing order is meanwhile safe, inasmuch as the faculty of making money is in America the commonest of all and fairly runs the streets: so simple a matter does it appear there, among vast populations, to make betimes enough *not* to mind. Yet the withdrawal of the considerable group of the pecuniarily disqualified seems no less, for the present, an assured movement; there will always be scattered individuals condemned to mind on a scale beyond any scale of making. The relation of this modest body to the country of their birth, which asks so much, on the whole—so many surrenders and compromises, and the possession above all of such a prodigious head for figures—before it begins, in its wonderful way, to give or to "pay," would appear to us supremely touching, I think, as a case of communion baffled and blighted, if we had time to work it out. It would bathe in something of a tragic light the vivid truth that the "great countries" are all, more and more, happy lands (so far as any can be called such) for

any, for every sort of person rather than the middle sort. The upper sort—in the scale of wealth, the only scale now—can to their hearts' content build their own castles and move by their own motors; the lower sort, masters of gain in *their* degree, can profit, also to their hearts' content, by the enormous extension of those material facilities which may be gregariously enjoyed; they are able to rush about, as never under the sun before, in promiscuous packs and hustled herds, while to the act of so rushing about all felicity and prosperity appear for them to have been comfortably reduced. The frustrated American, as I have hinted at him, scraping for *his* poor practical solution in the depleted silver-mine of history, is the American who "makes" too little for the castle and yet "minds" too much for the hustled herd, who can neither achieve such detachment nor surrender to such society, and who most of all accordingly, in the native order, fails of a working basis. The salve, the pecuniary salve, in Europe, is sensibly less, but less on the other hand also the excoriation that makes it necessary, whether from above or below.

From Chapter VII of The American Scene (1907)

Concord and Salem

1905

I felt myself, on the spot, cast about a little for the right expression of it, and then lost any hesitation to say that, putting the three or four biggest cities aside, Concord, Massachusetts, had an identity more palpable to the mind, had nestled in other words more successfully beneath her narrow fold of the mantle of history, than any other American town. "Compare me with places of my size, you know," one seemed to hear her plead, with the modesty that, under the mild autumn sun, so well became her russet beauty; and this exactly it was that prompted the emphasis of one's reply, or, as it may even be called, of one's declaration.

"Ah, my dear, it isn't a question of places of your 'size,' since among places of your size you're too obviously and easily first: it's a question of places, so many of them, of fifty times your size, and which yet don't begin to have a fraction of your weight, or your character, or your intensity of presence and sweetness of tone, or your moral charm, or your pleasant appreciability, or, in short, of anything that is yours. Your 'size'? Why, you're the biggest little place in America—with only New York and Boston and Chicago, by what I make out, to surpass you; and the country is lucky indeed to have you, in your sole and single felicity, for if it hadn't, where in the world should we go, inane and unappeased, for the particular communication of which you have the secret? The country is colossal, and you but a microscopic speck on the hem of its garment; yet there's nothing else like you, take you all round, for we *see* you complacently, with the naked eye, whereas there are vast sprawling, bristling areas, great grey 'centres of population' that spread, on the map, like irremediable grease-spots, which fail utterly of any appeal to our vision or any control of it, leaving it to pass them by as if they were not. If you are so thoroughly the opposite of one of these I don't say it's all your superlative merit; it's rather, as I have put it, your felicity, your good fortune, the result of the half-dozen happy turns of the wheel in your favour. Half-a-dozen such turns, you see, are, for any mortal career, a handsome allowance; and your merit is that, recognizing this, you have not fallen below your estate. But it's your fortune, above all, that's your charm. One doesn't want to be patronizing, but you didn't, thank goodness, make yours. That's what the other places, the big ones that are as nothing to you, are trying to do, the country over—to make theirs; and, from the point of view of these remarks, all in vain. Your luck is that you didn't have to; yours had been, just as it shows in you to-day, made *for* you, and you at the most but gratefully submitted to it. It must be said for you, however, that you keep it; and it isn't every place that would have been capable——! You keep the look, you keep the feeling, you keep the air. Your great trees arch over these possessions more protectingly, covering them in as a cherished presence; and you have settled to your tone and your type as to treasures that can now never be taken. Show me the other places in America (of the few that have *had* anything) from which the best hasn't mainly been taken, or isn't in imminent danger of being. There is old Salem, there is old Newport, which I am on my way to see again, and which, if you will, are, by what I hear, still comparatively intact; but their having was never a having like yours, and they adorn, precisely, my little tale of your supremacy. No, I don't want to be patronizing, but your only fault is your tendency to improve—I mean just by your duration as you *are;* which indeed is the only sort of improvement that is not questionable."

Such was the drift of the warm flood of appreciation, of reflection, that Concord revisited could set rolling over the field of a prepared sensibility; and I feel as if I had quite made my point, such as it is, in asking what other American village could have done anything of the sort. I should have been at fault perhaps only in speaking of the interest in question as visible, on that large scale, to the "naked eye"; the truth being perhaps that one wouldn't have been so met half-way by one's impression unless one had rather particularly *known,* and that knowledge, in such a case, amounts to a pair of magnifying spectacles. I remember indeed putting it to myself on the November Sunday morning, tepid and bright and perfect for its use, through which I walked from the station under the constant archway of the elms, as yet but indulgently thinned: would one know, for one's self, what had formerly been the matter here, if one hadn't happened to be able to get round behind, in the past, as it were, and more or less understand? Would the operative elements of the past—little old Concord Fight, essentially, and Emerson and Hawthorne and Thoreau, with the rest of the historic animation and the rest of the figured and shifting "transcendental" company, to its last and loosest ramifications—would even these handsome quantities have so lingered to one's intelligent after-sense, if one had not brought with one some sign by which they too would know; dim, shy spectralities as, for themselves, they must, at the best, have become? Idle, however, such questions when, by the chance of the admirable day, everything, in its own way and order, unmistakably came *out*—every string sounded as if, for all the world, the loose New England town (and I apply the expression but to the relations of objects and places), were a lyre swept by the hand of Apollo. Apollo was the spirit of antique piety, looking about, pausing, remembering, as he moved to his music; and there were glimpses and reminders that of course kept him much longer than others.

Seated there at its ease, as if placidly familiar with pilgrims and quite taking their homage for granted, the place had the very aspect of some grave, refined New England matron of the "old school," the widow of a high celebrity, living on and on in possession of all his relics and properties, and, though not personally addicted to gossip or to journalism, having become, where the great company kept by her in the past is concerned, quite cheerful and modern and responsive. From her position, her high-backed chair by the window that commands most of the coming and going, she looks up intelligently, over her knitting, with no vision of any limit on her part as yet, to this attitude, and with nothing indeed to suggest the possibility of a limit save a hint of that loss of temporal perspective in which we recognize the mental effect of a great weight of years. I had formerly the acquaintance of a very interesting lady, of extreme age, whose early friends, in "literary circles," are now regarded as classics, and who, toward the end of her life, always said, "You know Charles Lamb has produced a play at Drury Lane," or "You know William Hazlitt has fallen in love with such a very odd woman." Her facts were perfectly correct; only death had beautifully passed out of her world—since I don't remember her mentioning to me the demise, which she might have made so contemporary, either of Byron or of Scott. When people were ill she admirably forebore to ask about them—she disapproved wholly of such conditions; and there were interesting invalids round about her, near to her, whose existence she for long years consummately ignored. It is some such quiet backward stride as those of my friend that I seem to hear the voice of old Concord take in reference to her annals, and it is not too much to say that where her soil is most sacred, I fairly caught, on the breeze, the mitigated perfect tense. "You know there has been a fight between our men and the King's"—one wouldn't have been surprised, that crystalline Sunday noon, where so little had changed, where the stream and the bridge, and all nature, and the *feeling*, above all, still so directly testify, at any fresh-sounding form of such an announcement.

I had forgotten, in all the years, with what thrilling clearness that supreme site speaks—though anciently, while so much of the course of the century was still to run, the distinctness might have seemed even greater. But to stand there again was to take home this foreshortened view, the gained nearness, to one's sensibility; to look straight over the heads of the "American Weimar" company at the inestimable hour that had so handsomely set up for them their background. The Fight had been the hinge—so one saw it—on which the large revolving future was to turn; or it had been better, perhaps, the large firm nail, ringingly driven in, from which the beautiful portrait-group, as we see it today, was to hang. Beautiful exceedingly the local Emerson and Thoreau and Hawthorne and (in a fainter way) *tutti quanti;* but beautiful largely because the fine old incident down in the valley had so seriously prepared their effect. That seriousness gave once for all the pitch, and it was verily as if, under such a value, even with the seed of a "literary circle" so freely scattered by an intervening hand, the vulgar note would in that air never be possible. As I had inevitably, in long absence, let the value, for immediate perception, rather waste itself, so, on the spot, it came back most instantly with the extraordinary sweetness of the river, which, under the autumn sun, like all the American rivers one had seen or was to see, straightway took the whole case straightway into its hands. "Oh, you shall tell me of your impression when you have felt what *I* can do for it: so hang over me well!"—that's what they all seem to say.

I hung over Concord River then as long as I could, and recalled how Thoreau, Hawthorne, Emerson himself, have expressed with due sympathy the sense of this full, slow, sleepy, meadowy flood, which sets its pace and takes its twists like some large obese benevolent person, scarce so frankly unsociable as to pass you at all. It had watched the Fight, it even now confesses, without a quickening of its current, and it draws along the woods and the orchards and the fields with the purr of a mild domesticated cat who rubs against the family and the furniture. Not to be recorded, at best, however, I think, never to emerge from the state of the inexpressible, in respect to the spot, by the bridge, where one most lingers, is the sharpest suggestion of the whole scene—the power diffused in it which makes it, after all these years, or perhaps indeed by reason of their number, so irresistibly touching. All the commemorative objects, the stone marking the burial-place of the three English soldiers, the animated image of the young belted American yeoman by Mr. Daniel French, the intimately associated element in the presence, not far off, of the old manse, interesting theme of Hawthorne's pen, speak to the spirit, no doubt, in one of the subtlest tones of which official history is capable, and yet somehow leave the exquisite melancholy of everything unuttered. It lies too deep, as it always so lies where the ground has borne the weight of the short, simple act, intense and unconscious, that was to determine the event, determine the future in the way we call immortally. For we read into the scene too little of what we may, unless this muffled touch in it somehow reaches us so that we feel the pity and the irony of the *precluded* relation on the part of the fallen defenders. The sense that was theirs and that moved them we know, but we seem to know better still the sense that wasn't and that couldn't, and that forms our luxurious heritage as our eyes, across the gulf, seek to meet their eyes; so that we are almost ashamed of taking so much, such colossal quantity and value, as the equivalent of their dimly-seeing offer. The huge bargain they made for us, in a word, made by the gift of the little all they had—to the modesty of which amount the homely rural facts grouped there together have appeared to go on testifying—this brilliant advantage strikes the imagination that yearns over them as unfairly enjoyed at their cost. Was it delicate, was it decent—that is *would* it have been—to ask the embattled farmers, simple-minded, unwitting folk, to make us so inordinate a present with so little of the conscious credit of it? Which all comes indeed, perhaps, simply to the most poignant of all those effects of disinterested sacrifice that the toil and trouble of our forefathers produce for us. The minute-men at the bridge were of course interested intensely, as they believed—but such, too, was the artful manner in which we see *our* latent, lurking, waiting interest like, a Jew in a dusky back-shop, providentially bait the trap.

Beyond even such broodings as these, and to another purpose, moreover, the communicated spell falls, in its degree, into that pathetic oddity of the small aspect, and the rude and the lowly, the reduced and humiliated above all, that sits on so many nooks and corners, objects and appurtenances, old contemporary things—contemporary with the doings of our race; simplifying our antecedents, our annals, to within an inch of their life, making us ask, in presence of the rude relics even of greatness, mean retreats and receptacles, constructionally so poor, from what barbarians or from what pigmies we have sprung. There are certain rough black mementos of the early monarchy, in England and Scotland, there are glimpses of the original humble homes of other greatness as well, that strike in perfection this grim little note; which has the interest of our being free to take it, for curiosity, for luxury of thought, as that of the real or that of the romantic, and with which, again, the deep Concord rusticity, momentary medium of our national drama, essentially consorts. We remember the small hard facts of the Shakespeare house at Stratford; we remember the rude closet, in Edinburgh Castle, in which James VI of Scotland was born, or the other little black hole, at Holyrood, in which Mary Stuart "sat" and in which Rizzio was murdered. These, I confess, are odd memories at Concord; although the manse, near the spot where we last paused, and against the edge of whose acre or two the loitering river seeks friction in the manner I have mentioned, would now seem to have shaken itself a trifle disconcertingly free of the ornamental mosses scattered by Hawthorne's light hand; it stands there, beyond its gate, with every due similitude to the shrunken historic site in general. To which I must hasten to add, however, that I was much more struck with the way these particular places of visitation resist their pressure of reference than with their affecting us as below their fortune. Intrinsically they are as naught—deeply depressing, in fact, to any impulse to reconstitute, the house in which Hawthorne spent what remained to him of life after his return from the Italy of his Donatello and his Miriam. Yet, in common with everything else, this mild monument benefits by that something in the air which makes us tender, keeps us respectful; meets, in the general interest, waving it vaguely away, any closer assault of criticism.

It is odd, and it is also exquisite, that these witnessing ways should be the last ground on which we feel moved to ponderation of the "Concord school"—to use, I admit, a futile expression; or rather, I should doubtless say, it *would* be odd if there were not inevitably something absolute in the fact of Emerson's all but lifelong connection with them. We may smile a little as we "drag in" Weimar, but I confess myself, for my part, much more satisfied than not by our happy equivalent, "in American money," for Goethe and Schiller. The money is a potful in the second case as in the first, and if Goethe, in the one, represents the gold and Schiller the silver, I find (and quite putting aside any bimetallic prejudice) the same good relation in the other between Emerson and Thoreau. I open Emerson for the same benefit for which I open Goethe, the sense of moving in large intellectual space, and that of the gush, here and there, out of the rock, of the crystalline cupful, in wisdom and poetry, in Wahrheit and Dichtung; and whatever I open Thoreau for (I needn't take space here for the good reasons) I open him oftener than I open Schiller. Which comes back to our feeling that the rarity of Emerson's genius, which has made him so, for the attentive peoples, the first, and the one really rare, American spirit in letters, couldn't have spent his career in a charming woody, watery place, for so long socially and typically and, above all, interestingly homogeneous, without an effect as of the communication to it of something ineffaceable. It was during his long span his immediate concrete, sufficient world; it gave him his nearest vision of life, and he drew half his images, we recognize, from the revolution of its seasons and the play of its manners. I don't speak of the other half, which he drew from elsewhere. It is admirably, to-day, as if we were still seeing these things *in* those images, which stir the air like birds, dim in the eventide, coming home to nest. If one had reached a "time of life" one had thereby at least heard him lecture; and not a russet leaf fell for me, while I was there, but fell with an Emersonian drop.

From Chapter VIII of The American Scene (1907)

Washington

1905

I

I was twice in Washington, the first time for a winter visit, the second to meet the wonderful advance of summer, to which, in that climate of many charms, the first days of May open wide the gates. This latter impression was perforce much the more briefly taken; yet, though I had gathered also from other past occasions, far-away years now, something of the sense of the place at the earlier season, I find everything washed over, at the mention of the name, by the rare light, half green, half golden, of the lovely leafy moment. I see all the rest, till I make the effort to break the spell, through that voluminous veil; which operates, for memory, quite as the explosion of spring works, even to the near vision, in respect to the American scene at large—dressing it up as if for company, preparing it for social, for human intercourse, making it in fine publicly presentable, with an energy of renewal and an effect of redemption not often to be noted, I imagine, on other continents. Nowhere, truly, can summer have such work cut out for it as here—nowhere has it to take upon itself to repaint the picture so completely. In the "European" landscape, in general, some, at least, of the elements and objects remain upon the canvas; here, on the other hand, one seems to see intending Nature, the great artist of the season, decline to touch that surface unless it be first swept clean—decline, at any rate, to deal with it save by ignoring all its perceived pretensions. Vernal Nature, in England, in France, in Italy, has still a use, often a charmed or amused indulgence, for the material in hand, the furniture of the foreground, the near and middle distances, the heterogeneous human features of the face of the land. She looks at her subject much as the portrait-painter looks at the personal properties, this or that household object, the official uniform, the badges and ornaments, the favourite dress, of his sitter—with an "Oh, yes, I can bring them in; they're just what I want, and I see how they will help me out." But I try in vain to recall a case in which, either during the New England May and June, or during those of the Middle States (since these groups of weeks have in the two regions a differing identity and value), the genius in question struck me as adopting with any frankness, as doing more than passively, helplessly accept, the supplied paraphernalia, the signs of existing life. The business is clearly to get rid of them as far as may be, to cover and smother them; dissimulating with the biggest, freest brush their impertinence and their ugliness.

I must ask myself, I meanwhile recognize, none the less, why I should have found Mount Vernon exquisite, the first of May, if the interest had all to be accounted for in the light of nature. The light of nature was there, splendid and serene; the Potomac opened out in its grandest manner; the bluff above the river, before the sweep of its horizon, raised its head for the historic crown. But it was not for a moment to be said that this was the whole story; the human interest and the human charm lay in wait and held one fast—so that, if one had been making light, elsewhere, of their suggestion and office, one had at least this case seriously to reckon with. I speak straightway, thus, of Mount Vernon, though it be but an outlying feature of Washington, and at the best a minor impression; the image of the particular occasion is seated so softly in my path. There was a glamour, in fine, for the excursion—that of an extraordinarily gracious hospitality; and the glamour would still have been great even if I had not, on my return to the shadow of the capitol, found the whole place transfigured. The season was over, the President away, the two Houses up, the shutters closed, the visitor rare; and one lost one's way in the great green vistas of the avenues quite as one might have lost it in a "sylvan solitude"—that is in the empty alleys of a park. The emptiness was qualified at the most, here and there, by some encounter with a stray diplomatic agent, wreathed for the most part in sincerer smiles than we are wont to attribute to his class. "This"—it was the meaning of these inflections—"was the *real* Washington, a place of enchantment; so that if the enchantment were never less who could ever bring himself to go away?" The enchantment had been so much less in January—one could easily understand; yet the recognition seemed truly the voice of the hour, and one picked it up with a patriotic flutter not diminished by the fact that the speaker would probably be going away, and with delight, on the morrow.

The memory of some of the smiles and inflections comes back in that light; Washington being the one place in America, I think, where those qualities are the values and vehicles, the medium of exchange. No small part of the interest of the social scene there consists, inevitably, for any restless analyst, in wonder about the "real" sentiments of appointed foreign participants, the delegates of Powers and pledged alike to penetration and to discretion, before phenomena which, whatever they may be, differ more from the phenomena of other capitals and other societies than they resemble them. This interest is susceptible, on occasion, of becoming intense; all the more that curiosity must, for the most part, pursue its object (that of truly looking over the alien shoulder and of seeing, judging, building, fearing, reporting with the alien sense) by subtle and tortuous ways. This represents, first and last, even for a watcher abjectly irresponsible, a good deal of speculative tension; so that one's case is refreshing in presence of the clear candour of such a proposition as that the national capital *is* charming in proportion as you don't see it. For that is what it came to, in the bowery condition; the as yet unsurmounted bourgeois character of the whole was screened and disguised; the dressing-up, in other words, was complete, and the great park-aspect gained, and became nobly artificial, by the very complexity of the plan of the place—the perpetual perspectives, the converging, radiating avenues, the frequent circles and crossways, where all that was wanted for full illusion was that the bronze generals and admirals, on their named pedestals, should have been great garden-gods, mossy mythological marble. This would have been the perfect note; the long vistas yearned for it, and the golden chequers scattered through the gaps of the high arches waited for some bending nymph or some armless Hermes to pick them up. The power of the scene to evoke such visions sufficiently shows, I think, what had become, under the mercy of nature, of the hard facts, as one must everywhere call them; and yet though I could, diplomatically, patriotically pretend, at the right moment, that such a Washington *was* the "real" one, my assent had all the while a still finer meaning for myself.

I am hanging back, however, as with a sacred terror, from Mount Vernon, where indeed I may not much linger, or only enough to appear not to have shirked the responsibility incurred at the opening of these remarks. There, in ample possession, was masking, dissimulating summer, the envelope and disguise to which I have hinted that the American picture owes, on its human side, *all* its best presentability; and at the same time, unmistakably, there was the spell, as quite a distinct matter, of the hard little facts in themselves. How came it that if they could throw a spell they were yet so abject and so negligible? How came it that if they had no intrinsic sweetness, no visible dignity, they could yet play their part in so unforgettable an impression? The answer to this can only be, I think, that we happen here to "strike," as they say, one of the rarest of cases, a spot on which all sorts of sensibilities are touched and on which a lively emotion, and one yet other than the æsthetic, makes us its prey. The old high-placed house, unquestionably, is charming, and the felicity of the whole scene, on such a day as that of my impression, scarce to be uttered. The little hard facts, facts of form, of substance, of scale, facts of essential humility and exiguity, none the less, look us straight in the face, present themselves literally to be counted over—and reduce us thereby to the recognition of our supreme example of the rich interference of association. Association does, at Mount Vernon, simply what it likes with us—it is of so beautiful and noble a sort; and to this end it begins by making us unfit to say whether or no we would in its absence have noticed the house for any material grace at all. We scarce care more for its being proved picturesque, the house, than for its being proved plain; its architectural interest and architectural nullity become one and the same thing for us. If asked what we should think of it if it hadn't been, or if we hadn't known it for, Washington's, we retort that the inquiry is inane, since it is not the possessive case, but the straight, serene nominative, that we are dealing with. The whole thing *is* Washington—not his invention and his property, but his presence and his person; with discriminations (as distinguished from enthusiasms) as invidious and unthinkable as if they were addressed to his very ears.

The great soft fact, as opposed to the little hard ones, is the beauty of the site itself; that is definitely, if ever so delicately, sublime, but it fails to rank among the artificial items that I began by speaking of, those of so generally compromising an effect in the American picture. Everything else is *communicated* importance, and the magic so wrought for the American sensibility—by which I mean the degree of the importance and the sustained high pitch of the charm—place it, doubtless, the world over, among the few supreme triumphs of such communication. The beauty of the site, meanwhile, as we stand there, becomes but the final aspect of the man; under which everything conduces to a single great representative image, under which every feature of the scene, every object in the house, however trivial, borrows from it and profits by it. The image is the largest, clearest possible of the resting, as distinguished from the restless, consciousness of public service consummately rendered. The terms we commonly use for that condition—peace with honour, well-earned repose, enjoyment of homage, recognition of facts—render but dimly the luminous stillness in which, on its commanding eminence, we see our image bathed. It hangs together with the whole bright immensity of air and view. It becomes truly the great white, decent page on which the whole sense of the place is written. It does more things even besides; attends us while we move about and goes with us from room to room; mounts with us the narrow stairs, to stand with us in these small chambers and look out of the low windows; takes up for us, to turn them over with spiritual hands, the objects from which we respectfully forbear, and places an accent, in short, through the rambling old phrase, wherever an accent is required. Thus we arrive at the full meaning, as it were—thus we know, at least, why we are so moved.

It is for the same reason for which we are always inordinately moved, on American ground, I think, when the unconscious minor scale of the little old demonstrations to which we owe everything is made visible to us, when their disproportionate modesty is proved upon them. The reason worked at Mount Vernon, for the restless analyst, quite as it had worked a few months before, on the small and simple scene of Concord Fight: the slight, pale, bleeding Past, in a patched homespun suit, stands there taking the thanks of the bloated Present—having woundedly rescued from thieves and brought to his door the fat, locked pocket-book of which that personage appears the owner. The pocket-book contains, "unbeknown" to the honest youth, bank-notes of incredible figure, and what breaks our heart, if we be cursed with the historic imagination, is the grateful, wan smile with which the great guerdon of sixpence is received. I risk, floridly, the assertion that half the intensity of the impression of Mount Vernon, for many a visitor, will ever be in this vision there of Washington *only* (so far as consciously) so rewarded. Such fantastications, I indeed admit, are refinements of response to any impression, but the ground had been cleared for them, and it ministered to luxury of thought, for instance, that we were a small party at our ease there, with no other circulation—with the prowling ghosts of fellow-pilgrims, too harshly present on my previous occasion, all conveniently laid. This alone represented privilege and power, and they in turn, with their pomp and circumstance of a charming Government launch, under official attendance, at the Navy-Yard steps, amid those large, clean, protecting and protected properties of the State which always make one think much of the State, whatever its actual infirmities—these things, to say nothing of other rich enhancements, above all those that I may least specify, flung over the day I scarce know what iridescent reflection of the star-spangled banner itself, in the folds of which I had never come so near the sense of being positively wrapped. That consciousness, so unfamiliar, was, under the test, irresistible; it pressed the spring, absolutely, of intellectual exaltation—with the consequent loud resonance that my account of my impressions doubtless sufficiently translates.

II

Washington itself meanwhile—the Washington always, I premise, of the rank outsider—had struck me from the first as presenting two distinct faces; the more obvious of which was the public and official, the monumental, with features all more or less majestically playing the great administrative, or, as we nowadays put it, Imperial part. This clustered, yet at the same time oddly scattered, city, a general impression of high granite steps, of light grey corniced colonnades, rather harmoniously low, contending for effect with slaty mansard roofs and masses of iron excrescence, a general impression of somewhat vague, empty, sketchy, fundamentals, however expectant, however spacious, overweighted by a single Dome and overaccented by a single Shaft—this loose congregation of values seemed, strangely, a matter disconnected and remote, though remaining in its way portentous and bristling all incoherently at the back of the scene. The back of the scene, indeed, to one's quite primary sense, might have been but an immense painted, yet unfinished cloth, hung there to a confessedly provisional end and marked with the queerness, among many queernesses, of looking always the same; painted once for all in clear, bright, fresh tones, but never emerging from its flatness, after the fashion of other capitals, into the truly, the variously, modelled and rounded state. (It appeared provisional therefore because looking as if it might have been unhooked and removed as a whole; because any one object in it so treated would have made the rest also come off.) The foreground was a different thing, a thing that, ever so quaintly, seemed to represent the force really in possession; though consisting but of a small company of people engaged perpetually in conversation and (always, I repeat, for the rank outsider) singularly destitute of conspicuous marks or badges. This little society easily became, for the detached visitor, the city itself, *the* national capital and the greater part of the story; and that, ever, in spite of the comparatively scant intensity of its political permeation. The political echo was of course to be heard in it, and the public character, in his higher forms, to be encountered —though only in "single spies," not in battalions; but there was something that made it much more individual than any mere predominance of political or administrative colour would have made it; leaving it in that case to do no more than resemble the best society in London, or that in best possession of the field in Paris.

Two sharp signs my remoter remembrance had shown me the then Washington world, and the first met, as putting forth; one of these the fact of its being extraordinarily easy and pleasant, and the other that of one's appearing to make out in it not more than half-a-dozen members of the Lower House and not more than a dozen of the Upper. This kept down the political permeation, and was bewildering, if one was able to compare, in the light of the different London condition, the fact of the social ubiquity there of the acceptable M.P. and that of the social frequency even of his more equivocal hereditary colleague. A London nestling under the towers of Westminster, yet practically void of members of the House of Commons, and with the note of official life far from exclusively sounding, that might have been in those days the odd image of Washington, had not the picture been stamped with other variations still. These were a whole cluster, not instantly to be made out, but constituting the unity of the place as soon as perceived; representing that finer extract or essence which the self-respecting observer is never easy till he be able to shake up and down in bottled form. The charming company of the foreground then, which referred itself so little to the sketchy back-scene, the monstrous Dome and Shaft, figments of the upper air, the pale colonnades and mere myriad-windowed Buildings, was the second of the two faces, and the more one lived with it the more, up to a certain point, one lived away from the first. In time, and after perceiving *how* it was what it so agreeably was, came the recognition of common ground; the recognition that, in spite of strange passages of the national life, liable possibly to recur, during which the President himself was scarce thought to be in society, the particular precious character that one had apprehended could never have ripened without a general consensus. One had put one's finger on it when one had seen disengage itself from many anomalies, from not a few drolleries, the superior, the quite majestic fact of the City of Conversation pure and simple, and positively of the only specimen, of any such intensity, in the world.

That had remained for me, from the other time, the properest name of Washington, and nothing could so interest me, on a renewal of acquaintance, too long postponed and then too woefully brief, as to find my description wholly justified. If the emphasis added by "pure and simple" be invariably retained, the description will continue, I think, to embrace and exhaust the spectacle, while yet leaving it every inch of its value. Clearly quite immeasurable, on American ground, the value of such an assertion of a town-type directly opposed to the unvarying American, and quite unique, on any ground, so organized a social indifference to the vulgar vociferous Market. Washington may of course *know* more than she confesses—no community could perhaps really be as ignorant as Washington used at any rate to look, and to like to look, of this particular thing, of "goods" and shares and rises and falls and all such sordidities; but she knows assuredly still the very least she can get off with, and nothing even yet pleases her more than to forget what she does know. She unlearns, she turns her back, while London, Paris, Berlin, Rome, in their character of political centres, strike us as, on the contrary, feverishly learning, trying more and more to do the exact opposite. (I speak, naturally, as to Washington, of knowing actively and interestedly, in the spirit of gain—not merely of the enjoyed lights of political and administrative science, doubtless as abundant there as anywhere else.) It might fairly have been, I used to think, that the charming place —charming in the particular connection I speak of—had on its conscience to make one forget for an hour the colossal greed of New York. Nothing, in fact, added more to its charm than its appearing virtually to invite one to impute to it some such vicarious compunction.

If I be reminded, indeed, that the distinction I here glance at is negative, and be asked what then (if she knew nothing of the great American interest) Washington did socially know, my answer, I recognize, has at once to narrow itself, and becomes perhaps truly the least bit difficult to utter. It none the less remains distinct enough that, the City of Conversation being only in question, and a general subject of all the conversation having thereby to be predicated, our responsibility is met as soon as we are able to say what Washington mainly talks, and appears always to go mainly talking, about. Washington talks about herself, and about almost nothing else; falling superficially indeed, on that ground, but into line with the other capitals. London, Paris, Berlin, Rome, goodness knows, talk about themselves: that is each member of this sisterhood talks, sufficiently or inordinately, of the great number of divided and differing selves that form together her controlling identity. London, for instance, talks of everything in the world without thereby for a moment, as it were, ceasing to be egotistical. It has taken everything in the world to make London up, so that she is in consequence simply doomed never to get away from herself. Her conversation is largely, I think, the very effort to do that; but she inevitably figures in it but as some big buzzing insect which keeps bumping against a treacherous mirror. It is in positive quest of an identity of some sort, much rather—an identity other than merely functional and technical—that Washington goes forth, encumbered with no ideal of avoidance or escape: it is about herself *as* the City of Conversation precisely that she incessantly converses; adorning the topic, moreover, with endless ingenuity and humour. But that, absolutely, remains the case; which thus becomes one of the most thorough, even if probably one of the most natural and of the happiest, cases of collective self-consciousness that one knows. The spectacle, as it at first met my senses, was that of a numerous community in ardent pursuit of some workable conception of its social self, and trying meanwhile intelligently to talk itself, and even this very embarrassment, into a *subject* for conversation. Such a picture might not seem purely pleasing, on the side of variety of appeal, and I admit one may have had one's reserves about it; reserves sometimes reflected, for example, in dim inward speculation—one of the effects of the Washington air I have already glanced at—as to the amount of response it might evoke in the diplomatic body. It may have been on my part a morbid obsession, but the diplomatic body was liable to strike one there as more characteristically "abysmal" than elsewhere, more impenetrably bland and inscrutably blank; and it was obvious, certainly, that their concern to help the place intellectually to find itself was not to be expected to approach in intensity the concern even of a repatriated absentee. You were concerned only if you had, by your sensibility, a stake in the game; which was the last thing a foreign representative would wish to confess to, this being directly opposed to all his enjoined duties. It is no part of the office of such personages to assist the societies to which they are accredited to find themselves—it is much more their mission to leave all such vaguely and, so far as may be, grotesquely groping: so apt are societies, in finding themselves, to find other things too. This detachment from the whole mild convulsion of effort, the considerate pretence of not being too aware of it, combined with latent probabilities of alarm about it no less than of amusement, represented, to the unquiet fancy, much more the spirit of the old-time Legations.

What *was*, at all events, better fun, of the finer sort, than having one's self a stake in the outcome?—what helped the time (so much of it as there was!) more to pass than just to join in the so fresh experiment of constitutive, creative talk? The boon, it should always be mentioned, meanwhile went on not in the least in the tone of solemnity. That would have been fatal, because probably irritating, and it was where the good star of Washington intervened. The tone was, so to speak, of *conscious* self-consciousness, and the highest genius for conversation doubtless dwelt in the fact that the ironic spirit was ready always to give its very self away, fifty times over, for the love, or for any quickening, of the theme. The foundation for the whole happy predicament remained, moreover, of the firmest, and the essence of the case was to be as easily stated as the great social fact is, in America, whether through exceptions or aggravations, everywhere to be stated. Nobody was in "business"—that was the sum and substance of it; and for the one large human assemblage on the continent of which this was true the difference made was huge. Nothing could strike one more than that it was the only way in which, over the land, a difference *could* be made, and than how, in our vast commercial democracy, almost any difference—by which I mean almost any exception—promptly acquires prodigious relief. The value here was at once that the place could offer to view a society, the only one in the country, in which Men existed, and that that rich little fact became the key to everything. Superficially taken, I recognize, the circumstance fails to look portentous; but it looms large immediately, gains the widest bearing, in the light of any direct or extended acquaintance with American conditions. From the moment it is adequately borne in mind that the business-man, in the United States, may, with no matter what dim struggles, gropings, yearnings, never hope to be anything *but* a business-man, the size of the field he so abdicates is measured, as well as the fact of the other care to which his abdication hands it over. It lies there waiting, pleading from all its pores, to be occupied—the lonely waste, the boundless gaping void of "society"; which is but a rough name for all the *other* so numerous relations with the world he lives in that are imputable to the civilized being. Here it is then that the world he lives in accepts its doom and becomes, by his default, subject and plastic to his mate; his default having made, all around him, the unexampled opportunity of the woman—which she would have been an incredible fool not to pounce upon. It needs little contact with American life to perceive how she *has* pounced, and how, outside business, she has made it over in her image. She has been, up to now, on the vast residual tract, in peerless possession, and is occupied in developing and extending her wonderful conquest, which she appreciates to the last inch of its extent.

. . . .

IV

One might have been sure in advance that the character of a democracy would nowhere more sharply mark itself than in the democratic substitute for a court city, and Washington is cast in the mould that expresses most the absence of salient social landmarks and constituted features. Here it is that conversation, as the only invoked presence, betrays a little its inadequacy to the furnishing forth, all by itself, of an outward view. It tells us it must be there, since in all the wide empty vistas nothing else is, and the general elimination *can* but have left it. A pleading, touching effect, indeed, lurks in this sense of it as seated, at receipt of custom, by any decent door of any decent domicile and watching the vacancy for reminder and appeal. It is left to conversation alone to people the scene with accents; putting aside two or three objects to be specified, there is *never* an accent in it, up and down, far and wide, save such as fall rather on the ear of the mind: those projected by the social spirit starved for the sense of an occasional emphasis. The White House is an accent—one of the lightest, sharpest possible; and the Capitol, of course, immensely, another; though the latter falls on the exclusively political page, as to which I have been waiting to say a word. It should meanwhile be mentioned that we are promised these enhancements, these illustrations, of the great general text, on the most magnificent scale; a splendid projected and announced Washington of the future, with approaches even now grandly outlined and massively marked; in face of which one should perhaps confess to the futility of any current estimate. If I speak thus of the Capitol, however, let me not merely brush past the White House to get to it—any more than feel free to pass into it without some preliminary stare at that wondrous Library of Congress which glitters in fresh and almost unmannerly emulation, almost frivolous irrelevance of form, in the neighbourhood of the greater building. About the ingenuities and splendours of this last costly structure, a riot of rare material and rich ornament, there would doubtless be much to say—did not one everywhere, on all such ground, meet the open eye of criticism simply to establish with it a private intelligence, simply to respond to it by a deprecating wink. The guardian of that altar, I think, is but too willing, on such a hint, to let one pass without the sacrifice.

It is a case again here, as on fifty other occasions, of the tribute instantly paid by the revisiting spirit; but paid, all without question, to the general *kind* of presence for which the noisy air, over the land, feels so sensibly an inward ache—the presence that corresponds there, no matter how loosely, to that of the housing and harbouring European Church in the ages of great disorder. The Universities and the greater Libraries (the smaller, for a hundred good democratic reasons, are another question), repeat, in their manner, to the imagination, East and West, the note of the old thick-walled convents and quiet cloisters: they are large and charitable, they are sturdy, often proud and often rich, and they have the incalculable value that they represent the only intermission to inordinate rapacious traffic that the scene offers to view. With this suggestion of sacred ground they play even upon the most restless of analysts as they will, making him face about, with ecstasy, any way they seem to point; so that he feels it his business much less to count over their shortcomings than to proclaim them places of enchantment. They are better at their worst than anything else at its best, and the comparatively sweet sounds that stir their theoretic stillness are for him as echoes of the lyre of Apollo. The Congressional Library is magnificent, and would become thus a supreme sanctuary even were it ten times more so: there would seem to be nothing then but to pronounce it a delight and have done with it

—or let the appalled imagination, in other words, slink into it and stay there. But here is pressed precisely, with particular force, the spring of the question that takes but a touch to sound: is the case of this remarkable creation, by exception, a case in which the violent waving of the pecuniary wand *has* incontinently produced interest? The answer can only be, I feel, a shy assent—though shy indeed only till the logic of the matter is apparent. This logic is that, though money alone can gather in on such a scale the treasures of knowledge, these treasures, in the form of books and documents, themselves organize and furnish their world. They appoint and settle the proportions, they thicken the air, they people the space, they create and consecrate all their relations, and no one shall say that, where they scatter life, which they themselves in fact *are*, history does not promptly attend. Emphatically yes, therefore, the great domed and tiered, galleried and statued central hall of the Congressional, the last word of current constructional science and artistic resource, already crowns itself with that grace.

The graceful thing in Washington beyond any other, none the less, is the so happily placed and featured White House, the late excellent extensions and embellishments of which have of course represented expenditure—but only of the refined sort imposed by some mature portionless gentlewoman on relatives who have accepted the principle of making her, at a time of life, more honourably comfortable. The whole ample precinct and margin formed by the virtual continuity of its grounds with those expanses in which the effect of the fine Washington Obelisk rather spends or wastes itself (not a little as if some loud monosyllable had been uttered, in a preoccupied company, without a due production of sympathy or sense)—the fortunate isolation of the White House, I say, intensifies its power to appeal to that musing and mooning visitor whose perceptions alone, in all the conditions, I hold worthy of account. Hereabouts, beyond doubt, history had from of old seemed to me insistently seated, and I remember a short spring-time of years ago when Lafayette Square itself, contiguous to the Executive Mansion, could create a rich sense of the past by the use of scarce other witchcraft than its command of that pleasant perspective and its possession of the most prodigious of all Presidential effigies, Andrew Jackson, as archaic as a Ninevite king, prancing and rocking through the ages. If that atmosphere, moreover, in the fragrance of the Washington April, was even a quarter of a century since as a liquor of bitter-sweet taste, overflowing its cup, what was the ineffable mixture now, with all the elements further distilled, all the life further sacrificed, to make it potent? One circled about the place as for meeting the ghosts, and one paused, under the same impulse, before the high palings of the White House drive, as if wondering at haunted ground. There the ghosts stood in their public array, spectral enough and clarified; yet scarce making it easier to "place" the strange, incongruous blood-drops, as one looked through the rails, on that revised and freshened page. But one fortunately has one's choice, in all these connections, as one turns away; the mixture, as I have called it, is really here so fine. General Jackson, in the centre of the Square, still rocks his hobby and the earth; but the fruit of the interval, to my actual eyes, hangs nowhere brighter than in the brilliant memorials lately erected to Lafayette and to Rochambeau. Artful, genial, expressive, the tribute of French talent, these happy images supply, on the spot, the note without which even the most fantasticating sense of our national past would feel itself rub forever against mere brown homespun. Everything else gives way, for me, I confess, as I again stand before them; everything, whether as historic fact, or present *agrément,* or future possibility, yields to this one high luxury of our old friendship with France.

The "artistic" Federal city already announced spreads itself then before us, in plans elaborated even to the finer details, a city of palaces and monuments and gardens, symmetries and circles and far radiations, with the big Potomac for water-power and water-effect and the recurrent Maryland spring, so prompt and so full-handed, for a perpetual benediction. This imagery has, above all, the value, for the considering mind, that it presents itself as under the wide-spread wings of the general Government, which fairly make it figure to the rapt vision as the object caught up in eagle claws and lifted into fields of air that even the high brows of the municipal boss fail to sweep. The wide-spread wings affect us, in the prospect, as great fans that, by their mere tremor, will blow the work, at all steps and stages, clean and clear, disinfect it quite ideally of any germ of the job, and prepare thereby for the American voter, on the spot and in the pride of possession, quite a new kind of civic consciousness. The scheme looms largest, surely, as a demonstration of the possibilities of that service to him, and nothing about it will be more interesting than to measure —though this may take time—the nature and degree of his alleviation. Will the new pride I speak of sufficiently inflame him? Will the taste of the new consciousness, finding him so fresh to it, prove the right medicine? One can only regret that we must still rather indefinitely wait to see—and regret it all the more that there is always, in America, yet another lively source of interest involved in the execution of such designs, and closely involved just in proportion as the high intention, the formal majesty, of the thing seems assured. It comes back to what we constantly feel, throughout the country, to what the American scene everywhere depends on for half its appeal or its effect; to the fact that the social conditions, the material, pressing and pervasive, make the particular experiment or demonstration, whatever it may pretend to, practically a new and incalculable thing. This general Americanism is often the one tag of character attaching to the case after every other appears to have abandoned it. The thing is happening, or will have to happen, in the American way—that American way which is more different from all other native ways, taking country with country, than any of these latter are different from each other; and the question is of how, each time, the American way will see it through.

The element of suspense—beguilement, ever, of the sincere observer—is provided for by the fact that, though this American way never fails to come up, he has to recognize as by no means equally true that it never fails to succeed. It is inveterately applied, but with consequences bewilderingly various; which means, however, for our present moral, but that the certainty of the *determined* American effect is an element to attend quite especially such a case as the employment of the arts of design, on an unprecedented scale, for public uses, the adoption on this scale of the whole æsthetic law. Encountered in America, phenomena of this order strike us mostly as occurring in the historic void, as having to present themselves in the hard light of that desert, and as needing to extort from it, so far as they can, something of the shading of their interest. Encountered in older countries, they show, on the contrary, as taking up the references, as consenting perforce to the relations, of which the air is already full, and as having thereby much rather to get themselves expressive by charm than to get themselves expressive by weight. The danger "in Europe" is of their having too many things to say, and too many others to distinguish these from; the danger in the States is of their not having things enough—with enough tone and resonance furthermore to give them. What therefore will the multitudinous and elaborate forms of the Washington to come have to "say," and what, above all, besides gold and silver, stone and marble and trees and flowers, will they be able to say it *with*? That is one of the questions in the mere phrasing of which the restless analyst finds a thrill. There is a thing called interest that has to be produced for him—positively as if he were a rabid usurer with a clutch of his imperilled bond. He has seen again and again how the most expensive effort often fails to lead up to interest, and he has seen how it may bloom in soil of no more worth than so many layers of dust and ashes. He has learnt in fact—he learns greatly in America—to mistrust any plea for it *directly* made by money, which operates too often as the great puffing motor-car framed for whirling him, in his dismay, quite away from it. And he has inevitably noted, at the same time, from how comparatively few other sources this rewarding dividend on his invested attention may be drawn. He thinks of these sources as few, that is, because he sees the same ones, which are the references by which interest is fed, used again and again, with a desperate economy; sees the same ones, even as the human heroes, celebrities, extemporized lions or scapegoats, required social and educational figure-heads and "values," having to serve in *all* the connections and adorn all the tales. That is one of the liveliest of his American impressions. He has at moments his sense that, in presence of such vast populations and instilled, emulous demands, there is not, outside the mere economic, enough native history, recorded or current, to go round.

V

It seemed to me on the spot, moreover, that such reflections were rather more than less pertinent in face of the fact that I was again to find the Capitol, whenever I approached, and above all whenever I entered it, a vast and many-voiced creation. The thing depends of course somewhat on the visitor, who will be the more responsive, I think, the further back into the "origins" of the whole American spectacle his personal vision shall carry him; but this hugest, as I suppose it, of all the homes of debate only asks to put forth, on opportunity, an incongruous, a various, an inexhaustible charm. I may as well say at once that I had found myself from the first adoring the Capitol, though I may not pretend here to dot all the i's of all my reasons —since some of these might appear below the dignity of the subject and others alien to its simplicity. The ark of the American covenant may strike one thus, at any rate, as a compendium of all the national ideals, a museum, crammed full, even to overflowing, of all the national terms and standards, weights and measures and emblems of greatness and glory, and indeed as a builded record of half the collective vibrations of a people; their conscious spirit, their public faith, their bewildered taste, their ceaseless curiosity, their arduous and interrupted education. Such were to my vision at least some of its aspects, but the place had a hundred sides, and if I had had time to look for others still I felt I should have found them. What it comes to—whereby the "pull," in America, is of the greatest—is that association really reigns there, and in the richest, and even again and again in the drollest, forms; it is thick and vivid and almost gross, it assaults the wondering mind. The labyrinthine pile becomes thus inordinately *amusing*—taking the term in its finer modern sense. The analogy may seem forced, but it affected me as playing in Washington life very much the part that St. Peter's, of old, had seemed to me to play in Roman: it offered afternoon entertainment, at the end of a longish walk, to any spirit in the humour for the uplifted and flattered vision—and this without suggesting that the sublimities in the two cases, even as measured by the profanest mind, tend at all to be equal. The Washington dome is indeed capable, in the Washington air, of admirable, of sublime, effects; and there are cases in which, seen at a distance above its yellow Potomac, it varies but by a shade from the sense—yes, absolutely the divine campagna-sense—of St. Peter's and the like-coloured Tiber.

But the question is positively of the impressiveness of the great terraced Capitol hill, with its stages and slopes, staircases and fountains, its general presentation of its charge. And if the whole mass and prospect "amuse," as I say, from the moment they are embraced, the visitor curious of the *democratic assimilation* of the greater dignities and majesties will least miss the general logic. That is the light in which the whole thing is supremely interesting; the light of the fact, illustrated at every turn, that the populations maintaining it deal with it so directly and intimately, so sociably and humorously. We promptly take in that, if ever we are to commune in a concentrated way with the sovereign people, and see their exercised power raise a side-wind of irony for forms and arrangements other than theirs, the occasion here will amply serve. Indubitably, moreover, at a hundred points, the irony operates, and all the more markedly under such possible interference; the interference of the monumental spittoons, that of the immense amount of vulgar, of barbaric, decoration, that of the terrible artistic tributes from, and scarce less to, the different States—the unassorted marble mannikins in particular, each a portrayal by one of the commonwealths of her highest worthy, which make the great Rotunda, the intended Valhalla, resemble a stonecutter's collection of priced sorts and sizes. Discretion exists, throughout, only as a flower of the very first or of these very latest years; the large middle time, corresponding, and even that unequally, with the English Victorian, of sinister memory, was unacquainted with the name, and waits there now, in its fruits, but for a huge sacrificial fire, some far-flaring act-of-faith of the future: a tribute to the æsthetic law which one already feels stirring the air, so that it may arrive, I think, with an unexampled stride. Nothing will have been more interesting, surely, than so public a wiping-over of the æsthetic slate, with all the involved collective compunctions and repudiations, the general exhibition of a colossal conscience, a conscience proportionate to the size and wealth of the country. To such grand gestures does the American scene lend itself!

The elements in question are meanwhile there, in any case, just as the sovereign people are there, "going over" their property; but we are aware none the less of impressions—that of the ponderous proud Senate, for instance, so sensibly massive; that of the Supreme Court, so simply, one almost says so chastely, yet, while it breathes supremacy, so elegantly, so all intellectually, in session—under which the view, taking one extravagance with another, recurs rather ruefully to glimpses elsewhere caught, glimpses of authority emblazoned, bewigged, bemantled, bemarshalled, in almost direct defeat of its intention of gravity. For the reinstated absentee, in these presences, the mere recovery of native privilege was at all events a balm—after too many challenged appeals and abused patiences, too many hushed circuitous creepings, among the downtrodden, in other and more bristling halls of state. The sense of a certain large, final benignity in the Capitol comes then, I think, from this impression that the national relation to it is that of a huge flourishing Family to the place of business, the estate-office, where, in a myriad open ledgers, which offer no obscurity to the hereditary head for figures, the account of their colossal revenue is kept. They meet there in safe sociability, as all equally initiated and interested—not as in a temple or a citadel, but by the warm domestic hearth of Columbia herself; a motherly, chatty, clear-spectacled Columbia, who reads all the newspapers, knows, to the last man, every one of her sons by name, and, to the last boy, even her grandsons, and is fenced off, at the worst, but by concentric circles of rocking-chairs. It is impossible, as I say, not to be fondly conscious of her welcome—unless again, and yet again, I read into the general air, confusedly, too much of the happy accident of the basis of my introduction. But if my sensibility responds with intensity to this, so much the better; for what were such felt personal aids and influences, after all, but cases and examples, embodied expressions of character, type, distinction, products of the *working* of the whole thing?—specimens, indeed, highly concentrated and refined, and made thereby, I admit, more charming and insidious.

It must also be admitted that to exchange the inner aspects of the vast monument for the outer is to be reminded with some sharpness of a Washington in which half the sides that have held our attention drop, as if rather abashed, out of sight. Not its pleasant brightness as of a winter watering-place, not its connections, however indirect, with the older, but those with the newer, the newest, civilization, seem matter of recognition for its various marble fronts; it rakes the prospect, it rakes the continent, to a much more sweeping purpose, and is visibly concerned but in immeasurable schemes of which it can consciously remain the centre. Here, in the vast spaces—mere empty light and air, though such pleasant air and such pretty light as yet—the great Federal future seems, under vague bright forms, to hover and to stalk, making the horizon recede to take it in, making the terraces too, below the long colonnades, the admirable standpoints, the sheltering porches, of political philosophy. The comparatively new wings of the building filled me, whenever I walked here, with thanksgiving for their large and perfect elegance: so, in Paris, might the wide mated fronts that are of such a noble effect on either side of the Rue Royale shine in multiplied majesty and recovered youth over an infinite Place de la Concorde. These parts of the Capitol, on their Acropolis height, are ideally constructed for "raking," and for this suggestion of their dominating the American scene in playhouse gallery fashion. You are somehow possessed of it *all* while you tread them—their marble embrace appears so the complement of the vast democratic lap. Though I had them in general, for contemplation, quite to myself, I met one morning a trio of Indian braves, braves dispossessed of forest and prairie, but as free of the builded labyrinth as they had ever been of these; also arrayed in neat pot-hats, shoddy suits and light overcoats, with their pockets, I am sure, full of photographs and cigarettes: circumstances all that quickened their resemblance, on the much bigger scale, to Japanese celebrities, or to specimens, on show, of what the Government can do with people with whom it is supposed able to do nothing. They seemed just then and there, for a mind fed betimes on the Leatherstocking Tales, to project as in a flash an image in itself immense, but foreshortened and simplified—reducing to a single smooth stride the bloody footsteps of time. One rubbed one's eyes, but there, at its highest polish, shining in the beautiful day, was the brazen face of history, and there, all about one, immaculate, the printless pavements of the State.

From Chapter XI of The American Scene (1907)

Bibliographical Note

This note gives for each essay or passage included in this volume: (1) its first serial printing in case it was first published in a periodical; (2) its first and its subsequent appearances in book form in the volumes of travel writings Henry James published during his lifetime. In carrying his essays over from magazines and from one volume to another, James usually subjected them to incidental revision. The texts used here are the *final* texts James issued, as indicated below. The authorities on the bibliography of James are: (a) *A Bibliography of the Writings of Henry James* by LeRoy Phillips (New York: Coward-McCann, second and revised edition, 1930); and (b) *A Bibliography of Henry James* by Leon Edel and Dan H. Laurence (London: Rupert Hart-Davis: Soho Bibliographies, 1957).

The following are the books by Henry James referred to in the bibliographical notes. Those from which texts have been drawn in the present volume are marked with an asterisk:

Transatlantic Sketches by Henry James, Jr. (Boston: James R. Osgood and Company, Late Ticknor and Fields, and Fields, Osgood and Company, 1875).

Foreign Parts by Henry James (Leipzig: Bernhard Tauchnitz, 1883).

* *Portraits of Places* by Henry James (London: Macmillan and Company, 1883; Boston: James R. Osgood and Company, 1884: copyright 1883).

* *A Little Tour in France* by Henry James (Boston: James R. Osgood and Company; Leipzig: Bernhard Tauchnitz, 1885[84]). (Reissued London: William Heinemann; Boston and New York: Houghton, Mifflin and Company, 1900, with illustrations by Joseph Pennell). Texts here are taken from the last-named edition.

Essays in London and Elsewhere by Henry James (London: James R. Osgood, McIlvaine and Company; New York: Harper and Brothers, 1893).

° *English Hours* by Henry James, with illustrations by Joseph Pennell (London: William Heinemann; Boston: Houghton, Mifflin and Company, 1905).

° *The American Scene* by Henry James (London: Chapman and Hall, Ltd.; New York: Harper and Brothers, 1907).

° *Italian Hours* by Henry James, with illustrations by Joseph Pennell (London: William Heinemann; Boston and New York: Houghton Mifflin Company, 1909).

James's memoir, *William Wetmore Story and His Friends* (Edinburgh and London: William Blackwood and Sons; Boston and New York: Houghton, Mifflin and Company, 1903), includes much writing on the Italian and English scene.

The Paris letters which James contributed to the *New York Tribune* in 1875 and 1876 have now been collected as *Parisian Sketches* by Henry James, edited by Leon Edel and Ilse Dusoir Lind (New York: New York University Press, 1957).

Part I

"Saratoga": in *The Nation* (New York), August 11, 1870.

"Newport": in *The Nation*, September 15, 1870.

"Quebec": in *The Nation*, September 28–October 5, 1871.

"Niagara": in *The Nation*, October 12–19, 1871.

The above four essays were collected in °*Portraits of Places* (1883).

Part II

"Chester": in *The Nation*, July 4, 1872.

"Wells" and "Salisbury": combined as "Wells and Salisbury" in *The Nation*, August 22, 1872.

"Warwick": from "Lichfield and Warwick," *The Nation*, July 25, 1872.

The above essays were collected in *Transatlantic Sketches* (1875); in *Foreign Parts* (1883); and in °*English Hours* (1905).

"Rochester and Canterbury": from "An English Easter," *Lippincott's Magazine,* July, 1877.

"Abbeys and Castles": in *Lippincott's Magazine,* October, 1877.

"Oxford": from "Two Excursions," *The Galaxy* (where it first appeared as "Three Excursions"), September, 1877.

"Cambridge": from "English Vignettes," *Lippincott's Magazine,* April, 1879.

The preceding four essays were collected in °*Portraits of Places* (1883); and in °*English Hours* (1905).

"Old Suffolk": in *Harper's Weekly,* September 25, 1897.

Included in °*English Hours* (1905), where an apparent misprint dates the essay 1879.

"London": in *The Century Magazine,* December, 1888.

Included in *Essays in London and Elsewhere* (1893); and in °*English Hours* (1905).

Part III

"Occasional Paris": in *The Galaxy,* January, 1878 (under the title "Paris Revisited").

"Chartres": in the *New York Tribune,* April 29, 1876 (under the title "Chartres Portrayed").

"Rheims": from "Rheims and Laon: A Little Tour," first printed in *The Atlantic Monthly,* January, 1878 (under the title "A Little Tour in France").

The above three essays were included in °*Portraits of Places* (1883).

"Tours," "Toulouse," "Carcassonne," "Montpellier," "Avignon," "Arles," and "Nîmes" formed part of the series of essays contributed to *The Atlantic Monthly* under the general title "En Province," July to November, 1883, and February, April, and May, 1884.

Collected as *A Little Tour in France* (1885[84]); and in °*A Little Tour in France* (1900).

Part IV

"A Roman Holiday": in *The Atlantic Monthly,* July, 1873.

"A Chain of Cities": first printed in *The Atlantic Monthly,* February, 1874 (under the title "A Chain of Italian Cities").

These two essays were collected in *Transatlantic Sketches* (1875); in *Foreign Parts* (1883); and in °*Italian Hours* (1909).

"Siena": in *The Atlantic Monthly,* June, 1874; first collected as "Siena" in *Transatlantic Sketches* (1875) and in *Foreign Parts* (1883); revised and expanded with an additional section not included here in °*Italian Hours* (1909) under the title "Siena Early and Late."

"Florence": from "Italy Revisited," *The Atlantic Monthly,* April–May, 1878, this part as "Recent Florence."

"Venice": in *The Century Magazine,* November, 1882.

These two essays were included in °*Portraits of Places* (1883); and in °*Italian Hours* (1909).

"Capri and the Bay of Naples": from "The Saint's Afternoon," first printed in *The May Book,* compiled by Mrs. Aria in Aid of the Charing Cross Hospital (London: Macmillan and Company, 1901); revised and expanded with an addition not included here under the title "The Saint's Afternoon and Others" and dated by James 1900–1909 in °*Italian Hours* (1909).

Part V

"New England: An Autumn Impression": part of an essay of the same title in *The North American Review,* April–June, 1905.

"New York Revisited": parts of an essay of the same title in *Harper's Magazine,* February, March, and May, 1906;

and of "New York and the Hudson: A Spring Impression," *The North American Review,* December, 1905.

"The Sense of Newport": in *Harper's Magazine,* August, 1906.

"Boston": in *The North American Review,* March, 1906; and in *The Fortnightly Review* (London), March, 1906.

"Concord and Salem": first published as part of Chapter VIII of °*The American Scene* (1907).

"Washington": parts of an essay of the same title in *The North American Review,* May and June, 1906.

All the above essays formed chapters in °*The American Scene* (1907).

The dates given under the titles of essays in this book are as nearly as possible the dates of the original writing (often supplied by James himself when he dated the essays on their collection in book form), or of the travels they deal with where this can be determined.